Developing Democracy

Developing Democracy

Toward Consolidation

LARRY DIAMOND

The Johns Hopkins University Press
Baltimore and London

1999

© 1999 The Johns Hopkins University Press

All rights reserved. Published 1999
Printed in the United States of America on acid-free paper
9 8 7 6 5 4 3 2

The Johns Hopkins University Press
2715 North Charles Street
Baltimore, Maryland 21218-4363
www.press.jhu.edu

Library of Congress Cataloging-in-Publication Data will be found
at the end of this book.
A catalog record for this book is available from the British Library.

ISBN 0-8018-6014-8
ISBN 0-8018-6156-X (pbk.)

To my mother, a great democrat

CONTENTS

FIGURES AND TABLES

PREFACE AND ACKNOWLEDGMENTS

This is a book about the state and fate of democracy at the end of the twentieth century. What do we mean by democracy? How widespread is democracy? And how can we assess it? What determines the quality and stability of democracy? Why do democracies survive?

As these are the questions that have occupied my career since graduate school, it could be said that this book has been evolving for two decades. Important currents of my thinking were shaped in my graduate work at Stanford University and, subsequently, by interaction with teachers and advisors such as Alex Inkeles, Seymour Martin Lipset, and Gabriel A. Almond. The principal inspiration for this book, however, was Samuel P. Huntington's *The Third Wave: Democratization in the Late Twentieth Century*, in which Huntington tracks and explains the transition from authoritarian rule to democracy by some thirty countries between 1974 and 1990. He dubs this historical trend the third wave of global democratization and questions whether, like the previous two waves, it would end in a "reverse wave" of democratic breakdowns.

This book picks up where Huntington's left off. Its principal concern, theoretically and practically, is with the consolidation of the new democracies that came into being during the third wave. Conceptually, it seeks to refine our understanding of two pivotal terms, *democracy* and *consolidation*. Empirically, it tracks the continued momentum of democratic expansion in the 1990s, during which the number of third-wave democracies approximately doubled before expansion finally drew to a halt. Analytically, it asks the question: What will determine whether these new democracies survive and become stable?

Initially, I thought about the problem of democracy as persistence versus breakdown. Influenced strongly by the seminal four-volume work of editors Juan J. Linz and Alfred Stepan, *The Breakdown of Democratic Regimes*, I became convinced that the beliefs, choices, capacities, and alliances of key political actors played a crucial, autonomous role in determining the fate of democracy, even though I had been sensitized by my teachers to the constraining impact of cultural and social structural factors. I set out to study the general conditions for democratic stability and the historical causes of democratic failure in Nigeria's First Republic (1960–66). That experience, and the subsequent observation and analysis of the breakdown of Nigeria's Second Republic (1979–83), vividly conveyed to me the necessity of looking beyond the formal structures of democracy, to their depth and quality.

Although I did not fully appreciate it at the time, that realization was the beginning of a journey to a very different view of democracy: as a continuum and a process rather than a system that is simply either present or absent. This developmental view of democracy was heavily influenced by the thinking and writings of a leading Africanist political scientist and student of Nigeria, Richard L. Sklar, who had also advised me on my thesis. For my appreciation of the diverse and unpredictable sequences through which various elements of democracy can emerge, I owe him a considerable intellectual debt.

In sharp contrast to my early work on Nigeria, and then sub-Saharan Africa more broadly, this work is comparative in method and global in focus, spanning all the regions of the third wave: Southern, Central, and Eastern Europe, Latin America, and Asia. My familiarity with this wider terrain of global democratic development developed through two collaborative endeavors that have had a formative impact on my scholarship: the twenty-six-nation study, *Democracy in Developing Countries*, which I edited with Juan Linz and Seymour Martin Lipset, and my involvement with the *Journal of Democracy* and the National Endowment for Democracy. *Democracy in Developing Countries* (produced during the last half of the 1980s) was the first major comparative study during the third wave to examine the sources of democratic persistence, emergence, and failure across several regions. I was privileged in that endeavor to work with many of the finest country specialists and comparative students of democracy. In addition to renewing a deeply rewarding academic partnership with Seymour Martin Lipset, that project initiated a sustained intellectual relationship with the most tireless and knowledgable democracy scholar of our time, Juan Linz, who has since been for me (as for so many others) one of the most perceptive, motivating, and generous commenters on my work on democracy.

My knowledge of many of the practical and operational challenges of democratic development—and my appreciation that democratic change is produced not by abstract historical and structural forces but by individuals and groups choosing, innovating, and taking risks—has been deepened by my association since the mid-1980s with the National Endowment for Democracy. Through NED conferences and networks, I have become acquainted with many of the civil and political activists who made the democratic revolutions that produced the third wave. The insights and inspiration drawn from these exchanges permeate this book and shaped in particular my thinking in chapter 6 on civil society. I am most grateful to NED president Carl Gershman, and to other members of the National Endowment staff and network, for the involvement they have provided me and the confidence they have reposed in me.

Much in this book is gleaned from or inspired by articles in the *Journal of Democracy*, which I have had the privilege of editing with Marc F. Plattner since its founding in 1990. The *Journal* has been for me an indispensable source of information and ideas on the progress and travails of democracy around the world. It has also published early versions of portions of this book, which generated many useful responses. Through a decade of collaboration, first in co-editing the *Journal* and then in co-directing the NED International Forum for Democratic Studies, Marc Plattner has given me new angles of interpretation and unfailingly sound advice. No one in an ongoing relationship of mutual obligations and recurrent deadlines could hope for a more astute, conscientious, and unselfish partner.

Many other people in the United States and abroad have helped me to understand the practical challenges of developing democratic civil societies and political institutions. I would particularly like to acknowledge the assistance and support of Catharin Dalpino (former deputy assistant secretary of state for democracy), Kenneth Wollack (president of the National Democratic Institute for International Affairs), Barbara Haig (director of program) and David Peterson (senior program officer for Africa) of the National Endowment for Democracy, William Fuller (president) and Gordon Hein (vice president) of the Asia Foundation, Robert LaGamma (former director of the U.S. Information Service in Nigeria and South Africa), Peter Hakim (president) and Michael Shifter (director of the Governance Program) of the Inter-American Dialogue, Maria Rosa Martini (former president of Conciencia, Argentina), Chai-Anan Samudavanija (director of the Institute of Public Policy Studies, Thailand), Alex Boraine and Wilmot James (former and current executive directors of IDASA, the Institute for Democracy in South Africa), Olisa Agbakoba (former president of the Civil Liberties Organisation of Nigeria), and Clement Nwankwo (executive director of the Constitutional Rights Project of Nigeria).

The chapters in this book evolved through several drafts and numerous seminar presentations over the past few years. For these stimulating forums and for the feedback they and their colleagues gave me on these occasions, I thank Samuel Huntington at Harvard University, Guillermo O'Donnell at the Kellogg Institute of Notre Dame, Richard Gunther at Ohio State University, Joel Barkan at the University of Iowa; Prudhisan Jumbala at Chulalongkorn University in Bangkok, Naomi Chazan at the Harry S. Truman Institute of the Hebrew University of Jerusalem, Ergun Özbudun at Bilkent University in Ankara, Masipula Sithole at the University of Zimbabwe; in Taiwan, Huoyan Shyu and Mau-Kuei Chang at the Academia Sinica, John Fuh-Sheng Hsieh at National Cheng-chi University, and Yun-han Chu at National Taiwan University; in South Korea, Kyoung-Ryung Seong at Hallym University, Byung-Kook Kim at Korea University, Hoon Jaung at Chung Ang University, Young-Jo Lee at Kyunghee University, and Sook-Jong Lee at the Sejong Institute; and in South Africa, Steven Friedman at the Centre for Policy Studies, Wilmot James at IDASA, Vincent Maphai at the Human Sciences Research Council, Hermann Giliommee at the University of Cape Town, and Fanie Cloete at Stellenbosch University.

For providing me the more extended engagement of week-long seminars, where I presented draft portions of this book, I am especially grateful to Andreas Schedler at the Institute of Advanced Study, Vienna, José María Maravall, José Ramón Montero, and Mariano Torcal at the Center for Advanced Studies in the Social Sciences of the Instituto Juan March in Madrid, and João Espada of the Catholic University of Lisbon, as well as to former Portuguese president Mario Soares, whose invitation to lecture in the Democratic Invention series of his foundation sparked some of the ideas in chapter 7.

I am indebted to, and I hope will not with this book too much disappoint, many people who have read pieces of the manuscript and commented vigorously and candidly. I want in particular to thank Gabriel Almond, who read the entire manuscript in its penultimate form and provided countless clues, corrections, and suggestions that sharpened my argument, enlarged my view, and streamlined my style. At a crucial early stage in the development of chapters 2 and 3, I benefited from the extensive comments and incisive critiques of David Collier, Jonathan Hartlyn, Juan Linz, John W. Meyer, Guillermo O'Donnell, Marc Plattner, and Andreas Schedler. José Ramón Montero, Richard Rose, and Doh Chull Shin shared with me data, unpublished works, and detailed feedback that enriched chapter 5 on political culture. I owe a special thanks to Montero for his trenchant scrutiny of chapter 5, which (along with chapter 6) was released in earlier, abbreviated form as a working paper by the Juan March Institute.

I also thank, for providing me their data and papers, Geoffrey Evans, Marta Lagos, Robert Mattes, Ann Pincus (director of the Office of Research, United States Information Agency), and my colleagues in Taiwan, Yun-han Chu and Huoyan Shyu, as well as their senior collaborator at National Taiwan University, Hu Fu. Freedom House also repeatedly assisted graciously with provision of data. For their constructive comments on various portions of the draft manuscript and the stimulating feedback they have given me in related exchanges, I am grateful to Michael Coppedge, Shmuel Eisenstadt, Samuel Huntington, Scott Mainwaring, Celestin Monga, Oyeleye Oyediran, Minxin Pei, Adam Przeworski, Andrew Reynolds, Anibal Romero, Harald Waldrauch, and Eliza Willis; my colleagues John Dunlop, Alex Inkeles, Thomas Metzger, Ramon Myers, and Barry Weingast at the Hoover Institution; and my partners in organizing the ongoing Stanford seminar on democratiza-tion: Terry Karl, Philippe Schmitter, Michael McFaul, and Michel Oksenberg. My thinking about the nature and determinants of democracy has benefited considerably from many years of lively exchange with Karl and Schmitter.

Most scholars who both teach and write will concede that we often learn as much from our students as we give them and that the interactive process of teaching sharpens our thinking and widens our perspective. I owe a special debt to the students in my 1996 graduate seminar at Stanford on democratic consolidation, during which critical ideas for this book were aired, debated, and refined. For their comments on portions of the manuscript I thank several former and current students, in particular Sunhyuk Kim, Sanjeev Khagram, Rebecca Bill, and Svetlana Tsalik. During the writing of this book, I have benefited from the cheerful, devoted personal assistance of Marguerite (Petie) Kramer and the research assistance of Boris Wijkstrom, Stephan Wall, and Nathan Henson. Nathan Batto and Chin-En Wu assisted in analyzing the Taiwanese survey data summarized in table 5.7. Especially helpful and systematic research assistance was provided by Gabriel Goodliffe on chapter 3 and Svetlana Tsalik on chapter 4. Tsalik's contribution was so creative, energetic, and substantial that I proudly acknowledge her role as a full partner in the writing of chapter 4. For his unflagging interest in the project and wise counsel, I am especially indebted to Henry

Tom, executive editor of the Johns Hopkins University Press. I thank also copyeditor Diane M. Hammond, production editor Kimberly Johnson, and indexer Alexa Selph.

With sincere appreciation for the financial support that enabled me to complete research on this book, I thank the Carnegie Corporation of New York, particularly its recently retired president, David Hamburg, for his personal interest and encouragement of my work. Since 1985, my research and writing on democracy have been based at the Hoover Institution. It would be difficult to imagine a more challenging and supportive milieu in which to work on any of the major policy problems of our time, and I am deeply grateful to John Raisian, director of the Hoover Institution, and to Thomas Henriksen, the associate director, for their steadfast backing. I also appreciate the support of the National Science Council of the Republic of China, Taiwan, and the engaging hospitality of the Institute of Social Sciences and Philosophy of the Academia Sinica, which enabled me to finish writing this book while beginning research on a new book on democratic consolidation in Taiwan.

Finally, to all my friends and family who saw the light burning late into the night and understood, thank you. Thanks to my twin sister, Linda, for all the gentle pushes and encouragement. Most of all, I thank my mother, Lila Diamond, who kindled my interest in democratic politics at an early age, and to whom this book is dedicated.

Developing Democracy

1

Defining and Developing Democracy

The basis of a democratic state is liberty.
—Aristotle, *The Politics*

Since April of 1974, when the Portuguese military overthrew the Salazar/ Caetano dictatorship, the number of democracies in the world has multiplied dramatically. Before the start of this global trend, there were about forty democracies. The number increased moderately through the late 1970s and early 1980s as several states experienced transitions from authoritarian rule (predominantly military) to democratic rule. In the mid-1980s, the pace of global democratic expansion accelerated markedly. By the end of 1995, there were as many as 117 democracies or as few as 76, depending on how one counts.

Deciding *how* to count is crucial to some principal tasks of this book: refining what we mean by the term *democracy*; analyzing the degree of global democratic progress since 1974; considering whether democracy will continue to expand in the world; and determining what factors will shape the viability of the many new democracies that have come into being.

In a seminal formulation, Samuel Huntington termed this post-1974 period the "third wave" of global democratic expansion and has shown the central importance to it of regional and international demonstration effects.[1] The democratizing trend began in Southern Europe in the mid-1970s, spread to the military regimes of South America in the late 1970s and early 1980s, and reached East, Southeast, and South Asia by the mid to late 1980s. The end of the 1980s saw a surge of transitions from communist authoritarian rule in Eastern Europe and the former Soviet Union and a trend toward democracy in Central America as well. Finally, the democratic trend spread to Africa in 1990, beginning in February of that year with the sovereign National Conference in Benin and the release of Nelson Mandela and the unbanning of the African National Congress in South Africa. By 1998 there were between nine and seventeen democracies on the continent—again, depending on how one counts.

Huntington defines a "wave of democratization" simply as "a group of [democratic] transitions . . . that occur within a specified period of time and that significantly outnumber transitions in the opposite direction during that period."[2] He identifies two previous waves of democratization (a long, slow wave from 1828 to 1926 and a second, post–World War II wave, from 1943 to 1964). Each of the first two waves ended with a reverse wave of democratic breakdowns (1922–42, 1961–75), in which some but not all of the new (or reestablished) democracies collapsed. Each reverse wave significantly diminished the number of democracies in the world but left more democracies in place than had existed prior to the start of the democratic wave.

Will the new century bring a third reverse wave, challenging once again democratic ideas, models, and institutions?

The Best Form of Government

Why should we worry about the danger of a new reverse wave? Why study the determinants of democracy? Why democracy?

The normative perspective underlying this book is that democratization is generally a good thing and that democracy is the best form of government. However, democracy is not an unmitigated blessing. Dating back to Aristotle (and to Plato, who had even less sympathy for democracy), the key shapers of democratic political thought have held that the best realizable form of government is mixed, or constitutional, government, in which freedom is constrained by the rule of law and popular sovereignty is tempered by state institutions that produce order and stability.[3] Aristotle saw that, in a state of pure democracy, "where the multitude have the supreme power, and supersede the law by their decrees . . . demagogues spring up," and democracy degenerates into a form of despotism.[4]

Thus, as Locke, Montesquieu, and the American Federalists asserted, only a constitutional government, restraining and dividing the temporary power of the majority, can protect individual freedom. This fundamental insight (and value) gave birth to a tradition of political thought—liberalism—and to a concept—liberal democracy—that are central to this book. As elaborated below, I use the term *liberal* to mean a political system in which individual and group liberties are well protected and in which there exist autonomous spheres of civil society and private life, insulated from state control. Conceptually, a liberal polity is independent of the existence of a competitive, liberal economy based on secure rights of property, although in practice the two are related, in part by their common need to restrict the power of the state.[5]

Even if we think of democracy as simply the rule of the people, as a system for choosing government through free and fair electoral competition at regular intervals, governments chosen in this manner are generally better than those that are not. They offer the best prospect for accountable, responsive, peaceful, predictable, good governance. And, as Robert Dahl cogently observes, they promote "freedom as no feasible alternative can."[6] "Democracy is instrumental to freedom in three ways." First, free and fair elections inherently require certain political rights of expression, organization, and opposition, "and these fundamental political rights are unlikely to exist in isolation" from broader civil liberties. Second, democracy maximizes the opportunities for self-determination, "for persons to live under laws of their own choosing." Third, it facilitates moral autonomy, the ability of each individual citizen to make normative choices and thus to be, at the most profound level, self-governing. Consequently, the democratic process promotes human development (the growth of personal responsibility and intelligence) while also providing the best means for people to protect and advance their shared interests.

Up to a point consistent with the principles of constitutionalism and representative democracy, government is better when it is more democratic. This is not to argue that even electoral democracy is easily attainable in any country at any time.[7] However, more democracy makes government more responsive to a wider range of citizens. "The greater the opportunities for expressing, organizing, and representing political preferences, the greater the number and variety of preferences and interests that are likely to be represented in policy making."[8]

Normatively, I assume here that accountability of rulers to the ruled and government responsiveness to the diverse interests and preferences of the governed are basic goods. So also are the minimization of violence in political life and of arbitrary action by government. And so, above all, is liberty. Increasingly in the twentieth century, the freedoms of the individual to think, believe, worship, speak, publish, inquire, associate, and become informed, and the freedoms from torture, arbitrary arrest, and unlawful detention—not to mention enslavement and genocide—are recognized as universal and inalienable human rights. From the Universal Declaration of Human Rights (adopted by the U.N. General Assembly in 1948) to the 1993 World Conference on Human Rights in Vienna, these rights have been acknowledged and reaffirmed by more and more countries. At Vienna in 1993, all 111 countries in attendance agreed that "human rights and fundamental freedoms are the birthright of all human beings; their protection and promotion is the first responsibility of governments."[9] While intellectuals and social movements have been ready to surrender these liberties in utopian pursuits of rapid development or the perfect society, political experiments from fascism to communism (and myriad other mutations of dictatorship) have exposed the horrible costs and illusions of these models.[10]

Liberal democracy provides, by definition, comparatively good protection for human rights. However, there is no reason that electoral democracy and liberty must go together. Historically, liberty—secured through constitutional, limited government and a rule of law—came about before democracy both in England and, in varying degrees, in other European states. And today, as I demonstrate in chapter 2, there are many illiberal democracies, with human rights abuses and civil strife. These two facts have rekindled intellectual interest in liberal autocracy as a better, safer, more stable form of government for many transitional societies.[11]

In times of very limited education and political consciousness, when the franchise could be confined to a narrow elite, liberal autocracy was possible. In today's world, it is an illusion, a historical anachronism. Save for two island states with populations of 100,000 each (Tonga; Antigua and Barbuda), there are no autocracies in the world that could possibly qualify as liberal.[12] And there will not be any significant ones in the future, for liberalism insists upon the sovereignty of the people to decide their form of government—and these days, according to Marc Plattner, "popular sovereignty can hardly fail to lead to popular government."[13] In an age of widespread communication and political consciousness, people expect political participation and accountability much more than they did in the eighteenth, nineteenth, and early twentieth centuries. The only way the demand for meaningful political participation and choice can be suppressed is to constrain liberty. Thus, as noted above, there is a powerful association between democracy and liberty: "countries that hold free elections are overwhelmingly more liberal than those that do not."[14] Indeed, the more closely countries meet the standards of electoral democracy (free and fair, multiparty elections by secret and universal ballot), the higher their human rights rating.[15]

Reverse waves threaten not only political freedom and human rights but also world peace. The first reverse wave gave rise to the expansionist fascist regimes that brought on World War II. The second reverse wave spread during the peak of the Cold War and fed a number of regional conflicts and civil wars, in which the major world powers became directly or indirectly involved. Although regimes in transition may be prone to international conflict, and democratic regimes have a long history of war and conquest against nondemocracies, no two countries that have established liberal democracy have ever gone to war against one another. Bruce Russett notes that democracies "rarely fight each other even at low levels of lethal violence" and that they are much less likely to let their disputes with one another escalate.[16] This, he argues persuasively, is not only because of the institutional restraints on democracies' decisions to go to war but even more so because of democratic normative restraints on the use of force to resolve disputes.

In fact, the longer that democracies endure (and presumably consolidate these norms), the less likely it is there will be violent conflict between them. United Nations Secretary-General Boutros Boutros-Ghali observed that "a culture of democracy is fundamentally a culture of peace."[17] More generally, the relative openness of democracies to the free flow of information, and their valuing of law and constitutionalism, logically make them much more likely than authoritarian regimes to honor their obligations under international laws and treaties. The secretiveness, repression, and dubious legitimacy of authoritarian regimes make them "more likely to incite hostilities against other States in order to justify their suppression of internal dissent or forge a basis for national unity."

The norms that restrain institutionalized democracies from warring with one another also appear to foster peaceful conflict resolution within their societies. Although the *process* of democratization may stimulate ethnic conflict and induce weak states to meet communal rebellion with repression rather than accommodation, "the resolution of ethnopolitical conflicts in institutionalized democracies depends most fundamentally on the implementation of universalistic norms of equal rights and opportunities for all citizens ... and pluralistic accommodation of [group] desires for separate collective status."[18] In democracies, particularly ones with well-institutionalized representative processes, minority groups have the political scope to mobilize and to win response within the democratic process, and they lose support when they turn to violence and terrorism.

The policies and institutions that settle ethnopolitical conflicts and manage diversity peacefully include full political and civil rights for ethnic minorities, programs to alleviate their poverty, protection for them to use their languages and cultures, regional autonomy and devolution of power, and mechanisms or incentives for sharing power, constructing multiethnic coalitions, encouraging crosscutting alignments, and allowing broad access to power at the center.[19] Instituting these reforms and making them work involve processes of bargaining, accommodation, consensus building, and political learning that are not unknown in authoritarian regimes but are much more likely to exist in democracies.[20] Moreover, strategies for moderating conflict through the creative design of electoral institutions—and of terminating civil wars through a negotiated turn to the ballot box—inherently require meaningful, competitive elections.[21]

Beyond the violence between states and between or against ethnic groups within states lies a more stunning generalization: "Power kills, absolute power kills absolutely."[22] Rudolph Rummel's exhaustive study of deaths from war, genocide, mass murder, and domestic violence in this, history's most murderous, century, demonstrates that every instance of mass murder by a state against its own people has happened under authoritarian rule and that the more absolutist the regime the greater the tendency toward democide (genocide and mass murder of innocent civilians).[23] Thus, "the way to virtually eliminate genocide and mass murder appears to be through restricting and checking power. This means to *foster democratic freedom.*"[24]

Other dimensions of performance further distinguish democracy as the best form of government. With their protection for rights to protest and organize, their freer flows of information, their wider deliberation, debate, and transparency in policy making, their greater respect for law (including international conventions), and their mechanisms to hold rulers accountable, democracies do a much better job of protecting the environment.[25] And contrary to the myth that rests on the India-China comparison, they are also more effective at reducing population growth. Even when controlling for the level of development, populations grow much more rapidly under authoritarian rule.[26] While the relationship between democracy and economic growth remains at issue, a growing body of evidence suggests that, at a minimum, authoritarian regimes in general do not grow faster in per capita income than democracies.[27] Indeed, statistical analyses suggest that "there is no trade-off between development and democracy," that "democracy need not generate slower growth,"[28] and that in the poorest countries, the level of democracy is positively correlated with improvements not only in per capita income but also in infant survival rates and life expectancy.[29] Thus, while democracy may generate fewer economic miracles, it seems better suited to avoid or to correct disasters, as Adam Przeworski and Fernando Limongi observe, and also better suited to achieve steady progress in human well-being. Finally, while the relationship between democracy and inequality is also in dispute, democracies appear in the long run to respond better to the needs of the poor and the marginalized, because they enable such groups to organize and mobilize within the political process.

The above positive benefits of democracy derive, as Russett notes with respect to interstate peace, from both the norms and the political institutions that characterize democracies. But which democracies? For peace and development and for the just treatment of minorities, is it enough that governments come to power through free, fair, and competitive elections? Or do these objectives require other features of democracy—a rule of law, free information, civil liberties, and a distribution of power that produces a horizontal accountability of rulers to one another? What do we mean by democracy?

Conceptualizing Democracy

Just as political scientists and observers do not agree on how many democracies there are in the world, so they differ on how to classify specific regimes, the conditions for making and consolidating democracy, and the consequences of democracy for peace and development. A key element in all these debates is lack of consensus on the meaning of *democracy*. So serious is the conceptual disarray that more than 550 subtypes of democracy are identified in David Collier and Steven Levitsky's review of some 150 (mostly recent) studies.[30] Some of these nominal subtypes merely designate specific institutional features or types of full democracy, but many denote diminished forms of democracy.

The diminished subtypes of democracy vary greatly in terminology and conceptual emphasis. Some, such as bourgeois, or capitalist, democracy, identify the dominance of socioeconomic elites or extreme social inequality as the key barrier to full democracy. However, the incorporation of social and economic desiderata into the definition of democracy—an approach fashionable in the 1960s and 1970s—has waned considerably in the past two decades. By and large, most scholarly and policy uses of the term *democracy* today refer to a purely political conception of the term, and this intellectual shift back to an earlier convention has greatly facilitated progress in studying the dynamics of democracy, including the relationship between political democracy and various social and economic conditions.[31]

Where conceptions of democracy diverge today is on the range and extent of political properties encompassed by democracy. Minimalist definitions of what I call electoral democracy descend from Joseph Schumpeter, who defined democracy as a system "for arriving at political decisions in which individuals acquire the power to decide by means of a competitive struggle for the people's vote."[32] Huntington, among others, explicitly embraces Schumpeter's emphasis on competitive elections for effective power as the essence of democracy.[33] However, Schumpeter's concise expression has required periodic elaboration (or what Collier and Levitsky call "precising") to avoid inclusion of cases that do not fit the implicit meaning.

The seminal elaboration is Dahl's conception of *polyarchy*, which has two overt dimensions: opposition (organized contestation through regular, free, and fair elections) and participation (the right of virtually all adults to vote and contest for office). Yet embedded in these two dimensions is a third, without which the first two cannot be truly meaningful: civil liberty. Polyarchy encompasses not only freedom to vote and contest for office but also freedom to speak and publish dissenting views, freedom to form and join organizations, and alternative sources of information.[34] Both Dahl's original formulation and a later, more comprehensive effort to measure polyarchy take seriously the nonelectoral dimensions.[35]

Electoral Democracy

Minimalist conceptions of electoral democracy usually also acknowledge the need for minimum levels of freedom (of speech, press, organization, and assembly) in order for competition and participation to be meaningful. But, typically, they do not devote much attention to them, nor do they incorporate them into actual measures of democracy. Thus (consistent with most other efforts to classify or measure regimes), Przeworski and his colleagues define democracy simply as "a regime in which governmental offices are filled as a consequence of contested elections" (with the proviso that real contestation requires an opposition with some nontrivial chance of winning office and that the chief executive office and legislative seats are filled by contested elections).[36] Such Schumpeterian conceptions (common among Western foreign policy makers as well) risk committing what Terry Karl calls the "fallacy of electoralism." This flawed conception of democracy privileges elections over other dimensions of democracy and ignores the degree to which multiparty elections (even if they are competitive and uncertain in outcome) may exclude significant portions of the population from contesting for power or advancing and defending their interests, or may leave significant arenas of decision making beyond the control of elected officials.[37] Philippe Schmitter and Terry Karl remind us that, "however central to democracy, elections occur intermittently and only allow citizens to choose between the highly aggregated alternatives offered by political parties, which can, especially in the early stages of a democratic transition, proliferate in a bewildering variety."[38]

In recent years, electoral conceptions of democracy have expanded to rule out the latter element of ambiguity or misclassification; many now exclude regimes that suffer substantial reserved domains of military (or bureaucratic, or oligarchical) power that are not accountable to elected officials.[39] But still, such formulations may still fail to give due weight to political repression and marginalization, which exclude significant segments of the population—typically the poor or ethnic and regional minorities—from exercising their democratic rights. One of the most rigorous and widely used measures of democracy in cross-national, quantitative research—in the "polity" data sets—acknowledges civil liberties as a major compoment of democracy but, because of the paucity of data, does not incorporate them.[40]

Freedom exists over a continuum of variation. Rights of expression, organization, and assembly vary considerably across countries that do have regular, competitive, multiparty elections in which votes are (more or less) honestly counted and in which the winning candidates exercise (most of the) effective power in the country. How overtly repressed must a minority be for the political system to be disqualified as a polyarchy (a *liberal* democracy)? Is Turkey disqualified for its use of indiscriminate violence to suppress the ruthless Kurdish insurgency or for its historical constraints (recently relaxed) on the peaceful expression of Kurdish political and cultural identity? Is India disqualified for the extensive human rights violations by its security forces in secessionist Kashmir? Is Sri Lanka disqualified for the brutal excesses by both sides in the secessionist war of Tamil guerrillas; or Colombia, for its internal war against drug traffickers and left-wing guerrillas or for its frequent political assassinations and other human rights abuses? Was Russia democratic when it waged war against secessionists in Chechnya? Do democracies not have a right to defend themselves against violent insurgency and secessionist terror? Or do the above five polities all fail to meet the conceptual test of democracy—despite briskly competitive elections that have witnessed electoral alternation of parties in power—because of high levels of political violence, lawlessness, and corruption, by both state and nonstate actors?

By the minimalist definition, Turkey, India, Sri Lanka, Colombia, and Russia qualify as democracies. But by the stricter conception of liberal democracy, all (except perhaps India as a whole) fall short. In fact, the gap between electoral and liberal democracy has grown markedly during the latter part of the third wave, forming one of its most significant but little-noticed features. As a result, human rights violations have become widespread in countries that are formally democratic.

Liberal Democracy

Electoral democracy is a civilian, constitutional system in which the legislative and chief executive offices are filled through regular, competitive, multiparty elections with universal suffrage. While this minimalist conception remains popular in scholarship and policy, it has been amplified, or precised, to various degrees by several scholars and theorists. This exercise has been constructive, but it has left behind a plethora of what Collier and Levitsky term "expanded procedural" conceptions, which do not clearly relate to one another and which occupy intermediate locations in the continuum between electoral and liberal democracy.[41]

How does *liberal* democracy extend beyond these formal and intermediate conceptions? In addition to the elements of electoral democracy, it requires, first, the absence of reserved domains of power for the military or other actors not accountable to the electorate, directly or indirectly. Second, in addition to the vertical accountability of rulers to the ruled (secured mainly through elections), it requires the horizontal accountability of officeholders to one another; this constrains executive power and so helps protect constitutionalism, legality, and the deliberative process.[42] Third, it encompasses extensive provisions for political and civic pluralism as well as for individual and group freedoms, so that contending interests and values may be expressed and compete through ongoing processes of articulation and representation, beyond periodic elections.

Freedom and pluralism, in turn, can be secured only through a "rule of law," in which legal rules are applied fairly, consistently, and predictably across equivalent cases, irrespective of the class, status, or power of those subject to the rules. Under a true rule of law, all citizens have political and legal equality, and the state and its agents are themselves subject to the law.[43]

Specifically, liberal democracy has the following components:

— Control of the state and its key decisions and allocations lies, in fact as well as in constitutional theory, with elected officials (and not democratically unaccountable actors or foreign powers); in particular, the military is subordinate to the authority of elected civilian officials.

— Executive power is constrained, constitutionally and in fact, by the autonomous power of other government institutions (such as an independent judiciary, parliament, and other mechanisms of horizontal accountability).

— Not only are electoral outcomes uncertain, with a significant opposition vote and the presumption of party alternation in government, but no group that adheres to constitutional principles is denied the right to form a party and contest elections (even if electoral thresholds and other rules exclude small parties from winning representation in parliament).

— Cultural, ethnic, religious, and other minority groups (as well as historically disadvantaged majorities) are not prohibited (legally or in practice) from expressing their interests in the political process or from speaking their language or practicing their culture.

— Beyond parties and elections, citizens have multiple, ongoing channels for expression and representation of their interests and values, including diverse, independent associations and movements, which they have the freedom to form and join.[44]

— There are alternative sources of information (including independent media) to which citizens have (politically) unfettered access.

— Individuals also have substantial freedom of belief, opinion, discussion, speech, publication, assembly, demonstration, and petition.

— Citizens are politically equal under the law (even though they are invariably unequal in their political resources).

— Individual and group liberties are effectively protected by an independent, nondiscriminatory judiciary, whose decisions are enforced and respected by other centers of power.
— The rule of law protects citizens from unjustified detention, exile, terror, torture, and undue interference in their personal lives not only by the state but also by organized nonstate or antistate forces.

These ten conditions imply an eleventh: if political authority is to be constrained and balanced, individual and minority rights protected, and a rule of law assured, democracy requires a constitution that is supreme. Liberal democracies in particular "are and have to be constitutional democracies. The lack of a constitutional spirit, of an understanding of the centrality of constitutional stability, is one of the weaknesses" of many illiberal third-wave democracies in the postcommunist world, as well as in the Third World.[45] A constitutional state is a state of justice, a *Rechtsstaat* in the German, in which the state acts predictably, in accordance with the laws, and the courts enforce restrictions on popularly elected governments when they violate the laws or the constitutional rules.[46] This in turn requires a legal and judicial system and, more broadly, a state with some capacity. Thus Juan Linz's dictum: "no state, no *Rechtsstaat*, no democracy."[47]

The above elements of liberal democracy compose most of the criteria by which Freedom House annually rates political rights (of contestation, opposition, and participation) and civil liberties for the nations of the world. Political rights and civil liberties are each measured on a 7-point scale, with a rating of 1 indicating the most free and 7 the least free. Countries with an average score on the two scales of 2.5 or lower are considered "free"; those scoring between 3 and 5.5 are "partly free"; and those scoring between 5.5 and 7 (as measured by a more discriminating raw-point score) are "not free."[48]

The "free" rating in the Freedom House survey is the best available empirical indicator of liberal democracy. As with any multipoint scale, there is inevitably some arbitrariness in where one draws the line to establish the threshold for a concept. However, there are real differences even between the average scores of 3.0 and 2.5, which is the cutoff point for liberal democracy. In the 1997–98 survey, all eleven countries with the lowest freedom score (2.5) within the "free" category rated 2 on political rights and 3 on civil liberties. The difference between a 2 and a 3 on political rights is very real. Typically, a 3 indicates significantly more military influence in politics, electoral and political violence, or electoral irregularities—and thus political contestation that is appreciably less free, fair, inclusive, and meaningful. The difference between a 2 and a 3 on civil liberties is also significant, as the countries scoring a 3 have at least one area—such as freedom of speech or the press, personal security from terror and arbitrary arrest, or associational freedom and autonomy—in which liberty is significantly constrained. Still, political rights are strong enough to render the system "free" (if just barely). However, when a country (such as Brazil in 1995 and 1996) with a score of 2 on political rights has a score of 4 on civil liberties, then human rights violations are so serious and widespread, the military and police are so immune to accountability, the judicial system is so ineffectual and corrupt, or the poor and landless are so victimized by wealthy elites that the political system cannot be considered liberal and free.

Midrange Conceptions

Conceptual approaches are no longer easily dichotomized into electoral and liberal approaches. Some conceptions of democracy fall somewhere in between, explicitly incorporating basic freedoms of expression and association yet still allowing for constrictions in citizenship rights and a porous, insecure rule of law. The crucial distinction turns on whether freedoms are relevant mainly to the extent that they ensure meaningful electoral competition and participation or whether they are, instead, viewed as necessary for a wider range of democratic functions.

A good example of the midrange conception is Juan Linz's definition of democracies as "political systems that allow the free formulation of political preferences through the use of basic freedoms of association, information and communication for the purpose of a free competition between leaders to validate at regular intervals, by nonviolent means, the claim to rule without excluding any office of national decision-making from that competition."[49] Here, a Schumpeterian conception of democracy has been expanded to rule out reserved domains of power and to require that electoral competition be underpinned by basic political freedoms. But this leaves open the extent to which civil liberties will otherwise be protected. Thus, the scope of civil liberties in democracies might vary considerably depending on the wishes of the majority, as long as "basic freedoms to contest politically remain unquestioned and the rights guaranteed in the constitution are not restricted."[50]

Although Linz's conception encompasses the right to advocate alternatives, it could allow a democracy, by a constitutional process, to constrain civil liberties and minority rights more severely than would be consistent with the principle of liberal democracy. As Linz makes clear, democracies are the form of government least likely to violate human rights, but they may do so when under stress or confronted with terrorist or antisystem challenges. This is why violent, antidemocratic, or secessionist movements are a particular problem for a liberal democracy and why liberal democracies need to act early and creatively to meet potential challenges if they are to preserve their liberal character.[51]

In another prominent midrange conception, Guillermo O'Donnell carefully rules out the fallacy of electoralism and the inclusion of reserved domains by adopting Dahl's concept of polyarchy and adding further procedural requirements that elected officials have meaningful power.[52] On the basis of these criteria, he excludes from his list of polyarchies in Latin America a number of quasi democracies, such as the Dominican Republic, Haiti, Guatemala, and Paraguay. This brings his classification close to my list of liberal democracies in Latin America (see table 2.6). However, the cutting point in his articulation of polyarchy centers on the institutionalization of elections rather than more broadly on the rule of law.

Indeed, a key point of O'Donnell's essay is that many third-wave democracies are polyarchies, and apparently enduring polyarchies, even though clientelism and particularism undermine horizontal accountability and adherence to formal rules. Thus, all of O'Donnell's cases of polyarchy "are such because of a simple but crucial fact: elections are institutionalized."[53] The institutionalization of elections requires surrounding conditions of freedom, but the cutting point appears to be their relevance for ensuring democratic electoral competition. O'Donnell concedes that "in many of the new polyarchies, individuals are citizens only in relation to the one institution that functions in a manner close to what its formal rules prescribe—elections. As for full citizenship, only the members of a privileged minority enjoy it. . . . Informally institutionalized polyarchies are democratic in the sense just defined. . . . But their liberal and republican components are extremely weak."[54]

The question of how extensive liberty must be before a political system can be termed a liberal democracy is a normative and philosophical one. The key distinction is whether the political process centers on elections or whether it encompasses a much broader and more continuous play of interest articulation, representation, and contestation. If we view the latter as an essential component of democracy, then there must be adequate freedoms surrounding that broader process as well, and to use O'Donnell's language, individuals must be able to exercise their rights of citizenship not only in elections but also in obtaining "fair access to public agencies and courts," which is often denied in "informally institutionalized" polyarchies.

The distinction between political and civil freedom, on the one hand, and cultural freedom (or license), on the other, is often confused in the debate over whether democracy is inappropriate for Asia (or East Asia, or Confucian Asia, or simply Singapore) because of incompatible values. Liberal democracy does not require the comprehensively exalted status of individual rights that obtains in Western Europe and especially the United States. Thus, one may accept many of the cultural objections of advocates of the "Asian values" perspective (that Western democracies have shifted the balance too much in favor of individual rights and social entitlements over the rights of the community and the social obligations of the individual to the community) and still embrace the political and civic fundamentals of liberal democracy as articulated above.[55]

Pseudodemocracies and Nondemocracies

An appreciation of the dynamics of regime change and the evolution of democracy must allow for a third class of regimes, which are less than minimally democratic but still distinct from purely authoritarian regimes. This requires a second cutting point, between electoral democracies and electoral regimes that have multiple parties and many other constitutional features of electoral democracy but that lack at least one key requirement: an arena of contestation sufficiently fair that the ruling party can be turned out of power. Juan Linz, Seymour Martin Lipset, and I term these regimes *pseudodemocracies*, "because the existence of formally democratic political institutions, such as multiparty electoral competition, masks (often in part to legitimate) the reality of authoritarian domination."[56]

There is wide variation among pseudodemocracies. They include semidemocracies, which more nearly approach electoral democracies in their pluralism and competitiveness, as well as what Giovanni Sartori terms "hegemonic party systems," in which a relatively institutionalized ruling party makes extensive use of coercion, patronage, media control, and other features to deny formally legal opposition parties a fair and authentic chance to compete for power.[57] In the latter systems, the ruling party regularly wins massively and controls the overwhelming bulk of legislative seats and subnational governments. Mexico (until 1988), Senegal, and Singapore are classic examples of such a system. In its usage here, however, pseudodemocracy extends beyond such hegemonic party regimes to encompass multiparty electoral systems in which the undemocratic dominance of the ruling party may be weak and contested (as in Kenya), or in the process of decomposing into a more competitive system (as in Mexico), or highly personalistic and poorly institutionalized (as in Kazakhstan).

What distinguishes pseudodemocracies from other nondemocracies is that they tolerate legal alternative parties, which constitute at least somewhat real and independent opposition to the ruling party. Typically, this toleration is accompanied by more space for organizational pluralism and dissident activity in civil society than is the case in the most repressive authoritarian regimes. Invariably, pseudodemocracies are illiberal, but they vary in their repressiveness and in their proximity to the threshold of electoral democracy (which Mexico could well cross in its next presidential election, in the year 2000). Thus, pseudodemocracies tend to have somewhat higher levels of freedom than other authoritarian regimes.[58]

The distinction between these two types of nondemocratic regime is also important theoretically. Throughout this book, following on the work of Richard Sklar, I appeal for a developmental view of democracy, which emerges in fragments or parts, by no fixed sequence or timetable. From such a perspective, the presence of legal opposition parties, which may compete for power and win some seats in parliament, and of greater space for civil society constitute important foundations for future democratic development.[59] In Mexico in particular, but also in Jordan, Morocco, and a few states of sub-Saharan Africa where former one-party dictators fraudulently engineered their reelection, these democratic fragments have expanded the boundaries of what is politically possible, and they could generate breakthroughs to electoral democracy, as they did in Ghana in 1996. In a number of African countries both above and below the threshold of electoral democracy, the growing assertiveness of parliaments, the renewed emphasis on constitutionalism, and civil society initiatives to promote accountability, responsiveness, and human rights counterbalance or outweigh the trends toward authoritarian regression.[60] In a similar vein (in an earlier era), elite-dominated, restricted democracies in Chile, Venezuela, and Costa Rica gradually became more democratic as civil society organizations and capable, middle-class parties forged effective linkages.[61]

This framework leaves a fourth, residual category, of authoritarian regimes. They vary in their level of freedom (see appendix), and they may even hold somewhat competitive elections (as in Uganda and other previously one-party African regimes). They may afford civil society and the judiciary some modest autonomy. Or they may be extremely closed and repressive, even totalitarian. But they all lack a crucial building block of democracy: legal, independent opposition parties. All the most repressive regimes in the world fall into this category.

This four-fold typology neatly classifies national political regimes, but political reality is always messier. Level of democracy may vary significantly across sectors and institutional arenas (as would be expected if democracy emerges in parts). It may also vary considerably across territories within the national state. Thus, some states in India manifest not only better, more efficient, and more accountable governance than other states but also better protection for civil liberties and lower levels of electoral and political violence. The states of Karnataka, Kerala, Gujarat, and West Bengal are more liberally democratic than the states of Uttar Pradesh, Madhya Pradesh, and Bihar, for example.[62] The undemocratic treatment of African Americans in the southern states before 1965 is another case in point.

With large countries, in particular, it is necessary to disaggregate to form a more sensitive picture of the quality and extent of democracy. This is why Sklar and others are uncomfortable with summary measures of democracy in a country and why Schmitter suggests that we conceptualize modern democracy "not as 'a regime,' but as a composite of 'partial regimes,' each . . . institutionalized around distinctive sites for the representation of social groups and the resolution of their ensuing conflicts."[63] Unfortunately, this is a task we can only acknowledge and hint at from time to time in this work.

Democracy in Developmental Perspective

Even liberal democracies fall short of democratic ideals. At the less liberal end of the group, they may have serious flaws in their guarantees of personal and associational freedom. And certainly ongoing practices in Italy, Japan, Belgium, France, the United States, and most other industrialized democracies underscore that even long-established and well-institutionalized democracies with the most liberal average freedom scores of 1 or 1.5 are afflicted with corruption, favoritism, and unequal access to political power, not to mention voter apathy, cynicism, and disengagement.

There is not now and has never been in the modern world of nation-states a perfect democracy, one in which all citizens have roughly equal political resources and in which government is completely or almost completely responsive to all citizens. This is why Robert Dahl uses the term *polyarchy* to characterize the more limited form of democracy that has been attained to date. Important currents in democracy's third wave are the increased valorization of such limited political democracy as an end in itself and the growing tendency of intellectuals (even many who had once been on the Marxist left) to recognize the need for realism in what can be expected of democracy. Certainly, democracy does not produce all good things. As Linz observes, "political democracy does not necessarily assure even a reasonable approximation of what we would call a democratic *society*, a society with considerable equality of opportunity in all spheres."[64] As Schmitter and Karl argue, democracies are not necessarily more economically or administratively efficient, or more orderly and governable, than autocratic regimes.[65] But by permitting widespread liberty and the real possibility of selecting alternative governments and policies, and by permitting disadvantaged groups to organize and mobilize politically, democracies (particularly liberal democracies) provide the best long-run prospects for reducing social injustices and correcting mistaken policies and corrupt practices.

It is important, then, not to take the existence of democracy, even liberal democracy, as cause for self-congratulation. Democracy should be viewed as a developmental phenomenon. Even when a country is above the threshold of electoral (or even liberal) democracy, democratic institutions can be improved and deepened or may need to be consolidated; political competition can be made fairer and more open; participation can become more inclusive and vigorous; citizens' knowledge, resources, and competence can grow; elected (and appointed) officials can be made more responsive and accountable; civil liberties can be better protected; and the rule of law can become more efficient and secure.[66] Viewed in this way, continued democratic development is a challenge for all countries, including the United States; all democracies, new and established, can become more democratic.

Obviously, the improvement and invigoration of democracy will not solve all social and economic problems that societies face. But widening the scope of public deliberation, empowering historically marginalized and alienated groups, and increasing citizen competence and government responsiveness—reforms that deepen and extend democracy—may increase the sophistication of mass publics and the legitimacy (and hence the governing capacity) of elected officials.[67] Beyond this, increasing citizen competence and participation in the political process will spill over into other arenas of social life. Civic engagement, such as participation in voluntary associations and community networks, generates trust, reciprocity, and cooperation, which reduce cynicism, encourage political participation, and facilitate economic development, democratic stability, and the resolution of social problems. Increasingly, social scientists view such social capital as a critical resource for dealing with the seemingly intractable problems of poverty, alienation, and crime in the United States and other industrialized democracies. Otherwise, "mutual distrust and defection, vertical dependence and exploitation, isolation and disorder, criminality and backwardness [reinforce] one another in . . . interminable vicious circles."[68]

Viewed from a developmental perspective, the fate of democracy is open-ended. The elements of liberal democracy emerge in various sequences and degrees, at varying paces in the different countries.[69] Democratic change can also move in differing directions. Just as electoral democracies can become more democratic—more liberal, constitutional, competitive, accountable, inclusive, and participatory—so they can also become less democratic—more illiberal, abusive, corrupt, exclusive, narrow, unresponsive, and unaccountable. And liberal democracies, too, can either improve or decline in their levels of political accountability, accessibility, competitiveness, and responsiveness. There is no guarantee that democratic development moves in only one direction, and there is much to suggest that all political systems (including democracies, liberal or otherwise) become rigid, corrupt, and unresponsive in the absence of periodic reform and renewal.[70] Democracy not only may lose its quality, it may even effectively disappear, not merely through the breakdown of formal institutions but also through the more insidious processes of decay.

Overview of the Book

This insidious decay—the progressive hollowing out of electoral democracy—is one of several striking features of the latter period of the third wave that have been inadequately appreciated. The contradictory trends of global democratic development are traced in chapter 2, which considers whether the third wave of democratization has come to an end. Comparing the growth of liberal democracy with that of electoral democracy, we find a large and growing gap between the two and a leveling off of democratic expansion in the world. Some new democracies have become more substantially democratic in recent years, but a surprising number are less so, at least in important dimensions. In much of the postcommunist and developing worlds, democracy appears stuck in a twilight zone of tentative commitment, illiberal practices, and shallow institutionalization. These new democracies, and the overall global trend of democratization, are very far from the depth and stability that follow from consolidation.

The concept and process of democratic consolidation form the theme of chapter 3. The essence of democratic consolidation is a behavioral and attitudinal embrace of democratic principles and methods by both elites and mass. These behaviors and attitudes are observable, and attitudes at least can be measured by survey data (as we find in chapter 5). Legitimation is in turn linked to three key dimensions of the consolidation challenge. First, democracy must be deepened and made more authentic. Democracy is significantly more likely to become consolidated if it is liberal, and there is no third-wave democracy in the world today that is both illiberal (or less than "free," according to Freedom House scales) and consolidated. Second, the political institutions of democracy must become more coherent, capable, and autonomous, so that all major political players are willing to commit to and be bound by their rules and norms. Institutionalization is thus strongly linked to the third challenge of consolidation: that democracy effectively address society's most pressing problems and, perhaps more important, provide the liberty, accountability, and responsiveness that citizens uniquely expect from democracy and the order that they expect from any government. The political dimension of performance is thus closely linked to the first challenge of democratic deepening.

In contrast to those who see the emergence of stable democracy as a relatively rapid and decisive occurrence crafted by elites,[71] I emphasize here the generally extended nature of democratic consolidation and its close relationship to developing the institutional, behavioral, and cultural components of democracy. These include a rule of law (and thus an independent judiciary), autonomous legislatures, credible structures for controlling corruption, effective democratic governance at the local level, a vibrant civil society, and values and practices of tolerance, trust, participation, and accommodation. Some new democracies (Spain in the late 1970s and early 1980s, the Czech Republic in the early 1990s) inherited or quickly generated enough of this institutional and cultural foundation for democracy to facilitate rapid legitimation. But most democracies are building, if not from scratch, then at least from a patchwork of blocks and beams.[72] This hard reality demands of scholars and policy makers a longer time perspective, particularly in lower-income countries, and an appreciation for the multilayered and nonlinear nature of the process, which often involves progress on some fronts and regression on others or setbacks followed by increments of progress.

One of the challenges of democratic deepening is to provide citizens access to power and to make the institutions of democracy more responsive to their preferences. Chapter 4 explores an intriguing question raised by the relationship between size and democracy. Countries with populations of less than one million are much more likely to be democracies and especially more likely to be liberal democracies. Even the obvious correlate of Anglo-American colonial heritage cannot explain away this relationship. There are theoretical reasons to expect a link between democracy and size of the political system. Most independent states have populations considerably larger than a million, and it would hardly be practical (or peaceful) to reduce them much in scale. However, devolution of power to meaningful local and regional government can bring democracy closer to the people and deliver a number of the benefits that appear to accrue to small size. In much of the world this promise is only beginning to be realized, and there are real pitfalls and challenges to decentralization as well. Yet devolution—and in larger-scale and more ethnically complex states, a fully federal system—offers a route for deepening and consolidating democracy.

If the core process of consolidation is legitimation, then it must involve some transformation of political culture. The relationship between political culture and democracy is explored in chapter 5. Reviewing a wealth of survey data across numerous regions and countries, it assesses trends in public support for democracy, satisfaction with democracy, and other political attitudes and values that can affect the viability of third-wave democracies. Independent of a variety of economic and social factors, including the regime's economic performance and the country's level of development, politics determines the growth of legitimacy and other democratic values. How well a regime delivers the freedom, accountability, and responsibility that citizens expect of democracy significantly affects the level of support for democracy. That political experience and the quality of governance can shape the way citizens think, believe, and behave politically underscores the need for viewing democracy in a developmental perspective. A political culture may contain large residues of past authoritarian orientations, but it is open to democratic evolution through the practice of democracy.

Because people learn in large measure by practice, and because democratic accountability and responsiveness are rarely achieved without concerted pressure from below, civil society (the arena of organizations and media that are autonomous from the state but concerned with public affairs) plays a central role in the process of consolidation. Chapter 6 shows that a vigorous and democratic civil society is vital for the construction of a democratic culture and, more broadly, for "making democracy work" (as Robert Putnam puts it). But as that chapter suggests, civil society performs many other functions for democratic development, including often a much larger role in the birth of electoral democracy than the transitions literature recognizes.

The tentative conclusion of this book is that the third wave of expansion in electoral democracies is drawing to a close. The best that can be realistically hoped for in the next decade is the consolidation of many of the fifty or so electoral democracies that remain in a twilight zone of persistence without legitimation and institutionalization. Meeting that challenge (which forms the central concern of this book) would represent a global transformation no less profound than the wave of democratic transitions of the past two decades. Such a transformation, I argue, would preempt the reverse wave, which history and theory both predict is otherwise likely to occur in the coming years. Yet even if a reverse wave could be prevented, or diminished, the question of the longer-term future would remain. Are we headed toward a world of democracies? Will there be a fourth wave and, if so, when—and why?

The highest theoretical (and even, in a sense, normative) imperative in thinking about consolidation is, as I argue in chapter 3 and again in the concluding chapter 7, to avoid teleology. There is nothing inevitable about the triumph and persistence of democracy in the world. No hidden hand will deliver it. And there is much to suggest that, without constant effort, innovation, and rejuvenation, democracy may deteriorate in the core of the world system. The prospects for economic development, especially in East Asia, and the popular disgust with the waste and repression of authoritarian rule in Africa offer grounds for hope about the long-term prospects for democracy in the world. Sometime in the first quarter of the twenty-first century, these could well ignite a new round of global democratic expansion, perhaps emanating from China and Indonesia. Still, these and other East Asian countries may fashion a distinctive (less-democratic) path to national development. Much will depend on what the established, wealthy democracies do, not only to promote democracy abroad but also to offer through their own institutional functioning an appealing and viable example of democracy that works. Democracy must periodically revalidate not only its efficacy (its capacity to address the problems that society confronts) but also its openness to reform and renewal in the ongoing quest for political freedom, responsiveness, and transparency.

2

Is the Third Wave of Democratization Over?

By any conception, democracy has expanded dramatically since the third wave began, with the overthrow of the Portuguese dictatorship in April 1974. If we take a minimalist or formal conception of democracy (in which governmental offices are filled through competitive, multiparty elections that place incumbents at real risk of defeat), both the number of democracies in the world and the proportion of the world's regimes that are democratic have increased dramatically since the third wave began. In mid-1974, there were only thirty-nine democracies in the world; twenty-eight of these had populations of more than one million.[1] Only 27 percent of the independent states in the world were formally democratic—and only 22 percent of states with populations exceeding one million. This difference owes to the fact that eleven of the eighteen states (61%) with populations under one million were democracies.[2] This striking relationship between size and (liberal) democracy, which has held continuously throughout the third wave, is explored in chapter 4.

By the beginning of 1998, the number of electoral democracies in the world had increased to 117, and even though the number of independent states has steadily grown throughout the third wave (by more than a third), the proportion of countries that are formally democratic has more than doubled, to more than 60 percent. More striking still is how much of this growth (both proportionally and in sheer number of democracies) has occurred in the 1990s, with the collapse of Soviet and Eastern European communism and the diffusion of the third wave to sub-Saharan Africa. From 1990 to 1996, the number and percentage of democracies in the world increased every year, producing a democratic breakthrough without precedent in world history (see table 2.1). As recently as 1990, when he was writing *The Third Wave*, Huntington found only 45 percent of the world's states (with populations of more than one million) to be democratic, a proportion virtually identical to that in 1922, at the peak of the first wave.[3] Even if we similarly restrict our view to countries with populations of more than one million, the proportion of democracies in the world now stands at 57 percent.

What has been the trend with respect to *liberal* democracy? As one would expect, both the number and the proportion of countries in the world rated "free" by Freedom House have significantly increased, but not as dramatically as the number and proportion of electoral democracies. From 1972, when the Freedom House survey began, until 1980, the number of free states increased by only ten (and the proportion of free states in the world rose only slightly, from 29 percent in 1972 to 32 percent in 1980). Moreover, change was not only in one direction. During the first six years of the third wave (to 1980) five states suffered breakdowns or erosions of democracy that cost them their free status by the end of the decade. In fact, although the overall trend of regime change during the third wave has been toward significantly more democracy and freedom in the world, twenty-two countries suffered democratic breakdowns or recessions from the "free" status between 1974 and 1991, and further deterioration has occurred since then.[4]

Table 2.1   Electoral Democracies, 1974 and 1990–1997

Year	All Countries (N)	Democracies (N)	Democracies as Percentage of all Countries	Annual Rate of Increase in Democracies (%)
1974	145	39	26.9	
1990	165	76	46.1	n.a.
1991	183	91	49.7	19.7
1992	186	99	53.2	8.1
1993	190	108	56.8	8.3
1994	191	114	59.7	5.3
1995	191	117	61.3	2.6
1996	191	118	61.8	0.9
1997	191	117	61.3	−0.9

Sources: Data from Freedom House, *Freedom in the World: The Annual Survey of Political Rights and Civil Liberties, 1990–1991, 1991–1992, 1992–1993, 1993–1994, 1994–1995, 1995–1996, 1997–1998* (New York: Freedom House, 1991 and years following).

Note: Figures for 1990–1997 are for the end of the calendar year. Figures for 1974 reflect my estimate of the number of democracies in the world in April 1974, at the inception of the third wave.

In the latter half of the 1980s and beginning of the 1990s, political freedom took its biggest jump during the third wave. As we see in table 2.2, between 1985 and 1991 (a crucial period, since it encompasses the demise of both Eastern European and Soviet communism), the number of free states jumped from fifty-six to seventy-six, and the proportion of free states in the world increased from a third to more than 40 percent. Moreover, the proportion of blatantly authoritarian, "not free" states, declined, to barely over 20 percent. By contrast, in 1972 almost half of the independent states in the world were rated "not free."

Average levels of freedom in the world also experienced their biggest improvement in the period from 1985 to 1991. Although the third wave had been under way for a decade, by 1985 the median overall freedom score (which averages political rights and civil liberties) was 5, no different from what it had been in 1974. And the average overall freedom score was only slightly better (4.29) and virtually no different from the 1980 average (4.26). From 1985 to 1991, the average overall freedom score improved by more than 0.5 of a point on the 7-point scale (see table 2.3).

Since 1991–92, freedom in the world has increased only slightly—and very unevenly. During 1992 and 1993, the proportion of free states actually declined, and even with the modest increases in 1994 and 1996,

Table 2.2 Freedom Status of Independent States, 1972–1997, Various Years

Year	Free (N, %)	Partly Free (N, %)	Not Free (N, %)	Total N
1972	42 (29.0)	36 (24.8)	67 (46.2)	145
1980	52 (31.9)	52 (31.9)	59 (36.2)	163
1985	56 (33.5)	56 (33.5)	55 (32.9)	167
1990	65 (39.4)	50 (30.3)	50 (30.3)	165
1991	76 (41.5)	65 (35.5)	42 (22.9)	183
1992	75 (40.3)	73 (39.2)	38 (20.4)	186
1993	72 (37.9)	63 (33.2)	55 (28.9)	190
1994	76 (39.8)	61 (31.9)	54 (28.3)	191
1995	76 (39.8)	62 (32.5)	53 (27.7)	191
1996	79 (41.4)	59 (31.1)	53 (27.7)	191
1997	81 (42.4)	57 (29.8)	53 (27.2)	191

Sources: For 1972, 1980, and 1985, Raymond D. Gastil, ed., *Freedom in the World: Political Rights and Civil Liberties, 1988–89* (New York: Freedom House, 1989). For 1991–97, see table 2.1.

Note: Ratings refer to the status of the countries at the end of the calendar year. See text for an explanation of the basis of the ratings.

Table 2.3 Overall Freedom Scores, 1974–1997, Various Years

Year	Countries with Declining Freedom Scores (N)	Countries with Improving Freedom Scores (N)	Median Freedom Score	Average Freedom Score
1974	16	16	5.0	4.47
1980	24	25	5.0	4.26
1985	12	9	5.0	4.29
1990	18	36	4.0	3.84
1991	17	41	3.5	3.68
1992	31	39	3.5	3.61
1993	43	18	3.5	3.72
1994	23	22	3.5	3.69
1995	11	29	3.5	3.63
1996	13	31	3.5	3.58
1997	9	13	3.5	3.58

Sources: See table 2.2.

liberal democracies were no more common in 1996 than they had been in 1991 (table 2.2). Only in 1997 did the proportion of liberal democracies reach a new historic high. Since the late 1980s, several countries, such as the Philippines, Slovakia, and Venezuela, have moved in and out of the "free" category. Moreover, after 1992, the proportion of "not free" states jumped sharply, from 20 to 28 percent, where it has remained for five years. During the 1992–94 period, the number of countries gaining in freedom were offset or exceeded by those that lost ground. During 1995–98, the positive trend of the early 1990s resumed: more countries improved in their freedom scores than declined. However, the declines were of greater magnitude, as some countries went from electoral democracy to outright dictatorship. As a result, the aggregate level of freedom in the world during 1996 and 1997, as indicated by the average overall freedom score, was virtually identical to what it had been in 1992 (table 2.3). The incremental gains in the average freedom score since 1993 suggest the possibility of a renewed positive trend. This was further indicated by the significant gains in freedom, and the continued growth in the number of free states, noted by Freedom House for 1998 (as this book was going to press). However, the number of electoral democracies remained unchanged.

The first half of the 1990s witnessed two contradictory trends: continued growth in electoral democracy but stagnation in liberal democracy. Juxtaposed, these trends signaled the increasing shallowness of democratization in the late period of the third wave. During the first six years of the 1990s, the gap between formal and liberal democracy in the world steadily widened. As a proportion of all the world's democracies, free states declined from 85 percent in 1990 to 65 percent in 1995 (see table 2.4). The proportion inched back up to 69 percent in 1997 (and close to 74 percent in 1998). But it remains to be seen whether this is a harbinger of a new trend of democratic deepening or just oscillation within a new equilibrium. During the first half of the 1990s, the quality of democracy (as measured by levels of political rights and civil liberties) eroded in a number of the most important and influential new democracies of the third wave (Russia, Turkey, Brazil, and Pakistan), while an expected transition to democracy imploded in Africa's most populous country (Nigeria). At the same time, political freedom deteriorated in several of the longest-surviving democracies in the developing world, including India, Sri Lanka, Colombia, and Venezuela.

As Huntington argues in the *The Third Wave*, the demonstration effects that are so important in the wavelike diffusion or recession of democracy emanate disproportionately from the more powerful countries within a region and internationally. Table 2.5 shows the trends in overall freedom scores for 1986 through 1997 for twelve of the most powerful and prominent electoral democracies in the developing and postcommunist regions.[5] Collectively, their experience represents the mixed and contradictory nature of global democratic trends in recent years. In two of these twelve countries, South Korea and Poland, freedom scores have been continuously good ("free") since their transitions

Table 2.4 Formal and Liberal Democracies, 1990–1997

Year	Formal Democracies (N, %)	Free States/ Liberal Democracies (N, %)	Free States as Percentage of Formal Democracies	Total N
1990	76 (46.1)	65 (39.4)	85.5	165
1991	91 (49.7)	76 (41.5)	83.5	183
1992	99 (53.2)	75 (40.3)	75.8	186
1993	108 (56.8)	72 (37.9)	66.7	190
1994	114 (59.7)	76 (39.8)	66.7	191
1995	117 (61.3)	76 (39.8)	65.0	191
1996	118 (61.8)	79 (41.4)	67.0	191
1997	117 (61.3)	81 (42.4)	69.2	191

Sources: See table 2.1.

to democracy; in South Africa the overall score also has been continuously good since its transition.

However, in each of the six countries that have been electoral democracies for all or most of the period covered in the table, freedom levels have eroded. India deteriorated from a longtime status of "free" to "partly free."[6] Since its democratic transition in 1988, Pakistan declined from "partly free" to the edge of political chaos, with massive political corruption and heavy-handed presidential intervention forcing out one elected government after another. Brazil and the Philippines experienced deterioration in civil liberties that put them below the "free" category; subsequently, the Philippines crossed the threshold back to a "free" state, while Brazil slipped back to a more illiberal democracy as human rights violations persisted. Argentina remained "free" (with significant progress on economic reform), but its freedom scores edged downward from 1990, just after a president with less commitment to democratic procedures, Carlos Menem, succeeded Raúl Alfonsin. (In 1998, Argentina finally fell out of the "free" category.) Thailand has oscillated quite a bit due to military intervention, both overt and subtle. Only in 1996, as military influence continued to ebb, did it return to the nearly free score it had held in the late 1980s.

In the more recent (and unstable) electoral democracies of Russia and Ukraine, freedom scores have declined slightly since the transition and have remained stuck for several years in a state of illiberal democracy encompassing widespread crime and corruption and pervasive weakness of state institutions. The relative success of Russia's 1996 presidential elections was an important step toward institutionalizing electoral competition, but it may also be seen as more of an aversion of political disaster than a decisive gain for political freedom (as Russia's freedom score registered no change).

Turkey's political deterioration has been particularly striking and steep, a paradigmatic case of a third-wave democracy avoiding breakdown while experiencing sharp declines in freedom (from earning a nearly free average score of 3 for six years to becoming one of the most illiberal of all electoral democracies). These declines in freedom owe to the rising political influence of the military (which in mid-1997 executed what one editorial writer dubbed "the first post-modern coup," as it quietly forced from power a coalition government led by the Islamic Rifah Party) and to "widespread" and "appalling" human rights abuses.[7] Driving these developments are the rise of Islamic political mobilization, which challenges the secular foundations of Turkey's political system;

Table 2.5 Average Overall Freedom Scores, Twelve Influential Electoral Democracies and One Failed Democracy, 1986–1997

Country	1986	1987	1988	1989	1990	1991	1992	1993	1994	1995	1996	1997
India	2.5	2.5	2.5	2.5	2.5	3.5	3.5	4.0	4.0	4.0	3.0	3.0
Pakistan	4.5	4.5	3.0⊤	3.0	4.0	4.5	4.5↓	4.0	4.0	4.0↓	4.5	4.5
Brazil	2.0	2.0	2.5	2.0	2.5	2.5↓	2.5	3.5	3.0	3.0	3.0	3.5
Argentina	1.5	1.5	1.5	1.5	2.0	2.0	2.5	2.5↓	2.5	2.5↓	2.5	2.5
Turkey	3.5	3.0	3.0	3.0	3.0	3.0	3.0	4.0	5.0	5.0	4.5	4.5
Philippines	3.0⊤	2.0	2.5	2.5↓	3.0	3.0	3.0	3.5	3.5	3.0	2.5	2.5
South Korea	4.5	4.0	2.5⊤	2.5	2.5	2.5	2.5	2.0	2.0	2.0	2.0	2.0
Thailand	3.0	3.0	3.0	2.5↑	2.5	5.0	3.5	4.0	4.0	3.5	3.0	3.0
Russia③	7.0	6.5	5.5	5.5↑	4.5	3.0⊤	3.5	3.5	3.5	3.5	3.5	3.5
Ukraine③	7.0	6.5	5.5	5.5↑	4.5	3.0⊤	3.0	4.0	3.5	3.5	3.5	3.5
Poland	5.5	5.0	5.0	3.5	2.0⊤	2.0	2.0	2.0	2.0	1.5	1.5	1.5
South Africa	5.5	5.5	5.5	5.5↑	4.5	4.5	4.5	4.5	2.5⊤	1.5	1.5	1.5
Nigeria*	6.0	5.5	5.0	5.5	5.0	4.5	4.5	6.0	6.5	7.0	6.5	6.5

Sources: Freedom House, *Freedom in the World: The Annual Survey of Political Rights and Civil Liberties, 1986–1987*, and subsequent years (New York: Freedom House, 1987 and years following).

Notes: ⊤: year of transition to electoral democracy; ③: scores are for USSR until 1991; ↑↓: upward or downward trend in level of freedom without a change in score; *: failed transition.

mounting political alienation due to poverty, inequality, and the corruption and inefficacy of the country's mainstream politicians; and intense ethnic separatist mobilization and violence. As in other electoral democracies in which freedom declined in this period, such as India, Sri Lanka, and Colombia, violent insurgency generated terror and brutal atrocities by the forces of both the insurgents and the state, displacing an estimated half million Kurds from their homes in southeastern Turkey and killing some 28,000 people in thirteen years of violent conflict.[8] Under U.S. and especially European pressure, human rights abuses eased somewhat in 1995–97 with the passage of reform legislation, the release of some political prisoners, and a de-escalation of the civil war, but abuses remained very serious, subjecting to criminal prosecution, imprisonment, and banning a number of parties, politicians, publications, and journalists who criticized the state security apparatus or endorsed the demands of the Kurdish minority for political recognition. In addition, torture has remained "a routine method of police investigation."[9]

Democracy in Latin America: Progress or Erosion?

The disturbing undertow in the third wave has been particularly significant (if not more widely acknowledged) within Latin America. For some time now, it has been commonly assumed in policy and journalistic circles that—except for Cuba, perhaps Mexico, until recently Haiti, and for a brief time under presidential emergency rule, Peru—all of Latin America is democratic. "Senior officials of the Bush administration liked to claim that '96 percent of Latin Americans now live in democracy' and that the Americas are becoming 'the first completely democratic hemisphere in human history.'"[10] In justifying prospective American military action to restore President Jean-Bertrand Aristide to power in Haiti, President Clinton remarked: "Today 33 of the 35 countries in the Americas have democratically elected leaders."[11]

This claim of nearly universal democracy in the Americas, and of steady democratic progress over the past decade, is misleading if not illusory.[12] It was particularly untenable when, in the early 1990s, it began to become conventional wisdom. By 1993, there were significantly fewer "free" countries (eight) than there had been in 1987 (thirteen), among the twenty-two countries below the Rio Grande with populations of more than one million. Four years later, the number of "free" countries had recovered partially (to eleven), with significant gains for democracy in Central America. However, despite the remarkable breakthroughs for democracy in the Americas over the past decade (including the peace accords in Central America, the transitions in Haiti and Paraguay, and the rise of competitive elections in Mexico), gains in freedom have largely been offset by losses. Nine of the twenty-two (principal) countries in the region had higher levels of freedom in 1997 than they did in 1987, and nine had lower levels.[13] While five countries made transitions to formal democracy (Chile, Nicaragua, Haiti, Panama, and Paraguay) during this decade, only Chile became a "free" country, and five countries fell out of the "free" status because of substantive deterioration in democratic conditions. Even in Argentina, Jamaica, and Venezuela, Freedom House has observed a downward trend in freedom in recent years. By the end of 1997, only eleven of the twenty-two principal countries in the region were rated "free," compared with thirteen in 1987 (see table 2.6). Thus, while harsh and blatant authoritarian rule has receded in the hemisphere, so has liberal democracy, as the region has experienced a convergence toward "more mixed kinds of semi-democratic regimes."[14]

Some consider it remarkable that Latin American democracies have survived at all under the enormous stresses they have experienced since the mid-1980s: dramatic economic downturns and increases in poverty (only recently being reversed in some countries), the mushrooming drug trade, and the violence and corruption that flourish in its wake. Since the redemocratization of Latin America began in the early 1980s, the response to severe adversity and political crisis, including scandals that have forced presidential resignations in several countries, has primarily been adherence to constitutional process and electoral alternation in office (although the military did nearly overthrow democracy in Venezuela in 1992 and has rattled its sabres loudly elsewhere). In the practice of "voting the bums out" rather than mobilizing against democracy itself, Latin American publics have given many observers cause to discern a normalization and maturation of democratic politics unlike previous eras.[15]

Indeed, a number of democratic governments (in Southern and Eastern Europe as well as Latin America) have been able to make considerable progress in economic reform during the third wave, and in one sizable sample of such reform experiences, "the party that initiated cuts in working-class income has been defeated in less than half the cases."[16] This resilience and persistence of constitutional procedures is cause for hope about the future of democracy in Latin America. So are reforms that opened up the electoral process in Venezuela and Colombia, instituted

Table 2.6 Freedom Scores, Latin American Countries, 1987, 1993, and 1997

Countries and Freedom Scores (Political Rights, Civil Liberties)

Combined Freedom Score	1987	1993	1997
	Liberal Democracies		
2	Costa Rica (1, 1); Trinidad & Tobago (1, 1)⇑	Trinidad & Tobago (1, 1)	Costa Rica (1, 2); Trinidad & Tobago (1, 2); Uruguay (1, 2); Chile (2, 2); Bolivia (1,3)⇑
3–4	Venezuela (1, 2); Argentina (2, 1); Uruguay (2, 2); Jamaica (2, 2)⇑; Dominican Republic (1, 3); Brazil (2,2)	Costa Rica (1, 2)#; Uruguay (2, 2)#; Chile (2, 2)	Argentina (2, 3); Jamaica (2, 3); Panama (2, 3); Venezuela (2, 3); El Salvador (2, 3)⇑; Honduras (2, 3)⇑
5	Bolivia (2, 3); Colombia (2, 3); Ecuador (2, 3); Honduras (2, 3); Peru (2, 3)	Argentina (2, 3)↓; Bolivia (2, 3); Ecuador (2, 3)↓; Jamaica (2, 3)⇓	
	Electoral Democracies (and Pseudodemocracies)		
6–7	Guatemala (3, 3); El Salvador (3, 4)	Colombia (2, 4)↓; Dominican Republic (3, 3)↓; El Salvador (3, 3); Honduras (3, 3)#; Panama (3, 3)↓; Paraguay (3, 3); Venezuela (3, 3); Brazil (3, 4)⇓	Dominican Republic (3, 3)↑; Ecuador (3, 3)⇓⇑; Nicaragua (3, 3)↑; Brazil (3, 4)⇓; Guatemala (3, 4)⇑; Mexico (3, 4)⇑⇓; Paraguay (4, 3)↓
8–9	Mexico (4, 4)	Mexico (4, 4)↓; Nicaragua (4, 5)↓; Guatemala (4, 5)	Colombia (4, 4)↓; Haiti (4, 5)↓; Peru (5, 4)
	Authoritarian		
10–11	Chile (6, 5); Haiti (5, 6)↓; Nicaragua (5, 5)⇑; Panama (5, 5)↓; Paraguay (5, 6)	Peru (5, 5)⇑	
12–14	Cuba (6, 6)	Cuba (7, 7); Haiti (7,7)	Cuba (7, 7)

Notes: Table excludes countries with less than 1 million population. Figures in parentheses are Freedom House country scores (political rights and civil liberties, respectively). Each scale ranges from 1 to 7, with 1 being most free. #: rating was changed for purely methodological reasons. ⇓: shift downward from previous year. ⇑: shift upward from previous year; ↓: downward trend in level of democracy, not significant enough to change freedom rating.

Sources: Freedom House, *Freedom in the World: Political Rights and Civil Liberties, 1987–1988; 1993–1994; 1997–1998* (New York: Freedom House, 1988, 1994, 1998).

an independent electoral commission in Panama, strengthened civilian control over the military in Argentina and Chile (and eliminated the military altogether in Panama and Haiti), and improved judicial functioning in several countries. These currents of progress toward democratic consolidation are examined in the following chapter. Subsequently, in chapter 4, we look more closely at one of the most promising democratic developments in Latin America, the growing trend toward decentralization of state power and democratization of government at the local level. Civil society has also grown in strength and independence (and significance for democratic development), as we will see in chapter 6.

However, these positive developments have been counterbalanced and in many countries even outweighed by conditions that render electoral democracy increasingly shallow, illiberal, unaccountable, and afflicted. Particularly troublesome are the weakness of formal political institutions, as evidenced in what Guillermo O'Donnell terms the "delegative" nature of democracy and in the extensive, even growing, scope of human rights violations.[17]

Delegative Democracy

To a considerable degree, the gap between democratic form and substance in the world is an institutional gap. No political system in the world operates strictly according to its formal institutional prescriptions, but what distinguishes most of the democracies in Latin America, Asia, Africa, and the postcommunist states are political institutions too weak to ensure the representation of diverse interests, constitutional supremacy, the rule of law, and the constraint of executive authority. The terms *low-intensity democracy, democracy by default, poor democracy, empty democracy*, and *hybrid regimes* (among others) have been used to describe the institutionally weak and substantively superficial nature of most new and recently restored democracies in Latin America.[18] Rather more precisely circumscribed theoretically is O'Donnell's conception of *delegative democracy*, which hinges critically on the relative absence of horizontal accountability between the elected president and the other two branches of government.[19]

Although delegative democracies have the formal constitutional structures of democracy—and may even (barely) meet the empirical standards of liberal democracy, as Argentina does—they are institutionally hollow and fragile. Voters are mobilized by clientelistic ties and populist, personalistic (rather than programmatic) appeals; parties and independent interest groups are weak and fragmented. Instead of producing an effective means of ongoing representation of popular interests, elections delegate sweeping and largely unaccountable authority to whoever wins the presidential election. For his or her term of office, the (democratically) elected president can then govern by decree and even whim, claiming to embody the will of the nation while invoking an authority based more on personal charisma and the backing of a popular movement than on a political party or institution. In such plebiscitary systems, O'Donnell argues, change (including economic reform) can be implemented swiftly and decisively precisely because so much power is delegated to a single office. However, policy is also more likely to be erratic and unsustainable, because the very swiftness and lack of consultation generate "a higher likelihood of gross mistakes," because election campaigns do not produce any clear programmatic and policy commitments that subsequently constrain leaders, and because no effort is made after the election to build a broad and informed coalition of support for the new policies.[20] The only real platform of the elected president is, as Argentine president Carlos Menem said in his election campaign, "*siganme*" (follow me).[21]

Highly personalistic, populist, delegative presidents like Menem and Alberto Fujimori in Peru rise to power precisely because of the political institutional vacuum in their countries. But rather than seeking to strengthen the judiciary, political parties, congress, and other representative institutions, delegative presidents set out deliberately to weaken, fragment, and marginalize them further, as a means of further aggrandizing their own personal power. "In both Argentina and Peru, political deinstitutionalization has been a conscious strategy of personalist leaders, enabling them to establish unmediated relationships with atomized mass followings while overcoming institutional checks on the imposition of neoliberal reforms."[22] Elsewhere, as in Venezuela, such deliberate institutional marginalization has served political agendas opposed to economic reform. The key point is that delegative democracy is not only a structure but also a process, which over time tends to accentuate the enervation of political institutions and the personalization of political power. In the process, democracy becomes not simply different, or "persistent without consolidation," but weaker, more hollow, and more fragile.

Delegative democracies thus present a number of problems for the quality and stability of democracy. While truly representative systems also delegate authority from the people, they do so much more broadly, in ways that check and separate powers and establish accountability not just vertically and occasionally, at election time, but also horizontally and continuously, in the play between independently powerful branches of government.[23] Because they rest on well-developed political institutions (parties, legislatures, courts, local governments) and are much more inclined to engage organized forces in civil society (and thus to provide more *continuous* vertical accountability), representative democracies, in O'Donnell's scheme, are not only more likely to check the abuse of power, they are also more likely to produce stable, sustainable, and broadly acceptable policies (though ones perhaps less capable of "miraculous" progress in the short term). They are thus more likely to avoid repeated crises and to attenuate rather than swell popular cynicism. For all these reasons, democracies are more likely to function effectively and become consolidated the more they are representative rather than delegative in nature. Indeed, despite the widespread assumption that policy delegation and insulation from political pressures are necessary for successful economic reform under democracy, economic reform appears to be most effective, coherent, and sustainable over the long run when it uses democratic processes of deliberation, consultation, representation, and coalition building.[24] Certainly, such a style of policy making helps to develop democratic institutions and popular commitment to them.

O'Donnell depicts delegative democracy as a new species of political system, demanding a distinct conceptual place within a typology of democratic regimes. Yet the novelty of Latin America's delegative democracies may have more to do with their persistence, and with an international (and regional) context that generates powerful pressures against their displacement, than with their poor institutionalization and partially autocratic natures. As Jonathan Hartlyn and Arturo Valenzuela observe in their review of democracy in Latin America since 1930, "even in democratic periods many countries in the region may be more accurately characterized as semi-democratic . . . because of constraints on constitutionalism, contestation, or inclusiveness," and some regimes featured such "persistent interference in politics of the military and powerful economic interests" that they appeared to be "hybrid democratic-authoritarian."[25]

During the 1980s and early 1990s, the costs of delegative democracy have been abundantly apparent in a number of Latin American countries with weak political institutions unable to constrain executive authority. As Francisco Weffort notes, the purest examples of the delegative pathologies of personalistic leadership, plebiscitarian elections, and political clientelism have been Brazil and Peru.[26] In both cases, economic policy fluctuated unpredictably within and across administrations, and populism and policy incoherence produced hyperinflation and economic crisis. In Brazil, *personalismo* left a crippling vacuum when the newly elected president, Tancredo Neves, died in 1985, at the dawn of the restored democracy; lacking political skill or any reliable base of political support in the fragmented party system and congress, his successor, José Sarney, floundered economically and politically. Then, in 1989, the hollow, personalistic nature of Brazilian democracy was evidenced in the election to the presidency of a telegenic but shallow young governor, Fernando Collor de Mello, whose arrogance, inexperience, inefficacy, and corruption brought about his impeachment and resignation in midterm (and the country's political drift for most of the final two years of that term). Only with the 1994 election of President Fernando Henrique Cardoso, a qualitatively different type of politician—a respected and experienced moderate of extraordinary intellect, high integrity, and commitment to coalition building—has Brazil gained the chance to chart a more positive course. Yet even Cardoso has had to use some old-fashioned methods to try to gain passage of economic and political reforms by a congress congenitally prone to gridlock and corrupt patronage politics.

In Peru, delegative democracy fostered the meteoric rise and crushing demise of the young, charismatic, left-leaning president Alan García, whose populist, incoherent economic policies plunged the country into fiscal chaos during the last half of the 1980s, followed by the election in 1990 of a populist, antiestablishment political novice, Alberto Fujimori, who, like Collor in Brazil, had little political base. After two years of implementing severe austerity policies he had opposed in the campaign, having to deal with a congress controlled by opposition parties, and battling the ongoing terrorist insurgency of the ruthless guerrilla group, Sendero Luminoso (Shining Path), Fujimori apparently grew impatient with even the feeble constraints on his authority that Peruvian democracy could muster. On April 5, 1992, he assumed emergency powers in an *autogolpe* that "temporarily" suspended the 1979 constitution, dissolved the congress, dismantled the judiciary and the general accounting office, arrested prominent opposition leaders, and then delayed municipal elections.[27]

Independent observers saw little need or justification for Fujimori's self-coup against democracy. New economic policies were being implemented, the congress, while watchful, appeared willing to work with him, the economy was starting to turn around, and the international community was sympathetic.[28] Although the military appears to have been consulted and assented to the executive coup, neither it nor the business community was clamoring for it. Rather, the delegative nature of democracy—with its aggrandizement of personal leadership, its erratic succession of policies, its corrupt and ineffective parties, and its venal, incompetent judicial system—greatly contributed to twelve years of disastrous democratic performance, which discredited the formal institutions of democracy while leaving society craving for a strong ruler (a messiah) to rescue the country. The "crisis of Peru's representative institutions" provided the structural opportunity for an authoritarian personality (Fujimori) to seize power and then to reshape the constitution and manipulate the resumption of electoral politics in ways that dramatically heightened the delegative, Caesaristic powers of the presidency.[29]

Elsewhere in the Americas, the delegative nature of democracy also figured prominently in its travails. Particularly alarming were the two serious military coup attempts (in February and November 1992) by junior officers in Venezuela, whose two-party system had been regarded for thirty-five years as a pillar of democracy in Latin America. The coup attempts, and the subsequent signs of decay and destabilization in the country's politics, were the products of both long-term trends and recent shocks. The biggest shock, which triggered a massive riot in the capital and its bloody repression, was the announcement by President Carlos Andrés Pérez of harsh economic austerity measures shortly after he took office in February 1989, after a traditional campaign as a social-welfare populist. Yet the crisis was structurally long in the making. The profligate distribution of state petroleum revenues (and when these dwindled, foreign debt) through lavish patronage and corruption, high profits, high wages, and the lowest taxes on the continent (as well as the extreme protectionism characteristic of other countries on the continent) produced fiscal disarray and adjustment imperatives for which the country, politically and psychologically, was totally unprepared.[30]

Moreover, closer examination might have gleaned from the 1989 *caracazo* (explosion) in Caracas (which may have claimed as much as eight times the official death toll of 277) the warning sign "that no institutions existed to channel Venezuelans' discontent."[31] Mounting intraparty factionalism and personal rivalry, and steady erosion of the spirit of cooperation and compromise, "had weakened beyond recognition" the distinctive pattern of democratic pragmatism, collaboration, and incorporation initiated by the Pact of Punto Fijo with the rebirth of democracy in 1958.[32] The two strong, dominant parties increasingly appeared to constitute a venal, self-interested *partidocracia* that, in its extreme internal centralization and pervasive reach, monopolized power, limited accountability to the voters, and "blocked channels for representation outside the parties, within the parties, and among the parties."[33] In short, through institutional rigidity and decay, Venezuelan democracy had become more and more like the afflicted, delegative democracies of the region.

With deep structural economic and political problems, Venezuela remains a democracy in trouble. Although significant political reforms have been implemented to decentralize power and improve democratic accountability, and the Venezuelan public has consistently manifested overwhelming popular support for democracy (as opposed to military rule),[34] the impeachment and removal on corruption charges of President Pérez in May 1993 only partially and temporarily arrested the political crisis.

The election that December of aging former president Rafael Caldera with a skimpy plurality of 31 percent, in a decisive rejection of the two main parties (AD and COPEI, the latter of which Caldera had founded), turned the country back to populist and incoherent economic policies and highly personalistic presidential leadership. Perhaps enamored with the Fujimori model, Caldera, after taking office in 1994, suspended constitutional guarantees regarding arbitrary arrest, property rights, and freedoms of expression and movement. Unlike Fujimori, however, he embraced unsustainable statist, protectionist economic policies during the first two years of his term. But these old *caudillista* formulas did nothing to revive economic health or popular confidence. By mid-1996, public opinion polls continued to reflect "widespread popular passivity, apathy, and distrust of democratic institutions," and electoral abstention continued to rise (to more than 70% in the December 1995 local elections).[35] In its personalism, clientelism, corruption, and institutional erosion, with their consequent political alienation and cynicism, delegative democracy has become a major impediment to the reconsolidation of a tottering Venezuelan democracy—which may survive mainly for want of an alternative and fear of the unknown.[36]

In Latin America as a whole, both the degree of delegativeness and its impact on democracy have varied. But its fundamental ills—personalism, concentration of power, and weak, unresponsive political institutions—have prominently contributed to the turbulence and poor quality of democracy and to the consequent political cynicism and apathy among Latin American publics. At one extreme, the Dominican Republic appeared for many years the paradigmatic case of hollow democratic persistence (since 1978) without progress toward more accountable, responsive, effective governance. An overweening, centralized state, a highly presidentialist system, a weak, increasingly fragmented party system, and a long legacy of venal, patrimonial politics trapped the country in the most unseemly (and questionably democratic) features of *delegativismo*. In fact, the controversial, fraud-ridden nature of Dominican elections finally seemed to push the country back below the threshold of formal democracy in 1994, when the country's dominant political figure of three decades, the blind, eighty-seven-year-old former president Joaquín Balaguer, was declared reelected in a result "widely disbelieved by vast sectors of the population and by international actors."[37]

At the opposite end of the spectrum are the two countries that have made the most impressive democratic progress since the mid to late 1980s, the only two third-wave democracies in Latin America to have average freedom scores as liberal as 2: Uruguay and Chile. Not coincidentally, these (along with equally liberal Costa Rica, the oldest and most stable democracy in the region) are the countries that least manifest delegative features. Although each country has faced distinctive democratic problems (including a troubling reserved domain of power for the military in Chile), each has benefited from a strong tradition of democratic values, a rule of law, and relatively institutionalized political parties.[38] Moreover, posttransition governments have been able to mobilize some degree of national vision and consensus while rising above narrow partisan and factional divisions. The first posttransition presidents, Julio María Sanguinetti in Uruguay and Patricio Aylwin in Chile, governed in a style notably different from the *personalismo* and *decretismo* of delegative democracies. Rather than bypassing representative institutions and imposing personal policies, they sought to mobilize and maintain broad consensual support. The capacity of seventeen center-left parties to hold together in Chile's Concertación de Partidos por la Democracia has been particularly impressive and resulted in a decisive victory for the coalition in the December 1993 presidential election, when Eduardo Frei won with 58 percent of the vote (to 24% for his principal right-wing rival).

Finally, there is the archetypical case of Argentina. Next to Chile, Argentina has made the most dramatic progress toward economic reform in the region (and unlike Chile, under civilian, democratic governance). As we see in later chapters, there have been important currents of democratic progress in Argentina, as well. But the country's impressive economic stabilization and opening under Carlos Menem was accompanied by a highly delegative style of rule that diminished the quality of democracy significantly from the level that prevailed under the politically liberal (but economically ineffectual) President Raúl Alfonsín. An assessment by Freedom House paints a classic portrait of a delegative, abusive, barely constrained president and ruling party elite, who evince contempt for the spirit and practice of democracy:

> The separation of powers and the rule of law have been undermined by President Menem's propensity to rule by decree and his manipulation of the judiciary. He has invoked emergency laws to issue more than 250 "decrees of necessity and urgency," more than 90 percent of all such decrees issued since 1853. Attempts by legislators to challenge Menem in court have been blocked since 1990, when Menem pushed a bill increasing the number of Supreme Court justices from five to nine through the Peronist-controlled Senate and stacked the court with politically loyal judges.
>
> Menem has also used the Supreme Court to uphold decrees removing the comptroller general, whose main function is to investigate executive wrongdoing, and other officials mandated to probe government corruption. Some top prosecutors have been removed and replaced with officials who had been targets of their investigations. In late 1993, Menem forced a number of Supreme Court judges to resign as part of the deal with Alfonsín to secure presidential reelection [through a constitutional amendment backed by Alfonsín's Radical Party in exchange for certain political reforms and spoils]. Overall, the judicial system is politicized and riddled with the corruption endemic to all branches of the government, creating what Argentines call "juridical insecurity."
>
> Despite nearly two dozen major corruption scandals and the resignations of at least that many senior government officials since 1989, no investigation has ended in a trial. Polls show that more than 80 percent of Argentines do not trust the judicial system, and that corruption ranked second—behind low salaries—among issues that most concern them.[39]

These trends leave one to wonder what political, economic, and social costs Argentina may pay for the corruption and institutional degradation of the Menem era. It seems reasonable to conjecture that Argentina's economic turnaround, and its appeal to foreign investors, would have been far more rapid and decisive if it had managed to control corruption and institutionalize the rule of law. Indeed, the grossly dysfunctional character of the judicial system throughout Latin America—as evidenced in se-

vere problems of corruption, inefficiency, inaccessibility, and lack of resources, autonomy, professionalism, and training—now constitutes one
of the biggest obstacles to progress not only in democracy but in economic reform and vitality as well.[40]

Illiberal Democracy

The deterioration of democracy under Argentina's highly delegative
president Menem has been of a particular kind. As the above analysis
suggests, and as the trend in its freedom scores shows, the erosion has
been primarily in civil liberties: while Freedom House has judged political rights to have held relatively constant at a score of 2, civil liberties have declined from a score of 1 under President Alfonsin to a score
of 3 under Menem. The press in particular has come under pressure
and assault. "Since 1989 there have been an increasing number of inci-
dents of media intimidation, including more than fifty cases of of physical attacks by security forces and shadowy groups apparently linked to
the ruling Peronist party. Journalists and publications investigating official corruption are the principal targets."[41] In the run-up to the October 1993 Chamber of Deputies elections (which failed to give Menem's Peronist Party the two-thirds majority it needed to amend the
constitution unilaterally), "Peronists were implicated in a series of
death threats and physical attacks against prominent journalists critical
of Menem," and Menem himself sought to intimidate and demoralize
critical journalists with an assault of expensive lawsuits.[42] Although
freedom of speech and of the press are respected in general, and there
is considerable pluralism of views, blatant acts of press intimidation and
victimization continue.[43]

The Argentine case is not unusual. Wherever democracy is highly
delegative and mainly electoral in nature, and where political institutions
that constrain executive authority and produce transparency and responsiveness are weak, the rule of law is tenuous and human rights may
be seriously abused. In fact, no aspect of politics and governance so seriously challenges the image of sustained democratic progress in Latin
America as the persistence of grave human rights abuses. Liberal democracy requires protection for freedoms of conscience, expression, organization, and information and the ability of all individuals and groups—irrespective of their wealth and status—freely to pursue their interests and
seek redress of grievances from the state. There is no more fundamental
interest than the security of the person from arbitrary harm, and when

harmful acts—illegal arrest, imprisonment without trial, *desaparecid* (disappearance), torture, rape, murder—are committed, condoned, or excused by agents of the state, these become political acts, diminishing the quality of democracy. While such abuses are most serious, systematic, and immune to legal accountability in countries in which democracy has been absent or in suspension (as in Cuba and, during recent periods, Haiti and Peru), they exist to troubling degrees in many countries with civilian, constitutional rule, including some that Freedom House continues to classify (just barely, perhaps) as "free." Only due process under a true rule of law can reasonably minimize human rights abuses, but this is precisely what is lacking in many "democracies" in Latin America and other developing regions.

The democratic wave of the past decade has brought about a much freer, more vigorous and pluralistic civil society in Latin America, including mass media and human rights organizations that are better prepared to monitor human rights conditions and more assertively inclined to expose abuses.[44] Nevertheless, the trends in Latin America (and elsewhere), evident in the resurgence of authoritarian practices under elected civilian presidents in countries such as Peru, Venezuela, and Colombia and in a general erosion of the rule of law under pressure from the drug trade, confirm my thesis of a growing gap between electoral and liberal democracy. Even with their rather different political orientations, Human Rights Watch and Freedom House thus come to remarkably similar conclusions:

> Periodic elections and transfers of power have not automatically led to an improvement in the quality of democracy experienced on a daily basis by the majority of citizens. Impunity for serious human rights violations committed by state agents is still appallingly pervasive; for the most part, military and police forces are accountable to courts and to civilian authorities on paper only. The courts fail miserably in providing citizens with a fair and impartial forum for the resolution of private disputes, and even more miserably in protecting them from abuse at the hands of the state, or in redressing those abuses.

> The reality is that, in the region today, rule is still based more on power than on law. . . . In a majority of countries the traditionally dominant sectors of society—political elites, the wealthy, armies, police—continue to enrich themselves at public expense, while the human rights of ordinary people are violated with impunity. Judicial systems are less

about justice than providing protection for those who can pay for it and punishing those who cannot. Voters can chase presidents and legislators through the ballot box in most countries, but government remains a racket dominated by the powerful and the well connected.[45]

Unfortunately, these assessments of the early to mid-1990s remain valid as the decade draws to a close. In its 1998 report, Human Rights Watch observed, "Massive and serious human rights violations plagued the region in 1997 regardless of the regular alternation in power of elected governments." Even in such major South American countries as Colombia, Peru, Venezuela, Brazil, and Argentina, "massacres, extrajudicial executions, disappearances, torture, and other forms of police brutality . . . stubbornly continued."[46] The U.S. State Department's *Country Reports on Human Rights Practices* for 1995 through 1997 largely coincides with these other sources in documenting the persistence of serious and widespread human rights abuses in most of Central and South America, and with much less of the judicial independence and integrity that provide some means for reining in abuses in poorer but more institutionalized democracies such as India and Sri Lanka (their own problems notwithstanding). In fact, in most Latin American countries the judicial system is grossly overburdened, backlogged, slow, unreliable, inefficient, underfunded, and lacking in public faith and credibility. It is also typically heavily politicized, intimidated by powerful establishment or insurgent forces, poorly paid and trained, lacking in transparency and secure tenure, and thus corrupt and dispirited. As a result, the poor have slight access to justice (with little in the way of legal assistance or effective public defenders), and state officials have rampant impunity not only for past human rights violations but for ongoing crimes and abuses. The latter include arbitrary arrest and detention, torture and beatings, political and extrajudicial killings, and murderous "social cleansing" of street children and other "undesirable" elements, by the police, the military, and other agents of state security (as well as wealthy and well-connected private actors, especially in rural areas).[47]

In short, most of Latin America has stood in the 1990s at a distinctive historical juncture, combining what Guillermo O'Donnell dubs "polyarchy and the unrule of law." Over vast stretches of social and territorial space, "the legal state is limited" or altogether absent. "The resulting dominant informal legal system, punctuated by arbitrary reintroductions of the formal one, supports a world of extreme violence."[48]

With closer domestic and international scrutiny and certain institutional reforms, human rights conditions do seem to be somewhat improving in countries such as El Salvador and Honduras (whose special prosecutor for human rights initiated in 1995 "the hemisphere's first investigation of active-duty military officers for human rights violations").[49] Yet in Guatemala and Peru modest improvements still leave severe human rights abuses, including extrajudicial killings, disappearances, attacks on journalists and politicians, torture, and the routine violation of due process as a result of arbitrary arrest and detention, judicial inefficiency and corruption, and, in Peru, the continued sitting of "faceless" tribunals to summarily judge detainees accused of terrorist activities.[50]

In Haiti, neither the return of the democratically elected President Aristide, ending a brutal three-year reign of military and elite terror, nor his electoral replacement by René Preval, marking the first peaceful transfer of power under democratic auspices in the country's history, nor the presence of more than six thousand international peacekeepers, could erase a two-hundred-year legacy that left the judicial system virtually moribund and the people prone to vigilante violence and murderous retribution. Continuing problems of impunity of security force personnel and intimidation of journalists and orchestration of attacks against the private and public broadcast media testify to the tenuous state of democracy in Haiti.[51]

Even in countries in which the ongoing abuse of human rights has been substantially contained, the inability to establish accountability for past crimes violates what the Inter-American Commission on Human Rights identifies, in a report critical of the amnesty laws in Uruguay and Argentina, as the intrinsic right of victims to justice. The commission found that the laws were incompatible with countries' obligations under the American Convention on Human Rights, a ruling that prompted Argentina and Uruguay to seek to limit the commission's jurisdiction to de facto violations.[52]

We need to question what we mean by *democracy* when situations like the following prevail in Latin American countries regarded as constitutional democracies:

— Widespread violence, including torture and even murder, by police in Brazil, Colombia, and Venezuela (and to a lesser extent Argentina) against suspected common criminals and "lowlives" (including an estimated seven to ten million Brazilian street children) in impoverished, crime-ridden barrios;[53]

— Violence, murder, and forced labor inflicted on landless peasants and rural activists in Brazil and Central America by the private armies of powerful landlords, in complicity with local or regional authorities or even elements of the security forces;[54]
— Political assassinations, kidnappings, and indiscriminate attacks on civilian populations by guerrilla armies in Peru, Colombia, and (until recently) Guatemala, countered by indiscriminate aerial bombing and ground attacks and forced displacement of rural populations by security forces, as well as "dirty-war" tactics (murder, torture, disappearance) by military and paramilitary forces;[55]
— Massive violence, corruption, and terror, including murder of judges, prosecutors, journalists, and politicians, by drug cartels in Colombia and throughout the Andes (often allied with insurgents), countered by special courts and procedures (violating basic tenets of due process);[56]
— Shifting alliances among drug traffickers, guerrilla armies, large landowners, and the military and police, spawning and condoning further violence against community activists, trade union and leftist political leaders, peasant and indigenous leaders, and human rights activists;[57]
— The pervasive absence or inefficacy throughout the region of civilian-led procedures for independently scrutinizing and punishing the murderous misconduct of military, police, intelligence, and prison authorities, as well as army and police officials operating off duty as death squads.[58]

Respect for human rights constitutes a continuum, and different observers are bound to disagree about how far a country can fall short and still be considered democratic. In 1997, of the twenty-two Latin American countries with populations above one million, only four had a civil liberties rating of 2 (none had a 1; see table 2.6). Ten had a civil liberties rating of 3. Six of these qualified as democracies only because they rated a 2 on political rights (Bolivia scored 1 on political rights), but all ten had levels of human rights abuse that significantly marred the quality of democracy and its potential to garner deep, widespread, and enduring popular support.

The illiberal nature of democracy in Latin America today is cause for concern for several reasons. First, civil liberties are not only of intrinsic concern to those who value freedom but significantly affect the quality of democracy even in strictly political terms. Second, according to Freedom House ratings, civil liberties have deteriorated over the past decade in countries such as Peru, Argentina, Brazil, Venezuela, and Colombia. Third, a steep and prolonged deterioration in human rights (and the general political quality of democracy) renders a country more susceptible to a complete breakdown of the regime. Fujimori's *autogolpe* in Peru was preceded by four years of declining freedom ratings by Freedom House, from a 2, 3 in 1980 through 1987, to a 2, 4 in 1988, a 3, 4 in 1990, and a 3, 5 in 1991. The attempted coups in Venezuela and Guatemala also followed steady declines in political rights and civil liberties. "Civilian inability to control paramilitary death squads or sanction human rights violations has seriously diminished regime legitimacy by baring the limits of the rule of law and demonstrating the inability of governments to protect their own citizens."[59]

The system of justice and conditions of human rights constitute a partial regime, in which we can observe the close interconnection between three variables: democratic quality, democratic legitimacy, and democratic consolidation (and hence stability). Elaborating and explaining these interactions is the principal focus of the next chapter. Here, it suffices to underscore that democratic regimes, even if they persist for extended periods of time, will not be stable and secure until they are considered legitimate by all major sections of their populations. For at least three reasons, this is highly unlikely to happen with the levels of human rights abuse now prevalent in most of Latin America.

First, from any political system but perhaps especially from democracy, people expect more than economic growth and security. They also value political liberty and security: freedom from terror and violence by both state and nonstate actors. Regimes that cannot rein in systemic criminal and terrorist violence, while at the same time subjecting the police and military to accountability before the law, are unlikely to garner deep, widespread, and unconditional popular commitment. In such systems, only the rich and powerful can feel secure (and then only behind very high walls).

Second, when the military is not accountable to civilian oversight and justice, democracy is inherently limited by a reserve domain of power. This not only diminishes regime legitimacy but undermines the security and confidence of civilian democratic authority. A critical realm of power, official violence, lies beyond the effective control of citizens and their representatives and can be turned against them at any time. The very threat of this intimidates elected officials, which reinforces military autonomy and impunity while underscoring the need for the very civilian supremacy that is lacking. As I argue in chapter 3, shrewd, forceful, and even courageous political leadership must strategize and mobilize to break this historical pattern.

Third, human rights victims in these countries are not randomly distributed. They are disproportionately poor, landless, powerless, poorly educated (hence largely ignorant of their legal rights), and members of racial and cultural minorities. In Latin America, indigenous peoples, in particular, suffer. As long as discrete groups in society are more or less excluded from the promise and protection of democracy, the regime will be unable to achieve the comprehensive inclusion necessary for broad legitimation among both elites and masses. For even if the regime achieves the "consensually unified elite" that signifies for one theoretical school the consolidation of democracy,[60] there will eventually arise from the excluded sector, as there has in Colombia and Venezuela, a counterelite, which challenges the existing political settlement and demands inclusion. These demands may eventually exact a high price in blood and fear and in rapidly escalating human rights violations, as they have in recent years through insurgencies in Central America, Peru, and Colombia and through criminal violence in Brazil. Improved protections for civil liberties and minority rights are thus an essential condition for consolidating democracy and making it truly stable.

Normative support for democracy and positive evaluations of the democratic regime both appear related to the quality of democracy, including the conditions of human rights, within Latin America and other regions (see chap. 5). For example, democratic legitimacy is weaker in Brazil than in its more liberal Southern Cone neighbors of Uruguay, Chile, and Argentina. And it is weaker in Chile than in many other countries in the region. This is not what would be expected for such an economically prosperous country with such a long democratic tradition. Doubts about democracy in Chile appear related to the continuing reserve power of the military and lack of accountablity for crimes of the past.

It is conceivable and even likely that certain historical, institutional, and cultural factors generate greater levels both of civil liberties and of positive assessments of democracy. These same factors probably explain the much higher levels of democratic legitimacy in Spain, Portugal, and Greece (and other Western European democracies) as compared to Brazil (see chap. 5). But it is plausible that the marginalization of a large proportion of the Brazilian citizenry, and its significantly greater vulnerability to human rights abuses, reinforces and sharpens feelings of skepticism, apathy, and alienation toward democracy.

The Globalization of (Hollow) Democracy

Hollow, illiberal, poorly institutionalized democracy is by no means unique to Latin America. It is characteristic of many third-wave (and Third World) democracies. Political violence and disorder, human rights violations, overweening executives, legislative and judicial inefficacy, corruption, and military impunity and prerogatives diminish the quality of democracy not only in major third-wave electoral regimes such as Turkey, Pakistan, Russia, and Ukraine but also in a wide range of smaller ones, such as Georgia, Moldova, Zambia, Mozambique, and most of the other new democracies of Africa and the former Soviet Union. In Africa, as in Latin America, presidentialism tends to mean strongly personalistic, clientelistic rule with weak constraints on executive authority. Some regimes, such as Zambia's, have descended into pseudodemocracy because of the repression of opposition and aggrandizement of presidential power. Most of the semipresidential regimes of the former Soviet Union (most notably Russia) can at least be considered delegative in their personalization of executive authority and lack of horizontal accountability.

Interestingly, even parliamentary regimes may manifest these delegative features, when party control of the prime minister is weak and the form of cabinet government does not work in practice. As Ergun Özbudun observes, since its restoration in 1983, Turkish democracy has "displayed strong resemblances to delegative democracy."[61] Strong-willed prime ministers have often ignored the cabinet in decision making and have used executive decrees to bypass parliament. Elections increasingly stress the qualities of individual leaders, who are portrayed as saviors of the country. As in Venezuela, strong party discipline and the absence of intraparty democracy render members of parliament highly dependent on the nominations and patronage controlled by top party leaders and, thus, too docile to hold the executives accountable (although some check is exercised by an unusually independent and assertive constitutional court). The pathologies of delegative rule are even more apparent in Pakistan, where there is less party discipline but also a less effective judicial system to constrain executive action. Under both Prime Minister Benazir Bhutto and her rival and predecessor (as well as successor) Nawaz Sharif, power has been heavily personalized and abused, the courts have been packed, and the judiciary has been inefficient, dependent, and corrupt.[62] In mid-1997, sizable majorities of the Pakistani public said the country lacked an impartial judiciary (62%), freedom of the press (56%), and a government free of corruption (64%). "The bottom line: nine years into civilian government, half do *not* consider Pakistan a democratic state (about a quarter do)."[63]

The Turkish and Pakistani regimes also reflect the generally illiberal nature of electoral democracies born in the third wave or functioning in Third World conditions. Despite improvements (under intense European and international pressure) that have reduced the incidence of abuse, Turkey's democracy continues to be marred by chronic human rights violations: punishment of critical journalists, extrajudicial killings, disappearances, destruction of villages, and torture, accompanied by immunity for the security forces who commit them.[64] Like some other electoral democracies struggling with brutal insurgencies, Turkish democracy is a mix of free and repressive realms. While there is scope for vigorous political contestation and open debate on many issues, explicitly pro-Kurdish political parties are banned and pro-Kurdish politicians are targeted for prosecution. In recent years, "some efforts by journalists, authors, and intellectuals to discuss the Kurdish issue, human rights abuses by security forces, or the armed conflict in southeastern Turkey were met with severe repression, including censorship, imprisonment and torture of journalists and writers, and the banning of newspapers."[65] Modest reforms notwithstanding, the government continues to deny the Kurdish minority certain basic cultural and linguistic rights, banning several newspapers published in the Kurdish language and prohibiting radio stations that carry broadcasts in Kurdish.[66]

In Pakistan, human rights violations appear more endemic throughout the country, with its much weaker judicial system, poorly disciplined police, more severe inequality, and more dispersed militant religious and sectarian groups. Yet Pakistan follows the pattern that finds the epicenter of human rights abuses in areas where extremist ethnic or religious groups wage violent campaigns against state authority. In Pakistan, that epicenter is Sind province and especially its capital, Karachi, the site of militant mobilization and guerrilla violence by the Mohajir Quami Movement (MQM), which seeks greater economic and political power for the Mohajirs (Muslims who fled India after the partition in 1947).[67] The most serious problems include extrajudicial executions (five hundred political killings were recorded in 1996 and a similar number in

1997), widespread torture of detainees, rape of female prisoners by police, arbitrary arrests and detentions, denial of fair trial, and continued restrictions on freedom of the press.[68] The illiberal and unsettled nature of electoral democracy in Pakistan was underscored in 1997 by the passage of an antiterrorism act, which suspended constitutional safeguards while increasing police powers,[69] and by the constitutional crisis that saw Prime Minister Nawaz Sharif locked in a bitter power struggle with the president and the supreme court, which required the mediation of the armed forces chief of staff and the resignation of the president.

In Sri Lanka, human rights abuses such as torture, terror, rape, disappearances (some seventeen thousand over a decade), extrajudicial killings, arbitrary arrests, and restrictions on free expression are mainly associated with and occur in the area of the brutal insurgency waged between the Liberation Tigers of Tamil Eelam and the state's counterinsurgency. In Sri Lanka, however, the scope of terrorist activity has pressed out the boundaries of emergency rule to cover a much larger proportion of the country than in Turkey.[70]

The cases of Turkey and Sri Lanka (and Peru and Colombia) show how difficult it is to protect human rights and sustain a rule of law when the state is under violent challenge from well-organized and ruthless insurgent forces, whether their motivation is ethnic separatism or a class-based revolution. Yet the constitutional regimes in these cases hardly qualify as mere victims of violent assault. In each case, violent insurgency was a response to objective grievances, which could have been addressed peacefully with reforms devolving political power, cultural autonomy, and socioeconomic resources to disadvantaged areas and peoples. The inadequacies of democracy, in other words, were both cause and effect of the violence.

A similar pattern is evident in India, where a generally open and liberal political system, and long-standing traditions of judicial independence, coexist with widespread and severe human rights abuses in the principal areas of active, violent insurgency in the country: (predominantly Muslim) Kashmir, the tribal areas of the northeast, Andhra Pradesh (the site of a class-based insurgency), and (at a greatly reduced level from years past) Punjab, the site of violent Sikh separatism. The situation in Kashmir, especially, resembles that of Kurdish southeastern Turkey in its intensity of human rights violations and impunity for state security forces. In 1996, an estimated three thousand people were held in unacknowledged detention by military and paramilitary forces in Kashmir, while torture continued to be routinely employed by the army and other state security forces.[71] Yet violent insurgency is not the only source of India's human rights abuses. Despite its more autonomous and institutionalized judicial system, India resembles much of Latin America in the severe backlogging of its courts and their relative inaccessibility to the poor. Moreover, measures designed to widen the arrest and detaining powers of the security forces in insurgency-afflicted areas, such as the 1985 Terrorist and Disruptive Activities Prevention Act (TADA introduced to fight terrorism in Punjab), and the National Security Act, have taken on an illiberal life of their own, leading to torture of detainees and thousands of arrests in states free of terrorist activity.[72] Human rights groups have also been victimized by intimidation and harassment of their members in Tamil Nadu and Andhra Pradesh and by the "disappearance" and assassination of their activists by soldiers and progovernment paramilitaries in Kashmir and Assam.[73]

Judicial malfunctioning and serious human rights problems are evident as well in the only two electoral democracies within ASEAN (the increasingly powerful Association of Southeast Asian Nations), the Philippines and Thailand. In each case, extensive corruption by politicians, judges, and military and police officials has been a major factor in undermining the quality of democracy and the rule of law. Yet in both countries, reforms are slowly improving democracy, and perceptible improvements in the human rights situation are associated with a decline in the military's political influence (most notably in the Philippines) and a recession in insurgent activity (many years ago in Thailand and more recently in the Philippines).[74] A key lesson learned by both countries is that well-organized regional or ideological insurgencies cannot be extinguished by military means alone but require political reforms and negotiation. In the Philippines, the peace accord reached in September 1996 between the government and the Moro National Liberation Front established the basis for a more inclusionary state, reducing the political and socioeconomic alienation that had driven many Muslims to embrace the ethnic insurgency against the government. The accord provides for devolution of power and increases the political autonomy of the country's Muslim population through the creation of the Southern Philippine Council for Peace and Development.[75]

This is a lesson that the highly delegative presidential system of Russia was slow to learn in its brutal war against separatist forces in Chechnya, where the indiscriminate use of military force left thousands of civilians killed, displaced an estimated half million people, and resulted in egregious human rights violations, including widespread political killings, disappearances, torture, and arbitrary arrests and detention of suspected insurgents.[76] As in Latin America and South Asia, security forces guilty of human rights abuses were immune from prosecution and punishment—and even serious investigation.[77]

The most important postcommunist country, Russia is in many ways paradigmatic of the institutional obstacles to democracy after communism: rampant corruption and illegalism, powerful organized criminal syndicates and elite bureaucratic cartels, a weak judicial system still in the process of postcommunist reconstruction, extreme concentration and personalization of power in the presidency (with the classic delegative reliance on executive decrees), and resurgent state security agencies only faintly accountable to other branches of government. In late 1966, three-fifths of Russians interviewed said the country had made no progress at all toward the rule of law (only 9% saw "a great deal" or "a fair amount" of progress).[78] Alexander Motyl's characterization of Russia as "proto-fascist" seems extravagantly pessimistic, as competition among power cartels prevents power from congealing into a new, coherent authoritarianism. However, the constitution adopted at the end of 1993 (and the armed assault on the parliamentary insurgents in October) did enshrine the president "as the dominant, if not quite dictatorial, player in the political arena," with vast powers of appointment and control, and the bureaucratic apparatus of the executive branch "is actually larger now than it was in Soviet times."[79] Even in the wake of a successful 1996 presidential election that many doubted would be held—or that would be free and accepted—the road to legality, transparency, and institutionalization remains a long one.[80]

Yet if Russia is prototypical, it is because it serves as the midpoint in a range of freedom levels wider than those of Latin America or South Asia. With all of their economic pains and institutional challenges, the states of the former Warsaw Pact, as well as the three Baltic states, are today liberal democracies, generally averaging a score of 1.5 or 2 on the Freedom House scale. Freedom levels recede as one moves east and south. Moldova, Ukraine, and the Kyrgyz Republic are illiberal electoral democracies, resembling the Russian mix of emergent economic, civic, and political pluralism (and relatively vibrant mass media in the latter two cases) combined with domineering executives, weak countervailing institutions, feeble, politicized judiciaries, widespread constraints on civil liberties and the rule of law, abusive police, and high levels of corruption.[81] Even in the Kyrgyz Republic, once viewed as a beacon of hope for democracy in Central Asia, several factors gave democracy an increasingly hollow and illiberal character: irregularities in the December 1995 elections reelecting the increasingly autocratic president Askar Akayev; a dubious 1996 constitutional referendum enhancing presidential power; mounting pressure on critical media, independent associations, and political opposition; and the familiar litany of other human rights problems.[82]

The former republics of the Soviet empire are not the only post-communist countries in which formally democratic institutions are enervated or negated by autocratic executives and repressive state structures. In Croatia, political pluralism and freedoms have been battered by increasing concentration of power within the presidency, the unchecked dominance of the ruling party, obstruction of electoral opposition, and expanded government control over political activity within the society at large, particularly the mass media.[83] Extensive executive intrusions into and interference with the affairs of the judiciary have compromised its ability to deliver fair trials to defendants. This is especially true with respect to ethnic Muslims and Serbs, who continue to be the victims of ethnic bias in cases of residency and property claims in areas from which they were driven during the summer of 1995 Croatian offensive. By contrast, many Croatians implicated in egregious human rights violations against Serbs have been accorded virtual impunity for their crimes by the judiciary. In Serbia, Montenegro, and Bosnia-Hercegovina, the scope for opposition and civil liberties is even worse.

There is a clear and important distinction between illiberal electoral democracies and pseudodemocracies (see chap. 1). The former are more or less troubled, weak, and hollow in their democratic institutions. Nevertheless, they meet the Schumpeterian conditions for electoral democracy. However concentrated state power may be in abusive executives and however brutal and rampant may be the human rights violations of state security forces (and their guerrilla nemeses), electoral competition is real and its outcome uncertain. By contrast, as one moves toward the rim of the former Soviet Union, Africa, parts of Asia, and the Middle East, elections themselves become increasingly hollow and uncompetitive, a thin disguise for the authoritarian hegemony of despots and ruling parties. "As recognition grows of the right freely to elect one's governmental representatives, more governments [feel] compelled to hold elections in order to gain [international] legitimacy."[84] However, in 1995 alone, these contests descended into an electoral charade in Kazakhstan, Turkmenistan, Tajikistan, Armenia, and Azerbaijan (not to mention Iraq, Iran, Egypt, and Algeria) because of intimidation, rigging, and constriction (or in the extreme, utter obliteration) of the right of opposition forces to organize and contest.

In Armenia, power is so heavily concentrated in the president that he not only can dissolve parliament, appoint all judges, and declare martial law but also has banned a leading opposition party and enjoys "virtual control of all three branches of government."[85] Belarusian president Alexander Lukashenka has "praised Hitler, reintroduced censorship, banned independent trade unions, ignored the Supreme Court when it overturned his decrees, and banned candidates for parliament from putting up posters or appearing on state media."[86] In such a context, elections cannot bring free and meaningful choice, even when multiple parties compete. And such is the context in many countries outside the former communist world as well. In the six years following the onset of Africa's second wave of democratization, beginning in early 1990, sixteen (formally) civilian regimes held multiparty elections so flawed that they did not meet the minimal criteria for electoral democracy.[87] In 1996 alone, fraud and intimidation negated the promise of electoral democracy in eleven of these countries—including Zambia, which lost its democratic status as a result. Although Ghana crossed an important threshold with its reasonably free and fair December 1996 elections for president and National Assembly, democratic regression overtook progress in Africa in the mid-1990s. During 1995–97, second elections in the post-transitional African multiparty regimes were generally less free and fair than founding elections, deepening the dominance of ruling parties.[88]

There are thus, as suggested in chapter 1, two important types of empirical gap in democratic form: between liberal democracy and electoral democracy and, more radically, between liberal democracy and its pale shadow, pseudodemocracy. Perhaps the most stunning feature of the third wave of democratization is how few regimes are left in the world (only slightly more than 20%) that do not fit into one of these three categories of civilian, multiparty, electoral regimes. This growing contradiction—continued expansion of the form of electoral democracy (and even more widely, of multiparty elections), while levels of actual freedom within such regimes diminish—signals the ideological hegemony of democracy in the post–Cold War world system but also the superficial nature of that hegemony. The United States and the international community demand real electoral democracy in Latin America and the Caribbean but are not too fussy about human rights and the rule of law. For Africa, a lower standard is set by the major Western powers: opposition parties that can contest for office, even if they are manipulated, hounded, and rigged into defeat at election time. Half of the forty pseu-dodemocracies in the world are in sub-Saharan Africa, and even the no-party regime in Uganda has become a darling of Western powers eager to see economic reforms implemented under any kind of fig leaf of political legitimacy.[89]

Five models of diffusion can help us understand not only the spread of the electoral form of democracy but also its considerable shallowness. One is the power model implied above. With the demise of the Soviet-bloc communist states, the power of the United States and of its wealthy democratic allies has increased significantly. Acting partly out of principle, but also from the growing belief that more constitutional and accountable political systems will generally produce better governance and more legitimate and stable regimes, these powerful democracies have pressed the formal model of electoral democracy on the weaker states over which they hold sway. Huntington, in particular, attributes much of the responsibility for the third wave to the policies, pressures, and expectations of the United States and the European Community and views the future of global democratization as linked in no small measure to the power, will, and capacity of the United States.[90] Economic and political rewards have been offered for democratization and democratic persistence, while attempts to overthrow democracy by military or executive coup (the unsuccessful *autogolpe* in Guatemala in May 1993, the incipient military coup in Paraguay in 1996), or to repress domestic movements for democracy, have often been deterred or punished with economic and political sanctions. But historically, and still to some considerable extent in the 1990s, democracy promotion policies have been dominated by a highly minimalist, electoral conception of democracy, and even then they have been hollowed out when other interests have come into play.[91]

A second model of diffusion has rested on richer, more expansive conceptions of democracy and of the conditions for sustaining it. This has involved increasingly concerted, sophisticated, and resourceful efforts on the part of established democracies, particularly Germany and the United States, and now increasingly international organizations like the United Nations and the Organization of American States, to assist the development of the political and social infrastructure of democracy: effective legislatures, judicial systems, local governments, political parties and elections; and all manner of nongovernmental organizations and media in civil society. This proliferation of discrete assistance programs, involving not only official aid and democracy promotion organizations but hundreds of nongovernmental actors in the established democracies, is not only diffusing the technology and particular institutional structures of successful democracy but also, in the process, reinforcing the diffusion of democratic norms and values (model four, below), especially through its aid to civil society.[92]

A third model of diffusion involves a kind of imitation: the demonstration effects of some earlier democratic transitions upon later ones (what Huntington calls "snowballing"), or the more gradual political learning that may come from the emulation of political models that are perceived as highly successful, powerful, and prestigious. In the latter respect, there is some overlap with the power model of diffusion, but the impetus for democracy in this case is internal rather than external. As with the first process of diffusion, democratization by emulation depends on whether the world's democracies continue to be seen as worth emulating, as the means to success in the world system. This model, too, is not inconsistent with a wide but shallow spread of democracy. The more widely an organizational form is imitated by diverse actors, the more it is likely to be diluted and adapted to local circumstances. Moreover, the diffusion of the third wave of democracy in more recent years has been primarily to countries—particularly in Africa, Central and South Asia, and the Middle East—in which the socioeconomic conditions for democracy (relatively high levels of education and per capita income, low inequality, a bourgeoisie and a working class independent of the state, vigorous civil societies, limited ethnic diversity or conflict, a strong sense of nationhood) are much weaker. Juan Linz, Seymour Martin Lipset, and I explicitly reject any view of these variables as preconditions, preferring to treat them as facilitating or obstructing factors.[93] However, it would be absurd to deny that when countries have consistently unfavorable levels of these variables (particularly with respect to per capita income), the odds against democratic endurance are greatly lengthened.[94] Moreover, where multiparty elections do take place in such conditions, they are less likely to take the form of liberal democracy or to persist in that status.

A fourth model of diffusion is more purely normative: judgments about what is intrinsically good, right, and desirable. These may overlap to some degree with the emulation or imitation model, but they probably work more slowly in motivating elites, civil society groups, or both toward regime change. Normative change may be driven by contact with specific countries and cultures (especially powerful or successful models, which also creates some overlap with the first model of diffusion). In fact, the conditions for such cross-cultural diffusion of values, experiences, and models have become increasingly fertile in recent decades, as exchanges of goods, ideas, information, and people (most significantly, university students) have all grown at extremely rapid rates.[95] Increasingly, however, it appears that normative change also derives from cultural evolution at the level of the global system. Gradually, the world community is embracing a shared normative expectation that all states seeking international legitimacy should manifestly govern with the consent of the governed, in essence, a right to democratic governance, a legal entitlement.[96] Already effectively implied by the Universal Declaration of Human Rights and the International Covenant on Civil and Political Rights, this right to democratic governance has been articulated more and more explicitly in the documents of regional organizations like the OAS and the Organization for Security and Cooperation in Europe (OSCE) and is affirmed by the growing interventions of those organizations and the United Nations in the internal political affairs of sovereign countries.[97] These declarations and interventions not only exercise power (model 1), they also reinforce change at the level of norms.

A fifth model, which John W. Meyer dubs "world society," encompasses to some extent the other four but adds a distinctive mechanism. This is the general trend toward global standardization, or isomorphism, in the structure of states. As Meyer and his collaborators show, over time, and particularly since World War II, global "cognitive models defining the nature, purpose, resources, technologies, controls, and sovereignty of the proper nation-state" have produced increasingly similar state structures with respect to education, science, the economy, the environment, health and welfare, and even constitutionally defined citizen rights, state functions, and ministries.[98] If these models, pressed by world organizations, international consultants, and rational expectations in world culture, have been able to generate similar state structures in all of these other sectors, it should not be surprising that they now increasingly define the rational, or expected, structure of state power as one selected through regular, competitive, multiparty elections with universal franchise. However, precisely because this standardizing force of world culture involves principles of rational organization much more than shared norms, the structural isomorphism it produces is likely to be formal, symbolic, and ritualized, rather than substantive; thus, policies and practices are likely to diverge.

Of course, pure diffusion is not the only means by which democratic norms, expectations, and models may spread across countries. Parallel changes within countries may also lead them to converge in their social, economic, and political structures. In particular, there is much evidence that economic development, and the associated growth of education and mass communications, generates profound changes in individual values and social organization that are conducive to sustainable democracy.[99] For some time, convergence among industrial societies was much more apparent with respect to social forms and processes than political systems.[100] In fact, even though constitutions have gradually become more similar in their general form, in the century immediately preceding the third wave of democratization (1870–1970), the world's constitutions showed no evidence of growing universality in guaranteeing rights of due process to their citizens. With respect to this crucial foundation for constraining the state and protecting human rights, neither convergence theory nor the world society model seemed to explain much.[101] With the inauguration of the third wave, and especially the global collapse of communism beginning in 1989, convergence is now strikingly apparent in politics as well, with Singapore being the only case of a relatively wealthy, industrialized society that lacks even electoral democracy.[102]

Clearly, multiple processes of global democratic diffusion and convergence are at work. But as we have seen, at least some of these are prone to generate a gap between form and substance. As the pace of democratic diffusion has quickened in recent years, we should perhaps not be surprised that the gap has widened. The wealthy, established democracies and the international institutions they dominate expect other countries to have or move toward democratic institutions but seem willing to accept a low standard of empirical adherence to democratic principles. Thus, an excessive emphasis is placed on free and fair elections (for Africa, simply multiparty elections) as the key standard for democracy, and interest in democratic conditionality wanes after that electoral hurdle has been scaled. But even when chicanery is prevented on election day, how free, fair, and *meaningful* can elections be when the civil liberties of individuals and associations are routinely violated; when the legislatures that are elected have little or no power over public policy; when state power remains heavily centralized and people have virtually no control over policy and resources at the local level; when the judicial system is corrupt, ineffective, and unable to provide a rule of law; and when elites who are not accountable to any elected authority—the military, the bureaucracy, local political bosses—exercise substantial veto power or direct control over public policy? In these circumstances, elections, however much they freely and accurately reflect the preferences between given options of those who turn out to vote on election day, cannot in themselves signal the presence of liberal democracy.

Is The Third Wave Over?

With the proportion of electoral democracies now more or less stagnating; with many prominent third-wave democracies deteriorating in their actual democratic performance; with human rights abuses persistent or increasing in even long-standing Third World democracies; with a significant gap between the electoral form and liberal substance of democracy; and with many of the world's most powerful and influential authoritarian states (China, Iran, and Saudi Arabia) showing little or no prospect of democratization in the near term, the question arises: Is the third wave over?

In two senses, the evidence in the affirmative appears to be mounting. The rate of increase in the number of electoral democracies in the world has steadily declined from 1991 until 1997, when it halted. While some countries might complete incremental and fitful transitions to electoral democracy in the next few years (Mexico) or return to democratic status (Peru), there is not an obvious cluster of candidates to continue to feed a wave of transitions. Of course, in 1987 (or even 1988) few foresaw the imminent regional waves of democratization that were about to sweep through Central and Eastern Europe and sub-Saharan Africa. But precisely because electoral democracy has spread rapidly to a majority of the world's states, many of these new regimes are highly fragile, and most of the remaining nondemocracies have objective conditions that do not augur well for imminent transition. Instead, it is more likely that in the next five years democratic regressions (as in Zambia) or breakdowns (as in Niger and the Gambia) will largely offset new breakthroughs to electoral democracy and that some few transitions to democracy will be aborted (as in Nigeria in 1993) or otherwise largely drained of democratic content (as has happened through political violence, repression, and fraud in Cambodia and many of the former Soviet states). In short, the unprecedented expansion in electoral democracy has drawn to a halt, and new regime concessions to the global expectation of democracy seem likely to take the hollow and ritualistic form of pseudodemocracy.

If we look even more demandingly beyond the form of democracy (a form that is increasingly expected by world culture and organizations), we see erosion and stagnation offsetting liberalization and consolidation. Liberal democracy, and political freedom more generally, have also leveled off within a narrow range of variation in recent years. While it is too early to assess whether the upward trend of 1995–1998 will be sustained, oscillation along the border between the "free" and "partly free" categories is just as likely as a steady increase in the number of free states. Over the past decade, at least thirteen democracies that had attained a "free" rating slipped below that threshold at least temporarily.[103] Of the fifty-seven electoral democracies (with populations of more than a million) that have been born in the third wave, about half (twenty-nine) are below the liberal threshold, and another eleven have an average freedom rating of 2.5, just above the liberal threshold (see appendix). If we take seriously the content of democracy, we must closely watch what happens to these electoral democracies in which liberty is not very deep and secure.

When overall expansion in the number of democracies halts for a sustained period (say, five to ten years), it seems reasonable to conclude that a democratic wave has come to an end. At least, this marks the end of a short wave of democratization. The second wave of democratization lasted about two decades. The third wave appears to have lasted not much longer. Does this mean that a third reverse wave of democracy is inevitable? This more dramatic change is not yet apparent and may well be avoidable. It is theoretically possible for a wave of democratic expansion to be followed not by a reverse wave but by a period of stagnation or stability, in which the overall number of democracies in the world neither increases nor decreases significantly for some time and in which gains for democracy are more or less offset by losses. It is precisely such a period of stasis we seem to have entered.

Many of the new democracies of the third wave are in serious trouble today, and there are grounds for arguing that the erosion of democratic substance could be a precursor to the actual suspension or overthrow of democracy, whether by executive or military coup. President Alberto Fujimori's *autogolpe* in Peru was preceded by years of steady deterioration in political rights and civil liberties. Historically, the path to military coups and other forms of democratic breakdown has been paved with the accumulation of unsolvable problems, the gross corruption and malfunctioning of democratic institutions, the gradual aggrandizement of executive power, and the broad popular disaffection with politics and politicians that are evident today in many third-wave democracies (and a few of longer standing).

However, three things are different today, and these have so far prevented a new wave of democratic breakdowns:

1. Military establishments are acutely reluctant to seize power overtly because of the lack of popular support for a coup (due in part to the discredit many militaries suffered during their previous brutal and inept rule); because of their sharply diminished confidence in their ability to tackle formidable economic and social problems; because of the "disastrous effects on the coherence, efficiency, and discipline of the army" which they have perceived during previous periods of military rule;[104] and not least, because of the instant and powerful sanctions that the established democracies have shown an increasing resolve to impose against such democratic overthrows.[105] Thus, even where a government unable to maintain civil order was returned to power with a low turnout and "widespread vote-rigging that [left] its legitimacy . . . in doubt," as in Bangladesh in February 1996, the disgusted citizenry evinced no desire for a coup, and the military surprised many observers by failing to seize power.[106] In addition, many of the democracies of the third wave have made significant progress toward establishing the conditions of objective civilian control that prevail in the industrialized democracies: high levels of military professionalism, constrained military role conceptions, subordination of the military to civilian decision makers, autonomy for the military in its limited area of professional competence, and thus "the minimization of military intervention in politics and of political intervention in the military."[107] (In the more fragmented and illiberal postcommunist states, different dynamics also appear to have inhibited military coups).[108]

2. Even where, as in Turkey, Brazil, Pakistan, and Bangladesh, progress toward democratic consolidation has been partial and slow, crises have been repeated, and the quality of democracy has deteriorated in some respects, publics have shown no appetite for a return to authoritarian rule of any kind; culturally, democracy remains a valued goal.

3. Finally, and related to the above, no antidemocratic ideology with global appeal has emerged to challenge the continued global ideological hegemony of democracy as a principle and as a formal structure of government.

As a result, most constitutional regimes of the third wave appear " 'condemned' to remain democratic," at least in form.[109] Political, social, and economic stresses that induced the breakdown of democracy during the first and second reverse waves bring its diminution during the waning years of the third wave. In many countries, democracy, instead of expiring altogether, has been hollowed out, leaving a shell of multiparty electoralism, often with genuine competitiveness and uncertain outcomes, adequate to obtain international legitimacy and assistance.

Rather than topple or mobilize against the constitutional system, political leaders and groups who have no use for democracy—or who are, in Juan Linz's classic term, only "semiloyal" to the system—are more likely to choose and condone oblique and partial assaults on democracy, such as repressing particularly troublesome oppositions and minorities. Instead of seizing power through a coup, the military may gradually reclaim more operational autonomy and control over matters of internal security and anti-insurgency, as they have done in Guatemala, Nicaragua, Colombia, Peru, Pakistan, Turkey, and Sri Lanka.[110] Or they may constitutionalize their rule through the facade of rigged elections, as in Niger, the Gambia, and Chad. Instead of terminating multiparty electoral competition and declaring a one-party (or no-party) dictatorship, as in the first and second reverse waves, frustrated chief executives (like Alberto Fujimori in Peru) temporarily suspend the constitution, dismiss and reorganize the legislature, and reshape to their advantage a constitutional system that subsequently retains the formal structure or appearance of democracy. Or they engage in a cat-and-mouse game with international donors, liberalizing politically in response to pressure and repressing as much as they believe they need to and can get away with in order to hang on to power, as the former one-party regimes of Daniel arap Moi in Kenya, Omar Bongo in Gabon, and Paul Biya in Cameroon have done in Africa.

Is this, then, the way the third wave of democratization ends: the slow, bleeding death of a thousand subtractions? Not necessarily. The alternative course would entail a fundamental stabilization of the current global equilibrium of regimes. It would require first and foremost the improvement and consolidation of the dozens of third-wave democracies (and the few preexisting democracies) that are shallow, illiberal, or only tentatively liberal. The deepening and enlargement of the ranks of stable, liberal democracies would then generate a much more favorable global environment for renewed democratic expansion, with the cultural capital and institutional models to help launch a fourth wave. Getting from here to there is essentially what the rest of this book is about.

3

Consolidating Democracy

The third wave seems to be losing the tremendous momentum of democratic expansion that it had gathered over two decades. In all likelihood, the number of electoral democracies will not increase significantly in the next few years and could even diminish sharply. In 1995, Samuel Huntington already saw "indications that a new reverse wave may be gathering which could lead to the erosion of some third-wave gains."[1] It is possible that democracy in the world, quantitatively and qualitatively, could simply maintain its equilibrium for some time to come. But this is unlikely. In global terms (particularly for the twentieth century), it is difficult to dispute Huntington's assertion that "history unfolds in dialectical fashion." When we examine closely the character of most third-wave democracies (and some of earlier provenance), we find acute problems and vulnerabilities, which diminish and erode the quality of democracy. In the coming years, these defects could extinguish democracy altogether in many countries unless they are corrected.

My primary purpose here is to question the assumption that democracy will persist by default, for want of a better alternative. If the shallow, troubled, and recently established democracies of the world do not move forward, to strengthen their political institutions, improve their democratic functioning, and generate more active, positive, and deeply felt commitments of support at the elite and mass levels, they are likely to move backward, into deepening pathologies that will eventually plunge their political systems below the threshold of electoral democracy or overturn them altogether. The international environment may still powerfully discourage defections from democracy, but it is unrealistic to expect that this constraint will persist or retain its potency indefinitely.

If the historical pattern is to be defied and a third reverse wave avoided, democracies must be strengthened and improved from within. The

64

overriding imperative is to consolidate those democracies that have come into being during the third wave (and to reconsolidate those that have lost their institutional effectiveness in this period). As with democracy, there are many conceptual approaches to democratic consolidation in the literature. If we are to avoid tautology, consolidation must rest on conceptual foundations other than what we hypothesize to be its principal consequence: the stability and persistence of democracy.[2] At bottom, I believe consolidation is most usefully construed as the process of achieving broad and deep legitimation, such that all significant political actors, at both the elite and mass levels, believe that the democratic regime is the most right and appropriate for their society, better than any other realistic alternative they can imagine.[3] Political competitors must come to regard democracy (and the laws, procedures, and institutions it specifies) as "the only game in town," the only viable framework for governing the society and advancing their own interests. At the mass level, there must be a broad normative and behavioral consensus—one that cuts across class, ethnic, nationality, and other cleavages—on the legitimacy of the constitutional system, however poor or unsatisfying its performance may be at any point in time.[4]

Legitimation in this sense involves more than normative commitment. It must also be evident and routinized in behavior. Consolidation encompasses what Dankwart Rustow calls "habituation," in which the norms, procedures, and expectations of democracy become so internalized that actors routinely, instinctively conform to the written (and unwritten) rules of the game, even when they conflict and compete intensely.[5] It is the deep, unquestioned, routinized commitment to democracy and its procedures at the elite and mass levels that produces a crucial element of consolidation, a reduction in the uncertainty of democracy, regarding not so much the outcomes as the rules and methods of political competition. As consolidation advances, "there is a widening of the range of political actors who come to assume democratic conduct [and democratic loyalty] on the part of their adversaries," a transition from "instrumental" to "principled" commitments to the democratic framework, a growth in trust and cooperation among political competitors, and a socialization of the general population (through both deliberate efforts and the practice of democracy in politics and civil society).[6] Democratic consolidation can thus only be fully understood as encompassing a shift in *political culture* (see chap. 5).

The relevant political actors in the consolidation drama are not just individuals, either at the elite or mass level. A crucial intermediate level comprises the myriad of collective actors who wage the competition for power and interests: political parties, trade unions, business associations, professional groups, student organizations, women's groups, and the wide variety of other interest groups and social movements who hunt for votes and benefits, lobby for reforms, and contest in elections and policy arenas. These collective actors also have normative orientations and behavioral styles. Explicitly in their charters and rhetoric, and implicitly in the strategies they adopt and the tactics they use, they may endorse the legitimacy of democracy or they may question or even reject it. They may seek their goals and wage their conflicts within the legal and institutional boundaries of democracy, or they may use any means to pursue their ends.

Consolidation requires more than a commitment to democracy in the abstract, that democracy is "in principle" the best form of government. For a democracy to be consolidated, elites, organizations, and the mass public must all believe that the political system they actually have in their country is worth obeying and defending. This robust legitimacy involves a shared normative and behavioral commitment to the specific rules and practices of the country's constitutional system, what Juan Linz calls "loyalty" to the democratic regime.[7]

Consolidation thus takes place in two dimensions—norms and behavior—on three levels. At the highest level are the country's elites, the top decision makers, organizational leaders, political activists, and opinion shapers, in politics, government, the economy, and society. Because of their disproportionate power and influence, elites matter most for the stability and consolidation of democracy, not only in their behaviors but also in their beliefs. Elite beliefs and norms are unusually important because, as Robert Dahl observes, elites are more likely to have elaborate systems of political beliefs, more likely to be guided in their actions by their beliefs, and in any case they have more influence over political events.[8] Beyond their direct power over events and decisions, however, elites also play a crucial role in shaping political culture and in signaling what kinds of behavior are proper and improper. Elites lead partly by example (good or bad); when they are contemptuous of the rules and norms of democracy, their followers or audiences are more likely to be as well. While this point is generally widely accepted, there has been strangely little attention to the political culture of elites in new democracies and little thought on how to measure it.[9]

At the intermediate level, parties, organizations, and movements have their own beliefs, norms, and patterns of behavior. These may not be uniform among their members, but different collective actors do tend to manifest very different orientations toward democracy. A liberal political party or an organization of lawyers and clerics to defend human rights views democracy and treats its laws and institutions very differently from the diehard party hanging on from the authoritarian era or an ethnic separatist organization that blows up police stations. Moreover, while collective actors may be led by elites, they do not necessarily have the same normative and behavioral commitments as their leaders. The rank and file of an organization or union may be less inclined to compromise or to tolerate opposition. They may be tightly controlled by their leaders or operate in much more decentralized fashion. However, to the extent that they operate as collective actors with many members and some coherent goals and tactics, their actions have consequences for democracy.

At the level of elites and organizations, it is easier to observe the phenomenon of democratic consolidation in its inverse: the signs of fragility, instability, and nonconsolidation (or *de*consolidation). These include all the manifestations of "disloyalty" that Linz notes: an explicit rejection of the legitimacy of the democratic system or of the nation-state and its boundaries by (significant) parties, movements, or organizations; a willingness of political competitors to use force, fraud, or other illegal means to acquire power or influence policies; "knocking at the barracks" door for military support in a political struggle; a refusal to honor the right to govern of duly elected leaders and parties; the abuse of constitutional liberties and opposition rights by ruling elites; and a blatantly false depiction of democratically loyal opponents as disloyal ("instruments of outside secret and conspiratorial groups"). Fragility may be further indicated by "semiloyalty": intermittent or attenuated disloyal behaviors; a willingness to form governments and alliances with disloyal groups; or a readiness to encourage, tolerate or cover up their antidemocratic actions.[10]

Democracy can be consolidated only when no significant collective actors challenge the legitimacy of democratic institutions or regularly violate its constitutional norms, procedures, and laws. Any democracy will have its share of cranks, extremists, and rejectionists on the margins of political (and social) life. If democracy is to be consolidated, however, these antidemocrats must be truly marginal. There must be no "politically significant" antisystem (disloyal) parties or organizations.[11] Political significance is signaled by numerical support, intensity of support (activism), and strategic location. To the extent that an antidemocratic party has sizable support in the society (one standard might be more than 10% of voters), or more modest support but concentrated among soldiers, intellectuals, clergy, or civil servants; or to the extent that its followers are intensely activist and devoted, constantly mobilizing in the streets and challenging the system, an antisystem group becomes politically significant. For Richard Gunther, Hans-Jürgen Puhl, and Nikiforos Diamandouros, "significance" turns on the capacity of a group to have an impact on the character and functioning of the democratic system. A "regime may be regarded as sufficiently consolidated even if some of its citizens do not share in the democratic consensus or regard its key institutions as legitimate, as long as those individuals or groups are numerically insignificant, basically isolated from regime-supporting forces, and therefore incapable of disrupting the stability of the regime. The broader the scope of that democratic consensus, however, the closer the regime will be to full conformity with our ideal-type definition of democratic consolidation."[12]

At the level of the mass public, consolidation is indicated when the overwhelming majority of citizens believe that democracy is the best form of government in principle and that it is also the most suitable form of government for their country at their time. As with "political significance," any designation of a threshold of quantitative support is inevitably arbitrary. Still, I would argue that both logic and the empirical evidence (see chap. 5) suggest that two-thirds is a minimum threshold, and 70–75 percent is a more compelling indicator. Such overwhelming public support for democracy signals consolidation at the level of mass beliefs but only when two other conditions are met: when this level is sustained consistently over some period of time and when the opposing view, actively rejecting the legitimacy of democracy (rather than simply expressing apathy or confusion), is held by only a small minority (no more than 15% of the population). At the level of mass behavior, democratic consolidation requires the rejection of violence, fraud, thuggery, and lawlessness as routine methods of political action. Democracy can be consolidated even when voter turnout is low (though it may be a lower-quality democracy that gets consolidated). It cannot be consolidated when supporters of rival parties frequently kill and terrorize one another in the struggle for power.

Somewhat more formally, we can assess a democratic system's progress toward consolidation with a three-by-two table depicting the levels of elite, organization, and mass and the dimensions of norms (beliefs) and behavior.[13] When all six of these cells show substantial normative commitment to democracy and behavioral compliance with its rules and limits, democracy is consolidated (see table 3.1).

Table 3.1 Indicators of Democratic Consolidation

Level	Norms and Beliefs	Behavior
Elite	Most significant leaders of opinion, culture, business, and social organizations believe in the legitimacy of democracy. All major leaders of government and politically significant parties believe that democracy is the best form of government and that the rules and institutions of the constitutional system merit support. These beliefs are manifest in their public rhetoric, ideology, writings, and symbolic gestures.	Leaders of government, state institutions, and significant political parties and interest groups respect each other's right to compete peacefully for power, eschew violence, and obey the laws, the constitution, and mutually accepted norms of political conduct. Elites avoid rhetoric that would incite their followers to violence, intolerance, or illegal methods. Political leaders do not attempt to use the military for political advantage.
Organizations	All politically significant parties, interest groups, and social movements endorse (or at a minimum, do not reject) in their charters, writings, and declarations the legitimacy of democracy and of the country's specific constitutional rules and institutions.	No politically significant party, interest group, movement, or institution seeks to overthrow democracy or employs violence, fraud, or other unconstitutional or antidemocratic methods as a deliberate tactic in pursuit of power or other political goals.
Mass public	More than 70 percent of the mass public consistently believes that democracy is preferable to any other form of government and that the democracy in place in the country is the most suitable form of government for the country. No more than 15 percent of the public actively prefers an authoritarian form of government.	No antidemocratic movement, party, or organization enjoys a significant mass following, and ordinary citizens do not routinely use violence, fraud, or other illegal or unconstitutional methods to express their political preferences or pursue their political interests.

The six cells of table 3.1 may seem to constitute a severe test, but I think systematic study would show that these different dimensions and levels tend to move together. When elites and significant collective actors are contemptuous of democracy, a good section of the public is as well. When elites and mass organizations do not only conform behaviorally for the time being with democracy's rules but manifest a deeper normative commitment, that is likely sooner or later to be internalized by the broad bulk of the public. On the other hand, it is possible that the public may be well ahead of some of its elites. The obstacle to democratic consolidation in Argentina now appears to be not at the mass level, where 70 percent or more of the public believe democracy is the best form of government, but among the ruling elites (particularly President Carlos Menem and his cronies), who have not been unwilling to use undemocratic methods in their pursuit of power and advantage (personal and partisan) (see chap. 5).

Consolidation involves not only agreement on the rules for competing for power but also fundamental and self-enforcing restraints on the exercise of power. This, in turn, requires a mutual commitment among elites, through the coordinating mechanism of a constitution, related political institutions, and often an elite pact or settlement as well, to enforce limits on state authority, no matter which party or faction may control the state at any given time. Only when this commitment to police the behavior of the state is powerfully credible (because it is broadly shared among key alternative power groups) does a ruling party, president, or sovereign, develop a *self-interest* in adhering to the rules of the game, which then makes those constitutional rules self-enforcing. Crucial to this democratic equilibrium is that each party perceives its long-term interest to lie first and foremost in enforcing the rules governing the exercise of (and competition for) power, so that the party can be relied on to rally against a transgression even if the transgression is committed by one of its own leaders and offers the party immediate rewards. This involves not only tactical calculations of long-term benefit in a repeated game but, again, a normative shift as well. As Barry Weingast puts it, "limits become self-enforcing when citizens hold [them] in high enough esteem that they are willing to defend them by withdrawing support from" political officials who violate them. "To survive, a constitution must have more than philosophical or logical appeal; citizens must be willing to defend it."[14]

Defending a constitution entails more than defense against blatant overthrow. It means defending constitutional norms, limits, and procedures against subversion or encroachment. In Latin America, most new democracies have now survived for over a decade through harsh economic conditions, with no explicit challenges from the military or anti-system parties. Yet most of these regimes have yet to be consolidated. On what grounds can we make this judgment? One could point to the many shortcomings of delegative democracy surveyed in the previous chapter: overbearing executives, weak political institutions (parties, legislatures, judiciaries, and so on), little horizontal accountability, and consequently, high levels of corruption and clientelism. But this may be to confuse the phenomenon of nonconsolidation with some of its causes or facilitating factors. In fact, it is precisely because these third-wave democracies—particularly Brazil, Argentina, Bolivia, and Ecuador—have persisted in the face of weak institutionalization of formal democratic structures that Guillermo O'Donnell now vigorously questions the utility of democratic consolidation as a concept. "All we can say at present is that, as long as [competitive] elections are institutionalized [as they are in the above countries], polyarchies are likely to endure."[15]

O'Donnell is correct to question the theoretical equation of consolidation with political institutionalization. In principle, countries can have weak, volatile party systems but highly stable and legitimate democracies. Practically, however, some degree of political institutionalization appears to be crucial for democratic consolidation. Alternatively, established party systems can dissolve into considerable turbulence (as in Italy in the mid-1990s), with no visible sign that democracy itself is losing legitimacy and becoming less viable. The strength of formal democratic institutions and rules (as opposed to the informal practices of clientelism, vote buying, rule bending, and executive domination) no doubt facilitates the endurance and the consolidation of democracy. But as O'Donnell notes, the two are not the same, and other factors "have strong independent effects on the survival chances of polyarchies."[16]

To answer O'Donnell's important challenge, it is necessary to answer the following questions: Why have these persisting democracies not become consolidated? How can we tell if they are or are not? And does it matter? Without persuasive answers to these questions, the concept does indeed lose its utility.

The answers are signaled by the patterns of behavior and beliefs of *significant* power players in these systems. To elaborate on the framework in table 3.1, there are no explicitly antisystem players, but there are military and police establishments who remain, or have again become, unaccountable to civilian authority and contemptuous of legal and constitutional norms. There are presidents who not only are delegative but have openly abused the laws and the constitution. Some have been driven from office; others, like Fujimori in Peru and Menem in Argentina, have abused their office with such political cunning and economic success that they have thrived politically. There are corrupt and oligarchical local bosses, deeply corrupted legislatures and judiciaries. There is, in short, precisely what O'Donnell observes: the institutionalization of informal, indeed illegal and even unconstitutional, practices (especially between elections). The degree and distribution of these informalities vary across countries. When such departures from the formal democratic rules are not simply one feature of the system (as they are to some degree in virtually every complex democracy) but a defining and endemic feature, they signal a lack of commitment to the basic procedural framework of democracy: democratic disloyalty, semiloyalty, frailty, nonconsolidation, or in countries like Colombia, Venezuela, Sri Lanka, even in some respects India, *deconsolidation.*

The implication of these signs of uneven, ambivalent, or deteriorating democratic commitment is twofold. First, in those cases in which powerful state officials and nonstate actors behave in this way, civil liberties are abused, opposition forces are harassed, elections may be violent (and even fraudulent), and democracy becomes hollowed out. Second, if these abusive elites do not act against the constitutional form of democracy, their commitment to it nevertheless appears to remain contingent and instrumental, not routinized, internalized, and unconditional. And a good deal of the instrumental value they derive from sustaining the democratic form (or facade), one may speculate, owes to the international system, which imposes costs on countries (and on their militaries, their economies, and thus their rich elites) that overturn democracy. Thus the contingency: if this international pressure (or perceptions of it) ever recedes, so will the viability of frail democracies. International—and especially European regional—constraints ultimately helped to consolidate democracy in Southern Europe and are doing so today in parts of Central and Eastern Europe, because they quickened and reinforced enduring changes in elite and mass political culture. These normative changes are not occurring (or happen only faintly) among key elite groups in many third-wave democracies, even though those democracies continue to persist.

By way of illustration, consider this example. In a certain country, a "generally free and fair election" is held for the third time in the five years since a transition from authoritarian rule. And for the second time since the inauguration of "democracy," the opposition wins and constitutionally assumes power. Thus what Huntington identifies as the "two-turnover" test for democratic consolidation is satisfied.[17] However, within a year of that third election, the defeated prime minister creates "ungovernability" by organizing a series of paralyzing strikes to force early elections or to provoke the army (which still heavily influences the presidency) into dismissing his opponent, who has again become prime minister. In return, the current prime minister investigates her opponent's business empire and arrests his elderly father on charges of tax evasion. Both politicians come from a tiny land-owning elite, which dominates the country's economy, army, politics, and state, and their differences on policy issues are limited at most, but they are far from agreeing on the rules of the game. At the mass level, political, sectarian, and ethnic violence sweeps through the country's most populous city and also its most remote province, where religious fundamentalists stage an uprising to demand imposition of Islamic law. The prime minister ultimately concedes, in violation of the constitution. Around the country, security forces continue to violate human rights with impunity, through torture, brutal prison conditions, extrajudicial killings, and the rape of female detainees.

By the definitional standards I have outlined, this country—it is Pakistan—is an electoral democracy, and it remained so even after the president used his constitutional authority to once again displace Prime Minister Benazir Bhutto and even after her nemesis, Nawaz Sharif, was tapped to replace her again and then became embroiled in a constitutional conflict with both the president and the Supreme Court. With soldiers, bureaucrats, and politicians all looking for international approval and aid, Pakistan could remain an electoral democracy for many years to come. Yet it is a hollow democracy, rife with semiloyal and disloyal behavior on the part of important political actors. No one should confuse its persistence with consolidation or with liberal democracy.

Three Tasks of Democratic Consolidation

Democratic consolidation confronts a number of characteristic challenges in new and insecure democracies. The salience of these challenges varies across countries and over time, and it would be an overstatement to characterize the complete resolution of any one of them as necessary for democratic consolidation. Beyond (by definition) establishing and routinizing broad commitment to the rules of the democratic game, there are probably no strictly necessary conditions for democratic consolidation, except (again, by definition) removing the military (or other institutions) as a reserved domain of power that limits the electoral accountability of government to citizens. However, the more these challenges persist in acute form, and the more they cumulate unresolved, the less likely democratic consolidation will be.

Democratic regimes vary in the depth and nature of the challenges they face. Nevertheless, there are three generic tasks that all new and fragile democracies must handle if they are to become consolidated: democratic deepening, political institutionalization, and regime performance. A central thesis of this book is the intimate connection between the deepening of democracy and its consolidation. Deepening makes the formal structures of democracy more liberal, accountable, representative, and accessible—in essence, more democratic. Progress toward greater liberty and lawfulness is essential. Some new democracies have become consolidated during the third wave (and there are also some consolidated Third World democracies), but none of the nonliberal, electoral democracies that have emerged during the third wave has yet achieved consolidation. In fact, many of the electoral democracies that predate the third wave and that have declined from liberal to nonliberal status during it (such as Venezuela, Colombia, Sri Lanka, and Fiji) have shown signs of deconsolidation.[18] Admittedly, it is hard to separate the concept from some of its causes here. Deconsolidation is indicated by declining commitment on the part of significant actors to the rules of the constitutional game. Manifestations of this decline are elite illegal and unconstitutional behavior, political violence, human rights abuses, military autonomy, and constraints on freedom (which are reflected in the deteriorating Freedom House scores and various journalistic accounts and scholarly analyses). These developments may also diminish public support for democracy, as appears to have happened in Venezuela. Whether or not such declines are visible at the mass level, however, and whether or not these systems are in danger of breaking down, rising levels of disloyal and semiloyal behavior are apparent and are eroding the normative, behavioral, and constitutional consensus that signifies consolidation.

There is thus an intimate connection between democratic consolidation and democratic deepening and improvement. The less respectful of political rights, civil liberties, and constitutional constraints on state power are the behaviors of key political actors, the weaker is the procedural consensus underpinning democracy. Consolidation is, by definition, obstructed. Furthermore, the more shallow, exclusive, unaccountable, and abusive of individual and group rights is the electoral regime, the more difficult it is for that regime to become legitimated at the mass level (or to retain such legitimacy), and thus the lower are the perceived costs for the elected president or the military to overthrow the system (or to reduce it to a pseudodemocracy). Consolidation is obstructed or destroyed by the effects of institutional shallowness and decay. To become consolidated, therefore, electoral democracies must become deeper and more liberal. This requires greater executive (and military) accountability to the law, to other branches of the government, and to the public; a reduction in the barriers to political participation and mobilization by marginalized groups; decentralization of power to facilitate broader political access and accountability; more space, energy, and autonomy for independent action by civil society; and more effective protection for the political and civil rights of all citizens and law-abiding groups.

Beyond deepening, two other general processes foster consolidation. One is a move toward routinized, recurrent, and predictable patterns of political behavior. This involves the settled convergence around (and internalization of) common rules and procedures of political competition and action. And this, broadly, is what political institutionalization is all about: strengthening the formal representative and governmental structures of democracy so that they become more coherent, complex, autonomous, and adaptable and thus more capable, effective, valued, and binding.[19] By defining clear, workable rules of the game to which contending political forces can credibly commit themselves, and by establishing more authoritative, proficient, and dependable structures for mediating political conflicts and interactions, institutionalization enhances trust and cooperation among political actors, or what Dahl terms "mutual security."[20] Thus it helps to draw reliable boundaries around the uncertainty of politics and to facilitate political trust, tolerance, moderation, civility, and loyalty to the democratic system. Political institutionalization is thus fundamental for building a political culture of democracy and enhancing the legitimacy of the democratic system.

Political institutionalization is also crucial to the deepening of democracy. If individual and group rights are to be protected, and if abuses of power are to be constrained and punished, the judicial system must have a high degree of institutional coherence, capacity, and autonomy. If interests in society are to find meaningful representation in the process of governance, political parties require not only organizational coherence and complexity but also some stability in their bases of support, ongoing linkages to social groups and forces, and the ability to adapt to social changes and to incorporate new actors. At the same time, legislatures must have the ability to formulate laws, aggregate preferences, allocate resources, and weigh societal petitions and grievances independent of the executive branch. If the military is to be surbordinated to civilian control, then civilian institutional capacities to manage and oversee it must be strengthened in the executive and legislative branches. By deepening and invigorating the practice of democracy in these ways, political institutionalization also heightens normative commitments to the democratic system.

The third task of consolidation is regime performance. Over time and over a succession of specific governments, the democratic regime must produce sufficiently positive policy outputs to build broad political legitimacy or at least to avoid the crystallization of substantial pockets of resistance to the regime's legitimacy. The content of these policy outputs, and the judgment of what constitutes sufficiently positive outcomes, will vary across countries and over time. The greater the cultural predisposition of the society to value democracy intrinsically, the less successful policies will need to be in generating economic growth and relieving major social problems. It is important to emphasize, however, that economic growth and distribution do not constitute the only dimension by which regime performance is assessed. The political performance of democratic institutions and actors (in generating liberty, constitutionalism, transparency, and a rule of law) is no less important, and judgments about the quality of democracy may significantly shape beliefs about its legitimacy. Thus, political institutionalization and deepening can facilitate perceptions of effective functioning. With respect to economic performance and, in many countries, economic reform, coherent and workable political institutions, particularly in the political party system, may again play an instrumental role.[21] But no less important are the policy and procedural choices that political actors make. Even at the level of institutional innovation and strengthening, reform cannot occur without the choices and actions of political leaders in establishing new structures and patterns of behavior. Consolidation thus cannot be comprehended without the human element.

The challenges considered below are characteristic of new and fragile democracies, but they vary across these regimes not only in salience and intensity but also in the speed and success with which they are resolved. Democracies encompass a set of partial regimes, which may be liberal, representative, accountable, legitimate, and stable to different

degrees; and which may move toward consolidated liberal democracy se-
quentially and perhaps very unevenly.[22] Chile, for example, has a highly
institutionalized party system, a rule of law, effective economic institutions and performance, but still less-than-democratic civil-military relations. As with democratic development in general, each country must
chart its own path to the consolidation of democracy, taking careful account of the distinctive challenges and opportunities that confront it.

Regime Performance

If democratic legitimacy and procedural commitment form the principal foundation of regime consolidation, the performance of the regime
is a crucial variable affecting the development and internalization of beliefs about legitimacy. Indeed, if we construe performance broadly to include the political outputs and character of the regime, as well as the material conditions it generates (or for which it is seen to be responsible),
then regime performance appears as an intervening variable that may
substantially mediate the effects of other factors on regime legitimacy.

There is a reciprocal relationship between legitimacy and performance. Historically, the more successful a regime is in providing what
people want, the greater and more deeply rooted its legitimacy tends to
be. A long record of successful performance builds a large reservoir of legitimacy, enabling a democratic system to weather crises and challenges.[23] At the same time, legitimacy is also an independent variable affecting the performance of the regime. The deeper and more universal
the belief in democratic legitimacy and the commitment to abide by the
rules of the democratic system, the more efficacious the regime is likely
to be in formulating policy responses to the principal problems the society faces, because politicians are more likely to be willing to work with
one another and oppositions will behave in more loyal and responsible
fashion. Higher levels of legitimacy also facilitate greater public patience
with and support for governments facing formidable problems and thus
provide more scope for them to implement difficult but necessary policy initiatives (a consideration with respect to economic reform). As a result, democratic regimes and governments that enjoy high initial legitimacy, or deep levels of legitimacy internalized and affirmed over long
periods of time, tend to be more effective in their performance (and to
be evaluated as such). There are thus densely reciprocal relations between legitimacy, effectiveness, and democratic stability; and a consoli-

dated democracy is to some extent both evidence and product of this virtuous cycle.[24]

However, legitimacy is shaped by a wide range of historical and cultural variables, and the more these variables generate deep commitments to democracy, the less consequential for consolidation will be the performance (particularly the economic performance) of the regime. Because it is a comparative judgment (embracing the political system as better than any alternative that could be imagined), legitimacy heavily depends on retrospective assessments of previous (nondemocratic) regimes in the country, as well as the perceived viability and attractiveness of other institutional visions and models in the world. And because it is a judgment about what is right and appropriate, legitimacy—especially intrinsic, or diffuse, legitimacy—springs from the deeper value orientations of citizens and elites. Economic development tends to generate more democratic values and norms, particularly at higher levels of affluence, and thus relatively affluent countries appear to be able to achieve the diffuse legitimation of democracy relatively rapidly—and even independently of short-term economic performance. This was the experience of the three new Southern European democracies (Portugal, Spain, and Greece), which achieved broad legitimation and consolidation within ten years of their launching in the mid-1970s, despite frustration and disenchantment with economic performance (and skepticism about political parties).[25] The fact that these countries were relatively industrialized and were embedded in the cultural, political, and economic milieu of a solidly democratic European community probably helped to generate this diffuse legitimacy, to detach legitimacy from perceptions of regime efficacy, and to minimize feelings of nostalgia for the previous authoritarian regimes.

Economic Performance

It is by now a truism that the better the performance of a democratic regime in producing and broadly distributing improvements in living standards, the more likely it is to endure. Many truisms are specious, outdated, or misleading, but in contrast to some observers of Latin America and other regions of democratic development, I do not believe this generalization is ready yet for the junk heap of comparative politics theory. Beyond the examples of numerous democratic implosions during the Great Depression of the interwar years (the central period of Huntington's first reverse wave), and the historic vulnerability of Latin American democracies during hard economic times, powerful quantitative evidence for the argument emerges from the research of Adam Przeworski and his colleagues.[26] Their analysis of post–World War II regimes (1950–90) shows that, while the level of economic development powerfully shapes the survival prospects of democracy and affluent democracies survive no matter what, among moderate-income and especially poor countries democracy is much more likely to last when the economy grows rapidly and with only moderate inflation.

Good growth and low-to-moderate inflation are generally produced by macroeconomic policies and institutions that protect property rights, impose fiscal discipline, liberalize trade and financial markets, keep exchange rates competitive, reduce state ownership and intervention in the economy, collect taxes efficiently and fairly from a broad base (with limited marginal rates), and so encourage domestic savings and foreign direct investment.[27] The newly established and unconsolidated democracies of the 1980s and 1990s were generally deficient in these policies and, thus, had to impose painful and potentially destabilizing economic reforms in order to achieve them. Although progress toward economic reform in these democracies has been uneven, it has been substantial. Indeed, it is striking how few third-wave democracies have broken down in the face of sharp increases in poverty and unemployment due to economic crisis and reform. This suggests that, with the right institutions, policy mixes and sequences, and leadership strategies and coalitions, economic reform and democracy can be compatible.[28] If Karen Remmer and other optimists are right, this could represent a permanently altered dynamic.[29] If my analysis is correct, however, the persistence of electoral democracy does not negate the danger of sustained economic hardship.

In recent years, many societies seem to have engaged in economic learning. Informed by the disasters of state socialism, populism, and hyperinflation, they have apparently lengthened their time horizons and become realistic about what can be achieved in the near term. This patience is particularly visible (and well documented) in postcommunist Europe. In a number of Latin American countries, such as Brazil, Argentina, Bolivia, and Peru, controlling hyperinflation has proven a valued and positive dimension of economic performance, with broad benefits, and appears to have bought time. And some reforming economies, such as Poland, the Czech Republic, Argentina, Peru, the Philippines, and Turkey have also begun to register good or at least moderate economic growth rates. But most third-wave democracies are still far from consolidation and are unlikely to achieve it unless they generate the kind of sustainable economic growth that broadly improves incomes and reduces very high rates of poverty and unemployment.

This raises the second, distributive, dimension of economic performance. There is no evidence that further enrichment of the wealthiest stratum of society has, in and of itself, negative consequences for democracy. To the extent that a rising tide lifts all boats, economic gains for the rich should not be resented. However, what damages the political legitimacy and sustainability of economic reform programs, and perhaps of democracy itself, are perceptions that a few are benefiting while many stagnate and suffer and that the beneficiaries of reform have come upon their windfall earnings unfairly, as a result of political connections and corruption rather than honest enterprise and risk-taking initiative. The distributive implications of growth thus matter greatly. In Mexico and Russia as well as many other Latin American and postcommunist countries, privatization programs have become much more controversial than they need have been because of the political corruption and favoritism that has pervaded the selling off (or in some cases, virtual giveaway) of state assets.

In Latin America, South Africa, and to a lesser extent the Philippines and Turkey, income is very unequally distributed.[30] Poverty is pervasive and often severely degrading and politically marginalizing. During the 1970s and 1980s in Latin America, poverty rates overall remained stubbornly high (40% of the population) and even increased in some countries. Urban poverty rates in particular jumped sharply between 1970 and 1990 (from 26% to 34% of the population).[31] While the costs of economic crisis and adjustment were borne disproportionately by the middle class, the poor (already on the margin of existence) proved the most vulnerable. The wealthy had the most resources to adapt—and even thrived. Thus, income inequality increased sharply during the 1980s in a number of Latin American countries.[32]

With the temporary exception of Peru, these economic strains have not led to democratic collapse in Latin America during the 1980s and 1990s, but they have sharpened political tensions, generated periodic eruptions of urban rioting and political crisis, intensified crime and social anomie, heightened political disaffection and fragmentation, and so obstructed the consolidation of democracy. As the Inter-American Dialogue observed in 1994, "The failure of most Latin American and Caribbean countries to address effectively the problems of poverty, illiteracy, and malnutrition has placed the credibility of democratic institutions at risk and endangers macroeconomic progress."[33]

Socioeconomic obstacles to democratic consolidation have been most strikingly evident in Brazil, which has the worst income distribution of the sixty-five developing countries for which the World Bank presents comparative data.[34] Brazil's high incidence of poverty and its extraordinary, increasing economic concentration have been part of a complex of factors presenting formidable obstacles to democratic consolidation. Other elements of this self-reinforcing syndrome include extreme concentration of landed wealth, corrupt, clientelistic politics, inconsistent, crisis-ridden policies, statism and its attendant gross inefficiency, militant mobilization by rural and urban labor, and extensive human rights violations against the rural and urban poor.[35] Numerous elements of poor economic performance—persistent and increasing poverty and inequality, periodic bouts of hyperinflation, the succession of feeble, short-lived stabilization and economic reform plans in the 1980s and early 1990s—accentuated the political limbo of hollow, illiberal democracy in which Brazil has been stuck and the significantly higher levels of skepticism or apathy toward democracy than in neighboring South American countries.[36]

With the implementation of a much bolder stabilization and adjustment plan in 1993 under Finance Minister Fernando Henrique Cardoso and Cardoso's election as president in 1994, hyperinflation was conquered, economic growth was regenerated, and a new era of economic liberalization, privatization, and deregulation was inaugurated. This had perceptible effects on Brazil's political stability and governability, making possible a constitutional amendment to allow immediate reelection of the president, which was welcomed by most political scientists and observers. However, the new impulse for reform and responsible governance continued to confront a huge load of structural distortions and vulnerabilities: high public deficits, decaying public infrastructure, low investment, a fiscally unviable social security system, and the massive frustrations left over from a long decade (1981–92) of stagnation, during which per capita income declined by almost 8 percent.[37] Brazilian democracy cannot be consolidated until these remaining structural distortions are addressed. But reform on these fronts is in turn obstructed by Brazil's party system fragmentation and its extreme form of federalism (see chap. 4), which highlights again the crucial importance of institutional design.

Although its democracy is much newer and benefits from the hugely legitimating prestige of the ruling party's courageous, decades-long struggle for liberation from apartheid, South Africa faces a similar type of challenge. Next to Brazil and Guatemala, it has the worst index of income concentration of any developing country. While such comparisons are notoriously imprecise, inequality in South Africa is particularly staggering because (even much more than in Brazil) it is so heavily correlated with race: the per capita income of South Africa's Black population is one-eighth that of Whites,[38] and in contrast to Brazil, Blacks compose the overwhelming majority of South Africa's population.[39] Horribly squalid living conditions and a lack of economic opportunity are associated with high levels of political violence and intolerance, particularly in the politically embattled province of Kwazulu-Natal, and fearful levels of crime and random violence in the cities. The enormous political stature and integrity of President Nelson Mandela, the conciliatory skills forged by contending elites in the crucible of a high-stakes, pacted transition, and the revolutionary credentials of the ruling African National Congress brought the regime a high degree of legitimacy at its inauguration in 1994. During the founding presidential term of Nelson Mandela, the new democracy has been surprisingly liberal and stable. But progress toward fulfilling expectations for a decent material life—jobs, housing, infrastructure, and education—has been slow. In the years to come, the new democracy will be hard put to maintain political and social order and, thus, respect for civil liberties (much less to record progress toward consolidation) if it cannot fulfill some of these elementary expectations of the long-suffering Black majority.

For the most part, economic hardships have not toppled third-wave democracies. However, severe economic inequality and decline have contributed to political instability in Venezuela and democratic suspension in Peru. These conditions could augur serious trouble ahead for other democratic regimes as well if they cannot produce economic stability and growth with distribution.

In Venezuela, grossly wasteful economic management and populist distribution, dependent on the passive income from state oil rents, "generated an unsustainable increase in the external debt, then rising inflation, and finally economic collapse in 1989."[40] By then, a third of the population had been plunged into poverty (twice the ratio at the start of the decade), mean hourly real wages had declined by a third since 1980,[41] and the sudden imposition of unprecedented austerity measures by the newly returned populist president triggered furious urban rioting. Although economic growth resumed in 1991–92, the long-term decline in living standards and the resistance to reform on the part of a population accustomed to lavish state subsidies and entitlements helped to generate the climate of political cynicism that welcomed the February 1992 military coup attempt.[42]

The clearest recent example of linkage between economic crisis and democratic implosion is Peru. Irresponsible populist leadership and shallow political institutions were pivotal to Peru's democratic deterioration in the 1980s and early 1990s. But so were historic patterns of profound social and regional inequality and the disastrous economic downturn (the worst in all of Latin America) that began in the mid-1970s. Together, historic inequalities and economic crisis, which dramatically increased poverty and robbed the young of job prospects, helped to generate both the ruthless revolutionary political violence of the guerrilla movement, Sendero Luminoso (Shining Path), as well as the economic violence associated with the drug trade and ordinary urban crime. Thus was generated what Adolfo Figueroa calls a "distributive crisis," which left Peruvians "disaffected with the democratic system."[43] By the time Alberto Fujimori swept from nowhere into the presidency in 1990, real per capita income had declined almost 30 percent from the level of the previous decade, when the military handed over power, plunging the country back to the overall standard of living it had in 1960. Investment had fallen more than 40 percent from its 1980 level, and real wages had fallen "almost continuously since the mid-1970s" (in the public sector, to *10%* of their mean level a decade earlier). Between 1987 and 1990 the incidence of poverty more than doubled, and annual inflation ballooned from 1,722 percent in 1988 to 7,650 percent in 1990.[44]

With such dire economic adversity being accentuated rather than positively processed by the fragmented and discredited political class, with the country under assault from a vicious insurgency, and with an early victory over hyperinflation to his credit, it should not have been surprising that Fujimori was able to win military, business elite, and popular support for his *autogolpe* in April 1992. By the time he took office in July 1990, the legitimacy of key democratic institutions had dramatically declined, with only 21 percent of Peruvians expressing confidence in political parties and only 23 percent in the courts.[45] The long, agonizing economic descent had

> eroded Peru's democracy in various ways. Without resources, the state was no longer providing the services that are a customary source of legitimacy for the government. Dismally paid state employees (including soldiers, police, and judges) were demoralized, and more likely to be tempted by bribes and extortion schemes. Also, as workers were

more fearful of losing their jobs, they were less active in labor unions, traditionally a major mode of political participation. Increasingly compelled to work numerous jobs and/or offer services informally, Peruvians had little or no time for civic organization.[46]

It is difficult to imagine democratic consolidation occurring in Latin America (or other less developed countries) on the current foundations of severe poverty, inequality, and economic instability. In those countries in which hyperinflation has been whipped, such as Bolivia and Argentina, democratic governments have won political credit for this important achievement, not least from the poor, who suffer most from inflation because they are less able to protect what wealth they have through the most common hedges (domestic-indexed or foreign-denominated financial instruments).[47] Nevertheless, if one posits that democratic consolidation will ultimately require the gradual social and political inclusion of severely marginalized poorer classes and ethnic and regional minorities, this can only come from sustained economic growth with low inflation. For "recession hurts the poor more than any other group in society," and "reviving economic growth in a sustainable way is the only truly effective policy" for reducing poverty.[48] This in turn requires that the economic reform process continue beyond initial stabilization and adjustment measures to far-reaching liberalization of the tax system, the trade and regulatory regimes, and the overall size and structure of the state, so as to promote investment and competition.

Generating sustainable growth is not only necessary for reducing poverty and inequality but also compatible with poverty alleviation in the nearer term. Various social safety net programs (such as nutritional and health assistance and emergency employment), if well designed, can relieve the impact of adjustment on the poor and the lower middle classes without breaking national budgets. In some countries, such as El Salvador, Brazil, the Philippines, and South Africa, land reform may remain an urgent priority, but such redistribution of fixed assets is enormously difficult to accomplish under democracy, and in any case populations are becoming less rural. Redistribution will therefore need to focus on an expansive asset, human capital, by making substantial long-term investments in primary and secondary education and basic, preventive health care (including wide access to family planning services). Just as such equality-enhancing efforts to improve human capital have buttressed and invigorated economic growth in East Asia, so they may in Latin American and other developing countries,[49] as would such other socially progressive measures as improving the education and status of women (which would also reduce fertility rates), and simplifying and enforcing tax provisions, to increase state revenues in ways that enhance fairness while not diminishing incentives to invest. Given the abysmal state of public education in Latin America and the Caribbean, which has higher repetition rates for school grades than any other region of the world, improvement of primary and secondary education appears essential to enhancing international competitiveness.[50]

Economic inclusion is closely related to political inclusion and, thus, to democratic deepening. Many social safety net programs are most effective when the impoverished communities themselves are involved in the design and management of nutritional assistance and other poverty-alleviation programs.[51] And reform of the legal system can enable poor and marginalized groups to acquire legal titles to property, access to reasonably priced credit and insurance, and other dimensions of security and legal status, which will enable them to invest more confidently to improve their productivity and expand their output.

The severe economic circumstances of many other third-wave and Third World democracies should not counsel despair. There is no simple equation between economic crisis or stagnation and democratic instability or nonconsolidation. A great many other factors enter in, and as Juan Linz and Alfred Stepan emphasize, the key is how economic adversity is "processed" politically by party and government leaders.[52] Still, their premier example of successful political processing, Spain, can apply only so far to less developed countries. When Spain entered its crisis of extremely high unemployment (up to 20%) and economic recession after the transition in the mid-1970s, it was already a largely industrialized country. Although its economic growth rate dropped dramatically (from 7% in 1960–74 to 1.7% between 1975 and 1985), it was still an industrialized country, among the twenty richest in the world in per capita gross national product.[53] And crucially, it had much better *political* performance than many of the third-wave democracies struggling to consolidate. Similarly, the faithful and effective performance of democratic political institutions can mute the impact of economic decline in poorer countries as well, but the challenge is steeper and the room for maneuver more limited.

For a fortunate (but unfortunately small) minority of third-wave democracies, the prospects for consolidation are enhanced by the prior successful adoption of difficult stabilizing and liberalizing economic reforms. When democracy is initiated in an economy that is growing vigorously and is structurally (more or less) sound, a broad consensus on macroeconomic policy and institutions is likely to exist across contending parties and elites. Differences of priority may remain with respect to wage growth, social services, tax policy, and so on, but these are within the narrower band of variation that characterizes the mature, industrialized democracies, and they do not threaten to generate the severe political polarization or wide policy swings that often plague countries with more stagnant or crisis-ridden economies. Such broad consensus on economic policy has characterized the new democracies of Chile and Taiwan and has facilitated the moderation of their party politics and the continuation of their vigorous economic growth. The same was true of South Korea until the financial crisis of 1997 revealed deeper structural problems that had been hidden and exacerbated by political corruption and the delegative nature of South Korean democracy.

Although its income distribution shows the typical, severe Latin American inequality, Chile enjoyed a decade of rapid growth in per capita income (averaging 6.5% annually) between 1985 and 1994. This owed not only to the far-reaching economic reforms (emphasizing liberalization, privatization, and export growth) under General Augusto Pinochet's military regime but also to their continuation and deepening under the new democratic administration of centrist President Patricio Aylwin. As the new democracy took hold following the military's withdrawal in 1990, economic growth remained impressive (averaging 7.5% annually in gross domestic product from 1990 to 1994); inflation, though high relative to industrialized countries, declined to an average rate of about 15 percent in this period (compared to more than 20% annually during the 1980s); unemployment remained low (5% in 1992); and real wages rose (4.5% in 1992). As a result of this continued strong economic performance, and the economic (and political) learning throughout society over the previous decade, the new democracy enjoyed high levels of political support and "a period of national unity not seen before by even the most senior generation of Chile's political leadership."[54] This left other serious institutional problems for democratic consolidation, especially the reserve power of the military and the continuing core of right-wing and potentially antidemocratic sentiment, but it gave Chile one advantage that many of its neighbors lacked.

A similar story could be told for Taiwan, which has been lifted into the ranks of high-income economies (with a per capita gross national product of more than $12,000) by more than two decades of sustained rapid growth. Even as the country moved toward full democracy, the domestic economy continued its steady growth at 5–6 percent annually, inflation has remained low (under 5%), and the currency has remained strong (with one of the largest foreign exchange reserves in the world). The resilience of Taiwan's economy in the face of the 1997–98 East Asian financial crisis has been particularly impressive.[55] People are generally becoming more affluent (private consumption grew by more than 8% in 1994).[56] While social and economic issues are becoming more salient, they involve the types of issue—reform, distribution, social policy, environmental, and consumer—that dominate the agenda of stable, advanced democracies. The basic direction of economic policy is not at issue, and no major party or segment of public opinion argues that democratization in itself has imposed an unacceptable economic cost on the society.

Both South Korea and Taiwan suffer, however, from increasing inequality and domination of politics by monied interests, and this helped generate the conditions for financial crisis in South Korea in 1997. In both countries, democratization has accelerated the political ascendance of business in general and powerful business elites in particular (which have been much more concentrated in South Korea than in Taiwan). In Taiwan (but significantly, not in Korea) this encouraged economic liberalization and competition, reducing state regulation and domination of the economy. On the other hand, this growing political influence of business has, as in Japan, fostered political favoritism and corruption, which has led to sweetheart deals, windfall profits, skyrocketing real estate prices, and increasing disparities in income and, especially, wealth. In Taiwan, which has historically boasted one of the least skewed income distributions of any developing country, the ratio of mean income between the top fifth of households and the bottom fifth grew from 4.10 in 1980 (one of the lowest in the world at that time) to 4.98 in 1992, while the disparity in asset ownership between the top and bottom quintiles rose to a factor of 17.8.[57] Yun-han Chu identifies the increasing inequality, the growing national political sway of business and gangster elements, and Taiwan's "recurring scandals of corruption and influence-buying," as major causes of the widespread voter cynicism about politicians, which constitutes a key challenge for democratic consolidation.[58]

Prosperity does not provide a magic carpet ride to stable democracy. Chile, Taiwan, and South Korea (even before its financial collapse) each face serious and distinctive obstacles to the consolidation of their new democracies. Thus, favorable economic circumstances do not in themselves ensure consolidation. Even though Huntington finds a "ceiling" for coup attempts at the upper-middle income level of about about $3,000 per capita GNP,[59] and even though Przeworski and his colleagues find democracy to be "impregnable" at a higher level of affluence,[60] history continues to unfold, and democracy can diminish or disappear in more subtle ways. Moreover, a favorable economic inheritance may impose high expectations on a new democracy for continued good performance. The economic depression that descended on South Korea in late 1997 with the collapse of its currency and banking system and the bankruptcy of large conglomerates generated a crucial test of whether democracy in that country can withstand a severe economic downturn, and political performance will be crucial to determining the outcome. The lower the level of economic development at the start of a new democracy and the weaker its political institutions, the more the new democracy may be at real risk if it does not satisfy economic expectations raised by the authoritarian regime.

Still, there is no gainsaying the considerable benefit to consolidation that a sustained and broadly positive economic performance can provide. In itself, such performance does not produce a democratic transformation of political values and preferences, but it does provide a context in which such a transformation can gradually occur. If growth is distributed reasonably well and inflation is restrained, all classes gain a stake in the system, confident that democracy can work for them, and the range of ideological and political differences is lessened. At a minimum, such economic dynamism not only incurs for the regime a conditional performance legitimacy but also buys time for the regime to accumulate more intrinsic (unconditional) legitimacy and to inculcate democratic values and commitments through the other processes described in this book: the reform and deepening of democracy, the strengthening of political institutions, the mobilization of civil society, the gradual habituation to a constitutional system that other political actors honor and obey. In addition, if economic growth is sustained and distributed over a long period of time, there is considerable evidence that it will effect changes in political culture, class structure, state structure, and civil society that will be strongly conducive to democratic consolidation.[61]

Political Performance

Effective government and regime performance is most often thought of in economic terms. But it is not only material progress and security that democratic citizens value. They are no less concerned with their physical safety and security, which require protection from arbitrary harm by the state or criminal elements. They may have sufficient nationalist sentiment to value increased prestige for their country in world affairs, but most of all, most of the time, peace is the foreign policy output they value most. And they expect from democracy, if nothing else, political freedom, accountability, and constitutionalism. The ability of a new or recent democracy to deliver decent, open, relatively clean governance should not be underestimated as a policy output that can help consolidate democracy. Indeed, as Luis Carlos Bresser Pereira, José Maria Maravall, and Adam Przeworski eloquently argue, precisely because democratic publics highly value democratic responsiveness, deliberation, and accountability, extreme delegation and insulation of executive authority may be a very shortsighted and in the end counterproductive strategy for implementing economic reforms in a democracy.

> Democracy is an autonomous value for which many people made sacrifices when they struggled against authoritarian regimes. The quality of the democratic process, perhaps less tangible than material welfare, affects the everyday life of individuals: It empowers them as members of a political community or deprives them of power. And if democracy is to be consolidated, that is, if all political forces are to learn to channel their demands and organize their conflicts within the framework of democratic institutions, these institutions must play a real role in shaping and implementing policies that influence living conditions.[62]

Faithfulness to the spirit of the democratic process is an important factor in consolidating democracy and in consolidating economic reforms in a democracy. Simply providing the liberal substance of democracy is a key dimension of performance that can help to build deep and lasting legitimacy among both elites and mass.

But of course it is not enough in itself, and there remains the classic tension between freedom and order. More than anything else, order, as signified by the safety and predictability of the social environment, is the other dimension of political performance that citizens value most and, perhaps, that democratic consolidation theorists most often neglect. One who has not done so is Juan Linz, who reminds us that minimizing nonstate violence and, especially, punishing, constraining, and disarming those who organize private violence for political ends are key variables in determining whether democratic regimes will break down.[63] In the most challenging circumstances of ethnic, regional, or political insurgency (as in Turkey, India, Sri Lanka, Peru, and Colombia today), democratic commitments are sorely tested and easily trampled in the state's struggle to preserve its legitimate monopoly over the use of force and even its territorial integrity. If democracy is to be consolidated or reequilibrated, democratic constitutionalism cannot be used as an excuse for a failure to confront these illegitimate, terrorist, and typically very brutal armed challenges. Citizens have a right to be safe in their persons and not to have their state dismembered by armed force. But at the same time, reasons of state cannot be allowed to override constitutional guarantees of due process and human rights, as they have in the anti-insurgency campaigns of all five of the countries above.

Democracy presumes the notion of a *Rechtsstaat*, "a state bound by law and excluding arbitrary decisions not based on rules," of which democracy, while not synonymous with it, is an important foundation.[64] Quite literally, then, democracy requires law and order, not in the colloquial, repressive terms purveyed by populist demagogues but in the literal sense of a balance between two essential principles of state. This underscores, however, the importance of designing political institutions and exercising timely political statecraft so as to avoid the mobilization of ethnic or regional disaffection into armed violence. For once such disaffection is whipped up and mobilized into terrorism and armed insurgency, no good options remain: a negotiated settlement is likely to be much more difficult, and the struggle (even if waged with democratic restraint by the state) is likely to be bloody and protracted.

The other dimension of the order problem often neglected by democratic theorists (perhaps because it seems so mundane or so inviting of illiberal state response) is crime. Crime is a serious problem in both rich, established democracies and new or unconsolidated ones. But in the latter countries, it may threaten democracy itself, for three reasons.

First, because the state in many posttransition developing countries and postcommunist countries is weaker, poorer, and more fragmented, the crime problem may be of an entirely different order of magnitude from that in the established democracies. This may be especially so when, as in El Salvador, Cambodia, Mozambique, and in a more limited way, South Africa, a new democracy rises from the ashes of civil war, and the country is awash with small arms and demobilized soldiers or "freedom fighters" looking for a means to survive. The resulting violence and fear may thus be much more pervasive and socially destabilizing in new democracies than in established ones.[65] In such areas as Moscow and St. Petersburg, the Cali region controlled by Colombian drug cartels, and some of South Africa's townships, violence and fear may be so endemic as to negate the state's monopoly control of force and even to construct a powerful parallel economy that the state cannot tax and to which businessmen must pay tribute.

Second, by raising transaction costs and undermining the security of property rights, crime may also become a major drag on economic efficiency and growth, while it increases inequality by concentrating wealth in the hands of criminal empires with the money and nerve to organize private armies. Crime may further retard economic growth, as it has in South Africa, by discouraging foreign direct investment and tourism and encouraging the emigration of skilled workers.

Third, crime can undermine respect for law by both the state and noncriminal elements among the public. In the context of weak states and inefficient, poorly disciplined police, crime may inspire drastic, illegal, unconstitutional, and grotesquely sadistic responses to try to control it. These responses take various forms, including popular vigilante squads that mete out instant justice to suspected perpetrators, police torture and killing of prisoners and suspects, and police-led extermination squads, which aim to clear the streets permanently of nettlesome street youths, the homeless, and other suspicious "lowlives."[66] In such circumstances, the problem that crime poses for democracy may generate a fatal "cure."

Another crucial dimension of political performance is corruption. This is not unrelated to crime. When organized criminal elements have substantial power in society and relative immunity from prosecution, as they have enjoyed in Colombia, Mexico, Thailand, Russia, and (to a more modest but growing degree) Taiwan, they inevitably corrupt the political and judicial systems of democracy in order to buy protection and extend their privileged access to markets, property, and other resources. This does not inevitably bring down democracy; Italy's democracy persisted for decades with breathtaking levels of corruption and protection that involved the Mafia and politicians of many parties. However, such corruption does damage the quality of democracy and erode its legitimacy, potentially putting it at risk. Endemic political corruption is resented not only for the unfair privileges and wealth it bestows on its beneficiaries in business, party politics, and the state but also for the manifest inefficiencies and waste that tend to accompany it, such as hugely delayed or deficient public infrastructure projects, collapsing bridges and buildings that were not properly built or inspected, and social services delivered late or incompetently. Moreover, even when the public shares in the booty, through the purchase of votes and the distribution of largesse, this only undermines their respect for law and their confidence in parties and politicians. Furthermore, endemic political corruption often (as in Pakistan, India, the Philippines, and much of Africa) goes hand in hand with electoral malpractices and violence because it so dramatically escalates the personal stakes in holding political office.

Survey data from new and troubled democracies around the world suggest that mass publics give considerable weight to problems of corruption and lawlessness when forming judgments about their regimes. In Pakistan, lawlessness and corruption are two of the top three reasons people offer for why they think their country is not a democracy. From 40 to 52 percent of Pakistanis think that the military could handle these problems better, and only a narrow plurality (36%) favor democracy over military rule or "religious" government. In Turkey, seven in ten respondents say that politics "is dirty and too closely tied to or influenced by criminals." In both Russia and Ukraine, more than eight in ten see little or no progress toward the rule of law, and most people are also generally disillusioned about the state of democracy. In South Korea, two-thirds cite "widspread corruption in business and government" for the country's economic woes. In Argentina, Brazil, Bolivia, Ecuador, Venezuela, Colombia, and Mexico, large majorities (typically three-quarters or more) perceive that corruption has increased in the past five years, and in none of these countries was more than a third of the public satisfied with the way democracy is working in 1996.[67]

The impact of political corruption has been strikingly apparent in the demise or decay of many democracies during the third wave. The 1991 military coup that deposed Thailand's first clearly democratic and civilian government in more than a decade was justified and publicly accepted (if not exclusively caused) by the widespread "perception of unabashed and mounting corruption in high government circles."[68] One of the earliest and most important democratic breakdowns of the third wave, in Nigeria in 1983, occurred first and foremost because of the massive economic dislocation, electoral rigging, and public alienation generated by corruption. The corruption of both the civilian and military political establishments also heavily contributed to the failure of the country's attempted transition, in 1993, to a Third Republic.[69] Political corruption constitutes a principal threat to the new democracies of Africa. It has played a central role in the descent of Zambia's promising new democracy, inaugurated with such great promise in 1991, into a pseudodemocracy gripped by public alienation, cynicism, suspicion, ethnic conflict, cabinet instability, and press restriction and intimidation.[70]

Extensive political corruption was also a key factor in the coup attempts against Venezuelan democracy in 1992 and the parade of presidential scandals and forced departures in Brazil, Venezuela, Guatemala, and Colombia (where President Samper barely survived to complete his term). That public pressure and constitutional processes have forced incumbent presidents from office is a marked departure and hopeful sign for Latin America. But that corruption still dominates legislative deliberations, executive transactions, and local power dynamics in much of Africa and Latin America and in the Philippines, Thailand, South Asia, and Russia and other post-Soviet states is a troubling sign for the future of democracy's third wave. Combating corruption is a major performance challenge for democratic consolidation, and that in turn requires political institutionalization and an effective civil society.

Political Institutionalization

Democratic consolidation must address the challenge of strengthening three types of political institution: the state administrative apparatus (the bureaucracy); the institutions of democratic representation and governance (political parties, legislatures, the electoral system); and the structures that ensure horizontal accountability, constitutionalism, and the rule of law, such as the judicial system and auditing and oversight agencies. New or troubled democracies are invariably weak in at least one of these three arenas of political institutionalization, often in two or all three. Making political institutions effective involves not only strengthening them in terms of capacity and resources but also designing them to fit the circumstances. This is a particularly complex and controversial challenge with respect to the electoral and constitutional rules that shape representation and governance.

Strengthening the Bureaucracy

Successful economic reform entails what several scholars refer to as the "orthodox paradox": "For governments to reduce their role in the economy and expand the play of market forces, the state itself must be strengthened."[71] Successful economic reform is only one of many tasks for which new and fragile democracies require what Juan Linz and Alfred Stepan call a "useable state bureaucracy."[72] To be usable and ultimately effective, the state must have technical talent and training, which requires (particularly in its upper reaches) a professionalized, meritocratic bureaucracy with relatively good pay, competitive standards of recruitment, and ideally, an esprit de corps. Such a competent state is needed to improve education and other forms of human capital; to develop the physical, legal, and institutional infrastructure of a market economy; to manage the macroeconomy with fiscal discipline and intelligent budgeting priorities; to negotiate with international trade partners, creditors, and investors; to control for negative externalities of the market without overregulating it; to modernize and broaden the collection of taxes; and to maintain order and a rule of law.[73] The paradox is that, on the one hand, overall state employment and expenditures must be cut to restore fiscal balance and permit increased domestic savings but, on the other hand, the leaner state that remains must be smarter, more coherent, and more adept. These two changes are not entirely inconsistent, but to bring them off simultaneously requires strong and able political leadership that can justify to restless constituencies the higher salaries for state managers while overall state employment is reduced and wages in the general economy stagnate. Visible and credible measures to control political corruption and improve state services may help to make this dual overhaul of the state palatable.

A crucial and commonly overlooked arena of state strengthening involves the system of justice and especially the police. Not only do order and personal safety constitute one of the most basic expectations people have of government, but the police are the agents of state authority whom ordinary citizens are most likely to experience in their daily lives. If the police are corrupt, abusive, unaccountable, or even lazy and incompetent, this cannot but affect popular perceptions of the authority and legitimacy of the state. If new democracies are to deliver the balance of freedom and order their peoples want and to keep the military out of the business of internal security (and thus politics), they must develop professionalized, disciplined, resourceful, and accountable police forces.[74]

In much of Latin America, Africa, Turkey, South Asia, and the Philippines, where police violations of human rights are common if not systematic, the policing dimension of state building is closely related to the deepening of democracy, and the reforms needed to develop civilian control over the military apply to the police as well. However, the development of a professional and effective police also requires many of the same generic types of enhancement that are needed for other sectors of the state: more careful recruitment of staff, much more comprehensive

and appropriate training, better organization of personnel and procedures, greater specialization of functions, higher standards of discipline
that are more effectively enforced, and significantly better pay (both to
attract a higher caliber of recruit and officer and to deter corruption).

The experience of police reform in Central America and Haiti,
which has heavily involved U.S. and international assistance, points to a
number of specific priorities. Ideally, a reorganized police force should
recruit afresh and not simply absorb former military personnel (as was
done in Panama after the 1989 U.S. intervention). New recruits should
be rigorously vetted for evidence of prior involvement in crime or human rights abuses, and they should be trained in a professional police
academy. Training should develop skills in collection of evidence (to reduce the reliance on confessions, which are often extracted through torture), knowledge of and respect for the legal rights of suspects and detainees, "technical skills for nonlethal defense and handling of suspects
and prisoners," and commitment to a strict code of conduct. Training can
help to create "a cadre of police supportive of new concepts of human
rights and civilian leadership," but it can only go so far to reshape values
of police personnel, and this is why force restructuring, retirements, and
fresh recruitment are essential. Other reforms in the region include establishing an independent office to monitor police conduct, improving
technical forensics capabilities, integrating the police more effectively
into the criminal justice system, and removing it from military supervi-
sion and control (as has begun to happen in Guatemala, Nicaragua, and
Honduras).[75]

Developing a capable, professional, democratically oriented police
force takes time and resources. This is one arena in which international
assistance programs, if carefully designed (and clearly separated from any
military or intelligence involvement), can make a difference. So, crucially, can the provision of "some interim external security force . . . to provide time and opportunity to assist the legitimate government to construct an adequate security force."[76] Such external forces, including
international police monitors and advisors and a separate human rights
mission, helped to bridge the security gap as part of the multilateral
peacekeeping missions in El Salvador, Haiti, and Cambodia, but one of
the lessons of these recent experiences (particularly the latter two) is that
the international community must stay engaged (including with security forces on the ground) long enough for able and nonpartisan police
forces to emerge and take charge. In devastated countries like Haiti and
Cambodia, this (and all other dimensions of elementary state building)

must be calculated in years, not months, and so must international engagement.

Strengthening Institutions of Governance

Political Parties

Even though their dominance has been eroded by the growth of mass media and civil society organizations, political parties remain an indispensable institutional framework for representation and governance in a democracy. As their members come to share a more coherent sense of their program or mission; as they become more complex both horizontally in their range of specialized functions and subunits and vertically in their reach down to the level of ordinary citizens; and as they develop autonomy from other state agencies and sociopolitical power centers, so that they have independent capacities to realize their particular goals, political parties become more capable and effective. When, in addition, they adapt to changes in their environment, developing new functional specializations, substantive concerns, and technical capabilities and incorporating newly emergent groups, parties are able to maintain their effectiveness over extended periods of time. By giving political interests and demands stable, legitimate means of expression in the political process; by helping to protect individual rights and maintain orderly, lawful, and open government; and by aggregating, deliberating, and negotiating among competing demands, effective democratic institutions tend to produce more consensual, sustainable policies and, hence, greater governability and legitimacy.

All political institutions, however—and perhaps political parties especially—face a tension between the durability features of institutional strength (coherence around principles, programs, and policies; unified action in the legislature and political process; elaborate, well-ordered vertical and horizontal structures) and adaptability. From this perspective, there is a curvilinear relationship between institutionalization (as coherence, routinization, predictability) and both the stability (consolidation) and quality of democracy. Stronger is not necessarily better; political parties and party systems can be overinstitutionalized as well as underinstitutionalized. In the former instance, structural coherence, discipline, and regularity may become frozen into rigidity and loss of salience for important new (or newly salient) generational, regional, ethnic, or class groups; and extremely low electoral volatility may signify a lack of competitiveness, meaningfulness, or civic engagement in the party system.[77] This has been the case in the elite-pacted democracies of Colombia and, particularly, Venezuela, where political parties (controlled in very hierarchical fashion by entrenched leaderships) have monopolized the political process and thus so pervasively penetrated state and organizational life that they have robbed interest groups and other political institutions of their autonomy and left little space for the incorporation of new, marginal, or alienated constituencies into democratic politics. This extreme domination and institutionalization of political parties—*partidocracia*, or partyarchy—has been a central factor in eroding the effectiveness, legitimacy, and stability of democracy in Venezuela.[78]

As with so many other aspects of democracy, political parties and party systems must strike a balance between competing values: in this case, stability, or rootedness, on the one hand and adaptability on the other—and thus in a sense between over- and underinstitutionalization. For most new democracies, however, the danger is the opposite of Venezuela's: a weak, fragmented, inchoate, highly volatile party system that barely penetrates the society, commands few stable bases of popular and sectoral support, has few ties to established interest groups, is prone to populism and polarization, and thus cannot produce effective governments or governing coalitions. To be sure, newly emergent party systems (and even most established ones) will probably never have the strong parties with committed mass memberships, vigorous local branches, and strongly defined social bases and issue orientations that characterized the developing and consolidating democracies of earlier eras in this century.[79] Still, political parties remain "the most important mediating institutions between the citizenry and the state," indispensable not only for forming governments but also for constituting effective opposition.[80]

Diverse types of civil society organization are more important to the representation of interests and the invigoration of democracy than ever before.[81] However, "interest groups cannot aggregate interests as broadly across social groups and political issues as political parties can. Nor can they provide the discipline necessary to form and maintain governments and pass legislation."[82] Only political parties can fashion diverse identities, interests, preferences, and passions into laws, appropriations, policies, and coalitions. "Without effective parties that command at least somewhat stable bases of support, democracies cannot have effective governance."[83] Therefore, some degree of party system institutionalization—of parties with effective, autonomous organizations, and developed, relatively stable linkages to voting blocs and social organizations—

seems an important condition for democratic consolidation.[84] Furthermore, an aggregative party system with a limited number of significant parties—and particularly (if it can avoid ideological polarization, or *partidocracia*) a two-party-dominant system—appears to foster policy effectiveness and consistency. By contrast, "fragmented and polarized party systems have posed major impediments to sustained implementation of [economic] reform."[85] Indeed, fragmented and ideologically polarized party systems pose severe problems for democratic governability in general, and fragmentation into a large number of parties is especially destabilizing under presidentialism.[86]

Legislatures

In addition to political parties, elected legislatures (at all levels of governance) are a crucial institution for the representation of interests and horizontal accountability. However, if legislatures are to become meaningful forums for injecting the interests and concerns of their constituencies into the policy process, they must have sufficiently elaborated and resourceful organizational structures so they can engage, challenge, and check executive officials and state bureaucracies. This requires legal and technical skill in writing legislation and reviewing budgets; a system of functional committees with professional staffs who have specialized expertise in various policy areas, from macroeconomics and the environment to national security; a library and information service (preferably computerized); a research support function; and means for promoting citizen access to the legislative process, as through public hearings in local constituencies, public dissemination of legislative proceedings, public opinion polling on issues before the legislature, and effective media coverage of the legislature. Because a national legislature has neither the time nor the expertise to investigate and deliberate effectively as a whole on most specific issues, strong committees with stable memberships and resourceful chairmen (and women) are vital.

In most new and unconsolidated democracies, these functions are all very weak, and national legislatures lack the organization, financial resources, equipment, experienced members and staff to serve as a mature and autonomous point of deliberation in the policy process. This does not always mean they lack authority. However, a congress that is constitutionally powerful but institutionally weak, as in a presidential system, is tempted to exercise its authority in destabilizing ways, through confrontation, obstruction, extortion, and corruption. This raises a related dimension of professionalization, which Moisés Naím emphasizes with respect to executive branch bureaucrats.[87] States (and peoples) get what they pay for. If they want civil servants and legislative staff with professional skill and dedication, and legislators more interested in representing interests than collecting bribes, they need to pay these officials reasonably well—and then vigorously punish illicit income.

Electoral Systems

There is a vast and growing literature on institutional choice for democracies, or what Giovanni Sartori calls in his book title "comparative constitutional engineering."[88] The debates in this literature revolve around two issues in particular: the choice of executive structure (presidential, semipresidential, or parliamentary) and the choice of an electoral system for representation (especially in the national assembly or parliament). Although persuasive arguments and evidence show parliamentary systems to be more flexible, adaptable, and accountable, less crisis prone and zero-sum, and therefore more successful and long-lived than presidential regimes, there are very few instances of change from presidential to parliamentary government under democracy.[89] (Indeed, most changes have tended to go in the other direction, precisely to enable ambitious executives to aggrandize their power.) A switch from presidential to parliamentary government in Latin America might well enhance the prospects for consolidation, as Juan Linz, Arturo Valenzuela, and others argue, but since the proposal (for a semiparliamentary system) was defeated at the polls in Brazil and is hardly imminent elsewhere (with the possible exception of Bolivia's "assembly-independent" system), strategies for consolidating democracy will need to focus on other variables.[90]

Electoral systems, on the other hand, are somewhat more accessible to reform, as they may typically be revised by more conventional legislative action. To the extent that the obstacles to democratic consolidation appear to relate in part to institutional design, electoral system reform is therefore a more realistic target and has been achieved even in such long-standing democracies as Italy and Japan. However, even the electoral system is not an easy target, because the very members of the legislature who would need to adopt a new system have acquired a vested interest by getting elected under the old one. Moreover, precisely because political institutionalization entails routinization, predictability, and broad valuing of rules and processes, there *should* be a bias for continuity. Electoral systems should be changed only in the face of manifest flaws, and then reform should focus on correcting those flaws as specifically as possible.[91]

Democracies can become consolidated under institutional arrangements that are less than ideal, both in the abstract and for the individual country. Italy's highly proportional electoral system, which generated a fragmented party system with a long succession of short-lived governments, nevertheless achieved consolidation. So did Israel's parliamentary democracy, with one of the most proportional electoral systems in the world; its consolidation gave rise to a growing fragmentation in the party system, giving small fringe parties disproportionate political influence in forming governments. Still, in each case, compelling cases were made that the quality of democratic functioning could be enhanced by reducing the fragmentation of the party system (which Italy adopted in a major way, switching to a much more majoritarian electoral system, while Israel only raised its electoral threshold slightly). Part of the problem is that scholars do not agree on which institutional design best promotes stable democracy, either as a general model or for a particular country.[92] Neither do they agree on strategies for reform to repair or improve a poorly functioning democracy. The choice of an electoral system, or an executive structure—or an entire panoply of constitutional arrangements that may be characterized on a continuum from highly majoritarian to highly consensual—involves trade-offs between competing values, which suit different countries (and different intellectuals and constitution makers) differently.

Four normative trade-offs become salient in designing (or reforming) electoral systems for contemporary democracies. One is the tension between efficiency and governability, on the one hand, and representativeness, on the other. It is by now well established that plurality, single-member-district (or SMD) electoral systems (otherwise known as "first past the post") give rise to fewer parties and, especially in combination with presidentialism, are more likely to produce a two-party system; whereas systems of proportional representation tend to give rise to multiple parties. This is why the SMD plurality system and others (such as the alternative vote and the French double-ballot SMD system) that produce a smaller effective number of parties represented in parliament are considered majoritarian.[93] The more majoritarian the electoral system, the greater the distortion (disproportionality) between votes and seats, and the less representative the outcome (in giving parliamentary place and voice to all interests and views). However, the efficiency of democracy, "the ability of elections to serve as a means for voters to identify and choose among the competing government options available," is best served with a majoritarian electoral system, which can provide coherent governing alternatives known to the electorate in advance (ideally between two parties) and also a governing majority.[94]

Majoritarian (again especially plurality) systems are also seen to enhance governability, by avoiding the need to cobble multiple parties and interests together into shaky coalitions. Yet precisely for these reasons, majoritarian systems have a zero-sum character to them; one party (or narrow coalition) wins, while other parties and interests lose out. Presidentialism heightens this zero-sum effect because, unlike cabinet government, it gives control over the executive to a single individual and party, even if they command considerably less than majority support. Precisely by being efficient and decisive, then, majoritarian institutions concentrate power, narrow and streamline the process of governing, and are thus exclusionary. Consensual systems of government, with proportional representation and parliamentary rule as their twin centerpieces, are by contrast highly representative and inclusive of diverse interests (both in the parliament, in which diverse interests may have their separate parties to represent them, and in the executive cabinet, in which government is formed by a grand or broadly inclusive coalition). But for this reason, they may also be slow, indecisive, turgid, and stale, with more or less the same parties and faces forming one government after another.[95]

A second trade-off pits the representativeness and inclusiveness of proportional representation against the direct vertical accountability and accessibility provided by the single-member district system. Philosophically and normatively, representation in a democracy may be conceived in several ways. There is the issue of whether representatives should be selected to vote their conscience and principles or to mirror the wishes of their district. Either way, however, when representatives are chosen in individual, territorial constituencies, there are clear lines of communication, responsibility, and accountability (for both legislative votes and services) to the voters of that constituency.[96] The more members elected from the typical constituency, the more proportional the allocation of seats can be (if proportional representation is used), but the weaker will be the ties between specific representatives and specific voters. In very large districts (up to the maximum, where as in Israel and the Netherlands the entire nation is a single constituency under national list proportional representation), representativeness can be maximized, but accountability of individual representatives to the electorate is effectively absent.

Proportional representation systems can compensate for this problem by constructing districts of moderate size (three to five members), but each ideal must give some in the process. Accountability is less than perfect when several members represent the same constituency. And proportionality tends to diminish as district size shrinks, unless there are mechanisms to "top off" the representation in parliament by drawing from party lists (or from each party's "best losers" within the various constituencies) in order to achieve overall proportionality in distribution of seats. But this system, like the German two-tier system (which is fully proportional but elects half the lower house from state party lists and half from single-member districts), tends to create two classes of parliamentarians, those with specific territorial constituencies, to whom they are responsible, and those without such constituencies.

A different principle of representation raises a third trade-off in electoral system design, between party coherence and voter choice. One could argue that voter choice is maximized in single-member constituencies (especially when there are also party primaries to choose the candidates). An entirely different logic, however, is to hold representatives responsible not to territorial constituencies but to political, ideological, and interest-based constituencies, as they are reflected in political parties and their programs. This principle of responsibility gives rise to an important dimension of party system institutionalization: coherent, disciplined parties, whose members reliably back the party program. Its surest vehicle is proportional representation, using closed lists chosen and ranked by the party leadership. The more hierarchical the control of the party leadership over the selection and ranking of the lists, the greater the discipline and loyalty of party representatives in the assembly. As we have seen in the case of Venezuela, however, such extreme hierarchical control by the central party apparatus can contribute to an occluded, overinstitutionalized party system that is corrupt, arrogant, and poorly responsive to the wishes of the voters.

At the possible sacrifice of coherence and discipline, voter choice, and hence the democraticness of the system, can be enhanced if grassroots members of the party select the ranked lists of party nominees for each multimember district (or, as in Israel, for the national list) in an internal party ballot tantamount to a U.S. primary election. Even then, however, voters are constrained in the general election to a choice between alternative closed party lists, whose members are elected in the order they are ranked on the ballot. Voter choice as well as the independence of representatives and political openness are increased with open lists, in which voters can choose specific candidates from an unranked party list or can rerank the list if they prefer. These values are advanced even better under the single transferable vote, in which voters in multi-member districts cast their votes for individual candidates in order of their preferences. Under this system, the surplus votes of candidates who meet the quota for election are transferred to the next lower preferences of the voters, and the weakest candidates also have their preference votes redistributed, in a continuous process until the requisite number of candidates are elected.[97] This system maximizes voter choice, because voters may rank order the candidates across party lines, but it therefore diminishes party coherence and requires voter knowledge of individual candidates and a fair amount of political literacy.

This raises a fourth potential trade-off in electoral systems. Simplicity, or ballot accessibility, may thus conflict with the appropriateness of the system, in abstract theoretical terms. A system like the single transferable vote, which in theory may seem ideal in its capacity to reconcile competing goals, may in practice be complex, cumbersome, and confusing, especially for electorates composed mainly of illiterate and poorly informed voters. While evidence from southern Africa suggests that voters' political knowledge and sophistication often exceeds their general level of education and literacy, electoral systems that are complicated or opaque or that include a complex written ballot (listing possibly hundreds of candidates) may be ill-advised for some developing countries.[98] More generally, electoral system design "should aim for simplicity [and thus transparency], unless complications demonstrably yield a more-than-marginally better outcome." Many complexifying innovations wind up having "undetectably small" or obscure effects on the overall balance between parties, while making the system less comprehensible to the average voter.[99]

The biggest theoretical mistake is to assume that any one model is suitable for all cases. Precisely because one cannot maximize both efficiency and representativeness, the choice of electoral system should depend on the particular historical pattern of cleavage and conflict in each country and on which threats to democracy are judged to be most severe: the possible exclusion, alienation, apathy, and illegitimacy of majoritarian outcomes or the potential fragmentation, low governability, and even paralysis of proportional ones.[100] Depending on the political context, either system could give rise to political polarization, either between two or three well-defined political blocs under the majoritarian system or between ideological extremes that flank the more moderate parties and pull them away from the center, into the fragmented partisan array Sartori calls "polarized pluralism."[101]

The choice of institutional model must be sensitive to the political imperatives and constraints not only of each particular country but also of the historical moment. As Vincent Maphai argues, "Some institutions that may be workable or even necessary in the short term may undermine the long-term process of democratic consolidation."[102] Thus while the power-sharing features of the transitional South African constitution (which, for example, guaranteed cabinet representation to any party with at least 5% of the vote for parliament) were indispensable to the process of democratization, they could prove counterproductive to democracy in the long run. As in Colombia and Venezuela, it may be necessary to structure such consociational features as temporary bridges or confidence-building measures rather than open-ended arrangements.

If any generalization about institutional design is sustainable, given the bloody outcomes of countless political systems that appeared to exclude major cleavage groups from power, it is that majoritarian systems are ill-advised for countries with deep ethnic, regional, religious, or other emotional and polarizing divisions. Where cleavage groups are sharply defined and group identities (and intergroup insecurities and suspicions) deeply felt, the overriding imperative is to avoid broad and indefinite exclusion from power of any significant group.[103] Thus a concrete way that institutional design can mitigate the obstacles to democratic consolidation is by discouraging politically significant groups from becoming disloyal or even equivocal in their commitment to the system.

If defection or equivocation is to be avoided, each group must feel it has a stake in the system. This may not (and in most cases, should not) require the cumbersome institutional configuration of a fully consociational system, with its grand governing coalition, mutual veto, subgroup (segmental) autonomy, and elaborate proportionality in distribution of legislative seats and government posts.[104] But it does compel institutional designers to do several things. First, they need to provide incentives for groups to form coalitions or to pool votes in national politics, ideally in ways that will give rise to multiethnic parties. Second, they need to distribute power vertically, so that territorially based groups can have some control over their own affairs; this is an important way that federalism and decentralization of power serve the consolidation of democracy. And third, they need to ensure that all ethnic and nationality groups have political equality.

Proportional representation in some form generally provides the best tool for ensuring that all groups in a deeply divided society feel included in the political process and even for encouraging the development of cross-cutting cleavages that can moderate ethnic or regional conflict. As Andrew Reynolds demonstrates in his comparative study of five electoral systems in southern Africa, even where (as in Malawi) the single-member-district plurality system produces a highly proportional translation of votes into legislative seats, the very territorial concentration and cohesion of ethnic groups that ensures that proportional outcome also creates regional or ethnic fiefdoms, such that the favored party in a given ethnic group or region gains a monopoly of representation for that group. Analysis of actual results and simulations under alternative electoral system designs shows that under either of two types of majoritarian electoral systems, "regions constituting more than half the total seats would be one-party fiefdoms with no minority party representatives."[105] Such majoritarian systems have the particularly perverse effect of denying legislative representation to precisely those voters who represent the greatest hope for accommodation, the ones willing to vote for a party other than the one that dominates their group or region. At the extreme, they can facilitate the hollowing out even of electoral democracy by denying representation to a political opposition that is spread broadly but thinly across a number of electoral districts, thus creating a de facto one-party state (as in Zimbabwe). And even when such systems give birth to ethnically broad parties and governments, as in Zambia in 1991, they tend to give way more easily to polarization, as ethnic parties mobilize to gain hegemony in the particular territorial districts where their groups reside.

With proportional representation, as in South Africa, votes are not wasted, so parties have an incentive to construct ethnically (or racially, or regionally) inclusive lists of candidates and thus to reach out, integratively, to develop a political base among groups predominantly represented by rival parties.[106] In this way, South Africa's two largest political parties (the ruling African National Congress and the former ruling party under apartheid, the National Party) have developed surprisingly broad multiethnic or multiracial profiles, both in their lists of party candidates and in their profiles of voter support.[107] In South Africa, the principal problem with the system, however, is that proportionality has been achieved at the expense of accountability, as half of the four hundred members of the National Assembly were elected from national party lists and half from nine provincial lists that generally also constituted very large districts (too large to afford any direct ties between representative and voter).

As Reynolds wisely puts it, "The constitutional engineer who seeks to craft a dynamic and inclusive democracy must look somewhere in between the extremes of the remote and unaccountable representation that characterizes national list proportioinal representation and the exclusionary and all too often complacent representation provided by MP's elected from 'safe' SMDs."[108] The German two-tier system provides one option, by providing direct accountability for half the members who are elected in single-member districts, in a system that is proportional overall (by selecting the other half of parliament as needed from each of the party lists to achieve proportionality). However, this system may be excessively complicated in its requirement for separate ballots for the two tiers of representation; it also tends to give rise to two classes of representatives (those responsive to local concerns and those beholden to national party bosses), requires the drawing of a large number of equal-sized constituencies, and cannot effectivly hold accountable to specific voters the half of parliament elected from proportional representation lists (or even a good share of the single-member district representatives who come from uncompetitive districts dominated by one party).[109]

Probably a better alternative is the use of smaller, multimember constituencies with open lists, combined with some topping off from a national list or set of provincial lists, to achieve greater proportionality among the parties. This would provide more direct lines of communication and accountability between specific representatives and clearly demarcated constituencies; it would give voters more choice in the selection of individual candidates; it would help break the hegemony of individual parties within their presumed ethnic or regional strongholds; and it would also give each national party a better chance (through their regional or national topping off lists) to elect some candidates from ethnic groups and regions in which the party is not (yet) particularly strong.[110]

What, if anything, do the above issues and principles say to new and poorly functioning democracies in other parts of the world? One general lesson is that, in electoral system design as in the practice of democratic politics, there is value in moderation. Extreme, highly proportional, electoral formulas tend to produce extreme fragmentation of parties and even to elevate extremist politics. Thus, as a general rule, a moderately multiparty system, produced by a moderate system of proportional representation, makes more sense for most emerging democracies.[111] This can be achieved either by relying on moderately sized multimember districts or by choosing an electoral threshold, such as the German 5 percent barrier (and certainly no lower than 3%), which will weed out very small parties. The adoption of a 5 percent threshold for party representation (and 7% for coalitions) has accelerated the consolidation of the party system in Poland, helping to streamline the number of parties in the Sejm (lower house) from the twenty-nine winning representation in 1991 to six in 1993.[112]

Such consolidating reform in the electoral system appears particularly necessary in Brazil, where Latin America's most fragmented party system has contributed to chronic problems of governability. Because the only electoral threshold that parties must cross is to win a single seat on a party list at the state level, "parties can enter parliament by winning less than 2 percent of the vote in a large state like São Paulo, which has many seats, or as little as an eighth of the vote in one of the smaller states."[113] Further compounding the misfortune of this design is the fact that voters select not a party list but a single candidate from the statewide lists, thus generating the extreme individualism and lack of party discipline found in single-member district systems, "without the latter's requirement that representatives be accountable to geographical constituencies."[114] (Overrepresentation of small states, even in the lower chamber, is another problem.)

As a result of the extremely low threshold and weak incentives to party system institutionalization, in October 1990, 19 parties won seats in the Chamber of Deputies (the lower house), producing an "effective number" of 8.7 parties, the highest such figure in Latin America and one of the highest in the world.[115] Even with the broad coalition that gathered behind Fernando Henrique Cardoso in the October 1994 presidential election, lifting him to a first-ballot victory in an eight-candidate race, legislative fragmentation remained severe, with 18 parties winning seats in the chamber, and 10 of them failing to capture as much as 3 percent of the seats.[116] Although Cardoso crafted a more effective multiparty supporting coalition in the congress, the quest for economic and political reforms continues to be obstructed by the weakness and fragmentation of the party system.

In a system such as Brazil's, the reform imperatives are clear but far from easy. Somehow, the effective threshold for legislative representation must be raised to reduce the number of parties, either by substantially reducing district magnitudes or by establishing a threshold of the national vote that must be won for representation in the lower house.[117] Bolivar Lamounier recommends the 5 percent threshold of the German system (even perhaps the German two-tier structure, as well), reapportionment of seats to ensure equality of representation for citizens of all states, and closed lists for the chamber to generate more stable and coherent parties.[118]

In Israel, the need to reduce political party fragmentation has been apparent for some time. Although Israel's democracy has shown no signs of actually breaking down, the accumulating political stress of the Palestinian *intifada* (uprising) in the late 1980s and the growing political polarization within Israel on questions relating to peace and territory were associated with perceptible declines in attitudinal support for democracy.[119] The difficulties in forming governments and the tendency of the Israeli party system to display classic features of polarized pluralism, with extreme religious and ideological parties pulling the two principal parties away from the center on crucial issues, have led many political scientists to propose raising the electoral threshold from 1.5 percent (one of the lowest in the world) to 3.5 percent. This figure is low enough to allow for representation of the wide diversity of deeply held views and interests in the country but high enough to achieve a significant consolidation of the party system.[120]

Even the slight increase in Israel's electoral threshold from 1 percent to 1.5 percent reduced the number of parties winning representation in parliament from fifteen in 1988 to ten in 1992, not only because of the mechanical effect of removing smaller parties but also because of the psychological impact that induced some parties to coalesce in advance for fear of losing out entirely.[121] Unfortunately, in response to popular disgust with the blackmail techniques of small fringe parties during government formation after parliamentary elections, Israel took the unprecedented step in March 1992 of providing for direct election of the prime minister in 1996. As many political scientists predicted at the time, this only gave renewed stimulus to party fragmentation in the May 1996 general elections, leaving the two center parties, Labor and Likud, with less representation in parliament than ever and the religious parties stronger than ever, because voters separated their endorsement of a parliamentary party list from their selection of a candidate to head the government. This was a classic instance of a country *over*reforming in response to democratic stress, thereby diminishing rather than improving the quality and stability of democracy.[122]

If barriers to party fragmentation are generally desirable, they are not always so. There are times and places when weeding out small parties would do more harm than good. Several political parties representing key principles and constituencies did more poorly than many expected in South Africa's April 1994 founding election, and each would have been denied parliamentary representation altogether not only under single-member districts but even with a national threshold as low as

3 percent. Exclusion of the ultraconservative Afrikaaner Freedom Front and of the Black militant Pan-Africanist Congress could have meant a violent turn against the system by each of these volatile groups, whose radical constituencies felt the new political system had either surrendered too much or won too little. Exclusion of the Democratic Party, representing White (predominantly English-speaking) liberals, would have removed one of the most articulate forces pressing to institutionalize individual rights and horizontal accountability in democratic practice and in the permanent constitution.[123] Yet by 1999 or sometime thereafter, the need for such broad political inclusion of even very small groups may begin to be outweighed by the value of greater party aggregation, particularly among opposition forces.

Party system institutionalization may be undermined by proliferation not only of political parties but also of factions or personal followings within them. As we have seen, one of the weaknesses of the Brazilian system is the barrier to party coherence raised by asking voters to select a single candidate from the party list, thus pitting individual party candidates against one another. A similar inducement to personalism and a much stronger proclivity to party factionalism is generated by the single, nontransferable vote (SNTV), which differs from the Brazilian system in that it does not provide a party list of candidates nor any assurance of proportionality in the overall distribution of seats to parties (though the system is generally more proportional than SMD, particularly in districts of larger magnitude). Under SNTV, the voter casts a single vote for a single candidate in a multimember constituency. In a three-member district, the candidates with the three highest vote totals (from whatever party) are elected. If an individual party candidate in a multimember constituency gets a surplus of votes beyond the quota needed for election, these are not transferred to lower-order preferences of the voter but are simply "wasted."

SNTV has several potentially perverse effects. Precisely because of the nonproportionality and nontransferability of the vote, it can punish larger parties by fragmenting their vote if they nominate too many candidates in a district.[124] It also presents a very low threshold (whatever it takes to finish "nth" in an n-member district) and thus facilitates (even more than the single-member district system) the election of small parties and of independent candidates who have no party loyalty or may be prepared to align with the highest bidder. More generally, it personalizes the contest, diminishes party solidarity, encourages or entrenches party factionalization, and fosters corruption and vote buying by forcing candidates of the same party to compete against one another at the same time as they oppose candidates of other parties. Because the party as such cannot (in principle) favor any of its official nominees in a district, in order to attract votes candidates have to look elsewhere for assistance: to personal connections, factional ties, "radical gestures, money, or even physical force." As a result, in contrast to party list proportional representation systems, or the Westminster combination of parliamentary government with plurality elections, "candidates running under the SNTV system have little incentive to remain loyal to party discipline after election." Party indiscipline has therefore been a chronic problem in Taiwan.[125]

It is no wonder, then, that SNTV is rare and may be on its way to extinction. Dating back to the 1920s in Japan, it became a chief target of political reformers in that country and was replaced in 1994 with a two-tier system, which elected three hundred members of the lower house from single-member districts and two hundred by proportional representation from eleven large electoral districts. As one specialist notes, this is "a much more honest and representative electoral system that would give the people more say in governance."[126] In a period of even deeper political turmoil, Italy moved from extreme proportional representation toward a similar but more majoritarian system, which elects three-quarters of each house by plurality from single-member districts and the remaining one-quarter by party list proportional representation, with a 4 percent threshold. In these cases, mature but stressed democracies judged that vertical accountability, transparency, voter choice, and governability had become greater priorities than maximizing representativeness.

Taiwan is the only significant democratic system still utilizing SNTV, and for reasons similar to Japan's, democratic reformers in that country are seeking its replacement. In a limited sense, progress toward democratic consolidation may occur in Taiwan under any electoral system, given the growing strength of both opposition forces and civil society. Thus, defenders of the existing system could easily invoke Rein Taagepera and Matthew Shugart's bias for stability: "Most of the long-standing electoral systems do the job. Keeping the ills we know may be better than leaping into the unknown."[127] Yet Taiwan is a clear case in which the electoral system hinders the institutionalization of parties and the party system and, as a result, the consolidation of democracy. Political scientists and democratic reformers in the country are thus virtually unanimous in favoring its elimination, even though they do not agree on what should replace it.[128] These divisions, and the determination of local party factions to preserve the system that gives them power, will likely prevent electoral reform in Taiwan until there is a major political crisis or realignment.

As it was for Japan and Italy, a popular reform alternative for Taiwan is the two-ballot system, combining single-member districts with proportional representation. While this system does not secure overall proportionality the way the German system does, and thus the two components fit oddly (and even at cross-purposes), it may contribute to democratic consolidation in two ways. The large number of single-member districts should eventually breed greater transparency and accountability in relations between voters and their representatives, while encouraging a reduction in the number and significance of political factions and a rallying of party organization behind the single nominee in each constituency. At the same time, the proportional representation component will help develop greater party coherence, while attenuating the disproportionality that the single-member district system may generate.[129] The reduction of the size of districts and the simplification of competition within them should also reduce the increasingly enormous financial demands associated with electoral campaigns. Controlling corruption and vote buying, however, will require other reforms as well to regulate campaign spending and strengthen the legal system.

Strengthening Horizontal Accountability and the Rule of Law

An institutionally mature, resourceful, and autonomous legislature is an important instrument of horizontal accountability. Even in a parliamentary system in which government emerges out of the legislature, the latter is expected to question ministers and hold government accountable. However, elected executives, state bureaucrats, soldiers, and police cannot be held accountable without a judicial system that has the constitutional and political autonomy to ensure a genuine rule of law. Neither can civil liberties be protected and the power of the state constrained without such an institutionalized judicial system.

Such a judicial system requires more than independent and professional judges (who in turn require good pay, a secure and substantial term in office, and depoliticized procedures for selection). It demands that judges have the staffing and financial and technical resources to be effective and that they be served and petitioned by an infrastructure of institutions that compose an effective legal system: prosecutors, public defenders, police, investigators, legal aid programs, bar associations, law schools. It further requires a body of law (criminal and otherwise) that is clearly codified, widely accessible, and democratic in spirit. Finally, as with the constitution specifically, it requires that citizens commit themselves to the rule of law, independent of whatever immediate advantage may be derived from temporary transgressions. Only when organized actors in politics and civil society recognize their long-term collective interest in a strong, independent judiciary can that branch of government gain the authority and resources to impose accountability on other state actors. An effective judicial system thus depends on effective supporting structures and norms in civil society.

The courts can also play an important role in punishing and deterring corruption and abuse of office but only if other specialized agencies are available to monitor, expose, and bring charges against such wrongdoing. Autonomous audit agencies as independent arms of government are indispensable for controlling corruption. Such bodies, including, ideally, an agency to receive and monitor regular declarations of assets by public officials, must have particularly strong coherence and autonomy—both legally and in terms of professional mission and esprit de corps—if they are to resist the enormous pressures that will be visited upon them to ignore wrongdoing. Audit agencies, and ombudsmen to investigate citizens' complaints, also need the staff and technical resources to probe effectively and the statutory authority to punish wrongdoing. The single biggest frustration of the Control Yuan (which has the power to censure and impeach law-breaking and duty-neglecting public officials under the constitution of the Republic of China on Taiwan) is that they do not have the authority to impose concrete penalties on public officials but must rely on the judicial system, which is more susceptible to political influence and to its own problems of corruption.[130]

Deepening Democracy: Civil-Military Relations

Deepening democracy—making it more liberal, accountable, responsive, and representative—overlaps with several of the institutional challenges discussed above, but it also entails others. Power must be decentralized and devolved to lower levels (see chap. 4). Autonomous groups and media in civil society need to develop the energy, resources, and organizational capacity to check the abuse of power and constitute additional means for representing interests and stimulating participation (see chap. 6). For many new democracies in Asia, Africa, and Latin America, an urgent challenge is to reduce the autonomous and democratically unaccountable power of the military.

Most scholars of civil-military relations concede that the best way for a democracy to deter a coup is to govern effectively and maintain broad legitimacy. But good goverance and legitimation may take time to achieve, and in any case, some new democracies are born into circumstances of very substantial political power and prerogatives for the military. The challenge for democratic consolidation, then, is to gradually roll back these prerogatives and refocus the military's mission, training, and expenditures around issues of external security. By definition, democracy cannot be consolidated until the military becomes firmly subordinated to civilian control and committed to the democratic constitutional order. More specifically, as Felipe Agüero articulates it, "civilian supremacy" gives democratically elected government unquestioned authority over all policy arenas, including defining the goals and overseeing the organization and implementation of national defense. In such a system, the military role is constrained to matters of national defense and international security, the military is removed from all responsibility for internal security, and governmental structures (such as a civilian ministry of defense) exist to enable civilians to exercise effective oversight and control of the military (as well as the intelligence services).[131]

When the military as an institution has a long tradition of political intervention and retains extensive political and economic prerogatives, new democracies face a particularly difficult and dangerous challenge. In such circumstances, establishing civilian supremacy is a complex and typically protracted process, requiring many of the factors that promote democratic consolidation: skilled political leadership, unity among civilian political forces (across partisan and other divides), civilian expertise (both inside and outside government) on national security matters, and luck (in the form of divisions within the military, and military rebellions too partial and inept to succeed).[132]

Successful reform also requires a long-term policy vision, driven by political leadership.[133] The military must be steadily removed from the political realm, including from such nonmilitary responsibilities as rural development, "civic action," domestic intelligence, policing, and participation in the cabinet. Such involvement in domestic affairs, even in worthy goals such as developing the hinterland, erodes the military's distinct role as a defense force and immerses it in political conflicts and concerns.[134] Reorientation to a more narrowly defined mission of external defense takes time, because it would require several actions: pruning a bloated officer corps, reducing the size of the military (and hence its capacity to seize and exercise political power), devising new missions and doctrines, revising military officer training and education, and reorganizing force structures around weaponry better suited to performing the military's mission of defending the country's borders, air space, and sea lanes (as well as ancillary functions, such as assisting in times of national emergency or natural catastrophe).

Increasingly, these legitimate missions also include international peacekeeping. This is a fortunate development, because in the post–Cold War world large militaries are less needed to defend against conventional security challenges. Thus, it appears that one reason that the Bangladeshi army may not have intervened in the wake of the country's recent disastrous elections is that its forces were occupied in United Nations peacekeeping missions on four other continents.[135] Another new mission, however—the pressure on Latin American militaries to conduct a war on drug production and trafficking—takes the military in the wrong direction, toward a new involvement in internal security and in the corruption that invariably surrounds the drug trade.

Democratic consolidation typically requires a strategy by which military influence over nonmilitary issues and functions is gradually reduced and civilian oversight and control is eventually established over matters of broad military and national security policy (including strategy, force structure, deployment, expenditures, and—if armed conflict should come to pass—rules of engagement). Unless the military has been defeated or shattered, as with the transitions in Greece and Argentina and the U.S. invasions of Panama and Haiti, when outright elimination of the army becomes possible in a small country, this strategy usually pursues reforms incrementally, through bargaining, dialogue, and consensus building rather than blunt confrontation

The risks of military reaction can be reduced if civilians accord the military a position of status, honor, and income; if they never use the military as a power resource in political competition; if they avoid political interference in routine promotions; and if they avoid highly conflictual trials for crimes committed under authoritarian rule. Prosecution for past crimes is a noble and profoundly democratic goal, encompassing basic notions of accountability and lawfulness. But it is typically more than the fragile civil-military relations of new democracies can bear. In such circumstances, Samuel Huntington is unfortunately right that "the least unsatisfactory course may well be: do not prosecute, do not punish, do not forgive, and above all, do not forget."[136]

Timing is crucial in the politics of democratic consolidation. Moments of opportunity may arise (as in the early years of the Kim Young Sam presidency in South Korea), in which a democratic president has such widespread popular support and the military is sufficiently weakened domestically, divided internally, and embedded internationally that a civilian regime has unusual scope to weed out the officer corps and restructure civil-military relations. More often, however, time is needed for civilian and military elites to adapt to new structures of authority and to develop confidence and trust in one another. Military officers in particular need to be convinced that expanding civilian control will not compromise the nation's security or the institutional prestige and integrity of the military.

Time is also needed for what Alfred Stepan terms "democratic empowerment," by which civilians develop the substantive competence to manage and monitor military budgets, acquisitions, training, promotions, and operations intelligently and responsibly.[137] Building up sufficient civilian expertise to staff the defense ministry, the foreign intelligence bureau, legislative oversight committees, and the more informal inputs and scrutiny that must come from the academy, policy community, and mass media is a long-term process. So is the generational change that sees old-line commanding officers, who may bear responsibility for human rights violations under authoritarian rule, succeeded by younger officers better able to adapt to a more constrained military role. The overarching logic of incrementalism has been articulated by Agüero: "Untimely civilian effort to initiate military reform may prove counterproductive. The need to reassure the military during the first years [following a democratic transition] may . . . demand postponement of reform measures, particularly in those areas deemed most sensitive. Civilian expertise is most effective if put into practice when at least some degree of confidence between the new authorities and the military has developed."[138]

If democracy works in other respects, it is likely to make progress in civil-military relations as well. As democratic institutions sink roots and as popular commitment to the constitutional system deepens, the scope for the military to intervene in politics diminishes. As economic development proceeds, bringing a country to middle and upper-middle income status, the society becomes more educated and complex, and the plausibility of it ever being governable again by a centralized military re-cedes. The political culture also changes, promoting tolerance and peaceful conflict resolution and greater resistance to authoritarian styles of governance. These factors no doubt help to explain the national in-come ceilings on coups and coup attempts, which Huntington identi-fies.[139]

Moreover, if democracy can distribute development across the coun-try and resolve the society's key conflicts through peaceful accommoda-tion, it will preempt the forms of violent protest (left-wing guerrilla movements, ethnic secessionist movements, religious fundamentalist movements) that have brought military coups or political interference to many civilian regimes throughout the world. Finally, as new democra-cies become established and more economically developed, they become more viable partners for participation in democratic collective security arrangements that generate powerful additional pressure—political, normative, and structural—for civilian supremacy over the military. NATO has been the classic instrument of such influence, and it is likely that the incorporation of emerging Eastern European democracies like the Czech Republic, Poland, and Hungary as full members will advance consolidation in those countries, as it did in Spain, Portugal, and Greece.[140]

These positive concomitants of democratic change do not lessen the importance of a coherent reform strategy or the difficulty of imple-menting it in many new and troubled democracies. But democratic de-velopment—and thus consolidation—is an integrated process. In the end, the military threat to democracy will not be permanently contained without other changes that improve the effectiveness of democratic in-stitutions and the depth of popular involvement with, and commitment to, them. While causality may be reciprocal and intertwined, ultimately, civilian supremacy and democratic legitimacy go hand in hand.

4

Size and Democracy

The Case for Decentralization

with Svetlana Tsalik

One of the most striking features of the distribution of democracies (liberal and otherwise) around the world is also, curiously, one of its least discussed, theoretically: its significantly greater incidence in very small countries, with populations of less than about one million (in current numbers, for our purposes here). When the third wave began in April 1974, about half of these very small (independent) countries were democratic (compared to 23% of larger states). During the third wave, some seventeen new states with populations of less than one million (many with less than a hundred thousand) became independent, and most of them have become stable (and liberal) democracies.

Overall, close to 75 percent of the states that now have populations of less than one million were formally democratic at the start of 1998, compared to less than 60 percent of larger states. The difference in the incidence of liberal democracy is particularly stunning: two-thirds of states with populations of less than one million are rated "free" by Freedom House, compared to only about one-third of states with populations over one million. (Further, the small states have a more democratic median freedom score of 1.5, compared to 3.5 for the larger states, and a more democratic average score, 2.63 versus 3.86 for larger states.) Even more striking is the incidence of democracy among the thirty-three states with populations of less than half a million. Five in six of these "microstates" are democracies, and more than three-quarters are liberal democracies (see table 4.1). In fact, the greater incidence of democracy

117

in states under one million population is entirely due to the microstates.[1] These differences, which have been visible for some time, resurrect the intriguing question (which was raised in the seminal analysis of Robert Dahl and Edward Tufte in 1973 and then largely abandoned by the field) of whether democracy is not indeed easier to establish and create in small, less complex societies.[2]

Skeptics contend that the relationship between size and democracy is an artifact of British (and later American) imperial reach across the oceans. To be sure, it is hard to disentangle the two effects: two-thirds of the democracies with populations under one million are former colonies or dependencies of Britain, the United States, and Australia. Yet so are five of the eleven nondemocracies under one million population (and four of the five nondemocracies with population less than half a million). The incidence of democracy (both electoral and liberal) is higher in former Anglo-American colonies than in the entire population of states (compare tables 4.1 and 4.2); and thus it is higher still when compared only with other developing countries. However, as table 4.2 shows, it is the impact of Anglo-American colonialism that is an artifact of size. Among the fifty-three countries that were once Anglo-American colonies or dependencies (excluding the settler lands of the United States, Canada, Australia, and New Zealand), we find the same pattern

Table 4.1   All States, Distribution of Democracy by Size, 1997

	Electoral Democracies		Liberal Democracies	
Size of State	N	%	N	%
All states (N =191)	117	61.3	81	42.4
median freedom score = 3.5				
average freedom score = 3.58				
States > 1 million population (N = 150)	87	58	54	36.0
median freedom score = 3.5				
average freedom score = 3.86				
States < 1 million population (N = 41)	30	73.2	27	65.9
median freedom score = 1.5				
average freedom score = 2.63				
States < 500,000 population (N = 33)	28	84.9	26	78.8
median freedom score = 1.5				
average freedom score = 2.03				

Source: Freedom House, *Freedom in the World: Political Rights and Civil Liberties, 1996–1997* and *1997–1998* (New York: Freedom House, 1997, 1998).

Table 4.2   Former British, U.S., and Australian Colonies, Distribution of Democracy, by Size, 1997

Size of State	Electoral Democracies		Liberal Democracies	
	N	%	N	%
All former Anglo-American colonies	36	67.9	28	52.8
($N = 53$)				
median freedom score = 2.5				
average freedom score = 3.09				
States > 1 million population	16	57.1	9	32.1
($N = 28$)				
median freedom score = 4.0				
average freedom score = 3.89				
States < 1 million population	20	80.0	19	76.0
($N = 25$)				
median freedom score = 1.5				
average freedom score = 2.20				
States < 500,000 population	19	82.6	18	78.3
($N = 23$)				
median freedom score = 1.5				
average freedom score = 2.07				

Source: See table 4.1.

of variation as among the entire set of countries in the world: those with populations under one million are appreciably more likely to be electoral democracies and more than twice as likely to be liberal democracies (see table 4.2).[3] The former Anglo-American colonies above one million population have the same proportions of democracies and liberal democracies as other states in the world of the same size, and so do the former colonies with populations under half a million (compare tables 4.1 and 4.2). If causation is being confounded, it seems to be the other way around: at least part of the "credit" for democratic success that is ascribed to Anglo-American cultural and institutional influence owes to an accident of history: that so many British and U.S. colonies were so small.

If there is indeed a connection between the size of a country and its likelihood of maintaining democracy, then a powerful policy implication follows. Since most states are not likely to get smaller in size (given the enormous human, financial, and political costs typically imposed by secession or state disintegration), other ways must be found to reduce the scale of democracy as it is experienced by citizens in their daily lives. This means devolution of power: federalism and regional autonomy in countries whose scale and complexity call for it and whose culture and politics permit it; and in all countries, elected local governments with meaningful autonomy and capacity to mobilize and spend resources. Even at the level of municipalities, the afflictions and frustrations of urban life in huge metropolises (in rich and poor countries alike) increasingly generate demands for further decentralization to give people greater control (and to press officials toward greater accountability and responsiveness) with respect to education, sanitation, public safety, and other key services. If institutional arrangements such as federalism and decentralization can mimic in some important respects the conditions of small states, then perhaps larger states may benefit from some of the same favorable conditions for democracy that are intrinsic to very small states.

If decentralization enhances the efficacy, quality, and legitimacy of democracy, then worldwide trends in devolution provide cause for optimism. Since the 1970s, strong pressures for political and administrative devolution have appeared in both the developed and developing worlds. Concern for improving efficiency of service provision led to greater support for decentralization in Europe. Local governments, it was believed, would function like firms in a market, competing to provide the best services for their citizens.[4] When local officials are elected and citizens have to pay for the services they provide, local officials would have greater incentives for efficiency, it was argued. Moreover, the economic stagnation of the 1970s led to pressure to unload central budgetary responsibility onto local governments.

In the developing world, the performance of highly centralized postcolonial governments came under increasing criticism for corruption, rigidity, unresponsiveness, and inefficiency. Moreover, urbanization made it harder for a central government to meet the widely differing requirements of both village dwellers and the rapidly expanding urban populations. Urban centers will continue to grow, making it harder to provide the necessary infrastructure investments such as clean water, sanitation, and roads, from the center.[5] In countries emerging from authoritarian rule in Latin America, decentralization was seen as a means to dilute the power of the central state and thus undermine the political, social, and economic resource bases on which authoritarian rule could be rebuilt.

Pressure for decentralization in the developing world also came from international lending agencies. The International Monetary Fund shifted its lending portfolio toward promoting municipal development, hoping developing countries could alleviate their growing debt burden by tapping into local fiscal potential.[6] In the 1990s the World Bank also reconsidered its structural adjustment policies to emphasize that "ordinary people should participate more in designing and implementing development programs" and that "local governments are best suited to meet the needs of local communities."[7] Regional development banks such as the Inter-American Development Bank (IDB) also enthusiastically promoted decentralization and stronger municipal government. Bilateral aid donors such as the U.S. Agency for International Development and the Scandinavian aid agencies gave increasing emphasis to local initiative and grassroots participation in their programs and policy guidelines.[8] Political pressure for decentralization was also driven by demands from below, by increasingly mobilized and aware populations of the poor and marginalized who became active in a myriad of formal and informal community organizations.

These pressures led to a wave of political decentralization throughout the world since the 1970s. "Out of the seventy-five developing and transitional countries with population greater than five million, all but twelve claim to be embarked on some form of transfer of political power to units of local government."[9] However, the movement for devolution of power confronts powerful resistance from entrenched central bureaucracies, anxious national officials, lingering centralist and statist ideologies, and historical traditions of centralized state power dating from colonial rule, the Ottoman Empire, and the indigenous kingdoms of such countries as Thailand and Korea. Beyond these obstacles, effective local governments require resources to create their own structures of administration and representation and to provide services to their citizens. These resources are at a particular premium in poor countries, which have felt the need to concentrate power and spending authority in order to ignite development and ensure more even distribution.[10]

Why Promote Local Democracy?

How can we explain the greater success of democracy on a very small scale? And how can decentralization help deepen and consolidate democracy in larger states? In what follows we offer several propositions about how local government can improve democracy. Meaningful, representative, local government fosters democratic vitality in five broad, overlapping ways. First, it helps to develop democratic values and skills among citizens. Second, it increases accountability and responsiveness to local interests and concerns. Third, it provides additional channels of access to power for historically marginalized groups and thus improves the representativeness of democracy. Fourth, it enhances checks and balances vis-à-vis power at the center. Fifth, it provides opportunities (and in federal, three-tier systems, opportunities at two of these tiers) for parties and factions in opposition at the center to exercise some measure of political power. Each of these functions, we argue, enhances the legitimacy and hence stability of democracy. We consider each of these potential contributions to democratic vitality in turn below. Later in this chapter, we take up the potential additional benefits—and costs—of a fully federal system.

Citizen Development

Supporters of democratic local government value, above all, its educational potential. John Stuart Mill noted that, "except by the part they may take as jurymen . . . the mass of the population have very little opportunity of sharing personally in the conduct of the general affairs of the society."[11] Such political disengagement is dangerous, not only because it leaves citizens estranged from the decision-making process but also because it may translate into rejection of the democratic system if unpopular decisions are made. By serving on local bodies, citizens "have to act for public interests, as well as to think and to speak, and the thinking cannot all be done by proxy."[12] Involvement in democratic local government is a great educative force, Mill claimed, because it teaches citizens to look beyond their immediate interests, recognize the just demands of others, and if necessary, accept decisions they did not initially like.

The educative potential of local government is available however not only to those who serve in it, as Mill suggested, but to all local residents. Benjamin Barber emphasizes local government's vital role as "talk shop": "the objective is not to exercise power or make policy; it is to . . . instill civic competence."[13] Through local deliberation, citizens become aware of other interests and construct a more realistic conception of what is politically feasible than they would in the isolation of a ballot box. People "learn, by their direct involvement in local affairs, what is possible, practical, and expedient. Experience teaches them the use of power and authority" and the need for consultation and negotiation, practices vital to stable democracy.[14]

The powerful socializing impact of decentralized participation is one of the most striking findings of Robert Putnam's study of civic traditions in modern Italy. Those regions that have registered the best political and economic performance in democratic Italy evolved over centuries political traditions that, while not fully democratic in their inclusiveness, involved the active participation of a large number of adult males in town or city governance. This in turn bred the broad civic commitment and horizontal relations of trust, tolerance, cooperation, and solidarity that constitute what Putnam calls the "civic community." Indicators of "civic involvement"—of social solidarity and mass political participation— stretching over six decades in turn correlate highly not only with one another but with measures of economic development (and also with the quality of democratic life) at later points in time.[15] Over the past quarter century, political decentralization in Italy has broadly "transformed elite political culture" in a democratic direction. The creation of elected regional governments, which then won some significant autonomous power and control over resources, generated a less ideologically polarized, more moderate, pragmatic, tolerant, and flexible style of politics and a "greater mutual acceptance among virtually all parties."[16] And gradually, citizens came to identify with this level of government and even to regard it more favorably than the national government.

The prodemocratic socializing impact of decentralization is likely to be more potent the smaller the community to which power is devolved. As Dahl stresses that, with increasing scale of a society or political system, "knowledge of the public good becomes more theoretical and less practical." With increasing scale, it becomes more and more difficult for any citizen to know concretely any significant proportion of other citizens in the society and, thus, to apprehend their interests directly.[17] This loss of direct contact diminishes the possibility for "empathic understanding" that would lead citizens to a more altruistic, nonegoistic conception of "civic virtue."[18] In larger communities, the loss of direct contact makes people less disposed to appreciate the validity or reasonableness of other interests.

Beyond teaching citizens about the need for compromise and consideration of others' interests, local democracy also enables a much wider range of citizens to participate in setting the political agenda. When agendas are set by nationally elected officials and representatives, citizens are left with little control other than the decision to either reelect or oust every few years. As public choice theorists have recurrently demonstrated, the ability to structure an agenda—timing, wording, sequence, and rules of order—has a tremendous effect on which choices are made. Those who control the agenda also control the set of feasible alternatives.

When groups are underrepresented in national office, it is likely that issues of concern to them may never enter the policy debate. As Anne Phillips writes with regard to feminist consciousness, "the vote . . . has a built-in bias towards whatever is currently on offer," which may only be overcome with "more engaged interaction" at the local level.[19]

Decentralization and democratization of local government also have great potential to stimulate the growth of civil society organizations and networks. It is the arena of local and community life that offers the greatest scope for independent organizations to form and influence policy. At the local level, the social and organizational barriers to collective action are lower and the problems that demand attention—from social services to transportation and the environment—impact more directly on people's quality of life. Direct citizen involvement in the administration of public services at the local level generates an important opportunity to strengthen the skills of individual citizens and the accumulation of social capital, while making public service delivery more accountable. In Brazil, for example, oversight of local administration and communication of citizen concerns to public officials appear to be improving in some municipalities as a result of laws requiring local education and health officials to consult with *conselhos* (councils) made up of local citizens.[20]

For the new democracies undergoing sweeping social and economic changes, involving citizens in local government may prevent widespread disillusionment with new policies from turning into a rejection of the entire democratic process. Ordinary citizens will be more likely to accept policies that hurt their immediate interests if they understand and are involved in the decisions leading to these policy choices and in the efforts to implement them locally. As Putnam's evidence suggests, involving citizens actively in the democratic process (in horizontal relations of political equality), both through electoral politics and through civil society, is more likely to generate a "civic culture" of tolerance, trust, reciprocity, and cooperation.[21] This in turn cushions a new democratic system against popular alienation and polarization if government performs well below expectations.

Local government is particularly suited for giving citizens the opportunity to internalize democratic norms and practices because of its lower barriers to participation than at the national level. In Britain in recent years, for example, the proportion of women serving as local councilors has been roughly double the number in national office (until the sweeping gains of women candidates in the 1997 parliamentary elections). Importantly, it is not that excluded groups such as women are more likely than men to participate in local politics but that "when women *are* involved in politics, it is more likely to be at local rather than national level."[22]

Accountability and Responsiveness

Democratic local government can also boost legitimacy by making government more responsive to citizen needs. This is one of Mill's core arguments in support of local government. "It is but a small portion of the public business of a country which can be well done, or safely attempted, by the central authorities."[23] Local interest and knowledge is best qualified to make effective service provision at the local level. Although Putnam and his colleagues show evidence of systematic differences across Italy's regions in citizen satisfaction with regional government, related to a robust measure of the political and economic performance of these governments, they also found a strong relationship between satisfaction and the level of government. A 1988 survey showed that "from the point of view of most Italians, the three major levels of government form a ladder of increasing efficacy as one moves from the most distant and most distrusted level (national government) to the closest and most trusted (local government)," with regional government much closer to local in satisfaction.[24]

Data from developing democracies is more fragmentary and also less meaningful, given that democratic local government is often very new, or very weak, or not very democratic—or any combination of these. Yet the initial evidence supports the thesis that citizens generally feel closer to and more confident in lower-level government. Consistently, in three annual surveys, 1994–96, the Turkish public expressed more confidence in local government than in the national government, and this in a country that has historically been very centralized.[25] In four samples of new democracies in Central America and Eastern Europe, people felt somewhat more confident of their ability to influence the local government than the national government.[26] In a 1993 survey of four Russian provinces, a question about the ability to solve the concrete problems of the region elicited much more confidence in the governor (50%) and regional legislature (40%) than in the president (35%) and national parliament (15%).[27]

In a survey late in 1995 (some months after the election of new postapartheid local governments), 54 percent of South Africans perceived they could have some influence on their local town council, compared to 47 percent who felt they could influence the national parliament (and 47%, the provincial parliament).[28] Even though South Africans were less satisfied with provincial than national government, 39 percent favored increasing provincial powers and 32 percent favored maintaining them.[29] Seven in ten respondents thought that democratic elections would make local government work better.[30] However, by 1997, South Africans found that government was more responsive and deserving of approval the higher the level of government.[31] By contrast, in South Korea one year after the first direct elections for provincial governors and city mayors, 51 percent found the new local executives more diligent and responsive than the old officials appointed by the central government; only 4 percent found them worse. This conforms with qualitative reports of more efficient local public service delivery and of numerous reforms to make local administration more transparent, accountable, communicative, entrepreneurial, and flexible.[32]

To be responsive, a government must recognize the varying problems that localities face.[33] This is especially true in the developing world, where urban migration has caused cities to swell and villages to be depleted. It is doubtful whether a national administration has the capacity or the interest to subject local administration to the kind of scrutiny that citizens of each community expect. Focus groups of citizens in South Africa before the 1995 local elections illustrate the distance voters feel from national government, even after the election of a new postapartheid government. "Leaders don't come to us" and "We are living in an isolated and ignored place" were typical responses. As one woman put it, "If a candidate comes from our community at least we know he is going to help us."[34]

The smaller scale of legislative constituencies in the local government arena promotes not only greater responsiveness to local concerns but greater accountability as well. It is often difficult for a local community to turn a national legislator (much less a president or prime minister) out of office for failing to meet their distinctive local needs. Particularly if the community is small relative to the size of the electoral district, there may be simply too few votes at stake and, thus, little incentive for a national-level official to respond. Even if many local communities are similarly dissatisfied, the national legislator may bear little responsibility for the local problems, and the vote for national office includes too many other considerations to be an effective tool for the redress of inadequate local governance. Devolution of power to localities provides a more precise means of redress. Voters at the local level can replace a local government that is corrupt, insensitive to their demands and priorities, or merely incompetent at getting the garbage collected.

Local accountability is facilitated by smaller size of the ward or constituency. Whereas local legislators typically represent a few hundred or thousand people, national legislators can represent several hundred thousand. It remains the case today, as Dahl and Tufte observed a generation ago, that the average U.S. representative has a constituency roughly twice the population of Iceland or Luxembourg.[35] In fact, *a typical member of the U.S. Congress today represents a district larger than the entire populations of twenty-six of the world's liberal democracies.*

Table 4.3 compares the ratios of population to legislators in the lower (or unicameral) national assemblies of ten small democracies (including Mauritius, which is just slightly over one million population) and fifteen medium to large democracies from around the world. All of the microdemocracies have less than ten thousand people per national legislator (Mauritius has about fifteen thousand). The modal democracy among the fifteen larger countries has one national legislator for every hundred thousand persons, a ratio ten times as great as the microdemocracies (and of course, the ratios are much greater still in Brazil, the United States, and most of all, India).[36] Interestingly, Dahl and Tufte report that "the largest and most careful study bearing on the relation of size to democracy within a country" that they could locate (a study of thirty-six local government communes in Sweden) found that citizens' participation and sense of effectiveness were greatest in densely populated communes of under eight thousand people. Significantly, in those small-sized units, membership in political and voluntary organizations was greater and people were more likely to be acquainted with their local representatives.[37] The legislative districts in microdemocracies do not provide an exact parallel (in part because they are not all single-member), but the average population per legislator is in most cases about eight thousand or less.

Even at the local level, the size of the community may make a difference in facilitating political participation, efficacy, and knowledge. In surveys conducted in Slovakia, Poland, Hungary, and the Czech Republic one year after the first democratic elections, respondents in smaller localities were more likely than respondents in large cities to be knowledgable about local politics, to see local politics as relevant to their lives, and to feel that they had more influence than before on the way the municipality is run.[38]

The durable and ingenious solution that the American federalists devised for the problem of size and democracy was republican (representative) government. But the more the population increases (while assem-

Table 4.3 Average Population per Legislator in Lower (or Unicameral) House, in Selected Democracies

Small Democracies	Population (000s)	Seats in Lower House	Population Per Legislator (000s)
Small democracies			
Barbados	259	28	9.25
Cape Verde	396	79	5.01
Dominica	71	21	3.38
Iceland	263	63	4.17
Luxembourg	390	60	6.50
Micronesia	120	14	8.57
St. Lucia	140	17	8.24
Solomon Islands	346	47	7.36
Western Samoa	163	49	3.32
(Mauritius)	1,096	70	15.66
Medium and large democracies			
Australia	17,847	148	120.59
Brazil	159,622	503	317.34
Chile	13,829	120	115.24
Costa Rica	3,209	57	56.30
France	56,556	577	98.02
Hungary	10,313	386	26.72
India	880,338	545	1,615.30
Japan	125,046	511	244.71
Korea (South)	45,485	299	152.12
Poland	38,253	460	83.16
Russia	149,984	450	333.30
South Africa	40,388	400	100.97
Spain	39,141	350	111.83
United Kingdom	57,700	651	88.63
United States	260,884	435	599.73

Source: Arthur S. Banks, ed., *Political Handbook of the World, 1993* (Binghamton, N.Y.: CSA Publications, 1993).

Note: All population figures are for 1993, estimated. Assembly sizes are for 1993.

blies reach an absolute ceiling on their practical size), the greater the difficulty representatives will have communicating with their constituents, and vice versa. The mass media provide a partial solution for the first path of communication, but individual citizens (even operating via the Internet) face problems of access and response when their representative also must worry about a hundred thousand, a quarter of a million, or half a million other constituents. The difficulty increases in systems with proportional representation and larger (in some cases very much larger) multimember districts, even when interest groups enter the picture, because such groups then add another layer of mediation between representative and citizen, and in large-scale democracies the major interest groups are themselves large in scale. As Dahl and Tufte noted in 1973 (with considerable prescience), as the size of the constituency increases, chains of communication between the people and their representatives become longer and more bureaucratized, citizens have (by sheer numerical odds) less chance of having their own views and interests advanced by their representative, and representatives must spend more time (and mobilize more technical expertise) to maintain communication and services for their constituents.[39]

Representativeness

Local elections allow government to be more representative, in the sense of reflecting the diversity of the population. Members of a minority group, who stand less chance of garnering enough votes in a national district, can be elected at the local level, where the minority community is concentrated. In divided societies rife with ethnic conflict, holding power at the local level (and at an intermediate, provincial level) can give ethnic groups the assurance that they are represented and that there is a bulwark against abuse of their rights and interests by national leaders.

Not only members of minority groups but also individuals with ordinary occupational or educational backgrounds have a greater chance of occupying office at the local level. As focus groups in South Africa indicate, citizens wish to elect officials to local government who are ordinary people, "people we know" who are familiar with local problems and are approachable.[40] The higher costs of running for office at the national level, in larger constituencies, is another impediment to enhancing the representativeness of legislators. These high costs heighten the tendency toward the professionalization of politics as the size of the political unit (and the number and complexity of its demand groups) increases. "With increasing size, then, the part-time amateur is replaced in the representatives' ranks by the full-time professional. . . . In every country where constituencies have swelled, legislators have had to devote more and more time to politics."[41] In a democracy of even moderate size, professionalization among parliamentarians is almost inevitable in the contemporary era, and it helps to avoid excessive reliance on professional bureaucrats in the executive and the legislative staff, as well as on lobbyists. However, professionalization makes it more difficult for marginalized groups to win representation and reduces social diversity in the legislature. Most of all, it increases the social distance between citizens and their representatives.

Checks and Balances

The above opportunities that local government can provide strengthen democracy by developing civic competence and generating greater citizen satisfaction with elected authorities. In addition to these important contributions, local government can also act as a structural bulwark against a reversion to authoritarian rule at the national level. Alexis de Tocqueville, who applauded the "local spirit of democracy," believed that even if a despotic majority prevailed at the national level in the United States, its effect would be limited. "The townships, municipal bodies, and counties form so many concealed breakwaters, which check or part the tide of popular determination. If an oppressive law were passed, liberty would still be protected by the mode of executing that law; the majority cannot descend to the details and what may be called the puerilities of administrative tyranny."[42] Local power can figure prominently in an overall system of checks and balances over the exercise of power. For this reason, the postwar constitutions of Italy, Portugal, Spain, Belgium, and the federal countries of Europe have included constitutional guarantees for local government. And in Korea and Taiwan, devolution of power to municipal and county governments is seen as a major element in the deepening of democracy and the constraining of powerful national executives and central bureaucracies.

Contingent Consent

A critical step toward successful democratization is the development of contingent consent.[43] Contingent consent occurs when the losers of an election agree to accept the results on the condition that the election winner will not use their advantage to restructure the rules of the game to keep the opposition permanently out of power. But how can an opposition trust the winning party to keep its word?

When local governments (and even more so, state or provincial governments) are democratically elected and vested with meaningful authority, opposition parties have a chance to win some share of political power and thus to acquire some direct stake in the political system. Holding office at the subnational level may help reassure opposition parties that they are not permanently excluded from power at the center, or at least that they are not completely excluded from all the power that matters in a system. In India's federal system, "The existence of so many opportunities to capture at least some power persuades parties and politicians to remain engaged with elections and logrolling, even when they are defeated in some arenas."[44] Even in a unitary system like Botswana's, opposition party control of some local government councils (with significant power over community development) has been a significant source of democratic vitality, mitigating the effect of one-party dominance at the center and enhancing the legitimacy of the system.[45] But perhaps more important, it puts a check on the actions of the party at the national level. Local opposition victories show the winning party that the opposition has some popular support. This may induce the national government to cooperate and learn to share power with the opposition to preserve harmonious center-provincial (or center-local) relations. Competition for power at the subnational level might also lead to coalitions between groups in opposition to one another at the national level. In the Mexican state of San Luis Potosi, for example, rightist and leftist opposition parties came together in a broad civic movement,[46] and in the 1997 Mexican state-level elections, supporters of the left and right opposition parties crossed traditional divides to unprecedented degrees to defeat the ruling PRI in several states as well as the federal capital district.

Opposition victory at the subnational level also provides a good test of the party's platform and its performance in government. A party that is out of power can easily criticize the governing party and make untenable claims about what it would achieve if it were in office. However, if the opposition holds power at the local level, voters have an opportunity to assess its performance. For example, left-wing parties in Brazil, Peru, Uruguay, Paraguay, and Venezuela that had criticized the ruling party for lack of accountability moderated this criticism after winning key elections in large cities. "Their theoretical radicalism was usually overwhelmed by the practical realities of running major cities."[47] In Brazil, left parties have become more integrated into the political mainstream, and political polarization has been reduced as a result of the experience with municipal administration of left-leaning parties. Some of these parties have implemented programs of citizen participation in the administration of social services that are regarded as models even by centrist political forces.[48] The same moderating effect has been apparent with the victory of the leftist PRD in the race for mayor of Mexico City. And the increased democraticness of elections at the state and local level now constitutes a crucial foundation for the democratization of the national political system in Mexico.

Similarly, in Taiwan, the November 1997 victory of the opposition Democratic Progressive Party (DPP) in twelve of twenty-three races for city mayors and county chiefs was a milestone of democratic development, marking the first time the long-ruling Kuomintang finished second in the national vote total and giving the opposition control of local governments representing 72 percent of the country's population and more than 80 percent of its locally generated revenue. Voters were willing to take a chance on the opposition precisely because it was not a national election with foreign policy at stake, and the DPP had already demonstrated a capacity to govern after winning previous local elections. At the same time, DPP mayoral and county chief candidates abandoned militant rhetoric about national independence in an effort to meet voters' practical concerns about building roads and housing, generating jobs, collecting garbage, and making local government work honestly and efficiently. Following the election, the challenges of having to work with a Kuomintang national government figured to further moderate the DPP's posture.

Interestingly, virtually all five of the above means of improving democratic performance have been evident with the regional reform in Italy. Regional government has had its costs, both in the scope for maladministration in some less "civic" regions and in the apparent increase in regional disparities. But overall, it has had important benefits for the *quality* of democracy:

> On the positive side, the new institutions are closer to the people, as proponents had claimed they would be. The regional governments are more familiar with regional realities and more accessible to regional demands than the remote Roman ministries they replaced. They provide multiple laboratories for policy innovation. . . . They help to nurture a moderate, pragmatic, tolerant style of policy making and conflict management—"a new way of doing politics." They engage the interests of regional social groups and community leaders, and they are gradually earning cautious approval from their constituents.[49]

Pitfalls of Decentralization

The implications of decentralization for democracy are not all positive. There are five main dangers associated with decentralization of government power. It may entrench or create authoritarian enclaves, permit intolerance of certain minorities, exacerbate geographical inequalities, foster redundancy and inefficiency, and stimulate ethnic and nationality consciousness. We consider the first four of these in turn and discuss the last one in our more focused discussion of federalism below.

Authoritarian Enclaves

Regional elites of the ancien régime or the traditional social elite may feel threatened by the democratic change, and may try to hold on to power by illegally and even violently excluding other groups or individuals from political participation. A decentralized political system can create niches for authoritarian figures (or movements) to consolidate their fiefdoms, safe from intervention by central authorities. This process is perhaps most egregious in Colombia where, after ten years of local elections, candidates and members of the main opposition party, the Patriotic Union, were being murdered at the rate of one person every other day. Both right-wing paramilitary units and guerrillas banned electioneering in the areas they informally control and declared candidates "military targets."[50]

Enclaves of exclusion and repression exist throughout Latin America and the successor states of the Soviet Union. In these states, the "persistence of authoritarian enclaves under civilian rule prevents the effective extension of basic political rights to the entire population," leaving segments effectively disenfranchised.[51] In large developing democracies such as India and Brazil, state and local governments and local political bosses are responsible for the most serious and systematic human rights violations. This is a particular problem in highly federal Brazil, where state governments have great authority over public security. During 1996, the "tension between the generally pro-human rights position of the federal government and the entrenched, often violent policies of many states, constituted perhaps the greatest obstacle to the effective implementation of the National Human Rights plan" put forward by the reformist government of President Fernando Henrique Cardoso.[52] Enough such pockets of authoritarian practice can drain democracy of content and obstruct its consolidation at the national level.

The decentralization of political and economic authority may also exacerbate clientelism at the local level. Where hierarchical chains of particularistic, patron-client relations are already the dominant mode of politics, shifting discretionary financial authority from the central to the local level may simply shift the locus of clientelism and corruption from the central to the local arena, making these problems even harder to control because of the absence of the strong parties and countervailing interests that are found at the national level. "Where the municipal system is already subordinated to the logic of intraparty factionalism and is not accountable to the electorate, enhanced financial transfers could simply encourage the existing 'short-termism' of municipal management styles, leading to even poorer selection of investment projects and even greater inefficiency of service provision."[53]

Intolerance and Discrimination

One of the trade-offs of local government is that, while the small size of communities lowers barriers to participation, small size may also create strong pressures for conformity and intolerance of difference. Gerry Stoker reminds us that "local government *is* government and as such might have as damaging an effect on individual liberty as could central government"[54] The more intimate setting of small communities enables disempowered groups to discover their political preferences and forge a common agenda, but it may also exhibit intolerance of differences. "The smaller the community, the greater the hostility to radically different solutions."[55] The prolonged subordination of African Americans and the violent political resistance that met the civil rights movement in the southern United States provide dramatic evidence of how decentralization of power can facilitate intolerance and offer a haven for undemocratic practices. Similarly, in India, discrimination against the scheduled castes and scheduled tribes was only systematically reduced by central government action.[56] More recently, members of the Russian diaspora living in the successor states of the former Soviet Union have complained about discrimination. In the Lithuanian capital of Vilnius, where half of the population is Russian, they made up only 11 percent of the city's councilors.[57]

The problems of integration are more serious in Estonia and Latvia, where Russian speakers form much larger percentages of the overall populations. There, political decentralization—in the unusual form of the birth of new states (or more accurately, the rebirth of previously existing ones) and in the historical shadow of the Soviet Union's legacies of totalitarianism and suppression of national identities—gave scope for exclusionary language and citizenship laws. These laws discriminated against Russophones who had settled after 1940, disenfranchising "almost 40 percent of the population of Estonia during a key foundational moment of the new would-be democracy."[58] In one Estonian town near the Russian border, only 6,000 of the 77,000 inhabitants were eligible to vote in the June 1992 constitutional referendum.[59] In Nigeria, limitations on the political and economic opportunities of "nonindigenes," defined on ethnolinguistic grounds, have also grown, as the number of state and local governments "has proliferated, their territorial size has diminished, and the dominant ethnic groups in those constituencies have sought to maximize their access to power and resources. Discrimination by Nigerian state and local governments has even denied free education and other government benefits to longtime residents and taxpayers, and under Nigeria's federal constitution these measures have been legal.[60]

Exacerbation of Geographic Inequality

For local government to have real autonomy in decision making, it must be able to generate some revenue of its own. No local government can be entirely self-sustaining, but if it is heavily dependent on the central government for the bulk of its finances, its capacity for self-government becomes weakened.[61] However, those countries that do offer local governments enhanced powers of revenue generation experience growing disparities between richer and poorer municipalities.[62] This problem is particularly acute in the developing world, where modernization has created great disparities between town and country. Capital and labor are concentrated in a few swollen metropolitan areas like Bangkok, Manila, São Paulo, Mexico City, Lagos, and Johannesburg, while rural villages are left without industry and without sufficient provision of social services. Urban areas can draw adequate revenue from enterprises and expensive residential properties; but rural areas engaged in subsistence farming and barter trade have virtually no tax base. Thus, without some central government transfers even the most minimal levels of horizontal equity are unattainable.

Desmond King argues that the democratic advantages of small government should be weighed against the importance of distributive justice for democracy, which assumes that equality of opportunity requires maintenance of more or less uniform standards in education, health, and so on. This involves profound value judgments that each polity and society must make about the trade-offs between freedom and equality and, thus, the degree of fiscal federalism or devolution. For King, local autonomy can constitute "a danger to equality and the social rights of citizenship by providing the potential for malevolent variations" in services along geographic lines.[63] Yet true equality cannot be reached without dragging all government services down to a low common denominator. Effective decentralization must inevitably make some use of a core principle of fiscal federalism: the incentive for some subunits to excel over others by crafting better policies and mobilizing resources more effectively. Many democracies forge some compromise between competing values, setting decent, minimum floors for education and other national services and providing some of the necessary funding, while allowing richer and more enterprising jurisdictions to exceed these floors if they can marshal additional resources.

Waste, Redundancy, and Confusion

Decentralization devolves to local government responsibility for many of the tasks performed by central ministries. It thus requires the creation of many new smaller bureaucracies at the lower level. While smaller, local bureaucracies are more accessible to the citizens they serve, they also impose costs associated with the loss of economies of scale achieved when these services were provided at the national level. Local budgets may be hard-pressed to finance structures of local service provision. Moreover, poor coordination between local and federal agencies providing some of the same services may leave citizens lost in a labyrinth of redundant bureaucratic mazes.

Failure to specify precisely the division of jurisdictional responsibility between central and local authorities can create problems at two extremes: duplication of efforts or the failure to implement policies because both central and local agencies consider the task the other's responsibility. In Panama, where local government power is divided between elected councillors, mayoral appointees, a community board, and the mayor, the parallel structure of elected and appointed officers has resulted in "layer after layer of new laws and procedures . . . creating widespread confusion and confrontation."[64]

One of the most serious potential pathologies of decentralization is the kind of gross waste and corruption that can lead to fiscal disarray at the national level. When large amounts of centrally collected revenue are transferred automatically to lower-level authorities, with no room for central government discretion or conditions, administrative accountability for expenditures is weak, and great scope is opened for the transferred revenue to be dissipated in political patronage. When such lower levels of government are democratically elected, the dynamic can even intensify. Then, only the voters can hold state (regional) and local officials accountable; and in less developed, more rural areas in particular, social relations tend to be vertical and clientelist, and electoral success is driven more by patronage than good government. The ability of state or regional governments to incur debt on their own can generate even more severe fiscal strains, as the state government gets the cash (and gives the state's voters perhaps some short-term benefits), while the central government (and central bank) get the headache of mounting fiscal deficits and endless state pleas for still more revenue. All of these features coalesce in the extreme form of federalism that has played a major role in Brazil's chronic fiscal problems since the return to democracy in the mid-1980s.

Moreover, the very factor that drives this extreme decentralization—an electoral and party system that gives subnational governments enormous influence over nominations for office even at the national level—also obstructs its reform. When one considers as well the problems of authoritarian enclaves, and the ability of subnational actors (especially state governors) to block a wide range of national policy initiatives (through their sway over members of congress), it seems beyond question that the level of political decentralization in Brazil constitutes a major obstacle to democratic consolidation.[65]

It is not inevitable that political decentralization will foster corruption and waste, entrench authoritarian enclaves, permit discrimination against minorities, or exacerbate regional inequalities. Some redundancy is probably unavoidable, but federalist, or decentralized, systems need not be wasteful and inefficient, and indeed the incentives for accountability to local constituencies could potentially make them more efficient. Much depends on how power is decentralized and how well civil society and mass-level constituencies at the local and regional level are organized to press their interests and monitor what subnational governments do. In this respect, the solution to the pitfalls and pathologies of decentralization is not centralization but empowerment: more vigilant and widespread democratic participation at the local level and more transparency through open procedures and an effective, free press. Another condition for successful decentralization is balance, including the retention of strong constitutional authority for a democratic center to intervene at lower levels to protect the rights of minority citizens and ensure a rule of law. Mechanisms must also exist to recruit and train local government bureaucracies and to hold local government officials to high standards of ethics and performance. National government offices (and if necessary, prosecutors) must have the capacity to monitor what local government does and punish mismanagement or illegality.

Challenges of Decentralization for New Democracies

If developing democracies are to succeed in establishing effective, democratic local government, they must address several key challenges. These challenges include weak state capacity, financial viability of local governments, finding the proper size of local government, and overcoming citizen apathy and legacies of authoritarian rule.

Weak States

In the postcolonial world, independence was accompanied by the challenge of consolidating modern states. Tribal elders, *patrones*, bosses, princes, and other informal agents of authority compete with the state to define social opportunities, regulate exchange, extract revenue, distribute privilege, and establish order.[66] The state's capacity is extremely weak in many of these postcolonial countries, as it is in most of the successor states of the former Soviet Union. In the weakest states, including much of Africa, the effective reach of state authorities extends only very haphazardly beyond the capital. Implementation of state policies locally can be achieved only through compromises and payoffs to local bosses and chieftains, in a system of patron-client relations that fosters corruption. In such circumstances, central state leaders have been reluctant to devolve formal political authority, fearing this would only dissipate a thin stock of political power that, instead, needs to be concentrated and enlarged. A more general problem of incentive also exists. No politician likes to surrender power. "The resistance to change is built into the structure of administration itself—consciously and unconsciously, politicians and officials have a natural tendency to centralize power in their own hands and to resist measures of decentralization."[67]

Why, then, would democratic political leaders at the center want to decentralize power, or even reluctantly agree to do so? Political incentives again provide the key. They will do so to the extent they judge that there are political benefits to themselves and their parties from embracing decentralizing reforms and political costs to resisting them. This cost-benefit calculus is more likely to obtain when national politicians need the support of local political factions to govern effectively or to survive politically;[68] when strong political pressures for devolution of power accumulate among influential interest groups and grassroots constituencies; when fiscal deficits pressure central government leaders to cut spending; and when international assistance requires some measure of decentralization.

Of course, if central state leaders judge the price of decentralization to be the loss of their power and control, they may resist it anyway. But there is a growing recognition among many political leaders in developing democracies that power in a political system is not a zero-sum commodity and that the overall capability of the state at all levels can grow as its legitimacy increases. Separate and apart from the changing incentives of the political game, the global trend toward decentralization seems to be driven in part by the understanding that when government is closer to the people, its legitimacy will be greater; hence, its authority to mobilize resources, maintain order, and regulate social and economic life will be greater. In extreme cases, decentralization may seem to be the only means of restoring political order and holding the state together in the face of violent secessionist mobilization, as in the Basque region of Spain, the tribal hill states of northeastern India, and the predominantly Muslim southern Philippines.[69] Moreover, when government is decentralized, central state leaders shed some of the political responsibility for local scandals and disasters and for the intractable problems that characterize, in particular, large cities.

As Juan Linz and Alfred Stepan argue, the consolidation of democracy requires a state structure that is legitimate, "usable," and at least moderately effective.[70] In many third-wave democracies, part of the challenge of consolidation is to strengthen state capacity to collect revenue, to provide social services, to regulate conflict, to preserve the environment, to stimulate investment, to develop and manage the macroeconomy in an era of globalization, and to maintain a rule of law that preserves order while protecting human rights. In a few countries, such as Brazil, the relative power of the center vis-à-vis state and local government must be strengthened if state capacity overall is to increase. But for the most part, these challenges of state building are independent of the vertical distribution of powers. In fact, in most third-wave democracies, the administrative, technical, and financial capacities of the state need to be strengthened at all levels. Not only national governments but local governments as well need permanent staffs with the education and training to administer government resources and services effectively and the pay to attract capable people and to deter corruption. But as with central government, and even more so, local governments are hard pressed to find the financial resources to attract, develop, and retain capable, well-trained bureaucracies. This underscores the crucial variable of financial viability.

Financial Viability

Arguably, the most important determinant of the success of local self-government is the availability of adequate financing both from its own revenue sources and from the national budget. The delegation of new functions to local government without the accompanying resources or authority to raise revenue to pay for these services makes decentralization meaningless at best and dangerous for democracy at worst. If local governments are responsible for functions they do not have the resources to perform adequately, citizens may become disillusioned not only with their local officials but with the democratic process itself. One reason that Sudan's sweeping decentralization efforts failed in the 1970s and 1980s was the inability to fund proposals emanating from the new regional governments.[71] In the Dominican Republican province of Salcedo, an experiment to develop broad consultation and collaboration on development policy through community forums foundered when the decisions reached in the forums could not be implemented because neither the resources nor the authority to raise revenue were forthcoming from the central government.[72]

The problem of overburdened and underresourced local governments is particularly pressing in the postcommunist states. In these countries, the new national governments inherited a social system in which the state traditionally provided cradle-to-grave social services for every citizen. Eager to relieve themselves of the cost of these services but unwilling to incur the political fallout from eliminating them, many governments of these new states transferred responsibility for comprehensive social services to subnational governments, but without a corresponding shift in revenue sources. In Poland and Hungary, local governments have been given expenditure responsibilities in education, transportation, environment, and housing. These spending assignments violate the "benefit area" approach to local finance, which suggests that "each function should be assigned to the lowest level of government that encompasses all or most of the service benefits." The assignments in

Poland and Hungary allowed for major benefit spillovers and the under-provision of services in poorer localities.[73]

Without adequate resources and amenities, local (and provincial) governments will be unable to attract competent civil servants or to afford the infrastructure necessary to run a subnational government. Shortages of qualified personnel, finance, housing, office accommodation, transport, and other resources have dogged decentralization efforts in Africa. William Tordoff thus recommends a phased decentralization rather than a radical departure not grounded in available resources.[74]

While adequate revenue is critical for effective local self-government, it is important that not all of it come from the central government. Worldwide trends in devolution of responsibility make it impossible for all but the wealthiest subnational governments to be entirely self-supporting. However, central transfers should be balanced by authorization to generate local revenues. When local budgets are entirely dependent on central government financing, it is difficult to maintain local autonomy and, hence, accountability to local constituencies. In England, "the undermining of local democracy stemmed from central government wanting to control local spending and taxing." As the share of local government expenditures covered by local taxes declined from 60 percent in the mid-1980s to less than 20 percent by the mid-1990s, local spending patterns became largely determined by the central government's "standard spending assessments," and local authorities effectively became administrative agencies of the central government.[75]

An abundance of funding from the central budget can have the same deleterious effect on local autonomy. Nigeria's oil boom, which increased federal revenues fourteenfold in the 1970s, meant a huge rise in transfers to subnational governments. The vastly greater dependence on the center for revenue led to extensive federal involvement in major areas of local public policy.[76] It also led to a collapse of state and local government services when the national oil economy imploded in the 1980s and there was no sound base of locally generated revenue to fall back upon. Most of all, the dependence of local government on federal oil revenue for virtually all of its income undermines accountability and citizens' identification with local government, since it is not really "their" money that is being spent (or wasted and misappropriated). Responsible and accountable governance at the local level in Nigeria will thus only emerge under a principle of "no representation without taxation."[77]

Taxation represents a major potential source of revenue for subnational governments. Traditionally, in most market economies, the central government controls the more redistributive taxes, such as personal income tax, and charges local governments with collecting more stable sources of revenue, such as excise, retail, or property taxes.[78] Property taxes are potentially the most significant source of revenue and are most appropriate to be levied at the local level. "To the extent locally provided services increase property value, the beneficiaries of public expenditures are made to pay."[79] However, the yield from municipal taxation in Latin America has been disappointing because of the high administrative costs of tax collection.[80] Where own-revenue tax sources are insufficient, another option is tax sharing, in which one government collects tax revenue and shares it with other levels of government. Corporate and personal income taxes and the value-added tax have all been used in tax-sharing arrangements between central and subnational governments in many Eastern European and Soviet successor states.[81] While tax sharing guarantees some degree of revenue certainty to localities, it also gives local governments little incentive to be accountable or efficient in use of these funds, since the acquisition of those revenues is costless.[82] In addition to taxation, localities may introduce user charges for licensed activities and for private goods provided by public services, such as housing rents, water, heating, sanitation, solid waste management, public lighting, and transport fares. But any of these efforts at local revenue generation requires strengthening state structures at the subnational level. And local taxes and fees are unlikely to be imposed as long as local governments and publics expect that the central government will sooner or later bail them out of their fiscal deficits.

Size and Jurisdiction

One of the dilemmas of decentralization concerns the size of the jurisdiction for local government. On one hand, building local government around traditional communities such as small villages can preserve the lifestyle of self-contained historical communities and better educate citizens in the process of self-government. On the other hand, such small localities lack the revenue and infrastructure to adequately administer social services, education, and housing, and residents of small communities may simply transfer their demands for services to larger, neighboring cities, which get overwhelmed.[83] While larger districts can more effectively provide major services, they also increase the ratio of citizens to council members as well as the distance between citizens and representatives, thus reducing the role of citizens in local self-government.

This dilemma has hindered the process of creating functioning local self-governments in Eastern and Central Europe, where the new democratic regimes enthusiastically adopted principles of local democracy. These countries have chosen to preserve traditional communities, and thus the same legislation regulates local government in large cities and tiny hamlets.[84] These disparities have prevented transfer of responsibility for service provision from central ministries to local authorities, since very small municipalities lack the resources to administer specialized social services.

Several solutions are available to the dilemma of small size versus effective service provision. Small municipalities may join together to create administrations that provide services to all the contractors. Another approach, practiced in France, Germany, and the United States, is for small localities to contract for services with large jurisdictions that have developed highly professional departments. Services can also be contracted from the private sector (as in England and the United States).[85] Another alternative (popular in both Western and Eastern Europe) is to create an additional higher level of elected local administration, for populations of a hundred thousand or more.[86] However, such overlapping jurisdictions may generate rivalry and tension unless the functional responsibilities of each level of government are clearly defined.[87]

Authoritarian Legacies and Citizen Apathy

Democratic local government creates the opportunity for citizens to influence policy making at a smaller scale and more accessible level of the political system. But the opportunity to participate does not always translate into greater involvement. Citizen apathy diminishes local politics in both stable and new democracies. In England, only about 40 percent of the electorate votes in local elections. In the United States, voter turnouts have averaged slightly less than 40 percent at the state level (even combined with midterm national congressional elections) and about 25 percent in recent local elections. Voting in the first democratic local elections in Eastern and Central Europe also proved disappointing.[88]

In light of survey data showing that voters judge local government more accessible and more relevant to their daily lives, the lower turnout rates at the local level seem puzzling. However, local elections are typically much less penetrated by party politics and intensive media and mobilization efforts than national elections, and the issues in local elections are typically less clearly defined. In the case of Taiwan, where parties organize and invest intensively in the elections for city mayors and county chiefs, turnout is much higher (around 70%) and more comparable to national elections.[89] Turnout in local elections is also much higher (even exceeding 80–90%) in many European countries in which proportional representation is used and voting is compulsory.[90]

In countries emerging from authoritarian rule, democratic local government may be tainted by legacies of the ancien régime. In Latin America, for example, local government under military dictatorships or authoritarian regimes was often a tool used by rulers to extend control over society. Political activism was frequently met with violence, and corruption was pervasive. Consequently, in many countries—particularly those in which democratization has been most superficial—citizens continue to feel distrust and disdain for local government and often bypass these structures.[91] Resistance to greater citizen involvement comes from local authorities as well, even if they are formally elected. In fact, civic apathy and official arrogance interact in a symbiotic relationship that perpetuates narrow, opaque, and unresponsive government at the local level. Despite constitutional provisions for local citizen involvement throughout Latin America, few local governments have pursued these avenues. In Colombia a major municipal reform in 1986 permitted the creation of elected submunicipal administrative units. By 1990, only fifteen municipalities had created such units.[92]

In Eastern Europe, as well, attitudes changed only modestly in the years immediately after the downfall of the communist regimes. Interviews throughout the region in 1991 found continued mutual alienation between local officials and their constituents, with citizens seeing local councils as reluctant to seek their input and local officials complaining of citizen apathy and detachment.[93] A separate survey of local publics in four postcommunist countries found more mixed results. Typically a third to a half of the samples thought that local government administration had improved and that the influence of the average citizen had increased since the first democratic local elections. However, no more than one in five trusted their local councillors "to work for the good of the community," and while most people felt at least some confidence in their ability to understand local affairs, they remained skeptical about their ability to influence them.[94] In short, even if political efficacy and trust are higher for local government than for national, the absolute levels are still low.

Creating the formal institutions of democratic local government does not guarantee that elected officials will be open and responsive or that citizens will take the opportunity to get involved. The critical link between formal institutions of local democracy and more vibrant citizen involvement is civil society. In the Philippines, where nongovernmental organizations have become pervasive, powerful, and assertive, a far-reaching local government code, adopted in 1991, addresses many of the key challenges noted above. Subnational governments at all levels (provincial, city, municipal, and *barangay*) were collectively guaranteed 40 percent of the national internal revenue. They were also given the power to levy and collect various local taxes and to negotiate and transact directly with foreign donors and investors. Substantial authority and responsibility were devolved to local governments in several sectors.

But in addition to fiscal authority and resources, local governments were given an infusion of some seventy thousand experienced officials transferred from the central government. While implementation has been slow (and dependent on foreign donor support), the Philippine law represents one of the boldest experiments in political decentralization, and the importance of civil society mobilization for this initiative is indicated by the requirement that one-quarter of all the seats on local councils be reserved for nongovernmental organizations.[95] As this case shows, the growth of civil society and the decentralization of political power are parallel processes, closely intertwined in the development of democracy.

Steps to Increase Citizen Participation

While a thriving civil society can deepen citizens' democratic norms and stimulate and channel their active participation, there are also more formal steps that can be taken to enhance citizen involvement in local governance.

Holding Referenda and Open Meetings

One way of extending citizen involvement without making heavy demands on citizens' time is through the referendum. Commonly used throughout Europe, the referendum is an easy form of involvement for most citizens that does not heavily favor the politically active. Referenda may be initiated by citizens or local authorities, they may be binding or not, and they may be used to formulate policy or to vote on existing proposals. The primary objections to the referendum are two. First, it undermines the deliberative process of representative democracy in favor of a plebiscitary approach. Second, it simplifies complex decisions and thus promotes ill-informed policy making. Referenda offer a yes-no choice when most issues present a range of more nuanced options.[96]

While referenda facilitate the direct involvement of all concerned, they are less conducive to thorough and informed discussion of all the consequences of a proposed policy. Open meetings better encourage discussion and debate.[97] However, few people attend open meetings. Thus they privilege those who have the greatest interest in an issue.

Stoker suggests that some of the problems with open meetings can be overcome through public meetings to encourage debate and discussion of an issue (rather than to reach a decision), neighborhood forums, and co-optation of representatives to governing bodies.[98] These options for soliciting wider civic input seem more in keeping with the principles and restraints of representative democracy. A key goal, and possibility, of local democracy is to open up the policy-making process to community debate and participation as much as possible. But even at the local level, most communities are too large to be governed well along the Greek model of direct democracy.

Increasing Access to Local Representatives

Involvement in local governance is more likely to happen when citizens have easy access to decision makers. Size of local governments is a major factor determining ease of access. When a local government council member represents a hundred thousand people rather than two thousand, she or he has less time and less incentive to respond to the demands of a modest group. In turn, citizens may be deterred from trying to contact councillors who are pressed with such large workloads. "Local government is enhanced as local democracy by the closeness of council members to those they represent." A lower ratio of citizens to council members "embeds local government into the grass roots."[99] Indeed, there appears to be some connection between the size of local authority and the strength of democracy. In England, where local democracy has sharply diminished in recent decades, the size of local governments has increased. In comparison to France and Germany, which have average population sizes of local authorities of 1,320 and 2,694, respectively, England's average population size of local authorities is 122,740.[100] The similar problem of a low number of councillors and municipalities plagues Latin American local governments. In most cases, this is a legacy either of outdated municipal codes written when urban populations were a mere fraction of their current size or of electoral laws from the military era that limit the number of councillors that can be elected in a municipality. The number of citizens per councillor ranges between 20,000 and 80,000, much higher than international standards.[101]

To be sure, there are serious problems of financial and administrative viability that confront small local government jurisdictions in developing countries. But pooling and coordination of services can overcome some of these, and even in large metropolitan jurisdictions the challenge of accessible representation can be met by increasing the total number of representatives. Meaningful local democracy requires that citizens have access to their representatives and that representatives have an electoral incentive to be responsive to the communities they represent. Much more than at the state or national level, this also argues for single-member districts, in which individual representatives have clear accountability to specific and relatively small territorial constituencies.

Changing the Electoral Design

Perhaps the most effective way to combat low voting rates in local elections is through electoral design. Both the timing and structure of local electoral systems can have a large impact on turnout. When local elections are timed close to national elections, voter turnout is usually higher.[102] Voting in the first democratic local elections in Central and Eastern Europe varied between 39 percent (in Hungary) and 75 percent (in the Czech Republic), a variance largely related to the amount of time that elapsed between the first democratic national elections and the local elections.[103] Local turnout is highest when local elections coincide with national ones, so that local candidates can capitalize on the greater political attentiveness, structure, and energy generated by the national election campaigns of competing parties.

The type of electoral system employed also has a large impact on turnout. Unfortunately, this works in an opposing logic to the quest for access and accountability. As we noted earlier, countries which use proportional representation for subnational elections generally experience much higher turnout at that level, just as they do at the national level.[104] While more systematic study is needed to disentangle the effects at the local level of electoral system, timing of election, partisanship, and compulsory voting, it would not be surprising if proportional representation does indeed stimulate turnout at the local level and for the same reasons: by increasing representativeness and making every vote count. This raises the same trade-off between representativeness and accountability that was analyzed in chapter 3 for the national electoral system. And it may recommend a similar synthetic solution that combines features of proportionality and district representation (for example, single-member or small multimember districts, with a substantial topping off of representation on the local council from party lists in order to achieve proportionality). In the case of local government councils, however, the imperative of district representation in order to establish clear lines of access and accountability is even more important than at the national level.

Local party activity can sharpen the issues, clarify the electoral choice, and significantly stimulate voter participation. "Parties present policies for debate, attract media attention, and generally instill some vitality into the election atmosphere."[105] Political parties also provide a stepping-stone to greater involvement: they are always looking for new candidates and new activists, thus providing channels for citizens wishing to become more politically engaged. For parties to stimulate participation, however, there must be party competition. Voters turn out more often in marginal districts (and in PR systems), where they see the outcome to be in doubt and their vote to matter, than in safe districts, where the election seems a foregone conclusion.[106]

Simultaneous elections at the local, provincial, and national level, along with numerous contested offices at the subnational levels, generate party activity and build ties of mutual dependence between national and subnational candidates, both of which build stronger parties and an integrated government system. In simultaneous elections with a plethora of offices to fill, local and regional candidates draw more heavily on the party label and the coattails of national candidates, while national candidates rely on local candidates to mobilize voters, publicize the party's program, and raise funds for the national party coffers.[107] Simultaneous elections also diminish voter fatigue, which results from constant elections and campaigns. However, simultaneous elections may also result in national issues and contests overwhelming local (or provincial) ones. Political accountability at the subnational level may thus suffer. Each democracy must weigh the trade-off between party development and local accountability. Where parties are already strong and government has been historically centralized (as in Venezuela) local accountability may be the more compelling goal. To avoid voter fatigue and low turnout, however, elections should probably be constrained to two different time periods and calendars (where there is a fixed electoral calendar): national and local elections could be held at different times, and provincial or state elections could be combined either with the national or local ones.

However local elections are timed, it appears that the reformist instinct (periodically evident in U.S. politics) to take the party out of local politics is exactly the wrong approach for developing democracy. Nonpartisan elected officials are less likely to build alliances with higher authorities that will advance the interests of their community. They are also less likely to draw voter turnout and they certainly do nothing to develop the grassroots of a democratic party system. Political parties cannot be strong institutionally unless they are strong at the grassroots. Moreover, political parties may serve an important role in improving the accountability of local authorities. In a system with meaningful elected government at all levels, parties can generate common interests between central and local politicians. A local politician wishing to advance within the party or to hold office at a higher level must have a solid reputation, which can be demonstrated through good local performance. In Germany, for example, political reputations at the local level commonly lead to important positions at the *Land* and *Bund* levels.[108] Similarly, in the United States, politicians who succeed at the national level have frequently come up through the ranks of local and state office. This pattern is familiar in other federal systems, such as India, Argentina, and Brazil, and will probably become more so as new democracies with multiple levels of democratic power mature.

Federalism and Democracy

Democratic decentralization requires by definition the transfer of control to lower levels of elected government—the devolution of real authority over some aspects of the policy agenda. If local administrations merely implement central policies, then there is little reason for citizens to participate in local governance and little exercise of democratic control. Local democracy requires decisional autonomy.

Power may be devolved from the center to the locality, but it may also be taken back in a myriad of ways, from major recentralizing initiatives to a gradual slicing away of local authority and initiative. States transitioning from authoritarian rule are especially vulnerable to recentralization, because the rules of the game are still in flux and can easily be changed. Indeed, the more authoritarian the state and the weaker the rule of law, the more vulnerable are subnational governments to the arbitrary seizure of their powers by the center. Thus, autonomy is only one variable in the vertical distribution of power. No less important is the question of how local autonomy can be guaranteed.

Federalism is a means for institutionalizing local autonomy. In William Riker's classic definition, "Federalism is a political organization in which the activities of government are divided between regional governments and a central government in such a way that each kind of government has some activities on which it makes final decisions."[109] Federalism leaves certain matters exclusively within the scope of regional or local authorities and thus beyond the discretion of national government.[110] But for such local authority to be exclusive and final, it must be guaranteed. And this implies another condition: the protection of a written constitution that is enforced by an independent judicial authority and that cannot be amended without the consent of the subnational units themselves. In any democracy, a constitution serves as a coordinating device to enable citizens to cooperate in policing and constraining the behavior of their government officials.[111]

In a federal democracy, however, it is not only citizens but subnational governments that must be coordinated to defend the boundaries between central and regional or local authority. Once commitment to these boundaries is embedded in a constitution, it becomes largely self-enforcing, although not free of reliance on the occasional reinforcement and interpretation of a constitutional court. Because of this constitutional and judicial requirement, real federalism cannot exist in an authoritarian (much less totalitarian) regime, which is why Riker was wrong to take the Soviet Union and Mexico as cases of real federalism and to deny the association between freedom and federalism.[112] "In a strict sense, only a system that is a constitutional democracy can provide *credible guarantees* and the institutionally embedded mechanisms that help ensure that the law-making prerogatives of the sub-units will be respected."[113]

Beyond institutionalizing (by constitutionalizing) the autonomy of subnational units, federalism offers additional advantages. In countries of medium to large size, it offers a more comprehensive framework for political decentralization by adding a middle tier of government with certain distinctive powers. In such countries—and especially in continental-sized countries like the United States, Canada, Australia, Brazil, India, and Russia—local governments are simply too numerous and too small to counterbalance the power of the center, to provide an adequate arena for democratic determination of distinctive subnational needs and interests, and to perform the other functions that help reduce ethnic conflict, such as dispersing the arenas of political conflict and generating cross-cutting cleavage. In these countries, only a middle tier of democratic government can perform these functions, and only full-blown federalism can manage and secure the complexity of decentralized power relations among three tiers of government. It is by no means coincidental that the largest democracies in territory and most of the largest ones in population (including also, when they are democratic, Nigeria and Mexico) are federal states. Federalism also fosters regional competition and innovation and encourages productive activity by limiting predation by the central government (although subnational governments can certainly be predators themselves). Perhaps most crucially, federalism provides a more reliable framework for managing ethnic and nationality cleavages and generating mutual security in multiethnic states that confront real or potential secessionist pressures.

However, federalism has its drawbacks, including the danger of reifying the cleavages that gave rise to it in the first place. We discuss the pros and cons of federalism below, concluding with the critical question of design: What makes democratic federalism stable?

Why Federate?

Federalism serves a valuable role in strengthening democracy by institutionalizing decentralization and thus preserving the autonomy of regional and local governments. But it has other benefits as well, including its ability to provide better representation to minority groups and its potential to stimulate economic growth.

Democracy does not guarantee representation to national communities in a multinational state. Majority rule may permanently shut minorities out of power at the center if cleavages are ascribed by birth or otherwise unmalleable. In such circumstances of politically mobilized ethnic consciousness, a unitary state is liable to leave minority ethnic groups feeling powerless, excluded, alienated, and insecure. Perceiving no stake in a political system that does not seem to recognize their worth and legitimacy as a group, they are prone to look to secession as the only alternative.[114] Federalism may hold such a state together. It is a positive alternative to the violence and bloodshed that typically accompany attempts at secession in multiethnic societies and to the repression and discrimination that may victimize newly created minorities in a state formed from secession.[115] Federalism can reconcile nationalism and democracy in a multiethnic state by giving territorially concentrated minorities authority over matters of local concern, security in the use of their language, culture, and religion, and protection from the discretion of national leaders or the sentiments of the national majority. When intergroup conflict is severe, federalism can alleviate and contain it through Donald Horowitz's five famous conflict-reducing mechanisms:[116]

1. *Proliferating the points of power.* By compartmentalizing friction, the conflicts of one region need not polarize politics or cripple governance at the national level nor spill over into other regions.
2. *Generating intraethnic competition.* Regional elections can stir competition for power among members and factions of the same ethnic or nationality group, cutting across and softening the lines of interethnic political conflict.
3. *Generating interethnic cooperation.* Ethnically heterogeneous regions in a federal state may prompt intergroup cooperation, since groups must collaborate to win benefits from the center or may need to construct coalitions to win regional elections.
4. *Encouraging alignment on nonethnic issues.* States controlled by different ethnic groups may join together along functional lines of interest or rally as one against the center in defense of their prerogatives.
5. *Reducing disparities between regions through redistribution.* This may happen when ethnic groups can advance within the bureaucracies and universities of their own states.

In the two largest multiethnic federal states in the developing world, India and Nigeria, federalism has performed all five of these conflict-reducing functions, despite the many flaws in Nigeria's federal system and the other pathologies that have repeatedly frustrated its attempts at democracy.[117]

Federalism is unlikely to eradicate ethnic conflict and may in some instances exacerbate separatist aspirations. But conflict can be meaningfully reduced even when its eradication is unfeasible, and this reduction may be sufficient to make democracy viable. Much depends on the particular institutions of federalism and idiosyncrasies of the context in which they are adopted. As Horowitz shows, federal institutions can produce radically different results depending on the number of constituent states, their boundaries, and their ethnic composition.[118] The ability to creatively design federal or subunit boundaries to crack the solidarity of dominant groups and generate intraethnic cleavages and cross-cutting ties should not be underestimated.

Federalism also offers potential economic benefits. The most widely studied economic boon is federalism's tendency to spur competition among regions.[119] When capital and labor are mobile, federalism discourages the lower units of government from limiting or preying upon economic activity, since resources will relocate to other jurisdictions. Competition between subunits to attract investment and labor drives innovation. Another implication is that only the restrictions on economic activity that citizens are willing to pay for will survive. This reduces the pervasiveness of rent-seeking and patronage systems, which thrive in areas protected from market forces.[120]

In the view of Barry Weingast and his colleagues, undue state interference in the market is minimized, and incentives to invest, and thus economic growth, are maximized by a system of "market-preserving federalism," characterized by two levels of government (each with an institutionalized, autonomous scope of authority), a common market, hard budget constraints on the lower level of government, and significant delegation of regulatory responsibility over the economy to subnational governments. Such a system, in generating a "credible commitment to limited government," fosters economic growth by insulating investment at the subnational level from political volatility at the national level and by generating more attractive conditions for investment in various localities.[121] Regional governments that impose restrictions on their firms find themselves at a disadvantage: regions compete to provide the most favorable conditions for attracting investment, successful regional innovations are copied by others, and regions that wallow in rent seeking are at a competitive disadvantage. Even in a formally communist state such as China with still many statist features, these dynamics of market-preserving federalism have promoted extraordinarily high economic growth for well over a decade.[122] But China's future economic vitality is increasingly threatened by the failure to provide the critical national public goods—such as a common market, a unified monetary system, a law of commerce, and an independent judicial system—that underpin a truly market-preserving federalism. In economic as well as political aspects, federalism is only fully realized when it is institutionalized in a strong legal and constitutional framework.

The underprovision of public goods is only one of several problems that confront a "pure" model of market-preserving federalism, in which the central state plays a very limited role. As Rodden and Rose-Ackerman have recently shown, a highly decentralized federation is prone to experience problems of local protectionism, exportation of costs from one jurisdiction to another, and increasing inequality among the jurisdictions (partly due to structural problems that cannot be surmounted even with policy adaptation on the part of the poorer jurisdictions). These problems generate potential barriers to efficiency and economic growth (and threats to political stability) that can only be met by a central government with some significant fiscal and regulatory power. "A central government that cannot enforce a common market, redistribute resources, or provide public goods may not be able to survive or hold the federation together."[123]

This tension calls for a "delicate balance"[124] between decentralization and a common national market: a central government sufficiently constrained to enable states to innovate and compete and to compel them to take responsibility for their policies and budgets but strong enough to monitor and regulate the activities of subnational governments, to limit abuses (including corruption), to attenuate inequality, to make subunits internalize externalities, and to ensure mobility of goods and factors of production (a key assumption of the market-preserving federalism model). Thus, just as democracy is served by some degree of balance between federal and local power, in which each checks and constrains the other, economic development may be served by a federalism in which competition among subunits is fostered but the central state has the power to enforce conditions that make that competition meaningful and sustainable. Somewhat reformulated, market-preserving federalism has considerably greater potential to generate economic growth than its critics allow for, but in a system where nonmarket political logics have long been entrenched at all levels (as in India), competition may only generate its expected effects over a longer period of time, and only if the central government sets a vigorous reform context and if information about competing policies and outcomes flows across the constituencies of widely separated jurisdictions. Even with all of the political pathologies that Rodden and Rose-Ackerman identify in Indian state-level politics, Manor finds that Indian federalism has "aided the cause of economic reform by enabling New Delhi to 'off-load' some of the pain associated with liberalization to state-level arenas, where the resulting tensions are largely quarantined," while also giving scope for state governments to innovate in economic policy.[125]

The Limits of Federalism

Unless the rights of local governments and individuals are constitutionally protected, federalism may relegate the fate of either to the whims of regional governments. Federalism gives regional governments exclusive authority over a given set of issue areas. Regional leaders can use this discretion to rule undemocratically over local governments or oppress citizens within their jurisdiction. In fact, the same potential dangers of decentralization in general—authoritarian enclaves, discrimination against minorities, heightened geographical inequalities, inefficiency— are even more acute in a federal system, precisely because federalism entrenches the prerogatives of subnational governments. The autonomy afforded regional governments by a federal constitution can deprive victims of recourse to the national government, because the latter cannot intervene in the regions' domains.

Such a situation exists in Russia today, where governors, although democratically elected, exercise tight control over local government by dismissing and appointing mayors and by controlling all revenue collection and spending in their territory. Similarly, in a multiethnic country in which populations are geographically intermixed, the central government may not always be able to intervene to protect the rights of a region's minorities. If federalism is to foster the deepening and consolidation of democracy, the rights of individuals and local governments must be constitutionally inscribed as part of the federal bargain. Again, this means that the center must have the power to intervene in the subnational units to protect constitutional rights and procedures. In the United States, the historic advances in civil rights have come when federal policies superseded state legislation and practices.[126]

A distinctive pitfall of federalism is that it may provide the territorial blueprint for future separatism. When ethnic groups are territorially concentrated and federal boundaries are drawn around them to create homogeneous states or provinces, federalism may reinforce the cleavages that gave rise to it in the first place, for two reasons. First, federalism tends to accelerate the process of nation building among territorially concentrated nationalities. As Juan Linz argues, "The official recognition of the different languages, their introduction into the education system and other spheres of life assuring their diffusion, the subtle and not so subtle discrimination [against] those not accepting the nationalist cultural program or not ready to learn and use the local language, are all directed at nation-building."[127] Ronald Suny shows how the cultural policies of Soviet federalism transformed groups with little in common into the nations that ultimately fractured the Soviet Union.[128]

Second, any tension between the center and a region or among regions will take the form of ethnic politics, as has occurred in India when the center intervened to displace governments in Punjab and Kashmir. The threat of unleashing ethnic agitation can be a powerful bargaining tool of politicians striving to accomplish political ends. Moreover, economic inequality among regions may spur feelings of ethnic rivalry. Groups living in poorer regions may feel the central government is not doing enough for their welfare. Groups in wealthier regions, like the Basques in Spain or the Igbos in Nigeria, may resent having to support ethnic groups living in other regions. If regional wishes are not accommodated, ethnic groups may conclude that independence is the only way to accomplish their ends.

Because of the above tendencies, some argue that multinational federalism is a slippery slope to secession. This is slippery reasoning, however. Many multinational federations, such as Switzerland, Spain, and Canada, have persevered even through periods of nationality conflict. And in countries like India and Nigeria, federalism has done more to relieve or contain secessionist pressures than to stimulate them.[129] In India, "once Tamil speakers were given a state, English was retained as a language of the Union, and a regional party won control of the state legislature [of Tamil Nadu], secession became a nonissue."[130] In contrast, Sri Lanka's Tamil secessionist movement plunged the country into a bloody and protracted civil war, which probably could have been prevented had the state acted sooner to devolve power to local regions and give autonomy to the Tamil minority concentrated in the northeast. Timing can be crucial. As Horowitz remarks, "An early, generous offer of autonomy, made before extreme separatist organizations outflank moderate leaders, may avert secession. A similar offer, made after separatist violence has broken out, may well do what opponents of concessions fear: it may testify to the weakness or vacillation of the central government and the success of the separatists, thereby fortifying their will to fight on."[131] The sequencing of elections may also be crucial. In a new democracy, holding national elections before regional elections generates incentives for the creation of national (as opposed to regional) political parties.[132]

Three additional lessons may be derived from experience. First, a broader integrative process of constructing a multinational state identity must proceed simultaneously with the devolution of power. As Linz and Stepan argue, and as much research has demonstrated, citizens from minority ethnic and nationality groups can hold "multiple and complementary political identities" that bind them to a larger state even as they deepen the attachment to their own ethnic and linguistic roots. However, the crucial condition for this dual attachment is a "common roof" of equal and inclusive citizenship, in which the constitutional rights of all citizens are mandated and enforced by the central state. Second, even if substantial sentiment for independence persists as a symbolic goal, as it has in the Basque region of Spain, it may be sublimated in a practical "accommodation to a democratic multinational state" if that state functions to give the minority ethnic group a feeling of security and a political structure within the federal system.[133] Third, when it is possible to do so, there is a value to creating heterogeneous subnational units and, in particular, to breaking up the solidarity of the largest ethnic groups.[134]

The Institutional Design of Federalism

No consensus exists about the defining institutional arrangements of federalism. For Riker, it is simply some vertical division of government power in which the federal government and the governments of the member units each have "authority to make some decisions independently of the other."[135] Stepan does not go much further, except to specify that the policy-making authority of each level of government must be constitutionally guaranteed.[136] Arend Lijphart posits five features of federalism: a written constitution, bicameralism, the right of the component units to be involved in amending the federal constitution but to have the right to change their own constitutions unilaterally, equal or disproportionately strong representation of the smaller subunits in the federal chamber, and decentralized government.[137] To these, Ronald Watts adds the allocation of revenue resources to each order of government, with some autonomy for each, an umpire to rule on disputes between governments, and processes to facilitate intergovernmental relations for those areas in which responsibilities are shared.[138]

One way out of the debate over essential institutions is to focus on the basic principle of federalism — the division of power between central and subnational governments—and, from there, identify the institutions that uphold this principle. Such an approach identifies important sources of federal stability and integrity beyond the formal constitutional provisions traditionally labeled federal. The primary question driving this approach is, How can the autonomy of regional governments be protected against intrusion by the central government? Unless regional governments have assurances that their sovereignty is guaranteed under the federal system, they have little reason to go along with the federal bargain.

In making ambition counteract ambition, the framers of the American Constitution noted the role that fragmentation of power can have in restraining the expansiveness of the central government. By giving different institutions of government different constituencies and different means of ascending to power, they created a system of checks that makes it very difficult to introduce fundamental changes into the political system. Such a separation of powers at the national level protects the states. So does a written constitution that can only be amended through a difficult process involving special majorities of both federal houses (including the Senate, in which small states are overrepresented) and majority assent of three-quarters of the state legislatures. Plainly, no constitutional power grab by the center could survive this process. The requirement for bicameral approval of legislation gives states a say in national policy making. Impartial judicial enforcement of federalism is facilitated by lifetime appointments. Moreover, judicial appointees reflect both national and state interests because they are appointed by the president but confirmed by the Senate.[139] In short, what Riker termed the ability of the central government to "completely overawe the constituent governments" can be contained through institutional mechanisms.[140]

For Riker (and for Ordeshook), however, the most important institutional barrier to an "overawing" center is a decentralized party system. Because parties in the United States are decentralized and the presidency is an institutionally weak office, a U.S. president has to bargain constantly for the support of state leaders "to get the votes to get nominated, to get the votes to get elected, to get the votes to get bills through Congress, to get the votes to get renominated."[141] Stability results not only from the president's dependence on local authorities of his party but also from their dependence on the president to head a strong party ticket.[142] Certain institutional designs—simultaneous elections, numerous offices to fill through elections, and so on—can facilitate the mutual dependence of regional and national leaders. The more posts that are filled by election at the regional and local level, in which voters confront an array of candidates about which they know little beyond their party label, the greater the incentive for regional politicians to coordinate their election activities by developing an integrated party system. In countries like Canada and India, in which elections are not simultaneous, mutual dependence between the national, state, and local candidates is weakened.[143] In countries like Russia, in which nonsimultaneity is compounded by strong presidential powers and an electoral system that separates the fates of local and national candidates, an integrated federation and an effective party system seem unlikely to emerge.[144]

An alternative way of conceiving the fundamental objective of federalism is as a limitation on the ability of a politywide majority to make policy. Stepan identifies four spheres that determine where along the continuum of least to most majority-constraining a polity lies.[145] First, the more overrepresentation of small states and the more underrepresentation of large states, the greater the majority-constraining potential of the senate. Second, the greater the policy scope of the house that represents territories (e.g., the senate), the greater the potential to limit the lawmaking power of the chamber that represents population (the lower house). Third, the greater the area of jurisdiction (including residual powers) accorded to lower-level governments, the more policy areas that are beyond the lawmaking power of the central government and the more the majority is constrained. And fourth, the less disciplined and politywide the political parties, encompassing the entire country, the more the majority (or center) will be constrained. While some considerable constraint of a politywide majority may promote the security of territorially based ethnic minorities and thus the stability of democracy, this fourth mechanism is not a promising means for doing so. For when the electoral system and other institutions encourage regional and ethnic, as opposed to politywide, parties, they are more likely to generate polarized conflict and even state disintegration.[146]

Conclusion

Centralized government may or may not be more efficient, but it is intrinsically less democratic. Only if political power over certain issues and government functions is devolved to lower levels of authority that are democratically elected can government be truly responsive, representative, and accountable. The more ethnically heterogeneous the state, and the larger its size demographically and territorially, the more this is true. In the largest and most ethnically complex states, only the multiple levels and embedded arrangements of federalism are likely to provide the conditions for a liberal, peaceful, and stable democracy.

In a democracy, however, the vertical checks on abuse of power afforded by decentralization must be reciprocal. It goes without saying that local and regional governments cannot advance democracy if they are not democratic. Elections alone do not ensure the freedoms and protections of a liberal democracy. For that, other institutions are needed, including a well-crafted constitution, a strong and independent judiciary, and a vibrant civil society. As analysts are increasingly prone to recognize, a forceful constitutional and judicial framework is vital to the stability and democraticness of a federal system. The constitution must articulate the exclusive and concurrent powers of each level of government and the locus of residual power. It must forbid undemocratic and illiberal practices by subnational governments and must empower the federal courts and legal authorities to override and punish such laws and actions. It must empower a federal constitutional court to interpret and uphold its provisions, to adjudicate intergovernmental disputes, and to protect the constitutional rights of all individuals and groups. And it must be difficult to amend.

This again raises the issue of timing and returns us finally to the difficult case of Brazil. Federal democracies in particular face a constitutional paradox. Their federal nature makes the constitution especially vital to stability and, typically, especially difficult to amend. This puts a premium on getting the institutions right from the beginning, because once they are set in constitutional stone interests will crystallize to prevent their alteration by the democratic process. This leaves a country like Brazil, and to some extent Russia, saddled with arrangements that are unconducive to the consolidation of democracy but that are extremely difficult to change through democracy. One would hardly wish for the suspension of democracy, or a national political crisis, to generate more propitious institutional conditions for the consolidation of democracy. But that leaves a country either waiting for the rare conjuncture of gifted leadership and electoral realignment to break the Gordian knot of constitutional defect or limping slowly toward the consolidation of what will remain a less-than-effective democracy. Constitutional moments come rarely and must be seized with energy and vision.

For many developing democracies, however, the prognosis is encouraging. Institutional innovations are decentralizing power and making lower levels of power more democratic. And the context of democracy does make a difference. In contrast to authoritarian regimes, in which decentralization initiatives are largely superficial or perceived to be centralization measures in disguise, power really is devolving in a number of Third World and postcommunist democracies.[147] In many of these countries, the steady growth of civil society, educational levels, incomes, and civic awareness is also creating a more favorable context for local and regional government to function more effectively and democratically. Gradually—and to be sure, quite unevenly—an important foundation for a deeper and more liberal democracy is developing.

5

Political Culture

Few problems are riper for illumination from the political culture perspective than the sources of democratic emergence, consolidation, and persistence. Prominent theories of democracy, both classical and modern, claim that democracy requires a distinctive set of political values and orientations from its citizens: moderation, tolerance, civility, efficacy, knowledge, participation. Beliefs and perceptions about regime legitimacy have long been recognized as critical factors in regime change, bearing particularly on the persistence or breakdown of democracy.[1] The pathbreaking works of Gabriel Almond and Sidney Verba and of Alex Inkeles and David Smith show that countries differ significantly in their patterns of politically relevant beliefs, values, and attitudes and that within nations these elements of political culture are clearly shaped by life experiences, education, and social class.[2]

As early as the late 1950s, Seymour Martin Lipset presented extensive evidence demonstrating not only a strong positive relationship between economic development and democracy but also that political beliefs, attitudes, and values are an important intervening variable in this relationship.[3] In 1980, Inkeles and Larry Diamond presented more direct evidence of a relationship between a country's level of economic development and the prevalence among its people of such democratic cultural attributes as tolerance, trust, and efficacy.[4] Subsequently, Ronald Inglehart showed that life satisfaction, interpersonal trust, and rejection of revolutionary change are highly correlated not only with economic development but also with stable democracy and that "political culture may be a crucial link between economic development and democracy."[5]

Despite these considerable theoretical and empirical grounds for expecting that political culture plays an important role in the development and maintenance (or failure) of democracy, the post-1960s generation of work on democracy has tended, until rather recently, to neglect the phenomenon, particularly at the mass level. Political and intellectual trends in the social sciences during the late 1960s and 1970s challenged or dismissed political culture theory, from both the right and the left. The democratic transitions literature of the 1980s also tended to give short shrift to the political culture variable. Only with the surge in the 1990s of theoretical and empirical attention to the process of democratic consolidation (and to the growth of mass belief in democratic legitimacy as the core element of this process) has political culture recovered a central place in the comparative study of democracy.

This chapter makes the case for political culture—particularly, beliefs about democratic legitimacy—as a central factor in the consolidation of democracy. From the wealth of survey data across numerous regions and countries, it assesses trends in public support for democracy, satisfaction with democracy, and other political attitudes and values that could affect the viability of third-wave democracies. It also addresses three important theoretical questions in the study of political culture: Which elements of political culture matter for democratic consolidation? How and how much does political culture change over time in a developing democracy? And what are the sources of political culture change?

The most striking finding here is the autonomy of the political. No doubt, socioeconomic development does generate more "modern" attitudes and values: greater tolerance and valuing of freedom, higher levels of political efficacy, greater capacity to participate in politics and civic life. But political experience with democracy and alternative regimes, and how well a formally democratic regime functions to deliver the "political goods" of democracy, have sizable independent effects on political attitudes and values, often overpowering those of the country's level of socioeconomic development, the individual's socioeconomic status, and the regime's economic performance. That political experience and the quality of governance have such large autonomous effects on the way citizens think, believe, and behave politically underscores the need for viewing democracy in a developmental perspective. As new democratic experiments in deeply impoverished countries such as Nepal, Mongolia, Benin, and Mozambique are reaffirming, there is no developmental prerequisite for democracy. There is no better way of developing the values, skills, and commitments of democratic citizenship than through direct experience with democracy, no matter how imperfect it may be.

To advance our understanding of how political culture change and democratic development relate to one another, we must not only assess the available evidence but also weigh some of the methodological issues that arise from this new generation of public opinion studies. I begin with some essential conceptual and theoretical foundations.

Theories of Political Culture and Democracy

Conceptualizing Political Culture

The pioneering political culture work of the 1960s blazed important trails in articulating our understanding of what political culture is and how it is structured. That conceptual foundation has weathered well the test of experience. It treats political culture as *a people's predominant beliefs, attitudes, values, ideals, sentiments, and evaluations about the political system of their country and the role of the self in that system.* These components of political culture (which may be summarized simply as distinctive predispositions, or "orientations to action")[6] have been classified into three types of orientation: a *cognitive* orientation, involving knowledge of and beliefs about the political system; an *affective* orientation, consisting of feelings about the political system; and an *evaluational* orientation, including commitments to political values and judgments (making use of information and feelings) about the performance of the political system relative to those values.[7] Pure evaluations, of course, may change readily with empirical experience, but norms and values represent the most deeply embedded and enduring orientations toward political action and the political system. It is these affective and evaluational orientations to democracy that are the main concern of this chapter.

Lucian Pye observes that "the notion of political culture assumes that the attitudes, sentiments, and cognitions that inform and govern political behavior in any society are not just random congeries but represent coherent patterns which fit together and are mutually reinforcing."[8] But this does not mean that all social groups share the same political culture or that values and beliefs are evenly distributed throughout the population. Elites (politicians, intellectuals, business and associational leaders, media practitioners, and so on) typically have distinctive values and norms (and invariably, more information about the system), and they often lead the way in large-scale value change. Different ethnic and regional groups within a single country often have different value systems and worldviews. In addition, distinctive beliefs and norms may prevail in different institutional settings, such as the military, the bureaucracy, and the university. It may even be argued that differences in basic cultural biases are often greater within nations than between them.[9] The existence of these political subcultures compels us to disaggregate and to tread with caution in speaking of *the* political culture of a nation, except as a distinctive mixture or balance of orientations within a country.[10]

Why are these beliefs, attitudes, and values important for understanding democracy? A stereotype of political culture theory sees in it a causal determinism, that political culture more or less predetermines both political structures and political behavior and that the elements of political culture are resistant to change. To be sure, such perspectives can be found in the literature. Culturalist interpretations of Latin American politics have been openly deterministic in seeing the authoritarian, hierarchical, monistic cultural heritage of Latin America as greatly diminishing the prospects for liberal democracy.[11] Pye's treatment of Asian political culture recognizes its absorption of world culture, yet it approaches the deterministic model in its assumptions that political culture is "remarkably durable and persistent"; that this is so because of its rootedness both in distinctive national histories and in the personalities of individuals; that the latter are primarily shaped by powerful early socialization experiences in infancy and childhood; and that political culture is essentially causally prior, that "cultural variations are decisive in determining the course of development."[12]

Such culturally deterministic treatments should be viewed skeptically for three reasons. One is theoretical. Gabriel Almond argues that the cultural determinism stereotype is a distortion of his and other theories about the relationship between political culture and democracy. "The early advocates of political culture explanation . . . recognized that causality worked both ways, that attitudes influenced structure and behavior, and that structure and performance in turn influenced attitudes." Thus, "political culture affects governmental structure and performance—constrains it, but surely does not determine it." Three decades of research since *The Civic Culture* have shown that the cognitive, attitudinal, and evaluational dimensions of political culture are fairly "plastic" and can change quite dramatically in response to regime performance, historical experience, and political socialization. Deeper value and normative commitments have been shown to be more enduring and to change only slowly, in response to profound historical experiences and institutional changes.[13]

"Once established," says Inglehart, "these orientations have a momentum of their own, and may act as autonomous influences on politics and economics long after the events that gave rise to them."[14] The degree of culture plasticity is an empirical question. From the perspective of another leading theorist, Harry Eckstein, the "learning" of political values and beliefs is cumulative over a lifetime. Individuals adapt to changed conditions (and institutions), but "reorientation is always difficult" and "early learning limits greatly the extent and ease of later learning."[15]

A second reason for rejecting a deterministic approach to political culture is empirical. Considerable evidence has accumulated that, while political culture affects the character and viability of democracy, it is shaped and reshaped by a variety of factors, including not only the types mentioned above (political learning from historical experience, institutional change, political socialization) but also broad changes in economic and social structure, international factors (including colonialism and cultural diffusion), and of course the functioning and habitual practice of the political system itself.[16]

In the absence of clear evidence to the contrary, there is also a normative reason to avoid a deterministic approach: a "bias for hope." To argue that political culture is not at least somewhat plastic and open to evolution and change is to condemn many countries like the ones examined in this volume to indefinite authoritarianism and praetorianism. This brings us back to the compelling empirical grounds, where we find evidence of real and enduring cultural change in countries such as Germany, Italy, Japan, Spain, and Portugal, which were once written off as infertile soil for democracy. Recent survey data suggest that even the deeper, normative layer of mass political culture may respond fairly rapidly to major changes in a country's political system, making it possible to entrench democracy even when a country has little if any prior historical experience of it.

The Cultural Correlates of Democracy

Theories about the relationship between political culture and democracy date back at least to the classical Greek political thinkers. From Aristotle in particular, political culture theory has inherited concerns for the importance of moderation and tolerance and for the dangers of political extremism and unfettered populism, which continue to resonate in the contemporary literature. The development of a pattern, and ultimately a culture, of *moderation, accommodation, cooperation,* and *bargaining* among political elites has emerged as a major theme of the dynamic, process-oriented theories of democratic transition and consolidation. But well before this generation of work, theorists such as Gabriel Almond, Sidney Verba, Seymour Martin Lipset, Robert Dahl, and Alex Inkeles identified these orientations in political culture as necessary for the development and maintenance of democracy, to cope with one of the central dilemmas of democracy: to balance cleavage and conflict with the need for consensus.[17]

These orientations tend to fit together. They imply several important ingredients of liberal democracy: tolerance for opposing political beliefs and positions and also more generally for social and cultural differences; pragmatism and flexibility, as opposed to a rigid and ideological approach to politics; trust in other political actors and in the social environment; a willingness to compromise, springing from a belief in the necessity and desirability of compromise; and civility of political discourse and respect for other views. To be sure, these orientations may be induced by structural and institutional incentives and constraints, absent underlying norms; that is a key point of the transitions literature. But they will be difficult to sustain unless, for both elites and the mass, they become embedded in a deeper, more coherent and encompassing syndrome of beliefs and values.

The interrelationships among these factors are dense and intricate. Pragmatism, a quality Tocqueville identified as a distinct property of American democracy, facilitates bargaining and compromise by rendering goals negotiable and opinions and beliefs open to engagement and new information. Such intellectual openness promotes tolerance, by accepting "the idea that no one has a monopoly on absolute truth and that there can be no single, correct answer to public policy issues."[18] Thus, pragmatism restrains the role of ideology in politics and, hence, the danger of conflict polarization. Moreover, because the beliefs of democratic pragmatists are implicit and their goals adaptable to circumstances, these beliefs and goals are less likely to be abandoned under challenge or stress (in the way that a communist may suddenly become a fascist or some other "true believer"). From this perspective, the implicit and flexible character of democratic commitments is also their strength.[19]

Because pragmatism generates flexible goals, it is consistent with a commitment to democratic procedural norms that takes precedence over substantive policy objectives. This overriding commitment to democratic proceduralism is a critical political cultural condition for democracy. Democratic proceduralism, policy pragmatism, and political tolerance promote moderate partisanship and are the qualities most likely to limit the politicization of social life and the rancor of political intercourse. Similarly, a diffuse sense of political and social trust—what Harold Lasswell calls "confidence in the benevolent potentialities of man"—not only facilitates bargaining and compromise but encourages political discussion, makes political conflicts less threatening, and thus helps to transform politics into a non-zero-sum game, in which leaders and followers of defeated parties can accept exclusion from state power without fearing for their basic interests. Trust is also a key element of the social capital that, in facilitating cooperation through horizontal networks of civic engagement, leads to a more vibrant (and economically prosperous) democracy.[20]

Dispositions toward Authority

Dispositions toward authority drive to the very heart of what democracy is about. Early in the development of the political culture literature, Inkeles portrayed democratic political culture as the inverse of an authoritarian personality syndrome, which includes faith in powerful leaders, hatred of outsiders and deviates, a sense of powerlessness and ineffectiveness, extreme cynicism, suspicion and distrust of others, and dogmatism. A democratic culture thus encompasses flexibility, trust, efficacy, openness to new ideas and experiences, tolerance of differences and ambiguities, acceptance of others, and an attitude toward authority that is neither "blindly submissive" nor "hostilely rejecting" but rather "responsible . . . even though always watchful."[21] In the words of Sidney Hook, "A positive requirement of a working democracy is an intelligent distrust of its leadership, a skepticism stubborn but not blind, of all demands for the enlargement of power, and an emphasis upon critical method in every phase of social life."[22] Intimately connected to this is a belief in what Jacques Maritain called the "inalienable rights of the person" and Sidney Hook the "intrinsic worth or dignity" of "every individual."[23]

Because Pye sees Asian political cultures as generally lacking these orientations of individualism and suspicion of authority, he views the prospects for liberal, competitive democracy in Asia as limited. Treating conceptions of power (and authority and legitimacy) as the crucial cultural axis for understanding alternative paths of political development, Pye identifies (within the considerable political cultural variation in Asia) common tendencies to emphasize loyalty to the collectivity over individual freedom and needs; to favor paternalistic authority relations that "answer deep psychological cravings for the security of dependency"; and to therefore personalize political power, shun adversary relations, favor order over conflict, mute criticism of authority, and neglect institutional constraints on the exercise of power.[24]

"Distaste for open criticism of authority," writes Pye, "fear of upsetting the unity of the community, and knowledge that any violation of the community's rules of propriety will lead to ostracism, all combine to limit the appeal of Western democracy. As a result, the development of more open and enlightened politics in Asia is likely to produce a much more contained form of popular participation in public life. At best, it is likely to be a form of democracy which is blended with much that Westerners regard as authoritarian."[25] While Pye may impute more staying power to political culture orientations than is warranted, he offers a particularly lucid theoretical expression of the compatibility between democracy and core elements of political culture and of the way institutional forms like democracy may operate differently in different cultural contexts.

Nevertheless, political culture theorists do not assert that democracy is served by unqualified individualism. Common to all of these theoretical formulations, most notably that of Almond and Verba, is a concern for balance among conflicting values. Authority must be questioned and challenged, but it also must be supported. For J. Roland Pennock, democracy requires that individuals be "conscious of their rights and willing to stand up and struggle for them." Yet individualism must be balanced by a "public spirit" that offers commitment to the welfare of the collectivity and to a "unifying sentiment," such as nationalism.[26] Similarly, for Michael Thompson, Richard Ellis, and Aaron Wildavsky, democracy requires both "the participatory norms that come with the . . . cultures of individualism and egalitarianism" and the culture of "hierarchy to inculcate the norm that the parts should sacrifice for the whole."[27]

Legitimacy, Participation, and the Civic Culture

It is by now a cardinal tenet of empirical democratic theory that stable democracy also requires a *belief in the legitimacy of democracy*. Indeed, the growth of this belief and behavioral commitment is the defining feature of the consolidation process. Ideally, this belief should be held at two levels: as a general principle, that democracy is the best (or at least the least bad) form of government possible; and as an evaluation of one's own country's democratic regime: that in spite of its failures and shortcomings, it is better than any nondemocratic regime that might be established.[28] Both of these assessments, but particularly the latter, are relative judgments, rendered in comparison with known alternatives. Direct and recent experience with regime alternatives can powerfully shape the readiness of publics to embrace the legitimacy of democracy, not necessarily as an ideal form of government but as preferable to any other system that has been tried.[29]

Public opinion surveys have used several types of question to assess levels of democratic legitimacy (or what is sometimes termed "support for democracy"). At the most abstract level, they have explored support for "the idea" of democracy "in principle." Somewhat less abstract (and inevitably eliciting at least somewhat less support in established democracies) is the question of whether "democracy is the best form of government, whatever the circumstance" or whether "sometimes an authoritarian government can be preferable."

Much more concrete, and less stable, is the question of whether citizens are "satisfied with the way democracy is working" in their country. This is frequently taken as a measure of support for the democratic system and is the measure most widely and systematically available across many countries and time points. Yet this is not a measure of legitimacy or system support per se.[30] For one thing, identical responses to this question can have different meanings in different institutional contexts; depending on how democratic the country is (and the respondent as well), dissatisfaction could mean support for democratic reform or preference for a nondemocratic regime.[31] Citizens may be dissatisfied with the way democracy works in their country but still be deeply committed to the principle of democracy and unwilling to countenance any other form of government. This was the case in Italy throughout the 1980s and early 1990s, and this is one reason Italy's political earthquake over revelations of systemic corruption led to political reform and a reorganization of the party system rather than a diminution or suspension of democracy.

Alternatively, a citizen may see democracy as functioning reasonably well at the moment but may nevertheless be prepared to support an authoritarian regime at the first sign of trouble. In this case, the belief in legitimacy is not intrinsic—that is, internalized and deeply rooted, or what José María Maravall calls "autonomous"[32]—but instrumental, or conditional on effective performance. This is not real legitimacy, certainly not the kind that sustains and consolidates democracy. For at some point, democracy is likely to experience problems and public perceptions of decline in its effectiveness. Only when support for democracy has become intrinsic and unconditional can democracy be considered consolidated and secure. As Lipset argues, a long record of effective performance may generate a deep reservoir of intrinsic legitimacy, but the two are different, and legitimacy has many potential sources.[33] Historical survey data from Western Europe supports Lipset's thesis that once public support for democracy becomes deeply rooted, it does not soften in the face of poor economic performance, even if trust in political leaders or institutions declines.[34]

At the same time, publics may be committed to the idea of democracy in principle but be so disillusioned and disgusted with its failures in their own country that they may judge it an inappropriate form of government *for their country, at the time.* They may thus support and rally behind a temporary suspension of democracy, with the expectation that subsequent structural reforms will enable it to work better. This was close to the sentiment that appeared to prevail among the public in Nigeria when the military overthrew the Second Republic in December 1983, after four years of escalating abuse; and among the public in Peru in April 1992, when Alberto Fujimori staged his *autogolpe* amid terrorism and economic stagnation; and among the public in Thailand in February 1991, when the military overthrew a notoriously corrupt party-based government. In each case, the public supported the suspension of democracy with real and spontaneous enthusiasm, but that support was limited and pragmatic, not a philosophical rejection of democracy itself.

In a consolidated democracy, judgments of legitimacy must therefore refer to the political system as it actually operates, with its real institutions and informal rules, and not merely to its legal form.[35] Legitimacy thus reflects the depth of commitment to the substance of the political system and process (and to the boundaries and identity of the state that democracy governs). All of this suggests that the most revealing measure of democratic legitimacy would probe the extent to which a public views democracy as the best, the most appropriate, or the most suitable system for the country at the current time. Strangely, few surveys have posed the question this way.[36] Neither have they made the notion of democracy very concrete or probed very far to determine whether people's understanding of democracy matches the conception of multiparty electoral competition with constitutional freedoms, which is assumed by the researchers designing the questionnaire.[37]

Democratic legitimacy derives partly from the performance over time of the democratic regime. It is also influenced (especially in its early life) by how specific democratic institutions articulate with traditionally legitimate forms of authority and, later, by socialization, expanding education, and other types of social and cultural change. Regime performance is assessed in terms of not only economic growth and social reform but also several crucial *political* dimensions: the capacity to maintain order, to govern transparently, to maintain a rule of law, and to otherwise respect and preserve the democratic rules of the game.

One factor that seems to enhance the legitimacy of democracy among citizens is personal experience with it. For this reason, as well as for the quality and authenticity of democracy, participation is another central element of the ideal-typical mass democratic culture. This implies both valuing popular participation as a norm of political life and a disposition to actually participate in politics, based on an informed interest in public affairs.[38] For Almond and Verba, a "participant political culture" involves "an 'activist' role of the self in the polity,"[39] manifested not only through voting but also through political interest, information, knowledge, opinion formation, and organizational membership. Underlying a participant orientation is political efficacy, the self-confidence and sense of competence on the part of the citizenry that their political action may produce a change in policy or a redress of grievances.

Almond and Verba argue that the distinctive property of a civic culture is not its participant orientation but its mixed quality: the participant role is fused with and balanced by the political subject role (which embodies acceptance of political authority and allegiance to it) and the parochial role (which binds the individual to traditional, nonpolitical groups, such as family and church, and absorbs some of the energy and affect that might otherwise be focused on politics). This mixture of roles moderates the intensity of political participation by giving it (for most citizens) an "intermittent and potential character." It provides the system with legitimacy and support and yet preserves institutions outside the state that might check the abuse or excessive accumulation of power by the state. The civic culture also tempers the intensity of politics with social trust and cooperativeness and overarching commitments to the system, the nation, and the community. All of these moderate the conflicts and bridge the cleavages of politics; and trust also facilitates the vertical ties between elites and their constituencies that keep politics functioning within the institutional boundaries and constraints of democracy.[40]

Elite versus Mass Culture

How important are the above political cultural conditions for democracy? Terry Lynn Karl makes a compelling case that "there may be no single precondition for the emergence of a democratic polity" and that "the preconditions for democracy may be better conceived as the outcomes of democracy."[41] With the exception of a commitment among political elites to the legitimacy of democracy and its procedural norms (which may be initially quite instrumental and contingent), none of the above elements of political culture seems necessary for the establishment of democracy; most of them appear to be important mainly to the elite, especially early on. But once democracy formally emerges, mass political culture becomes increasingly important in shaping the character and viability of democracy.

Many theories of democratic transition recognize the importance for democracy of developing a moderate, accommodating style of political behavior, but important differences characterize the earlier and more recent generations of theory. Theorists of the 1960s and early 1970s believed political culture was an autonomous factor shaping the evolution of democracy, emphasizing the formative role of elite patterns and decisions in the early phases of system evolution or transition. Based on the historical experience of England and Sweden, Almond and Verba, Dahl, and Dankwart Rustow note how democratic culture emerged incrementally as a result of the instrumental, strategic choices of a relatively small number of political actors.[42] Such gradual evolution was successful because "the rules, the practices, and the culture of competitive politics developed first among a small elite," which shared ties of friendship, family, and class that restrained the severity of conflict. Dahl calls the resulting shared norms a system of "mutual security," based on cultural norms of tolerance, trust, cooperation, restraint, and accommodation. Almond and Verba term this a "civic culture," which blends tradition and modernity, consensus and diversity, permitting change but moderating it. Once this culture took hold, the admission of lower social strata was less threatening because "they were more easily socialized into the norms and practices of competitive politics already developed among elites."[43] For Rustow in particular, the choice of democracy by contending elites is contingent and instrumental, not normative, but the subsequent rooting of democracy in a "habituation phase" is very much a process of cultural learning, in which both elites and mass become committed to the norms and values of democracy through the successful practice of it.

The second generation of theory on democratic transitions, led by the multivolume work of Guillermo O'Donnell, Philippe Schmitter, and Laurence Whitehead and the writings of Adam Przeworski, advanced the analysis of the choices and strategic interactions of contending elites in an authoritarian regime and its democratic opposition.[44] Implicit was a shift by key elements of both sides toward a more flexible, instrumentalist set of norms. Their treatment of the political culture variable suffers from three defects, however. First, they generally neglect or altogether ignore mass culture. Second, they focus mainly on behavior and little on the complex processes by which behavior sheds its contingent, instrumental quality and becomes rooted in enduring values.[45] Finally, they ignore completely elements of political culture that are relevant mainly at the mass level and that have been theorized as important for maintaining democracy.

By contrast, Michael Burton, Richard Gunther, and John Higley take culture seriously, identifying the "restrained partisanship" of "a largely tacit consensus about rules and codes of political conduct" as one of the defining features of a "consensually unified elite," which is in turn the key factor in democratic consolidation.[46] Like Rustow, they are little concerned with the prior value orientations that impel or motivate elites to forge their mutual understandings. But unlike Rustow, they largely ignore the role of political culture change at the mass level, blinding them to the potentially exclusionary, and thus democratically destabilizing, nature of some elite settlements.[47] Other treatments of democratic consolidation, such as those by Whitehead and Giuseppe Di Palma, pose the challenge of democratic consolidation mainly in terms of "democratic crafting" on the part of elites.[48] Among scholars of the politics of democratic transition and consolidation, Juan Linz and Alfred Stepan stand out for their appreciation of the importance of mass-level changes in political culture and for their efforts to link the elite and mass levels of behavior and belief.[49]

Because the mass level has been so much neglected in recent democratic theorizing, it is worth recalling here John Stuart Mill's seemingly self-evident observation that "the people for whom the form of government is intended must be willing to accept it; or at least not so unwilling as to oppose an insurmountable obstacle to its establishment. They must be willing and able to do what is necessary to keep it standing. And they must be willing and able to do what it requires of them to enable it to fulfil its purposes. The word 'do' is to be understood as including forbearances as well as acts."[50]

Without question, elite political culture is crucial to democratic consolidation. Unless elites accept, in a regular and predictable way, the rules and limits of the constitutional system and the legitimacy of opposing actors who similarly commit themselves, democracy cannot work. But this is not the whole story. Ultimately, if democracy is to become stable and effective, the bulk of the democratic citizenry must develop a deep and resilient commitment to it. This is why democratic civil society leaders in so many emerging democracies have placed such a high priority on civic education and mobilization efforts that seek to inculcate democratic values, knowledge, and habits at the mass level.

Political Culture and Democratic Consolidation

If popular legitimation is a core component of democratic consolidation, then mass-level survey data on popular support for democracy provide an indispensable measure of progress toward democratic consolidation. National sample surveys can also tell us how mass publics evaluate the performance of their (fledgling) democracies, to what extent they manifest other attributes of democratic culture, such as trust, tolerance, efficacy, and engagement, and how these other attitudes and values are related to beliefs in the legitimacy of democracy. Most of the relevant survey data on third-wave democracies is relatively recent (as are many of the third-wave democracies, themselves), and much remains to be done to achieve a degree of standardization in survey items that would permit clear comparisons across regions as well as countries. Nevertheless, more and more explicitly cross-national survey work is being undertaken, and comparisons are now possible at least within regions and in some cases over several points in time.

Support for Democracy: Legitimacy

Spain, Greece, and Portugal were not only the first third-wave democracies but also the first to become consolidated. Numerous surveys show that Portugal within a decade and Spain and Greece well before that developed political cultures highly supportive of democracy, separate and apart from its material benefits. By 1985, 70 percent of Spaniards, 61 percent of Portuguese, and 87 percent of Greeks responded that "democracy is preferable to any other type of regime," while no more than 10 percent in any of these countries believed that "in some cases an authoritarian regime, a dictatorship, is preferable."[51] Within three years, these levels of democratic legitimacy had risen to 75 percent in Spain, 84 percent in Portugal, and 90 percent in Greece. By 1992, the Greek figure was the second highest of the twelve countries of the European Community (most of which had at least several decades of democratic experience), while Portugal also exceeded and Spain equaled the EC average of 78 percent agreement (see table 5.1). Considering that support for democracy ranged from 76 to 81 percent in such long-established and obviously secure democracies as Britain, France, Germany, and the Netherlands, the figures for Southern Europe point to a firm cultural rooting of democracy. In fact, in each of the three Southern European democracies, support for "the idea of democracy . . . in principle" was nearly universal by the end of the 1980s: Spain, 95.5 percent; Portugal, 98.5 percent; Greece, 98.7 percent. The latter percentages were the two highest of the twelve EC countries.[52]

Other survey data amplify the picture of resilience in the Spanish public's commitment to democracy. From 1978 (shortly after the completion of the transition) to 1993, the proportion of the Spanish public agreeing that "democracy is the best political system for a country like ours" ranged as high as 87 percent and never dipped lower than 69 percent, even at times of economic decline and terrorist violence. Immediately following the failed military coup attempt in February 1981, only 2 percent of the population expressed a preference for the principal alternative to democracy, a military government (and only 5% favored a civil-military government). These data led Linz and Stepan to conclude that, once the 1981 military coup plotters had been tried and punished, in 1982, democracy in Spain was consolidated.[53] Leonardo Morlino and José Ramón Montero essentially concur, showing that while dissatisfaction with the way democracy was working increased sharply in 1980, belief in democratic legitimacy held firm.[54] The absence of any significant electoral support for antisystem or antidemocratic parties since the mid-1970s further confirms the consolidation of Spain's democracy.[55]

Democratic consolidation is most evident and secure when support for democracy is not only unconditional but also widely shared by all major political groups and tendencies. Although citizens on the political right in each country (Portugal, Greece, and especially Spain) are more skeptical of the efficacy of democracy and more often willing to entertain an authoritarian regime, in all three countries clear majorities on all 5 points of the left-right spectrum believe democracy is always preferable, and only small percentages reject both the legitimacy and the efficacy of democracy.[56] In fact, by the 1990s in Spain, "democratic legitimacy was spread fairly evenly throughout society," and ideology does little to explain the variance in this belief.[57] Legitimacy is not linked to income, education, age, occupation, or religion in any of the three countries, and across all the principal political parties in each country, clear (and usually very large)

Table 5.1 Legitimacy and Support for Democracy, by Country, 1985–1997, Various Years

Country	1985	1988	1991	1992	1993	1995	1996	1997
Spain	70[1a]	72[1a] 87[2a]	76[1a]	78[1a] 73[1a]	81[1a] 79[2a]	74[1a]	81[1b]	
Portugal[1a]	61	84		83				
Greece[1a]	87	90		90				
EC avg.[1a]				78				
Uruguay[1]		73[a]	73[c]			80[c]	80[b]	
Argentina[1]		74[a]				77[c]	71[b]	
Chile		57[1a]	87[2c]	79[2c]		52[1c]	54[1b]	
Brazil[1]		43[c]	39[c]	42[c]		41[c]	50[b]	
Panama[1]							75[b]	
Venezuela[1]							62[b]	
Peru[1]							63[b]	
Nicaragua[1]							59[b]	
Colombia[1]							60[b]	
El Salvador[1]							56[b]	
Latin America avg.							63	
Czech Republic			77[1h] 88[3d]	71[1h] 78[3d]	72[1h] 82[3d]	74[1h] 75[3d]		
Slovakia			67[1h] 85[3d]	68[1h] 81[3d]	60[1h] 76[3d]	66[1h] 78[3d]		
Hungary			69[1h] 75[3d]	69[1h] 75[3d]	70[3d] 54[4e]	67[1h] 74[3d]		
Poland			60[1h] 67[3d]	48[1h] 57[3d]	71[3d] 49[4e]	65[1h] 68[3d]		
Slovenia			85[3d]	89[3d]		81[3d]		
Bulgaria			79[3d]	72[3d]	75[3d] 56[4e]	78[3d]		
Romania			90[3d]	81[3d]	76[3d] 81[4e]	88[3d]		
CEE avg.			81[3d]	76[3d]	75[3d]	79[3d]		
Belarus				68[3d]	57[3d]	60[3d]		
Ukraine				58[3d]	56[3d] 40[4e]	39[3d]		

(Continued)

Table 5.1   (*Continued*)

Country	1985	1988	1991	1992	1993	1995	1996	1997
Russia					49^{5d}			
					49^{4e}	41^{4e}		
South Korea							65^{1f}	69^{1f}
								81^{1f}
South Africa						47^{6g}		56^{6g}
						72^{7g}		

Sources:

a. José Ramón Montero, Richard Gunther, and Mariano Torcal, "Democracy in Spain: Legitimacy, Discontent, and Disaffection," *Estudio/Working Paper* 1997/100, Centro de Estudios Avanzados en Ciencias Sociales Instituto Juan March, tables 1, 2, 3.

b. Marta Lagos, "Latin America's Smiling Mask," *Journal of Democracy* 8, no. 3 (1997): table 3.

c. Juan Linz and Alfred Stepan, *Problems of Democratic Transition and Consolidation* (Baltimore: Johns Hopkins University Press, 1996), tables 10.1, 11.2, 11.4, 13.1, 14.1, 16.8.

d. Richard Rose and Christian Haerpfer, "Change and Stability in the New Democracies Barometer," Studies in Public Policy 270, Centre for the Study of Public Policy, University of Strathclyde, 1996, fig. 2.7; and Richard Rose and Evgeny Tikhomirov, "Trends in the New Russia Barometer, 1992–1995," Studies in Public Policy 256, 1995, Figure II.4.

e. Geoffrey Evans and Stephen Whitefield, "The Politics and Economics of Democratic Commitment: Support for Democracy in Transition Societies," *British Journal of Political Science* 25 (1985): Table 1; Stephen Whitefield and Geoffrey Evans, "Support for Democracy and Political Opposition in Russia, 1993–1995," *Post-Soviet Affairs* 12, no. 3 (1996): table 2.

f. Doh C. Shin and Richard Rose, "Koreans Evaluate Democracy: A New Korea Barometer Survey," Studies in Public Policy 292, 1997.

g. Robert Mattes and Hermann Thiel, "Consolidation and Public Opinion in South Africa," *Journal of Democracy* 9, no. 1 (1998): table 1.

h. Fritz Plasser, Peter A. Ulram, and Harald Waldrauch, *Politischer Kulturwandel in Ost-Mitteleuropa. Theorie und Empirie Demokratischer Konsolidierung* (Opladen: Leske and Budrich, 1997): table 9, 123.

Notes: Numbered superscript notations indicate the measure of legitimacy as follows:

1. Choose "Democracy is preferable to any other form of government" instead of "Under some circumstances, an authoritarian regime, a dictatorship is preferable to a democratic system" or "For people like me, a democratic and nondemocratic regime are the same."

2. Agree "Democracy is the best system for a country like ours."

3. Disapprove "If parliament was suspended and parties abolished."

4. Support "the *aim* of introducing democracy in [respondent's country], in which parties compete for government."

5. Disagree "We do not need parliament or elections but instead a strong leader who can make decisions and put them into effect fast."

6. Choose "Even when things don't work, democracy is always best" instead of "When that happens we need a strong leader who does not have to bother with elections."

7. Agree "Democracy may have its problems, but it is better than any other form of government."

Table 5.2   Approval of Previous Authoritarian Regime,
Sixteen Countries

Country and Year	Approve Authoritarian Regime (%)	Approve Current Regime (%)	Percentage Difference in Approval
Spain, 1985[1]	17		
Portugal, 1985[1]	13		
Italy, 1985[1]	6		
Greece, 1985[1]	6		
Brazil, 1989[2]	46[3]		
Czech Republic, 1995	24	77	+53
Slovakia, 1995	52	61	+9
Hungary , 1995	56	50	−6
Slovenia, 1995	36	66	+30
Poland, 1995	25	76	+51
Romania, 1995	28	60	+32
Bulgaria, 1995	58	66	+8
Belarus, 1995	77	35	−42
Ukraine, 1995	75	33	−42
Russia, 1995	67	26	−41
Korea, 1997	46	21	−25

Sources: Juan J. Linz and Alfred Stepan, *Problems of Democratic Transition and Consolidation: Southern Europe, South America, and Post-Communist Europe* (Baltimore: Johns Hopkins University Press, 1996), table 11.3.

For Southern Europe, José R. Montero and Mariano Torcal, "Voters and Citizens in a New Democracy: Some Trend Data on Political Attitudes in Spain," *International Journal of Public Opinion Research* 2, no. 2 (1990): table 6. For Central and Eastern Europe, Rose and Haerpfer, "Change and Stability in the New Democracies Barometer," figures 2.1, 2.2; table 5.1. For Korea, Shin and Rose, "Koreans Evaluate Democracy: A New Korea Barometer Survey," questions 16a and 16c.

1. Rate authoritarian regime as "mostly good."

2. Rate overall situation better under military regime than current regime.

3. Only 17 percent rated the overall situation better in the current regime of the New Republic, while 28 percent rated the two regimes as equal. Linz and Stepan, *Problems of Democratic Transition and Consolidation*, table 11.3.

majorities see democracy as legitimate and believe that it "works well" in their country.[58]

　　Two other measures further substantiate the picture of deep and resilient legitimacy (consolidated democracy) in Southern Europe by the mid-1980s. First, there was little nostalgia for the authoritarian past. By 1985, less than a fifth of citizens in Spain and Portugal and only a tiny fraction in Greece considered the previous authoritarian regime as good, on balance. This compares with much higher favorable evaluations of the previous authoritarian regimes in most of the postcommunist countries and Korea (see table 5.2). Second, the belief in democracy as always preferable was only weakly related to the perception of system efficacy (how well democracy is seen to be working in the country). In none of the three countries did the correlation between these two items exceed .30. Thus, one could "conclude that efficacy 'explains' less than 10 percent of the variance in the diffuse legitimacy variable."[59]

In other third-wave democracies, legitimation has generally not proceeded as far as in Southern Europe. Among the third-wave democracies of Latin America, probably only Uruguay could be classified today as consolidated (and Linz and Stepan judge it "a 'risk-prone' consolidated democracy," at that).[60] Elsewhere in the region, support for democracy either does not reach the two-thirds level (a minimum threshold of mass support for democracy in a consolidated regime) or there remain serious doubts about the stability of this support or the depth of elite commitment to the rules of the democratic game.

The 1996 Latinobarometro provides the most comprehensive comparative portrait to date of public opinion about democracy in Latin America. It confirms the picture that Linz and Stepan present of an Uruguayan public broadly and firmly committed to democracy. Unconditional support for democracy stood at 80 percent in Uruguay in 1996, identical to the stable and long-consolidated democracies in Costa Rica and Spain (table 5.1).[61] Moreover, this support was not new but had been almost as high (73%) in 1991 (six years after the transition), when support for democracy was well distributed regionally and across the ideological spectrum, with the political right having the lowest level (69%) but one still higher than the corresponding figures for the right in any of the Southern European democracies in 1985.[62]

This impressive level of support for democracy is only one dimension of what appears to be (along with Costa Rica's) the most democratic political culture in Latin America. Among the eighteen countries in the Latinobarometro (which includes Spain and Costa Rica), Uruguayans manifest the highest frequencies of satisfaction with democracy (57%) and perception of full democracy (34%) (see table 5.3). They are also the most likely to trust other people in general and (by large margins) to perceive their fellow nationals as honest and law-abiding; indeed, Uruguay appears to be virtually the only democracy in the region that departs from a sweeping "regional heritage of distrust."[63] Not surprisingly, this mass survey evidence is complemented by numerous indications of convergence toward democratic behavior and what Linz terms

Table 5.3 Freedom Score and Percentage of Population Supporting Democracy, Spain and Latin American Countries, 1996

Country	Freedom Score	Support for Democracy	Satisfaction with Democracy	Defend Democracy	Average Commitment	Perceive Full Democracy
Spain	1.5	81	57	76	71.3	29
Costa Rica	1.5	80	51	85	72.0	23
Uruguay	1.5	80	52	78	70.0	34
Argentina	2.5	71	34	73	59.3	12
Panama	2.5	75	28	75	59.3	13
Bolivia	2.5	64	25	84	57.7	13
Venezuela	2.5	62	30	74	55.3	16
Ecuador	3.0	52	34	80	55.3	20
Peru	3.5	63	28	75	55.3	14
Nicaragua	3.0	59	23	72	51.3	7
Colombia	4.0	60	16	74	50.0	7
El Salvador	3.0	56	26	60	47.3	10
Honduras	3.0	42	20	80	47.3	13
Paraguay	3.5	59	22	59	46.7	9
Brazil	3.0	50	20	69	46.3	4
Chile	2.0	54	27	53	44.7	10
Mexico	3.5	53	11	66	43.3	10
Guatemala	3.5	51	16	56	41.0	6

Source: Marta Lagos, "Latin America's Smiling Mask," *Journal of Democracy* 8, no. 3 (1997): 133, table 3; Freedom House, *Freedom in the World: The Annual Survey of Political Rights and Civil Liberties, 1996–1997* (New York: Freedom House, 1997, 579–80.

Note: Freedom Score is the average combined Freedom House rating on political rights and civil liberties for 1996. *Support* is the percentage agreeing that "democracy is preferable to any other kind of government." *Satisfaction* is "with the way democracy works in [nation]." *Defend* democracy is willingness "to defend democracy if it was under threat." *Commitment* averages these three percentages. *Perceive* is the percentage who "think that democracy is fully established in [nation]" rather than "it is not fully established and there are still things to be done for there to be a full democracy."

Table 5.4 Satisfaction with the Way Democracy Works in the Country, 1985–1997, Various Years

Region	Country	1985	1989	1993	1996	1997
Southern Europe, Latin America, Korea, and Taiwan	Portugal	34	60	54[1]		
	Spain	51	60	39[1]	57	
	Greece	51	52	45[1]		
	Italy	28	27	32[1]		
	EC avg.	58	66	41[1]		
	Uruguay				52	
	Argentina				34	

(*continued*)

Table 5.4 *(Continued)*

Region	Country	1985	1989	1993	1996	1997
	Bolivia				25	
	Brazil				20	
	Colombia				16	
	Chile				27	
	Ecuador				34	
	Mexico				11	
	Peru				28	
	Venezuela				30	
	Korea					49
	Taiwan				51[2]	

Region	Country	1990	1991	1992	1993	1994
Central and	Czech Republic	40	35	40	53	40[3]
Eastern Europe	Slovakia	26	17	24	27	19[3]
	Hungary	21	34	23	29	24[3]
	Poland	50	35	37	26	
					17[3]	
	Bulgaria				25[3]	
	Romania				17[3]	
	Estonia				29[3]	
	Lithuania				23[3]	
	Russia				19[3]	
	Ukraine				12[3]	
	CEE avg.				29	

Sources: Leonardo Morlino and José Ramón Montero, "Legitimacy and Democracy in Southern Europe," in *The Politics of Democratic Consolidation: Southern Europe in Comparative Perspective*, edited by Richard Gunther, P. Nikiforos Diamandouros, and Hans-Jürgen Puhle (Baltimore: Johns Hopkins University Press, 1995), table 7.4; Marta Lagos, "Latin America's Smiling Mask," *Journal of Democracy* 8, no. 3 (1997): table 3; Doh Chull Shin and Richard Rose, "Koreans Evaluate Democracy: A New Korea Barometer Survey," Studies in Public Policy 292, Centre for the Study of Public Policy, University of Strathclyde, 1997, question 34; Gábor Tóka, "Political Support in East-Central Europe," in *Citizens and the State*, edited by Hans-Dieter Klingemann and Dieter Fuchs (Oxford: Oxford University Press, 1995), table 12.3; Richard Rose, William Mishler, and Christian Haerpfer, *Democracy and Its Alternatives: Understanding Post-Communist Societies* (Oxford: Polity, 1998), fig. 5.1; Geoffrey Evans and Stephen Whitefield, "The Politics and Economics of Democratic Commitment: Support for Democracy in Transition Societies," *British Journal of Political Science* 25 (1995), table 4; Geoffrey Evans, "Mass Political Attitudes and the Development of Market Democracy in Eastern Europe," Discussion Paper 39, Centre for European Studies, Nuffield College, Oxford University, 1995, table 1.

1. Average levels of satisfaction over time are as follows: Portugal (1985–91), 63%, Spain (1985–91), 58%, Greece (1980–91), 56%, Italy (1976–91), 24%, EC overall (1976–91) 57%.

2. Mean level of satisfaction in two 1996 surveys in Taiwan, one showing 60%, the other 41%.

3. Percentage who answer "Positively" or "Very positively" to the question, "How would you evaluate the *actual practice* of democracy in [respondent's country] so far? Very positively, Positively, Negatively, Very negatively, Neither positively nor negatively."

"loyalty" to the democratic system on the part of political party elites, and both these attitudinal trends accord with Uruguay's history of freedom from political crisis since the 1989 referendum approving the government's amnesty for human rights abuses committed by the previous military regime.[64]

Among Latin American third-wave democracies, only Uruguay shows levels of public support for democracy that are unambiguously high. Although in 1996 more than 70 percent of the publics in Argentina and Panama supported democracy as the best system, it is not clear how stable these levels of support were. In both countries (in fact, in all Latin American democracies save for Uruguay and Costa Rica), substantial majorities of the public in 1996 were dissatisfied "with the way democracy works" in their country, and in Brazil and Venezuela more than a quarter said in 1996 they were "not at all satisfied" (see table 5.3). Satisfaction with democracy is much more sensitive to fluctuations in short-term economic, social, and political conditions than are public assessments of legitimacy or system efficacy. Satisfaction with democracy can dip to low levels in consolidated democracies (like those of Southern Europe) as policy effectiveness temporarily wanes. In the case of Italy, dissatisfaction was substantial and prolonged throughout the 1985–93 period. However, in Italy, high levels of dissatisfaction were counterbalanced by a deeper perception of system efficacy, with about two-thirds of Italians saying that "democracy works" or that "our democracy has many defects, but it works."[65] In the other three Southern European democracies, equivalent or higher proportions also perceive some degree of system efficacy.

A similar measure of system efficacy showed much more skepticism in South America in 1995, with only about half of the people in each country feeling that "democracy allows the solution of the problems" of the country (see table 5.5), while 34–46 percent say "democracy does not solve the problems." Since 1980, levels of skepticism have been similar in Spain (fluctuating between 42% and 56% on this question), but Spain has had higher levels of both legitimacy and satisfaction. In fact, it is precisely the large gap between high levels of legitimacy and only moderate levels of system efficacy (a gap of 43 percentage points in the capital of Montevideo in 1990) that led Linz and Stepan to worry that Uruguay's democracy is "risk-prone," unless it demonstrates an ability to formulate effective policy responses to the country's serious economic and institutional problems.[66] Yet, among Latin America's third-wave democracies, only Uruguay has a level of satisfaction with democracy that falls within the historic normal range for Western Europe of 50–60 percent.[67] As

Table 5.5 System Efficacy: Percentage Saying that Democracy Works, 1978–1995, Various Years

Country	1978	1980	1982	1985	1988	1993	1994	1995
Spain	68[1]	45[1]	55[1]		56[1]	42[1]	50[1]	
Spain				69[2]		75[2]		63[2]
Portugal				68[2]				
Greece				81[2]				
Italy				65[2]				
Uruguay								54[1]
Argentina								53[1]
Chile								48[1]
Brazil								46[1]

Sources: José Ramón Montero, Richard Gunther, and Mariano Torcal, "Democracy in Spain: Legitimacy, Efficacy, and Disaffection," paper presented to the conference on "The Erosion of Confidence in Advanced Industrial Democracies," Brussels, 1996, tables 4 and 5; Leonardo Morlino and José Ramón Montero, "Legitimacy and Democracy in southern Europe," in *The Politics of Democratic Consolidation: Southern Europe in Comparative Perspective*, edited by Richard Gunther, P. Nikiforos Diamandouros, and Hans-Jürgen Puhle (Baltimore: Johns Hopkins University Press, 1995), table 7.1; Juan J. Linz and Alfred Stepan, *Problems of Democratic Transition and Consolidation: Southern Europe, South America, and Post-Communist Europe* (Baltimore: Johns Hopkins University Press, 1996), table 14.1.

1. "Democracy allows for the solution of our problems" (versus "Democracy does not solve the problems").

2. "Democracy works well," or "It has many defects but it works acceptably well," (versus "It works rather badly," or in the 1985 surveys, "It is getting worse and soon will not work at all").

survey data accumulate in the coming years, we will learn how much of a problem low levels of satisfaction represent for democratic consolidation in Latin America—and how they fluctuate in response to economic and political developments.

How do these trends in support for and evaluation of democracy compare with those in Central and Eastern Europe and the former Soviet Union since the fall of communism? Unfortunately, opinion surveys are only beginning to be standardized across regions.[68] Our comparisons are thus presented tentatively and with caution. Table 5.1 mainly presents, as an indicator of democratic legitimacy for the postcommunist states, disapproval of the prospect of suspending parliament and abolishing political parties, which has the advantage of being available for nine countries for each of four years in which the New Democracies Barometer (NDB) was conducted between 1991 and 1996. However, data for the Czech Republic, Slovakia, Hungary, and Poland show that this indicator is closely associated with the most conventional measure of democratic legitimacy. Another revealing NDB measure is the percentage of respondents who reject all plausible authoritarian alternatives: army rule, a return to communist rule, and "getting rid of Parliament and elections in favor of a strong leader."

The data for both NDB measures show divergent trends among two sets of postcommunist states. The seven states of Central and Eastern Europe (CEE) appear to be heading toward democratic consolidation, at least at the level of mass attitudes and norms. The post-Soviet states, however, with the exception of the Baltic states (which are moving toward Europe culturally, politically, and economically), are stalled or moving backward.

In all seven CEE countries, more than two-thirds of the public have consistently (across four annual surveys) said they would disapprove if

Table 5.6 Freedom Score and Percentage of Population Supporting Democracy, Central and Eastern Europe, 1995, Korea, 1997

Country	Freedom Score	Reject All Authoritarian Alternatives	Approve Current Regime Minus Approve Old Regime	Representative Democrats
Czech Republic	1.5	80	49	75
Slovakia	2.5	71	9	69
Hungary	1.5	69	−6	65
Slovenia	2.5	68	30	69
Poland	1.5	63	51	51
Romania	3.5	61	32	66
Bulgaria	2.0	55	8	65
Belarus	5.0	31	−42	36
Ukraine	3.5	23	−42	22
Russia	3.5	28	−41	n.a.
Korea	2.0	70	−25	65

Sources: Richard Rose and Christian Haerpfer, "New Democracies Barometer IV: A 10-Nation Survey," Studies in Public Policy 262, Centre for the Study of Public Policy, University of Strathclyde, 1996, 21, 86; Rose and Haerpfer, "Change and Stability in the New Democracies Barometer," Studies in Public Policy 270, figures 2.1, 2.2, table 5.1; Stephen White, Richard Rose, and Ian McAllister, *How Russia Votes* (Chatham, N.J.: Chatham House, 1997), 48; Doh C. Shin and Richard Rose, "Koreans Evaluate Democracy: A New Democracy Barometer Survey," Studies in Public Policy 292; Doh C. Shin, private communication with author.

Notes: Rejection is of all three authoritarian alternatives: army rule, a return to communist rule, and "to get rid of Parliament and elections in favor of a strong leader who can quickly decide everything." Relative approval is the percentage approving of the current regime minus the percentage approving of the previous communist regime. "Representative democrats" (as Rose and Haerpfer term them) prefer parliamentary democracy to a "strong leader" *and* disapprove the suspension of parliament and abolishment of parties. For note and source of freedom score, see table 5.3.

parliament was suspended and parties were abolished. In six of the seven countries, three-quarters or more now would disapprove of this (table 5.1). Except in the Czech Republic (the most normatively democratic), somewhat smaller but still sizable majorities reject all three authoritarian alternatives (see table 5.6), and in each country support for any particular authoritarian alternative is limited. Although earlier surveys found considerable support (up to 45% in Bulgaria) for getting rid of parliament and elections in favor of a strong leader, sentiment for a "strong man" to solve the countries' problems has visibly diminished, from an average of 39 percent in 1992 to 24 percent in 1995. Moreover, there is strong support for liberal freedoms.[69] As early as 1991, large majorities said they would disapprove of placing greater constraints on what newspapers print.[70]

At varying paces and to somewhat varying degrees, the trends in attitudinal support for democracy in Central and Eastern Europe are matched by a stabilization of politics and by an apparent growing elite commitment to the rules of the democratic game. The most important political development in this regard was the defeat of the communist successor party in Romania in the 1996 elections and the peaceful, constitutional transition to a more liberal government. By that time, alternation of parties in power had taken place in all of these countries. (And even though this was less so in the Czech Republic, it had the most liberal government and arguably the regime closest to consolidation.)

On measures of attitudes, perceptions, and values, the Central and Eastern European countries appear headed toward democratic consolidation, albeit with some caveats or concerns. In each of these countries except Poland, "representative democrats" (those who disapprove of suspending parliament and also prefer the parliamentary system to a "strong leader") constitute two-thirds or more of the public, and if Poles are somewhat more tentative (51% "representative democrats"), they also have the highest positive margin of difference in approval of the current regime as opposed to approval of the previous one (table 5.6). Levels of satisfaction with democratic performance have been much lower in the Czech Republic, Hungary, Poland, and Slovakia than in the new Southern European democracies, resembling instead the levels in Latin America (table 5.4). But when the question of "how government works" compares the new democracy to the old communist system, all but one of the seven countries are more favorable about democracy, and usually by huge proportions. (Hungary is the exception, but it had the most liberal communist regime, and Hungarians are second highest in rejecting undemocratic alternatives.)[71]

In Russia, and especially Belarus and Ukraine, support for democracy is much more limited. Majorities of the public (51% in Russia, 56% in Belarus, 67% in Ukraine, compared to an average of 24% in the seven countries of CEE) would support terminating parliament and elections in favor of a strong leader, and larger minorities than in CEE (generally about a quarter) support a return to communist rule.[72] In fact, by 1995, fully three-quarters of the public in both Belarus and Ukraine and two-thirds in Russia looked back favorably on the old communist regimes.[73] In Belarus and Ukraine, in contrast to CEE, support for abolishing parties and parliament has actually increased, and by autumn 1995 only 39 percent of Ukrainians said they would disapprove of that (table 5.1).[74]

Similarly, in Russia between 1993 and 1995 support for building democracy declined from 49 percent to 41 percent, and positive evaluations of the actual practice of democracy declined from an already anemic 19 percent to 14 percent.[75] In each of these three post-Soviet countries, the old communist regime is much more popular than the current regime, and democracy is still a very long way from consolidation. While normative commitment to democracy played a vital role in motivating mass opposition to the August 1991 coup attempt in the Soviet Union,[76] the recent trends in public opinion foreshadowed the slide to outright dictatorship in Belarus and point ominously toward a similar vulnerability in Ukraine and Russia. These data help us to understand why, outside the Baltics, none of the other twelve former republics of the Soviet Union is "free," and only four are electoral democracies.[77]

Political attitudes and values have been extensively surveyed in both Korea and Taiwan. Most of these surveys measure legitimacy with markedly different questions from those above. A 1997 application of the (postcommunist) New Democracies Barometer to South Korea shows comparatively strong levels of support for democracy: 81 percent of Koreans would disapprove if parliament was suspended and parties abolished, a proportion that slightly exceeds the average for the seven democracies of CEE. And measuring legitimacy with the question used in the Latinobarometro, whether "democracy is preferable to any other form of government," shows a level of support for democracy (69%) higher than in most Latin American countries.

This strong support for democracy holds across a number of questions: 78 percent agree that "the best way of choosing our government is an election that gives every voter a choice of candidates and parties"; 92 percent endorse (at least "somewhat") "the idea of democracy" in principle;[78] 72 percent reject both of the plausible authoritarian options (army or strong-man rule), a proportion that again compares favorably with most postcommunist countries.[79] Moreover, the preference for democracy has risen since the beginning of the decade and (through mid-1997) held firm at a rather high level. On a 10-point scale, with 1 representing "complete dictatorship" and 10 "complete democracy," the mean level of democracy desired by Koreans rose from 6.8 in November 1991 to 8.4 two years later. In three surveys over the subsequent four years, it remained between 8.4 and 8.6.[80]

Support for democracy in Korea does seem, however, to have eroded with the perceived poor performance of the Kim Young Sam government. At this writing, it is too soon to tell how attitudes about democracy will be affected by the financial collapse that gripped Korea at the end of 1997, but even by mid-1997, following continued revelations of large-scale corruption (one involving President Kim's son), the belief that democracy was suitable for Korea had fallen 13 percentage points in three years, to 63 percent.[81] Although this is still a substantial majority, when democracy is evaluated not as an abstract principle or ideal but as a concrete regime, support for democracy in Korea further declines.

Koreans in mid-1997 expressed considerable disenchantment with the workings of their own democracy, and almost half had a favorable view of the authoritarian "system of government under the presidency of Chun Doo Hwan." Only a quarter viewed the system under Kim Young Sam favorably, a negative balance that is in marked contrast to the pattern among CEE countries. In fact, when offered the concrete alternative of "dictatorial rule like that of a strong leader like Park Chung-Hee," the rejection of an authoritarian alternative melted away. Fully two-thirds of Koreans in 1997 (up from 61% in 1994) felt that a dictator like Park "would be much better than a democracy to handle the serious problems facing the country these days." Political corruption under Kim Young Sam was rated "high" or "very high" by 85 percent, and a stunning 96 percent blamed him "a lot" or "somewhat" "for our country's political problems." Given these numbers, it may be surprising that more than half the public in 1996 was satisfied "with the way democracy works in Korea," a proportion roughly equivalent to that of Spain and Greece in 1985 and Uruguay in 1996 (and considerably greater than most Latin American democracies). By 1997 that proportion had plummeted to 36 percent.[82] Taken together, these data indicate overall progress toward the legitimation of democracy at the mass level but also some elements of decay, instability, reservation, and even contradiction.

The ambivalence in Koreans' support for democracy is underscored by their responses to several questions that assess public attitudes toward political pluralism and democracy. Only 39 percent of Koreans (in 1997) and 43 percent of Taiwanese (in 1996) disagreed with the proposition: "If a government is often restrained by an assembly, it will be unable to achieve great things." In 1993, 39 percent of Koreans and 40 percent of Taiwanese disagreed with the statement: "We can leave things to morally upright leaders." In 1996, only 34 percent of Koreans and 43 percent of Taiwanese disagreed with the statement: "Too many competing groups would undermine social harmony."[83] But although majorities of the public in both countries gave responses embracing nondemocratic values or beliefs, there are positive signs of democratic value change.

On some measures, majorities of Taiwan's public still manifest fear of disorder and a preference for communal harmony over individual freedom (which Pye takes to be generally characteristic of Asian attitudes toward power and authority and, much more polemically, which Lee Kuan Yew identifies as quintessential Confucian or East Asian values).[84] However, what is most striking about Taiwan is the generally steady increase, since democratization began in the mid-1980s, in the proportions of the public expressing prodemocratic sentiment and rejecting the paternalistic, collectivist, illiberal norms associated with the "Asian values" perspective. Between 1985 and 1991, support for authoritarian political norms declined, and on some measures the change was huge: those who reject the notion that "elders should manage politics" rose from 49 percent in 1985 to 81 percent in 1991; those who disagree that "many political parties lead to bad politics" rose from 34 percent in 1985 to 78 percent in 1991. This growth in liberal value orientations, driven by modernization and political liberalization, contradicts notions of a stable political culture rooted in traditional values and reproduced through early socialization experience.[85]

Different survey data, covering a longer time period, elaborate the picture of a political culture undergoing a process of democratic transformation. In tracking between 1984 and 1993 five dimensions of democratic belief and commitment in Taiwan (using eleven measures), Hu Fu and Yun-han Chu conclude that beliefs about political legitimacy overall conform "more to the modern authoritarian than democratic typology."[86] Yet, as they note, support for political equality was high from the beginning, and endorsement of popular sovereignty rose dramatically from 1984 to 1993. Moreover, several other beliefs continued to become substantially more democratic between 1984 and 1996 (see table

Table 5.7 Democratic Attitudes in Taiwan, 1984–1996, Various Years (%)

Survey Item[1]	1984	1987	1990	1991	1993	1996
Disagree: Different opinions lead to chaos[2]	24	34	35		34	40
Disagree: Too many groups lead to chaos[2]	25	36	38		49	43
Disagree: Too many parties lead to chaos[2]	24	32	33		49	53
Disagree: Government can't act with strong legislature[2]	37	47	38		47	43
Disagree: Government should decide what issues are allowed[2]	42	55	49		60	65
Disagree: All matters should be decided by government	44	59	—		67	72
Disagree: Women shouldn't participate	81	87	79		83	81
Disagree: Judges should accept executive opinions[2]	45	57	53		60	57
Disagree: Society is already democratic enough				44	51	53
Agree: Opposition improves politics				56	69	67
Democratic orientation on the Shyu scale[3]	12	27	27		32	34

Sources: Huoyan Shyu, "Empowering the People: The Role of Elections in Taiwanese Democratization," paper presented to the workshop, Power and Authority in the Political Cultures: East Asia and the Nordic Countries Compared, Nordic Institute of Asian Studies, Copenhagen, 1997; National Taiwan University, Department of Political Science, surveys of political systems and electoral behavior, directed by Professor Hu Fu, supported by the National Science Council of the Republic of China.

1. The survey items are the percentage saying that they strongly, moderately, or slightly disagree (or agree) with the following (as translated, with slight variations over time):

— "Everyone's thinking should be in the same vein, otherwise society won't be stable."

— "In any place (society), if groups proliferate everywhere, it will influence stability and tranquility in that place."

— "If a country has too many political parties, it will influence (impede) political stability."

— "If the government is often checked by the legislature, it can't possibly accomplish great things."

— "Whether or not a concept should be allowed to flow through society should be decided by the government."

— "Government executives are the equivalent of the head of a household all matters large or small should be decided by them."

— "Women shouldn't participate in political activities like men do."

— "When judges rule on important cases that influence law and order, they should accept the opinions of executive organs."

— "Our society is already democratic enough, we really shouldn't be greedy for more."

— "Politics will only improve if there is a strong opposition party."

2. Items in Shyu's scale of democratic orientations.

3. Items are scored from +3 (strongly disagree) to −3 (strongly agree with the authoritarian item). The total scale thus ranges from +18 to −18. Respondents were distributed into four categories, including: authoritarian, −18 to −6; democratic, +6 to +18.

5.7). Taiwan's citizens are markedly less likely today to fear political and social differences and to defer to government. On seven of the ten measures, majorities manifest a pluralist, democratic orientation, and on the other three, democratic norms increased. On the one norm that has remained basically stable, the vast majority rejects the notion that women should play a lesser role in politics. An analysis merging six of the measures into a 4-point scale of democratic orientation found that the most authoritarian category of response declined from 44 percent in 1984 to 15 percent in 1996, while the most democratic category increased from 12 percent to 34 percent.[87]

The evolution of political culture in Taiwan is particularly impressive when one recalls that martial law was lifted only in July 1987 (about the time of the survey conducted that year); the first multiparty national election did not take place until 1989; the first comprehensive reelection of the Legislative Yuan did not occur until 1992; and direct election of the president was only introduced in 1996.[88] The data for 1987 show a surge of democratic sentiment on some measures, with the lifting of martial law. As democracy matures, public sentiment sobers on some questions, such as what government can accomplish in the face of a strong legislature (which Taiwan now has). But even in the mid-1990s, values were more democratic, and since the breakthrough democratic reform in 1991, electing a new National Assembly to amend the constitution, the public has consistently favored the expansion of democracy.[89] All of this attitudinal change reflects the steady growth in Taiwan of an ideological marketplace, permitting vigorous debate on a wide range of issues, policies, and philosophies, from national identity to human rights to the environment to the very structure of the political system.[90]

Weighing the trends in public opinion about democracy over the past decade, Doh Chull Shin and Huoyan Shyu find "political ambivalence" in both Korea and Taiwan. There is support for the ideal of democracy in both fledgling East Asian democracies, but values and beliefs are not fully democratic, and much traditional suspicion of the slow, uncertain give and take of the democratic process persists. Even with the financial crisis and economic depression that has befallen South Korea, there seems little prospect of a reversion to outright authoritarian rule, and there are signs of growth in mass democratic commitment. Yet at the level of mass political culture, democracy has yet to become consolidated. "Obviously, eight years of democratic rule have not enabled a majority of the Taiwanese and Korean peoples to overcome the authoritarian political tendencies in which they have long been socialized. Consequently, they still live in a state of political ambivalence—desiring freedom from political oppression while simultaneously wanting to be ruled by a strong leader."[91] Part of the reason, they speculate, may be because, in contrast to Latin America and the former communist states, the authoritarian regimes in South Korea and Taiwan were successful in bringing economic development and, in their later years, more restrained in their use of repression.

My own interpretation is more optimistic. Even if democracy does not enjoy enormous legitimacy by default—in contrast to other regions—a gradual rooting of democracy in mass beliefs and practices is now occurring in South Korea and Taiwan. If it lags behind the pace of cultural change in Southern Europe, it is nevertheless following the same trajectory. After all, the percentage embracing democracy as "always preferable" was only 49 percent in Spain in 1980, but rose to 70 percent by 1985. Although democratic orientations and demands were more fully formed in Spain by the time of the transition, there, too, they evolved over time from a more authoritarian culture and continued to grow after the transition.[92] In processes of democratization, political learning occurs beyond the elite level. Democratic change in mass political culture occurs not only through the socialization of new generations but also through the resocialization of older generations. Any viable model of political culture dynamics must appreciate the lifelong character of the political socialization process, and thus the potential even for quite mature citizens to adapt their political beliefs and preferences in response to actual experience.[93] Although Korea's (and Taiwan's) democratic culture change may be set back by economic crisis or political turmoil, it will probably continue, however slowly and unevenly, and will no doubt have features unlike North American or European political beliefs. Nevertheless, the prediction that "remolding authoritarian cultural norms . . . may take several generations" seems to me pessimistic.[94] Given the enormous cultural and institutional changes the two countries have undergone in the past decade, it is not too much to expect that, if democracy continues to function in a reasonably democratic and even modestly effective manner, another decade may bring its consolidation at the level of mass beliefs and values.

Of the regions experiencing democratization during the third wave, Africa has been the least systematically surveyed. However, the largest and most influential democracy in Africa, South Africa, has been the subject of intensive public opinion study in the last few years. These surveys show a mixed picture. A measure of legitimacy somewhat comparable to (but slightly more demanding than) "democracy is always preferable" shows increasing, and now majority, support. The proportion of South Africans saying that democracy is "always best, even when it does not work," rose from 47 percent in 1995 to 56 percent in 1997. However, during those two years, there was a dramatic racial bifurcation in beliefs. While in 1995, Whites and Blacks had both been about at the national average, two years later Black support for democracy had increased to 61 percent while White support had declined to 39 percent.[95]

South African support for democracy is also heavily correlated with political party (which is also correlated with race). Fully two-thirds of Black supporters of the ruling African National Congress affirm the legitimacy of democracy, while only a quarter of White supporters of the conservative Freedom Front do so. The pattern of racial and party difference in political opinions and evaluations holds across a number of other measures. Satisfaction with democracy, trust in political institutions, and related assessments are heavily correlated with race and, to a lesser extent, party. Blacks are more likely to be satisfied and positive about how democracy is doing; Whites much less so. Yet mean levels of satisfaction with democracy among Blacks are significantly higher than the levels in Central and Eastern Europe at a comparable period of time after the transition.[96]

Explaining Support for Democracy

What causes public commitment to democracy? This is one of the most important analytical challenges in understanding democratic consolidation and one of the most difficult. Support for democracy is not strongly correlated with a perception of its systemic efficacy or with satisfaction with its near-term performance. Yet measures of efficacy and satisfaction typically capture, or are interpreted as capturing, the performance of the system in dealing with economic and social policy problems. The growing evidence from many countries and regions suggests that, in forming beliefs about regime legitimacy, citizens weigh independently—and much more heavily—the political performance of the system, in particular, the degree to which it delivers on its promise of freedom and democracy.

One source of support for this thesis is an innovative analysis by Doh Chull Shin and Peter McDonough of what causes change over time in Koreans' beliefs about the suitability of democracy for their country. The most powerful predictor of growth in this belief is not Koreans' assessment of economic performance (either their own personal condition or the country's). Nor is it their personal (egocentric) or national (sociotropic) assessment of change in the quality of life. Rather it is a scale of measures of democratic political experience. And of these, the single most powerful measure is Koreans' perception of change in the character of the regime from the military authoritarian era to the present. The more substantially democratic that Koreans judge their country to have become, the greater is the increase in how "suitable" they judge democracy to be for their country. The next most powerful predictor is satisfaction with the way democracy works in Korea. The more satisfied they are, the greater is their increase in support for democracy. Thus, while assessments of economic conditions (and slightly more so, of changes in the quality of life) significantly affect change in this support for "democracy in practice," the growth of this dimension of legitimacy in Korea has much more to do with how democratically the system is perceived to be functioning. From this, Shin and McDonough infer that a "political learning" model of democratic practice and internalization best explains change in support for democracy.[97]

Evidence from public opinion surveys in South Africa points in the same direction. There appears to be "a close association between people's beliefs about ethics and corruption . . . and their views on parliament and democracy." Of those who believe that "almost all officials" are corrupt, only 22 percent are "satisfied with democracy." As perceptions of corruption abate, the level rises, to 51 percent "satisfied" among those seeing "a few officials" as corrupt, and to 68 percent "satisfied" among those who believe "no officials are corrupt."[98] Assessments of the performance of parliament and the national government, plus a variety of other political factors such as the feeling that "government represents people like me," are also strongly associated with satisfaction with democracy.[99] To be sure, satisfaction is not the same as legitimacy, but perceptions of corruption and unresponsiveness have similar effects on democratic satisfaction in Spain, and when such public cynicism combines with economic crisis, it "can lead to a serious erosion of legitimacy and a tendency towards demagogic economic policies."[100]

Two studies of support for democracy in the postcommunist world confirm the thesis of the causal primacy of political factors. Richard Rose, William Mishler, and Christian Haerpfer analyzed through multiple regression analysis the determinants of two measures of regime support in nine Central and Eastern European countries: rejection of all authoritarian alternatives and positive evaluations of the current regime on their "heaven/hell" scale of minus 100 to plus 100.[101] For rejection of au-

thoritarian alternatives, a battery of eight political attitudes and evaluations explains substantially more of the variance (19.3%) than does a set
of nine objective and subjective economic measures (14.3%). When this
measure of support for democracy is regressed on all seventeen measures
simultaneously, five of the political variables and four of the economic
variables prove significant.[102]

Rose, Mishler, and Haerpfer found that the most powerful determinants of rejection of authoritarian alternatives are political: a negative
evaluation of the former communist regime and the perception of greater
political freedom in the current regime. Another political variable, patience, has about as strong an effect as any economic variable. The patient, who believe it will take years for government to deal with the problems inherited from communist rule, are twice as likely to reject all
authoritarian options as those who are "definitely" impatient. This pattern of causation holds when objective measures of a country's political
context are included in a regression with twenty-seven variables. Political variables remain the most powerful factors (accounting for more than
half of the total variance explained), and of the four objective country
variables, the three political measures are each more powerful than the
economic one (change in gross domestic product). Moreover, the objective indicators reinforce the subjective. The degree of increase in the
Freedom House rating of freedom in the world has an independent positive effect on this measure of support for democracy. And the single most
powerful predictor (strongly negative) is the political experience of having been part of the Soviet Union. Still, it is important to recognize that
in postcommunist Europe (as in Korea) economic experiences and perceptions are not irrelevant to the growth of democratic legitimacy. Absolute deprivation of necessary food, heat, or electricity in the previous
year in particular depresses support for democracy. To a lesser but still
significant extent, higher household income and future expectations for
the household and the country's economy increase support for democracy.

For the second measure of regime support, approval of the "present
system of governing with many parties and free elections," the single
most powerful predictor is in fact economic: evaluation of the current
economic system (with evaluations of the old economic system, expectations for the future, and change in gross domestic product also showing
significant effects). But many more political variables than economic
ones have significant effects, and these effects are remarkably robust no
matter how the regression test is structured. In particular, both the real-

ity and the individual perception of increased political freedom have independent and relatively sizable positive effects on regime approval, and political efficacy and trust in institutions are equally significant. Only slightly smaller is the positive effect of the perception of increased fairness.[103] In Russia, especially, the widespread perception that privileged ties to the state are unfairly benefiting a narrow, parasitic capitalist elite is suppressing the growth of popular support for the new democracy. In fact, the Russian state is heavily penetrated by superrich monopolies and organized crime, and this derives from the objective weakness of democratic institutions: parties, labor, civil society, and the judicial system.[104]

In the same year (1993), using data for a different measure than that of Rose and colleagues (support for "the *aim* of introducing democracy") and an overlapping set of countries in Central and Eastern Europe, Geoffrey Evans and Stephen Whitefield find political beliefs and perceptions—in particular, positive evaluations of "the actual practice of democracy"—explain considerably more of the variance in support for democracy than do evaluations of economic circumstances. Moreover, the effect of economic evaluations virtually disappears when support "for the *aim* of creating a market economy" is added to the regression model. Reinforcing the findings of other studies, they thus conclude that "people support democracies because they are seen to work, reflecting respondents' experience of the pay-offs from democracy itself, rather than on the basis of a simple 'cash nexus.'"[105]

Data from the Latinobarometro are also consistent with this theoretical interpretation. If we join Marta Lagos in averaging three responses (support for democracy, willingness to defend democracy, and satisfaction with the way democracy works) into a scale of democratic commitment, we find that levels of democratic commitment appear closely associated with levels of democracy.[106] The three countries that rank clearly highest and that are consolidated democracies (Costa Rica, Spain, and Uruguay; see table 5.3) also have the most liberal average freedom scores in 1996 from the Freedom House annual ratings. Levels of democratic support and overall commitment tend to decline with lower freedom scores, and the lowest democratic support levels are in the least democratic countries—Mexico and Guatemala—both of which had lower freedom scores before 1996.

The two exceptions to this pattern are telling. Colombia (which plummeted to the lowest freedom score of any South American democracy) shows middling levels of democratic support. That they are not lower may be due to the country's four decades of formal democracy.

However, Colombia also has the second lowest level of satisfaction with "the way democracy works" (second only to Mexico, which did not begin to cross the threshold to electoral democracy until the July 1997 midterm elections). A more striking exception is Chile, which is near the bottom in democratic support and overall commitment, even though it has the second most liberal freedom score. This skepticism seems to derive from two factors: the persistence of a proauthoritarian element, which views with favor General Pinochet's past military rule and supports his (or the military's) continued institutional role in politics, and broader popular frustration with the "authoritarian institutional lags," including General Pinochet's continued command of the army and the military's constitutional role in government seven years after the transition to democracy. In fact, as Linz and Stepan argue, the interlocking system of prerogatives for the military and its civilian appointees, embedded in Pinochet's 1980 constitution, so constrains the authority of elected governments and so insulates the military from democratic control that, until it "is removed or greatly diminished, the Chilean transition cannot be completed, and, by definition, Chilean democracy cannot be consolidated."[107] Chile's freedom score thus understates an institutional problem with its democracy that is deeply felt by its citizens and that continues to divide the society.

This returns us to the relationship between democratic deepening and democracy. Given wide disenchantment with corruption and "money politics" around the world, most citizens of most new democracies would not be inclined to think they have attained full democracy. The percentages of the public in Latin America who believe their country has achieved full democracy are generally low, but they are higher in those countries with higher levels of democratic legitimacy (especially the three consolidated democracies; see table 5.3). It is telling that Chile ranks so low here (10%, the same as Mexico and El Salvador) and that Brazil has the lowest percentage of all.

As Linz and Stepan show with regard to Spain and other third-wave democracies, citizens of a new democracy distinguish between the political and economic dimensions of regime performance and may value democracy for the political goods it produces even when its economic performance is perceived as poor and costly in the short term. Part of this is owing to the fact that citizens of postcommunist Europe have proven to be more patient and realistic in their time horizons for economic improvement than many observers expected. But much of it owes as well to the real improvements they perceive in what Linz and Stepan call the "political basket of goods" during the first few years of democracy. By late 1993 and early 1994, 60–98 percent of citizens in the Czech Republic, Slovakia, Slovenia, Hungary, Poland, Bulgaria, and Romania saw the current political system as better than the previous one in giving people freedom to join any organization they want, to say what they think, to travel and live wherever they want, to live without fear of unlawful arrest, to decide whether to take an interest in politics, and to choose whether or not to practice a religion. On these six dimensions of freedom the percentage recognizing a better political life was often 85–90 percent. The perception of increased freedom averaged 94 percent in Bulgaria, 91 percent in Romania, and 82 percent overall for the seven CEE countries. It was roughly as high in Lithuania and Estonia as well. By contrast, Russian perceptions (in mid-1993) of greater freedom on these six dimensions were less clear-cut, ranging from 29 percent (less fear of unlawful arrest) to 83 percent, with a mean of 62 percent (about the same as Belarus and Ukraine).[108] In a different, more recent survey (late 1996), 83 percent of Russians perceived little or no progress toward a rule of law, only slightly more than a third thought elections were honest and the media truly free, and only 15 percent believed the judicial system treats everyone equally.[109]

Widespread perceptions of greater freedom have done much to legitimate the new democracies of Central and Eastern Europe. The fuller the sense of greater freedom, the greater the likelihood that a postcommunist citizen will positively evaluate the current regime and reject all undemocratic alternatives. On each measure of support for democracy, there is a clear step pattern, as the number of dimensions on which the individual feels freer increases. Those perceiving greater freedom in all respects are four times more likely to be positive about the current regime and three times as likely to reject all authoritarian alternatives as those who perceive no change at all from the past.[110] Support for democracy is thus related to the "sense of freedom from state oppression [that] is felt throughout the postcommunist societies of Central and Eastern Europe. People may be dissatisfied with their current living standards or fearful of losing their jobs, but they have not forgotten the great gains made in freedom from fear and censorship."[111]

The statistical analysis of Rose and his colleagues confirms the apparent relationship in the postcommunist states (as in Latin America) between attitudinal support for democracy and actual levels of democratic freedom (table 5.6). People who live in liberal democracies are more likely to reject all authoritarian alternatives and to approve the current regime while disapproving the previous (communist) one. More generally, the data confirm the perception of rapid progress toward the entrenchment of democratic legitimacy and the consolidation of democracy in the six states of the former Warsaw Pact as well as Slovenia. These seven CEE states stand in sharp contrast to the former Soviet states of Russia, Ukraine, and Belarus. The latter have significantly lower freedom levels, and their citizens are significantly more likely to favor at least one authoritarian alternative to democracy.[112] In most of the other non-Russian successor states, the heavy weight of the Soviet legacy more closely matches the oppressive situation in Belarus, with a shapeless institutional terrain dominated by corrupt elite clans, authoritarian presidents, and local mafias.[113]

Romania appears as an anomaly in that its levels of public commitment to democracy rank it much higher among the postcommunist countries than would be predicted by its relatively low freedom score in 1995 and preceding years. This may help to explain its embrace of a more democratic alternative in the 1996 presidential elections and its movement during that year into the "free" category (followed by further improvement in 1997 to an average freedom score of 2). Romania's shift raises the question of the direction of causality. Once a formal transition has occurred, does the underlying political culture play a substantial role in pushing a country toward a certain level of democracy (or as in Belarus, back to dictatorship)? Or (as the transitions school maintains) do objective conditions and institutions of democracy generate appreciation for democracy that may then become embedded in the political culture?

The geographic patterning of human rights performance around the world appears to reflect a major role for culture. Using 1990s data, Russell Bova shows that, among electoral democracies, Western countries (or those influenced by Western cultural traditions valuing individual freedom and autonomy) have better human rights records than non-Western (African and Asian) countries.[114] This analysis does not control for economic development, which is correlated with regional and cultural blocs, nor does it adequately recognize how much (and how rapidly) culture can evolve in response to structural changes. Nevertheless, it suggests that culture does play an independent role in shaping a political system. Moreover, as we see in South Korea and Taiwan, some substantial residues of illiberal value orientations may persist and coexist with strong support for democracy in general and even with support for civil liberties. Thus, while habituation reshapes political norms and values to fit democratic institutions, underlying cultural dispositions may slow or accelerate this process.

As has long been argued by modernization theory and demonstrated by such studies as Almond and Verba's *The Civic Culture* and Inkeles and Smith's *Becoming Modern*, socioeconomic variables, both macro and micro, also help to explain democratic orientations and values. However, from the limited causal analysis that is so far available, social structural factors are not as powerful or as numerous as might have been expected. This augurs well for democratic consolidation, if by that we mean that there are no "socially cohesive pockets of resistance to democratization."[115] In the comprehensive study that Rose and his colleagues conducted during the 1990s in Central and Eastern Europe, the one social structural variable that appears to have some real power in explaining support for democracy (and especially, rejection of authoritarian alternatives) is education. (This was also the most powerful structural variable identified in the above two classic studies.) The more educated are more likely to embrace democracy, even when many other factors are controlled for. Education is one of the three most powerful factors predicting the rejection of authoritarian alternatives.[116] Education also has positive effects on a broader scale of liberal, prodemocratic social and political values in every one of ten postcommunist countries studied by Geoffrey Evans.[117] Even more strikingly (and in contrast to the findings of Rose et al.), so does youth.[118] Indeed, when one considers that youth and education and higher-status occupation are all associated with support for the market, the prognosis for the postcommunist states appears more encouraging, in that "the main opposition to both markets and democracy is among declining groups."[119]

Education appears to be strongly correlated with democratic values in Taiwan, also. William L. Parish and Charles Chi-hsiang Chang find that the more educated were appreciably more likely to disagree with authoritarian political ideas and, between 1985 and 1990, to manifest democratic value change. Beyond education, a more modern (professional) occupation, urban residence, and youth also contribute independently to more liberal values.[120] Consistently across five time periods, education emerges as the single most powerful determinant of a scale of democratic values encompassing many of the measures in table 5.7.[121] Within greater China, Yun-han Chu found that "level of education consistently exerts the most significant impact on the transformation of political culture at the individual level." The higher the educational level, the more likely respondents were in each of the four Chinese samples

(Hong Kong, Taiwan, China, and urban China) to manifest prodemo-cratic value orientations (as well as political efficacy).[122] Other studies of Hong Kong also show that the more educated are more likely to be tolerant of social conflict and to value political freedom.[123]

Evaluating Democracy: The Role of System Performance

We have seen that beliefs about the legitimacy of democracy are shaped more by political than economic performance and, in fact, have many causal sources, some of which do not relate to performance of the system at all. Still, even if citizens come to value democracy over the long run for its political qualities, shorter-run assessments of the system (like those tapped by questions about satisfaction with the way democracy works in the country) can presumably affect the ability of a democratic regime to mobilize support and govern effectively. These more immediate performance assessments appear much more sensitive to economic conditions. José Ramón Montero, Richard Gunther, and Mariano Torcal show that, in the first two decades of Spanish democracy (1976–96), public assessments of economic and political conditions covaried "almost perfectly" and that supposedly more general evaluations of system efficacy also follow closely in step with assessments of the economic and political situation. When these various evaluations of performance, however, are juxtaposed with the stability of public belief in the legitimacy of democracy, no clear association is apparent. Dissatisfaction with democratic performance appears to reflect partisan opposition to the government in power and policy dissatisfaction, while "the basic legitimacy of democracy is relatively autonomous."[124]

This detachment of legitimacy from evaluations of performance (satisfaction and system efficacy) took place in a democracy that had early on built up a strong foundation of legitimacy in several ways: rejection of the authoritarian past, socioeconomic development and generational change, integration into the sociocultural milieu of a democratic Europe, and perhaps most significantly, the institutionalization of democratic structures and procedures, as a result of which the democratic system functioned democratically, in adherence to constitutional rules and individual rights. In parts of Latin America, and even more so in the former Soviet Union, legitimacy has not yet firmly taken root, and support for democracy appears much more conditional on assessments of how the regime is performing.

The countries of Central and Eastern Europe appear to be following the Spanish model but with important distinctions. Levels of external efficacy are low, as people generally judge their elected officials as distant and unresponsive, but external efficacy is similarly low in Spain and other Western European democracies.[125] Overall levels of satisfaction with the way democracy works are much lower than in Spain, Portugal, and Greece, but the trends respond similarly to economic evaluations. At the individual level and especially the aggregate level of national surveys, satisfaction with democracy is strongly influenced by personal economic assessments (current and future); the greater the economic optimism, the greater the satisfaction with the way democracy is working.[126] Similarly, across five postcommunist samples, satisfaction with the way democracy is developing in their country is consistently correlated with expectations for progress in both personal and national conditions.[127]

Data from the New Democracies Barometer depicts a similar picture. Although they do not encompass as many time points as the data on Spain, the mean levels of political and economic approval for Central and Eastern Europe vary in association with one another, while legitimacy (support for democracy) moves somewhat independently. Noteworthy is the high level of legitimacy, even during periods when economic satisfaction is very low. In contrast to satisfaction in Spain, however, approval of the political system consistently hovers about 20 percentage points higher than approval of the economic system (see figure 5.1). This may be owing to the high levels of hope citizens of postcommunist Europe consistently manifest for the future economic system. For the seven Central and Eastern European countries, the average proportion expecting they will approve of the economic system in five years' time remained between 70 and 74 percent across the four surveys, 1991–95.[128] Even slightly larger proportions expect to approve of the political regime in five years' time.

The huge gap between current and future economic ratings (which narrowed from 40 percentage points in 1991 to 26 in 1995, as approval of the current system rose) is due to the patience of CEE publics. Two-thirds of Central and Eastern Europeans on average reject the proposition: "If our system can't produce results soon, that's a good reason to try some other system"; and instead accept the proposition: "It will take years for government to deal with the problems inherited from communists." Moreover, patience increased 10 percentage points between 1993 and 1995. Although CEE governments have frequently been voted out of office in response to economic pain, "people are not voting against the new

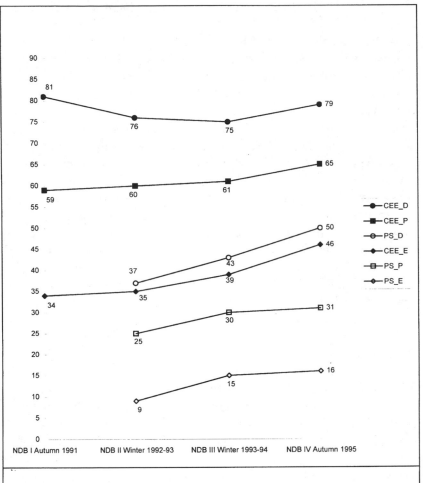

Central and Eastern Europe
CEE_E Approval of Current Economic System
CEE_P Approval of Current Political System
CEE_D Support for Democracy (reject suspension of parties and parliament)

Post-Soviet States
PS_E Approval of Current Economic System
PS_P Approval of Current Political System
PS_D Support for Democracy (average for Ukraine and Belarus only)

Figure 5.1 Trends in Support for Democracy and System Approval, Central and Eastern Europe and Post-Soviet States

Source: Richard Rose and Christian Haerpfer, "Change and Stability in the New Democracies Barometer: A Trend Analysis," Studies in Public Policy 270, Centre for the Study of Public Policy, University of Strathclyde, 1996.

regime, but endorsing a trial-and-error search for a government that will make the new system work better."[129] This political patience has important consequences. It not only increases support for democracy but also produces more positive evaluations of the current regime.[130]

Post-Soviet publics—who had the longest, most total experience with communism and who confront the steepest and most dislocating challenge of transition from state socialism to the market—are not nearly so patient or so approving of the current economic or political system. By 1995, only about a third of Russians and Ukrainians were prepared to see the system "take years" to deal with inherited problems.[131] Disenchantment with the current economic system in Russia, Ukraine, and Belarus is sweeping; by 1995, no more than 16 percent in any country approved of the way the economy was working. Political regime approval never exceeded 36 percent. Even expectations for the future were well below the CEE mean.[132]

While statistical analysis confirms the positive effect of patience on support for democracy in the postcommunist states, there are few statistical tests for the effect on democratic legitimacy of satisfaction with democracy or regime approval. Satisfaction has a positive effect on legitimacy in Korea. Because democratic legitimacy in Spain is only weakly correlated with satisfaction, Montero, Gunther, and Torcal conclude that it has "acquired increasing autonomy from . . . economic discontent or political dissatisfaction."[133] However, this finding was for a democracy that had significant public support at its birth and that rather quickly became legimated by, in part, its political performance. Given that economic as well as political factors shape regime approval, and given as well the degree to which political dissatisfaction in the post-Soviet states is grounded in objective realities of lower freedom and greater crime, lawlessness, and corruption, it seems plausible that (at least in some countries) low levels of regime performance depress satisfaction with the way the new political system is working, which in turn diminishes support for democracy. At the same time, political and historical factors clearly have an independent impact on regime legitimacy.

Economic performance can affect legitimacy indirectly, through the intervening variable of satisfaction with democracy (or regime approval), but the democraticness of the regime has an autonomous and more direct effect on legitimacy (through the perception of increased freedom and responsiveness) (see figure 5.2). While it cannot be fully confirmed by the above data and analysis, this model is consistent with much of that evidence. Certainly, the impact of economic performance on satisfaction with democracy is by now well established.[134] To be sure, causal dynamics are not everywhere the same. Although in Spain, "democratic legitimacy has not been inevitably undermined by economic discontent, political pessimism, political scandals or other unpopular aspects of a government's performance,"[135] in the post-Soviet states precisely the reverse appears to be true. In short, in systems in which democracy has not functioned well from the start, economically or politically, democracy must work better if it is to legitimate itself.

Can the same be said for Latin America? In Uruguay, support for democracy has been consistently high and satisfaction with the way democracy works is also relatively high. In Argentina, support for democracy has remained over 70 percent even though satisfaction is low. But elsewhere, even a decade and more beyond the democratic transition, levels of support for democracy lag well below those of Southern Europe in the mid-1980s (or today), well below those of Central and Eastern Europe, and below the two-thirds level one would expect to see in a consolidated democracy. In these Latin American countries, high levels of political dissatisfaction and distrust (which have apparently prevailed for some time) contribute to doubts about democratic legitimacy among sig-

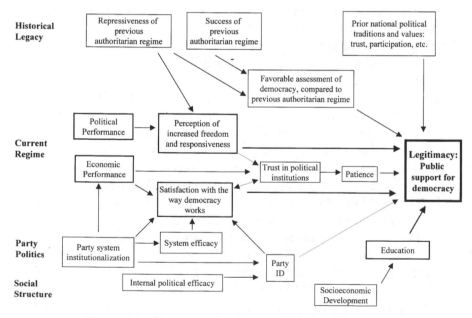

Figure 5.2   Democratic Legitimacy: A Model of Causation

nificant segments of the population. The 1996 Latinobarometro shows large majorities in many countries (more than 60% in Brazil, Argentina, Peru, and Venezuela) worried about being unemployed in the next twelve months (compared with only 29% in Spain). Although majorities (barely) in most countries believe voting "can change the way things will be in the future," only in Chile, among eight South American democracies, do most voters believe that elections are clean. More than a third in Argentina, Bolivia, Brazil, and Colombia and half the public in Venezuela say that politicians offer no solutions (not even "a few") to the problems of the country. Substantial proportions choose distrust, boredom, and indifference to describe how they feel about politics. Distrust was commonly expressed in Spain as well (40%), but in Brazil and Ecuador (two of the countries with the lowest levels of support for democracy), it was felt by roughly 60 percent of the public.[136]

How important is economic performance for the judgments citizens make about their democracy? The evidence to date is only partial and somewhat contradictory. Political performance appears much more important than economic performance in shaping deep-seated beliefs about democratic legitimacy, while economic performance becomes salient (possibly more than political performance or on a par with it) in shaping satisfaction with democracy. However, prolonged economic disaster can magnify the impact on legitimacy of middling-to-poor political performance, and the long-run effects of economic deprivation and stagnation are not yet apparent. In Latin America—and most of all in the postcommunist states—third-wave democracies enjoy a considerable amount of "legitimacy by default," as citizens still vividly remember the repression of the preceding regimes. These memories have made people patient and sober in their expectations about what democracy can deliver in the short run. But what will happen when these memories fade with generational change? To the extent that a foundation for economic stability has not been laid and democratic commitments locked into place, these regimes figure to become vulnerable to rising discontent over their protracted incapacity to deliver (and distribute) some material progress.

Trusting Democracy: Confidence in Institutions

In democracies new and old, much has been made of declining public trust, or confidence in institutions—what Seymour Martin Lipset and William Schneider label the "confidence gap."[137] Yet, democracies do not need high levels of trust in political leaders and institutions in order to function effectively. The ideal democratic culture is neither blindly trusting nor hostilely rejecting but is inquisitive and skeptical. What a healthy democracy must avoid is cynicism, a sweeping distrust of political and social institutions. Even if Western publics have become much less trusting of their parties and politicians, their societies are so richly endowed with autonomous and functioning institutions that they can find at least some to believe in.[138] By contrast, distrust is much more pervasive in Latin America and the postcommunist states.

Of fifteen political and social institutions that Rose and his colleagues inquired about in postcommunist countries, not a single one is trusted by a majority of the public. Even the most trusted institutions, the army and the church, have the explicit confidence of no more than 30 percent of the people across the nine countries surveyed. With the exception of the presidents of these countries (generally the most trusted political actor), political institutions enjoy little trust. Parties are trusted by only 5 percent of the people, parliament by 9 percent, the courts by 17 percent. Yet the alternative to trust is not necessarily distrust but skepticism, a kind of middling response (of 3, 4, or 5 on a 7-point scale of trust), which signals wariness rather than outright loss of confidence or alienation.[139] The good news from the surveys of postcommunist Europe is that skepticism, rather than distrust, is the modal feeling with respect to every institution; it is usually much larger, and even twice as large (for example, for civil servants and the courts), as feelings of distrust. The bad news is that every institution except the army and the church elicits more distrust than trust, and in some cases the ratios of the two are more than two to one, or four to one (for parliament and trade unions), or even (for parties) nine to one in favor of distrust.

The second piece of bad news is the evidence of a direct relationship between trust and democratic legitimacy, at least for some fledgling democracies. Institutional trust has significant positive effects both on support for the current regime and on rejection of authoritarian alternatives, and this positive effect appears to be linear. Those who generally trust in institutions are much more likely to support the current regime (76%) than skeptics are (58%), not to mention the distrustful (39%).[140] Trust in government may also affect satisfaction with the way democracy works.[141] Thus, improving levels of trust (or at least reducing levels of distrust) is part of the challenge of legitimating, and thus consolidating, democracy. The challenge is particularly serious in Belarus, Ukraine, and Bulgaria, in which distrust in institutions equals skepticism (44% in the latter two countries).[142]

Trust (both in institutions and, more diffusely, in people in general) also appears to be shaped to some extent by the more enduring cultural features. Differences in interpersonal trust across countries and regions can be enormous. In South America and in Russia, less than a quarter of the public believes most people can be trusted, but in Korea three-quarters do (which exceeds Scandinavian levels). Yet Koreans' trust does not carry over to politics: only one in five Koreans trust parties or the National Assembly.[143] In line with a long tradition of political culture research, Montero, Torcal, and Gunther conclude that in Spain distrust forms part of a syndrome of "political disaffection," which includes cynicism, inefficacy, disinterest, and general estrangement from politics.[144] This syndrome appears entirely independent of legitimacy and satisfaction but is remarkably durable. To Lagos, widespread interpersonal distrust has deep cultural roots in Latin America and is an archetypical feature of its political culture, underlying the very low levels of confidence in institutions.[145] To Rose, low levels of trust in postcommunist countries are more the result of the atomizing structures and politically alienating experiences of communism.[146]

Political and economic performance also affects levels of trust in institutions, and in Central and Eastern Europe the perception that freedoms have improved exerts "a substantial and positive effect on trust in postcommunist institutions" (both political and market).[147] That perception, the perception of the increased fairness of the system, and expectations for the future national economy are the three most important factors explaining variation in overall levels of trust in institutions. But other economic evaluations are also important, and they become even more so when explaining trust in political institutions alone. Against the alienating backdrop of communism and its collapse, trust grows when the economy is seen to be doing better.

Interpersonal trust may seem tangential to the stability of democracy. Political trust would seem on the surface much more relevant. Indeed, there is statistical evidence that levels of interpersonal trust do not affect change in the level of democracy: low levels do not seem to impede democratic transition or to undermine democratic persistence, nor do higher levels necessarily promote democratization.[148] But trust in people may merit more sustained investigation. Theoretically, trust is a foundation of cooperation. If rival political elites do not trust one another to honor agreements, it will be much more difficult for them to institutionalize the pacts, settlements, understandings, and mutual restraints that stabilize politics and consolidate democracy at the elite level. Of course, rational choice theories insist that it is precisely lack of trust that requires the coordinating mechanism of a constitution and legal institutions for democracy to be stable. From this perspective, trust is more the consequence of, than the prerequisite for, effective institutions.[149] But if trust is low and expectations of fellow citizens are pervasively cynical, institutions will be mere formalities, lacking compliance and effectiveness, as most people defect from obedience in the expectation that most everyone else will.

This is in fact a central problem in Latin America today, where laws are hollow, courts are feeble, and delegative presidents run roughshod over the constitution. Data from the Latinobarometro suggests a strong linkage between culture and the institutional hollowness of democracy. In most Latin American countries, most people (from 57% in Venezuela to 85% in Peru) do not consider their fellow nationals to be honest, and huge majorities (more than 80% in Argentina, Brazil, and Peru) believe their fellow nationals obey the law little or not at all. The only country that clearly departs from this pattern is Uruguay. Elsewhere in Latin America, lawlessness and distrust appear deeply embedded in social expectations, driving everything from tax evasion to ponderous bureaucratic regulations.[150] The attendant weakness of both the state and the rule of law, and the resulting poor quality of democracy, is a major obstacle to democratic consolidation.

Efficacy and Other Orientations

Political culture theory predicts that democracy should be more legitimate and stable when there are high but not polarizing levels of political efficacy, participation, and information. When citizens are knowledgeable, informed, and participant; when they are confident that their engagement can have some impact on political outcomes (internal efficacy); and when they believe the political system is responsive to their concerns (external efficacy), we should expect high levels of support for and satisfaction with democracy. It is not possible to test this assumption with the available data. However, there are grounds to question whether the expected relationships hold. There does appear to be some broad association in Latin America between political distrust

and alienation and the middling progress toward democratic legitimation. But better democratic performance would, our findings suggest,
advance legitimation even if individual political efficacy and interest remained low.

Evidence from Spain suggests that political disaffection, in the form
of low political interest and engagement and low political efficacy (both
internal and external), is stable across generations and can coexist for a
long time with high levels of democratic legitimacy. Since the early
1980s, the proportion of Spaniards expressing little or no interest in politics has generally ranged from 70 to 80 percent. On several measures
dating from 1978, solid majorities (usually 60–70%) have lacked political efficacy, finding politics too complicated to understand and politicians not caring what they think. Yet legitimacy has been consistently
high and even rising, while satisfaction has fluctuated with objective conditions. Statistically, low political interest, engagement, information, and
efficacy cluster in a syndrome of "affective estrangement," which is distinct from legitimacy and satisfaction and appears to be "a stable, if not
permanent, feature of Spain's political culture."[151]

This puts the high levels of inefficacy and cynicism in other new
democracies, including those in Southern and Eastern Europe,[152] in a
less apocalyptic light. The 60 percent of Taiwanese who believed (in
1996) that people like themselves cannot influence government policies
is almost identical to the proportion giving this response in Spain (64%
in 1993).[153] The one quarter of Taiwanese who disagree that "people
like me can't possibly influence government policy" may seem like a tri-
fling level of political efficacy, but it is twice as large as the typical proportion of postcommunist publics who so respond, even in democratically consolidating Hungary and Poland (see table 5.8). Yet, on other
indicators of efficacy, Hungary and Poland (and to some extent other
countries) show higher levels of efficacy, raising the question of measurement.

In fact, it is much too early to dismiss individual political efficacy and
engagement as inconsequential in shaping overall attitudes toward the
democratic system. Evans and Whitefield found a significant effect of efficacy on normative commitment to democracy in postcommunist countries. People who disagree that there is "no point in voting because the
government can't make any difference" are more likely to support
democracy, as are those who perceive some potential to influence the
government through elections and also those who support a political par-

Table 5.8 Individual Political Efficacy

Country	Statements and Percentages Claiming Individual Political Efficacy		
		Latinobarometro, 1996	
	Voting can change the way things will be in the future.	Votes of people like me have "a lot" or "some" influence on the way the country is governed.[1]	Disagree: People like me don't have any say in the making of government policy.
Spain	67	78[2]	47[2]
Argentina	63		
Brazil	61		
Ecuador	58		
Peru	52		
Bolivia	51		
Venezuela	49		
Chile	49		
Mexico	46		
Colombia	43	68	
Korea 1997			
Taiwan 1993, 96		25	27

Postcommunist states, 1991 and 1993

		Disagree: There is no point in voting because the government can't make a difference.	Everyone has an influence on the election of the government.	Disagree: People like me have no say in what government does.
Hungary	1991	53[2]		14
	1993	58	50	11
Poland	1991	44[3]		10
	1993	43	50	11
Romania	1993	76	39	11
Bulgaria	1991	86[3]		22
	1993	49	44	14
Estonia	1993	39	20	8
Lithuania	1993	39	47	11
Russia	1993	33	24	15
Ukraine	1993	23	23	11

Sources: Marta Lagos, "The Latinobarometro: Media and Political Attitudes in South America," paper presented to the annual meeting of the American Political Science Association, San Francisco, 1996; Doh Chull Shin and Richard Rose, "Koreans Evaluate Democracy: A New Korea Barometer Survey," Studies in Public Policy 292, Centre for the Study of Public Policy, University of Strathclyde, 1993, question 14; National Taiwan University, Department of Political Science, surveys of political system and electoral behavior, directed by Professor Hu Fu, supported by the National Science Council of the Republic of China; Geoffrey Evans and Stephen Whitefield, "The Politics and Economics of Democratic Commitment: Support for Democracy in Transition Societies," British Journal of Political Science 25 (1995): table 4; Max Kaase, "Political Culture and Political Consolidation in Central and Eastern Europe," Research on Democracy and Society 2 (1994): table 7.

1. Wording in 1991 was "Voting gives people like me some say about how the government runs things."

2. 1991.

3. Item was the same as in note 1 above, and thus efficacy is indicated by agreement rather than disagreement.

ty. As in other surveys, citizens of Russia and Ukraine show the lowest levels of both personal and system efficacy and the lowest levels of commitment to democracy.[154]

Conclusion

Despite the recent proliferation of data, we are still at an early stage in understanding both the trends and the causal dynamics underlying democratic legitimacy and other dimensions of political culture in third-wave democracies. First, most of these democracies are either recently established or have only recently begun to be surveyed intensively. It will thus be some time before we have a clear picture of longitudinal trends. Second, mountains of survey data have yet to be thoroughly analyzed. Many interesting indicators of democratic attitudes and beliefs have yet to be analyzed systematically, and little has been done to establish a comprehensive causal structure among subjective and objective indicators.

Third, causal dynamics probably vary across historical and cultural legacies, periods of time, and stages of development. We cannot assume that the determinants of democratic legitimacy in the immediate aftermath of a transition will be the same in ten or twenty years, once the historical context has changed, generational replacement has occurred, and democracy has to some degree become routinized. Thus, legitimacy and other democratic norms may have different correlates and causes in new democracies than in established ones. Neither is it obvious that the determinants of legitimacy will be the same in a relatively rich Western country and a relatively poor non-Western one, even at similar points in the transition process. Differences in causation might also be expected between postcommunist states, with their much more comprehensive and heavily discredited legacies of dictatorship, and the East Asian newly industrialized states, where authoritarianism was more successful and democracy came into being in large part because of that success. Even among the postcommunist states, economic factors may matter more in the post-Soviet states that are more deeply mired in economic crisis.

The biggest problem with comparison and generalization lies with the specific measures used. The lack of standardization across countries and studies is one of the biggest challenges confronting cross-national analysis of political culture. Seven measures of legitimacy (support for democracy) were used in various countries and regions (table 5.1). Many of these measures seem similar, if not nearly identical, and all seem to be tapping the commitment to democracy as the best form of government. Yet, responses are very sensitive to the wording of the question. In several cells of table 5.1 we observe different levels of support for democracy in the same country in the same year—but between two different questions. Spaniards were much more likely to agree in 1988 that "democracy is the best system *for a country like ours*" (my emphasis) than that "democracy is preferable to any other form of government," though both measures elicited broad support. Poles were much more likely in 1992 to reject the preference for a strong leader instead of parliament and parties than they were to positively affirm that democracy is always preferable. Similarly, postcommunist publics in 1993 were generally much more likely to say that they would disapprove "if parliament was suspended and parties abolished" than to support the more general "*aim* of introducing democracy" in their country (table 5.1). And still different levels of support—generally lower than the former question but higher than the latter—obtain in postcommunist societies when people are asked if they approve of the current system of government "with free elections and many parties." Different measures of internal political efficacy also register sharply different responses in most nations (table 5.8).

The problems of comparability and, more fundamentally, inference derive not only from questionnaire wording but from the possible responses proffered. To what extent will surveys find the same level of support for the democratic regime when one measures approval with a 5-point scale (strongly or moderately approve, strongly or moderately disapprove, and neither approve nor disapprove), one with a 4-point scale (the 5-point scale but without the "neither" option), one with a 7-point scale (adding the options of "slightly" approve or disapprove), one with a 6-point scale (the 7-point scale but without the "neither" option), and yet another with a 201-point scale (Rose's famous "heaven/hell" index)? To what extent are approval levels measured by the wider-scale options higher than those uncovered with the narrower scales merely because they suck up respondents with a slight feeling that is otherwise classified as sitting on the fence?

The same problems apply to all Likert, or thermometer-scale, measures. Similarly, does it matter whether respondents are asked simply to agree or disagree (strongly or not) that "democracy is preferable to any other form of government," instead of being offered the option that "in some cases an authoritarian regime is preferable" or even the option that "for people like me it's all the same"? In all likelihood, the levels of legitimacy observed vary depending on the response options the respondent is given. And this is even prior to the question of substantive difference, including whether it is unconditional or instrumental, specific or diffuse legitimacy that is being tapped. There is also the well-known problem of "acquiescence bias," the tendency of respondents to want to agree with the question asked (or the statement read), and thus the greater likelihood of a value or policy being embraced if the indicator of it is agreement rather than disagreement. In a recent Russian survey, James Gibson shows this to be a serious problem.[155]

All of this is to underscore a methodological point that may be tedious to some readers but that is vital to understanding how the culture of democracy evolves. We need much more systematic research with these political items to determine how responses vary according to the wording of the question and the structure of the response, and we need much more collaboration across countries and surveys to apply standardized items that can be confidently compared. (Even then, there are limits to confidence, given the challenge of trying to convey precisely the same meanings across languages and cultures.)

These problems particularly complicate the task of comparing levels of support for democracy (whereas other items, such as satisfaction with the way democracy works, tend to be more standardized in wording). The many sources of divergence, error, and "noise," combined with additional errors that can occur in sampling, interviewing, and coding, should make it less likely that we would find any regularities in the structure of causation. Yet, as we saw, across several widely different studies and regions, a similar pattern emerges: political factors, especially relating to how democratically the regime is performing or being seen to perform, are more important than economic factors in shaping perceptions of legitimacy.

Given the evident differences in causal patterns, and the rather scanty causal analysis available, it may seem foolhardy to advance a comprehensive model to explain how the political attitudes and values reviewed in this chapter relate to one another. Nevertheless, there is sufficient theory and evidence at least to propose a model for further testing. This model (see figure 5.2) posits that regime political performance (in terms of increased freedom, responsiveness, and transparency as mediated through public perceptions) has a direct positive effect on democratic legitimacy, while economic performance and economic evaluations most affect satisfaction with the way democracy works (but also probably trust in institutions). Support for democracy (as well as internal efficacy) is also increased by education but not by other objective individual attributes. Exposure to Western culture, which is stimulated to some extent by socioeconomic development, may have a further modest effect on the commitment to democracy; although this remains to be tested generally, it has been demonstrated for East Germany.[156]

Whether out of perceived interest or a more coherent ideology, those who support the market are also more supportive of democracy in the postcommunist states (a relationship that does not appear to hold in Latin America).[157] Trust, both as a generalized social phenomenon and as confidence in political institutions, increases political patience and the readiness to compromise and cooperate. At least indirectly, it should smooth the way to democratic consolidation by improving the stability and performance of the political system, although Rose's study finds direct positive effects of institutional trust on support for democracy.[158] Logically, it should also be the case that trust or confidence in political institutions is related to satisfaction with the way democracy works, although causation here could well be reciprocal. Satisfaction is increased by identification with the ruling party (and that relationship, in turn, appears to be mediated by political institutions, with consensual systems showing less decline in satisfaction among losers than systems with majoritarian institutions).[159]

Political institutionalization, particularly the strength and coherence of the party system, also has an important impact on democratic satisfaction (and by extension, possibly legitimation) both directly and through its positive effects on economic performance and assessments of system efficacy (the overall capacity to deal with the problems of society).[160] Internal political efficacy should increase the likelihood of party identification (and other forms of participation), and both efficacy and participation will tend to increase (or be correlated with) support for democracy.[161] These latter effects and associations (and some others) appear in Central and Eastern Europe but not in Spain. Only further analysis will tell us how universal these causal linkages are.

In an important respect, however, the data from Spain and the postcommunist states agree. Normative commitment to democracy (much more than satisfaction and related performance evaluations) is heavily shaped by history and by early socialization experiences. Thus, in Spain (and one may also surmise, Greece), favorable views of democracy formed before the transition, partly through generational transmission from the democratic past, partly through social change, and partly through an "intense process of learning" and "collective reflection" by various social groups.[162] These beliefs were then quickly increased and hardened by the initial period of democratic functioning after the transition. However, considerable differences existed and persisted between generations in Spain, based on different formative experiences and collective memories. In Spain, "the younger the cohort, the greater the support for democracy."[163]

No effect of age is apparent in the merged postcommunist samples of Rose, Mishler, and Haerpfer (although younger voters are more likely to support democratic party alternatives in Russia).[164] However, they do find that earlier life experiences, arising from the social structure (especially level of education) and the national context in which one comes of age, account for a third to a half of the variance explained in support for democracy (depending on which measure of support is used). Adding in another historical variable (evaluation of the previous communist regime) raises to three quarters the proportion of the causal explanation (for rejection of authoritarian alternatives) from historical or structural factors (as opposed to current political and economic performance). From this analytic perspective (and for this measure of "authoritarian rejection" more than support for the current regime), legitimacy is heavily historically determined (depicted by the arrows from the top variables in figure 5.2). Using different measures of support for democracy, Weil comes to a similar conclusion for postunification East Germany, which "appears to have been born strongly democratic" as a result of its unappealing past regime and its familiarity with prestigious foreign models of democracy that serve as a "reference group."[165]

The implications of this finding appear salutary for some countries and disquieting for others. For Spain, Greece, the Czech Republic, and Uruguay—in which national political traditions, social structure, and the experience of the prior regime all confer a huge democratic legitimacy bonus at the inception of the new regime—democratic consolidation (although it may not be historically determined) is greatly advantaged by the legacy from the past. Even then, however, initial democratic legitimacy depends on how the historical legacy is distilled, recreated, and shaped into founding myths by intellectuals, political elites, and the mass media.[166] Other countries—Brazil, Peru, Russia, and Ukraine—are clearly haunted by the authoritarian, alienating, distrusting past. Are they therefore condemned to relive it?

It would seem that history and early socialization constitute a powerful determinant of culture. But they are not destiny. Later life experiences also shape beliefs about democracy, and the evidence from Taiwan suggests that this posttransition political learning can gradually shift even more deep-seated values (not to mention more pragmatic assessments of a regime) toward a democratic value system. Those regimes that do not enjoy a legitimacy bonus from the moment of transition (the vast majority of third-wave democracies) are not condemned to public cynicism and hostility. But they will have to struggle to legitimate themselves, and they will be able to do so only gradually, through political and economic performance. For these less fortunate democracies, the quest for consolidation will likely be protracted and will succeed only if they demonstrate their capacity to deal with their major economic and social problems and to deliver the political freedom, fairness, transparency, and order that their people expect from democracy. This, in turn, demands from politicians some attention to the "moral and pedagogical aspects of politics."[167] And it requires building the institutions of a democratic state, party system, and civil society—in other words, developing democracy.

6

Civil Society

In the burgeoning theoretical and empirical literature on democratization, few issues are more central and diffuse than the question of elite versus mass influence. Is it primarily elites who make, shape, and consolidate democracy? Or does the public matter? If so, how, when, and to what degree?

Since the early 1980s, most scholarly studies of democratization have given primary emphasis to the divisions, choices, calculations, and strategic alliances among elites in both the authoritarian regime and its democratic opposition. A prominent line of work on democratic consolidation has also centered explicitly and unapologetically on the behavior, organization, and culture of political elites. It considers that democratic consolidation occurs once there emerges a "consensually unified elite" that shares a common commitment to the rules of the democratic game, a broader set of norms about the rules of political conduct, and a dense structure of interaction that fosters personal familiarity and trust.[1] This line of thinking bears a strong kinship to theories that locate the origins of democracy in political pacts among contending, even violently opposed, political elites.[2]

Without question, political elites—and thus politicians—are indispensable to bringing about democracy and making it work. Particularly in the delicately balanced, unstable, and highly uncertain periods of authoritarian breakdown and regime transition, the choices made and alliances forged among a relatively small set of leaders and strategists in the government, the military, political parties, trade unions, other interest groups, and various types of civic organizations do play the key role in shaping whether regime change will occur, and *how* it will occur—violently or peacefully, gradually or abruptly, to democracy or to some new authoritarian or hybrid regime.

218

✓ Beyond the transition, elites have a profound—and I would even concede, preeminent—impact in determining whether new democracies become stable, effective, and consolidated. This impact goes well beyond the cultural dimension of forging a common commitment to democracy and its specific constitutional rules. It encompasses the types of institutions and rules that elites craft, whether the system is parliamentary or presidential; whether it facilitates majoritarian or consensual government; whether it concentrates power at the center or disperses it to multiple levels of government; whether it provides for strong, autonomous institutions of accountability—or "agencies or restraint," such as a constitutional court, auditor-general, and central bank—to check the power of elected officials and ensure good governance. And it has to do with how government, party, and interest group leaders exercise their power—not just their commitment to democracy in principle, but their ability to bargain with one another, form coalitions, mobilize public support, and respond to public pressures and preferences.

✓ As these latter two criteria suggest, elites may be preeminent, but they are not the whole story. Democracy is not just a system in which elites acquire the power to rule through a competitive struggle for the people's vote, as Joseph Schumpeter defined it. It is also a political system in which government must be held accountable to the people, and in which mechanisms must exist for making it responsive to their passions, preferences, and interests. If it is *liberal* democracy that we have in mind, then the political system must also provide for a rule of law, and rigorously protect the right of individuals and groups to speak, publish, assemble, demonstrate, lobby, and organize. There must exist multiple avenues for "the people" to express their interests and preferences, to influence policy, and to scrutinize and check the exercise of state power continuously, in between elections as well as during them.

✓ The mass public matters for democratization in two senses: in its often pivotal role (too little appreciated by the scholarly literature) in helping to effect a transition to democracy, and in the never-ending quest to deepen democracy beyond its formal structure. If we think of democracy in developmental terms, as a political system that emerges gradually in fragments or parts, and is always capable of becoming more liberal, inclusive, responsive, accountable, effective, and just, then we must see democratization not simply as a limited period of transition from one set of formal regime rules to another, but rather as an ongoing process, a perpetual challenge, a recurrent struggle.

✓   In many of the third-wave democracies, competitive elections do not ensure liberty, responsiveness, and a rule of law. To varying but often alarming degrees, human rights are flagrantly abused; ethnic and other minorities suffer not only discrimination but murderous violence; power is heavily if not regally concentrated in the executive branch; and parties, legislators, executives, and judicial systems are thoroughly corrupt. In such countries, democracy (if we can call it that) will not become broadly valued, and thus consolidated, unless it also becomes more liberal, transparent, and institutionalized. In these circumstances, governing elites must be made accountable to one another and to the people, not only in theory but in fact. And institutions must be constructed or reformed to ensure that this will happen. In such circumstances of entrenched corruption and repression, the elites who come to govern have a stake in the existing system, and those who favor real reform are too weak to accomplish it by themselves. Only the mass public can generate the political pressure and power necessary to bring about reform.

✓   Even when democracy is firmly consolidated and its survival not in doubt, its quality may deteriorate and the need for adaptation and reinvigoration may become increasingly manifest. Students of democratic development should not ignore the serious problems of democratic functioning in the United States, Western Europe, and Japan: the deeply corrosive influence of big money in politics; the political alienation of large (and in some countries, growing) segments of the population; the decline of political parties as effective instruments of interest articulation and aggregation and the waning of popular attachment to them; the entrenchment of a culture of entitlements that is fiscally unsustainable; the rising hostility to immigrants and outsiders. In some of these respects, the mass public itself, in its expectations and patterns of behavior, constitutes a major source of the problem. But when the decay of democratic institutions is accompanied by (or even provokes) growing public disengagement from politics, democracy may settle into a low-level equlibrium that persists until it is shaken by genuine crisis. In the absence of such fiscal or political crisis, political leaders themselves typically cannot muster the will, courage, or power to bring about change on their own. They need the stimulus and the support of a mobilized public.

✓   "The public," like "the people," is a concept that is diffuse, and easily misused or abused. Politicians invoke it for their own ends. Demagogues manipulate it in attempting to ride to power. Without organization, structure, and principles, the public may not matter for democracy, or its impact may be negative. Certainly, a politically active public is not all that matters. Democracy—in particular, a healthy liberal democracy—also requires a public that is organized for democracy, socialized to its norms and values, and committed not just to its myriad narrow interests but to larger, common, "civic" ends. Such a civic public is only possible with a vibrant "civil society."

What Civil Society Is and Is Not

✓ *Civil society is the realm of organized social life that is open, voluntary, self-generating, at least partially self-supporting, autonomous from the state, and bound by a legal order or set of shared rules.* It is distinct from "society" in general in that *it involves citizens acting collectively in a public sphere* to express their interests, passions, preferences, and ideas, to exchange information, to achieve collective goals, to make demands on the state, to improve the structure and functioning of the state, and to hold state officials accountable. Civil society is an intermediary phenomenon, ✓ standing between the private sphere and the state. Thus, it excludes parochial society: individual and family life and inward-looking group activity (recreation, entertainment, religious worship, spirituality); and it excludes economic society: the profit-making enterprise of individual business firms. Parochial society and economic society do not concern themselves with civic life and the public realm, and yet they may help generate cultural norms and patterns of engagement that spill over into the civic realm. Similarly, civil society is distinct from political society, which encompasses all those organized actors (in a democracy, primarily political parties and campaign organizations) whose primarily goal is to win control of the state or at least some position for themselves within it. Organizations and networks in civil society may form alliances with parties, but if they become captured by parties, or hegemonic within them, they move their primary locus of activity to political society and lose much of their ability to perform certain unique mediating and democracy-building functions.

✓ Being essentially market-oriented, *actors in civil society recognize the principles of state authority and the rule of law* and need the protection of an institutionalized legal order to prosper and be secure. Thus, civil society not only restricts state power but legitimates state authority when that authority is based on the rule of law. However, when the state itself is lawless and contemptuous of individual and group autonomy, civil society may still exist (albeit in tentative or battered form) if its constituent elements operate by some set of shared rules (which, for example, eschew violence and respect pluralism). This is the irreducible condition of its "civil" dimension.[3]

Civil society encompasses a vast array of organizations, formal and informal, including

— *Economic:* productive and commercial associations and networks
— *Cultural:* religious, ethnic, communal, and other institutions and associations that defend collective rights, values, faiths, beliefs, and symbols
— *Informational and educational:* organizations devoted to the production and dissemination (whether for profit or not) of public knowledge, ideas, news, and information
— *Interest:* groups that seek to advance or defend the common functional or material interests of their members (e.g., trade unions, associations of veterans and pensioners, and professional groups)
— *Developmental:* organizations that pool individual resources and talents to improve the infrastructure, institutions, and quality of life of the community
— *Issue-oriented:* movements for environmental protection, land reform, consumer protection, and the rights of women, ethnic minorities, indigenous peoples, the disabled, and other victims of discrimination and abuse
— *Civic:* groups that seek (in nonpartisan fashion) to improve the political system and make it more democratic (e.g., working for human rights, voter education and mobilization, election monitoring, and exposure and reform of corrupt practices).

In addition, civil society encompasses what Thomas Metzger calls "the ideological marketplace," the flow of information and ideas, including those which evaluate and critique the state. This includes not only independent mass media but the broader field of autonomous cultural and intellectual activity: universities, think tanks, publishing houses, theaters, filmmakers, and artistic performances and networks.

Civil society is not some mere residual category, synonymous with "society" or with everything that is not the state or the formal political system. One of the most misleading and even trivializing conceptualizations of civil society is to treat it as simply "organizations independent of the state." Beyond being voluntary, self-generating, autonomous, and rule-abiding, civil society organizations are distinct from other groups in society in five respects.

First, *civil society is concerned with public ends* rather than private ends. It is distinct from parochial society. And it is "accessible to citizens and open to public deliberation—not embedded in exclusive, secretive, or corporate settings."[4]

Second, *civil society relates to the state* in some way but does not seek to win control over or position within the state; it does not seek to "govern the polity as a whole."[5] Rather, civil society actors pursue from the state concessions, benefits, policy changes, institutional reforms, relief, redress, justice, and accountability to their scrutiny. Organizations, movements, and networks that seek to displace ruling authorities from power, to change the nature of the state, and in particular to democratize it, remain part of civil society if their goal is to reform the structure of power rather than to take power themselves as organizations. Thus, a liberation party like the Indian National Congress in preindependence India or the African National Congress of South Africa is acting essentially in political society; it seeks not only a democratic transition but control of the state. Supporting movements and allied organizations, however, like the Congress of South African Trade Unions (COSATU), spring from civil society.

Third, *civil society encompasses pluralism and diversity.* To the extent that an organization, such as a religious fundamentalist, ethnic chauvinist, revolutionary or millenarian movement, seeks to monopolize a functional or political space in society, crowding out all competitors while claiming that it represents the only legitimate path, it contradicts the pluralistic and market-oriented nature of civil society.[6]

Fourth, *civil society does not seek to represent the complete set of interests* of a person or a community. Rather different groups represent or encompass different aspects of interest.[7] This partiality is crucial to generating one of the important consequences of a truly civil society: the profusion of different organizations and, for individuals, multiple organizational ties that cut across and complicate existing cleavages and generate moderating cross-pressures on individual preferences, attitudes, and beliefs. By contrast, parties or organizations of integration seek to encapsulate their members within a totalistic environment that isolates them from alternative views and ties, inculcates a rigid, comprehensive ideological or philosophical belief system, and demands total obedience. As Lipset argues, following the work of Sigmund Neumann, such totalistic parties or movements weaken democracy and, I would argue, are fundamentally uncivil, while pluralistic organizations strengthen democracy.[8]

✓   Confusion about the boundaries of civil society and the location of particular actors derives in part from the multiple and shifting nature of organizational goals. A religious congregation or establishment (a church or mosque or synagogue) may mainly function to cater to the spiritual needs of its members in parochial society. But when it becomes engaged in efforts to fight poverty, crime, and drug addiction, to improve human capital, to organize efforts for community self-improvement, or to lobby legislatures (or join constitutional cases) about public policies on abortion, sexuality, poverty, human rights, the legal treatment of religion, or a myriad of other issues, then the religious institution is acting in civil society. Many times, organizations based in one sphere temporarily cross the boundary into another. Trade unions may constitute themselves as virtual campaign organizations for particular candidates or parties at election times. The church may throw its leadership, resources, and moral authority into a broad national movement for democratic change, as has occurred to varying degrees in Brazil, Chile, Nicaragua, the Philippines, South Korea, Poland, South Africa, Zambia, Malawi, and elsewhere during the third wave. Recreational organizations may become politicized into civic action, if for example the birds they watch or the trails they hike become threatened by pollution or business development. Frequently, organizations and networks pursue multifaceted agendas that straddle the boundary between parochial and civil society, or between civil and political society, or even between all three sectors (as with religious organizations, when religion gets politicized).

✓   The balance of organizational activities tells us something about the character of a political system. A stable democracy, according to Gabriel Almond and Sidney Verba, requires, a "mixed political culture" in which a participant orientation—to vote and demonstrate and lobby and organize on the basis of rational interests—is tempered by a subject orientation of loyalty to the political community and constitutional order and by a parochial orientation that involves the individual in private and non political concerns, and that "expects nothing from the political system."[9] As a result of this mix, citizens do not participate incessantly and with equal intensity on all issues. Rather, they exercise "a reserve of influence" with a disposition to political activity that is "intermittent and potential." It is precisely the "comparative infrequency of political participation, its relative lack of importance for the [typical] individual, and the objective weakness" of the average citizen that "allow governmental elites to act" and preserve a healthy balance between conflict and consensus. Democratic governability and democratic responsiveness and accountability are facilitated by "cycles of citizen involvement, elite response, and citizen withdrawal."

✓   Although Almond and Verba's theory has been criticized as conservative in its structural-functional emphasis on system maintenance, it can comprehend change and reform as well as stability. And it has a parallel at the broader level of organizational life. Democracy differs in form across countries: some are more structured and dominated by elites, some more pluralistic, competitive, and conflictual. But in every democracy, effective governance requires some restraint in the number and intensity of demands upon the state and in the intensity with which conflicting parties and organizations press incompatible public policy agendas. When organizations that are primarily (or in theory) parochial become drawn into repeated and intense public policy debates, and when organizations in civil society become intensely and enduringly politicized along partisan lines of division, society may polarize, as the cross-cutting bonds of solidarity and civility dissolve. Such polarization may be creative and advantageous for social justice and democracy at moments of political crisis, bringing the downfall of an authoritarian regime, the reform of a decadent and occluded democratic system, the permanent expansion of participation and enlargement of civil liberties, the impeachment and removal of a corrupt president from office, the cancellation of a fraudulent election. But democracy cannot function indefinitely on the basis of crisis, polarization, and pervasive civic and political mobilization by every type of organization imaginable. Eventually, democratic governability requires a return to normality—not to apathy or withdrawal but rather to a boundary between civic and parochial society.

✓   Fifth, *civil society should be distinguished from the more clearly democracy-enhancing phenomenon of civic community.* Robert Putnam's model of the civic community has profound implications for the quality and consolidation of democracy. It also has great potential to bridge the literatures on political culture and civil society, with its concept of social capital, which Putnam defines as the "features of social organization" and of culture "that can improve the efficiency of society by facilitating coordinated actions." Both for economic development and effective democracy, voluntary cooperation (to pool resources, to engage in exchange, to organize for common ends) is crucial. Voluntary cooperation is greatly facilitated by interpersonal trust and norms of reciprocity, and these cultural orientations in turn are fostered by (but also deepen) "networks of civic engagement," in which citizens are drawn together as equals in "intense horizontal interaction."[10] The key to constructing a civic community is not whether an organization has an explicitly civic (public) or political purpose. Mutual aid organizations (e.g., rotating credit associations), neighborhood associations, choral societies, cooperatives, sports clubs, and mass-based political parties may all be constituent elements of a civic community. The key is whether associational life is structured horizontally so as to generate trust, cooperation, free flows of communication, and generalized, "robust norms of reciprocity."

✓ Viewed in this way, civic community is both a broader and narrower concept than civil society: broader in that it encompasses all manner of associations (parochial included); narrower in that it includes only associations structured horizontally around ties that are more or less mutual, cooperative, symmetrical, and trusting. By contrast, there are many organizations active in democratic civil societies—even civic organizations whose goal is to reform the polity or advocate human rights—that are not civic in Putnam's sense. Instead of bringing together people as trusting equals cooperating in relations of "generalized reciprocity" and mutual benefit and respect, these organizations tend to reproduce within themselves hierarchical cultural tendencies of the wider society: vertical structures of authority and flows of information, asymmetrical patterns of exchange between patron and clients, scant horizontal ties among the general membership, and weak levels of trust (at best). To the extent that hierarchy and suspicion rule the organization, cooperation becomes difficult, both among members of the organization and between it and other organizations. The organization then becomes dependent on a leader or ruling clique and may manifest a debilitating contradiction between its internal style of governance and the goals its professes to seek for the polity. As a result, the organization cannot widen its base; or it loses support and credibility in society; or it descends into fractious and internecine conflict with similar organizations professing similar ends and characterized by similar patterns of hierarchical, unaccountable, internal leadership. In the most extreme cases, civil society organizations may become hobbled and hollowed out by the personalistic, dependent, coercive, and exploitative authority relations of the "uncivic community" and its consequent vulnerability to "defection, distrust, shirking, exploitation, isolation, disorder, and stagnation."[11]

✓ Putnam's notion of civicness (reciprocity, cooperation, and trust versus hierarchy, fragmentation, and distrust) is not simply a tidy and appealing theoretical construct or a regression into cultural determinism. It is a powerful perspective for understanding why organizations that may be considered (and certainly consider themselves) part of civil society nevertheless fail to function effectively to develop democracy. The problem has been particularly severe in many African countries, where even many human rights organizations have been unable to build broad antiauthoritarian fronts because of paralyzing divisions, which prevent organizations from coalescing and encourage old organizations to divide around leadership disputes and new organizations to form (hierarchical- ly) around alternative leaders. To some extent, these types of divisions account for the weakness of the prodemocracy civic organizations in Nigeria, particularly since the annulment of the (largely successful and democratic) June 1993 presidential elections and the abortion of the democratic transition that the military had pledged to complete that year. Indeed, most African dictators who managed to withstand the winds of democratic change in the early 1990s did so in part by using money and manipulating ethnicity to entrench the uncivic tendencies that civil so- ciety organizations inherited from the larger society and, thus, to foment suspicion, division, co-optation, and defection.

The distinction between civic community and civil society under- scores a more general theoretical caveat. If civil society is to be a theo- retically useful construct for studying democratic development, it is important to avoid the tautology that equates it with everything that is democratic, noble, decent, and good. Civil society must be refined to a degree that distinguishes it from the much wider and more general are- na of (independent) associational life. But an association may be inde- pendent from the state, voluntary, self-generating, and respectful of the law and still be not only undemocratic, paternalistic, and particularistic in its internal structure and norms but also distrustful, unreliable, dom- ineering, exploitative, and cynical in its dealings with other organiza- tions, the state, and society. To the extent that such organizations char- acterize civil society, it will be less effective and liberal, and so will democracy. Alternatively, to the extent that civil society is characterized instead by civic norms and structures that induce trust and cooperation, this pattern will probably be reflected in parochial society as well. In this sense, Putnam (like Tocqueville) sensitizes us to the importance of the nature and intensity of associational life in general—of social capital— as a crucial cultural foundation of liberal democracy.

The Features of a Democratic Civil Society

Clearly, not all associations, and not even all associations in civil society, have the same potential to foster and deepen democracy. Five features of civil society generally and of individual organizations are important:

self-government, goals and methods, organizational institutionalization, pluralism, and density.

✓   One feature concerns how (indeed whether) an organization formally governs its own internal affairs. To what extent does it practice democratic principles of constitutionalism, transparency, accountability, participation, deliberation, representation, and rotation of leaders in the way it makes decisions and allocates its own power and resources? An organization may be able to represent group interests, check the power of the state, and perform many other democratic functions even if it is not internally democratic.[12] But if, in its own patterns of governance, it perpetuates norms that penalize dissent, exalt the leader over the group, and cloak the exercise of power, one thing it will not do is build a culture of democracy. If civil society organizations are to function as "large free schools" for democracy (in Tocqueville's term), they must function democratically in their internal processes of decision making and leadership selection. And they should encourage and institutionalize multiple avenues for active participation among the members. The more their own organizational practices are based on political equality, reciprocal communication, mutual respect, and the rule of law, the more civil society organizations will socialize members into these democratic norms and the more they will generate the social trust, tolerance, cooperativeness, and civic competence that undergird a vibrant and liberal democracy.[13]

✓   A second feature concerns the goals and methods of groups in civil society, especially organized associations. The chances to develop stable democracy significantly improve if a society's array of organizations and movements does not contain maximalist, uncompromising interest groups, or groups with undemocratic goals and methods. To the extent a group seeks to conquer the state or other competitors or rejects the rule of law and the authority of the democratic state, it is not a component of civil society at all, but it may nevertheless do much damage to democratic aspirations. Powerful, militant interest groups pull parties toward populist and extreme political promises, polarizing the party system, and are more likely to bring down state repression that may have a broad and indiscriminate character, weakening or radicalizing more democratic elements of civil society. Even within civil society, some groups are more inclined to cooperation and compromise than others. This returns us to Putnam's variable of "civicness."

✓   A third feature of civil society is its level of organizational institutionalization. As with political parties, institutionalized interest groups contribute to the stability, predictability, and governability of a democratic regime. When interests are organized in a structured, stable manner, bargaining and the growth of cooperative networks are facilitated. Social forces do not face the continual cost of setting up new structures. And if the organization expects to continue to operate in the society over a sustained period of time, its leaders will have more reason to be accountable and responsive to the constituency, and may take a longer-range view of the group's interests and policy goals, rather than seeking to maximize short-term benefits in an uncompromising manner. Institutionalization has a strong affinity with constitutionalism. It involves established procedures that are widely and reliably known and regularly practiced, as opposed to personalized, arbitrary, and unpredictable modes of operation.

✓   As with the structures and organizations in political society and the state, so with civil society we can measure the institutionalization of civil society actors with Samuel Huntington's four criteria: autonomy, adaptability, coherence, and complexity.[14] Autonomy must insulate a civil society actor from dominance or control not only by the state but by an individual leader, founder, or ruling clique. To the extent the purpose and functioning of the organization are subverted by other social or political actors, hijacked to their agendas, or subordinated to the whims and interests of a personalized ruler or a particular faction, a civil society organization's effectiveness is undermined, its potential base of support is narrowed, and its ability to develop a democratic culture is compromised. This relates also to the criterion of coherence. A civil society organization will be most effective and will best contribute to the development of democracy when it has a coherent purpose, structure, and organizational identity broadly shared among its members. Coherence requires consensus about the mission of the organization, its functional boundaries, and its procedures for resolving disputes. Consensus about goals, priorities, projects, and methods is more likely to be broad and sustainable if it emerges organically from a deliberative process and if it is transparent and codified in a constitutional framework.

✓   Complexity involves elaboration of functions and subunits, and this can potentially diminish coherence. But it need not negate it. A key element of complexity for civil society organizations at the national level is vertical depth: the extent to which they are able to organize provincial and local chapters that pursue the same goals at lower levels of public life. This is important not only for interest groups (trade unions and chambers of commerce have long perceived the need to be organized across a range of sectors and levels) but also for civic organizations. The most effective civic education, human rights, environmental, and democratic reform organizations in developing democracies have established local chapters and field offices in many or most of the states or provinces of their countries. This dispersed presence broadens the membership base of the organization, increases active participation in its affairs, and enables it to pursue a more complex policy agenda. This is especially vital when power is at least somewhat decentralized and government decisions or activities bearing on the organization's goals are made at the provincial and local levels. Decentralized structures of national civil society organizations also build social capital by bringing citizens together in face-to-face interaction concerning the problems of their immediate communities.

Complexity can also emerge, from the bottom up, through the growth of local organizations into more broad-based national structures, or it can come through the horizontal aggregation of many distinct organizations that share underlying interests or a common purpose and functional identity. Both of these processes have characterized the institutional growth of Korean civil society in the past decade. The Citizens' Coalition for Economic Justice (CCEJ) was established by reformers in the Seoul metropolitan area and then initiated other local and regional branch organizations. Only somewhat later did it formally come together as a national-level association. And national-level associations in Korea have established (on their own initiative and control, not that of the state) loose confederations to coordinate their sectoral activities and formulate common strategies. In 1995, the Korea Coalition of Citizen's Movements (KCCM) was founded with the participation of fifty-four national organizations, including eight civic organizations. The KCCM screens all applicant organizations to ensure that they are truly independent of government, political parties, and commercial enterprises. Such a formal coalition increases the moral and political clout of its constituent parts. The KCCM is frequently consulted by the government and has greater stature to mediate disputes and propose political reforms than does any one of its member organizations.[15]

Institutionalization also requires that civil society organizations adapt their missions, functions, and structures to an altered political and social context, new imperatives, and different opportunities. This, too, overlaps with other criteria, in particular complexity. Adaptation partly involves elaborating the functional agenda of the organization and deepening its local substructures. This adaptation has been vividly evidenced in the growth of election monitoring organizations beyond their original mission of ensuring free and fair elections, forged in the crucible of tense and uncertain transitions from authoritarian rule.

Such highly successful groups as the National Citizens Movement for Free Elections (NAMFREL) in the Philippines, the Crusade for Civic Participation in Chile (which later evolved into PARTICIPA), the Bulgarian Association for Fair Elections (BAFECR), the Paraguayan organization SAKA (a Guarani word for "transparency"), and the Civic Alliance in Mexico have moved beyond their original urgent purpose of educating voters and mobilizing volunteer poll watchers in crucial transitional or founding elections. While continuing their election monitoring work, they have also broadened the scope of their activity (either themselves or by spawning new, affiliated civic organizations) to encompass more comprehensive programs to educate, inform, and empower citizens, to foster and mediate debate on public issues, to train candidates and local government officials, to advocate institutional reforms to improve democracy and transparency, to promote dialogue between citizens and public officials, and to monitor the performance of elected officials.[16]

Similarly, the Institute for Democracy in South Africa (IDASA) has expanded from its focus on voter education and general civic education before the April 1994 founding elections in South Africa to undertake a much broader range of activities, including a Parliamentary Information and Monitoring Service, a Budget Information Service, and a Public Opinion Service that collects, analyzes, and disseminates public opinion survey data on current public issues and perceptions of democratic performance. In this way, as it becomes more functionally complex and institutionalized, IDASA is not only growing in resources, staff, influence, and connectedness, it is also working on a greater variety of fronts, with growing technical sophistication, to improve the functioning of democratic institutions.[17]

As a country moves from the exigencies and drama of a transition struggle to the more prosaic challenges of governance, incorporation, enculturation, and service delivery, civil society organizations must often evolve and adapt if they are to remain relevant and viable.[18] The course of adaptation, however, is not necessarily an unmixed blessing, as it may risk taking the organization far from its original mission while compromising its autonomy from the state.

A fourth feature of civil society is pluralism. Of course, some degree of pluralism is necessary by definition for civil society: no organization that is civil can claim to represent all the interests of its members. Still, within various sectors and issue arenas, there is an obvious tension between strength of combined numbers and the vitality of diversity. On the one hand, to the extent that advocates of particular interests unify into a single organization or confederation possessing what Philippe Schmitter calls "strategic capacity" (to define and sustain a course of action independent of immediate member preferences, as well as outside pressures) and "encompassing scope" (in the domain of interests represented), they will be more powerful actors and will produce more stable "partial regimes" of interest mediation. Indeed, Schmitter argues that civil society contributes most positively to democratic consolidation not in pluralist systems, in which "a great multiplicity of narrowly specialized and overlapping organizations emerge with close dependencies upon their members or interlocutors," but in corporatist systems, in which interest associations with monopolistic scope in specific interest domains are nationally focused and hierarchically coordinated into sole peak associations, with clear capacities for "class governance."[19]

✓   No doubt, corporatist associations with broader memberships and a representational monopoly make for stronger interest intermediaries and more stable bargaining as well. But they also tend to be less democratic in their internal governance. Before long, independence from member preferences not only opens wider space for bargaining but also activates Michels' "iron law of oligarchy"—the tendency of organizational leaders to entrench themselves or their faction indefinitely in organizational power and become unaccountable to their members.[20] Apart from political parties, trade unions have been particularly vulnerable to this tendency (given the especially large gap between the time and resources of their members and those of the leaders), and the larger and more bureaucratic the scale of the organization the more vulnerable it is to an oligarchy of power at the top.[21] The value of corporatism for democratic consolidation is also rendered dubious by the fiscal strains and barriers to global competitiveness such bargaining relations have imposed on European economies, as a result of the benefits that have been extracted by labor and capital.

✓   Extreme pluralism, in which a great multiplicity of groups compete to represent the same narrow interests, can produce disempowering fragmentation. But that is not the only alternative to corporatism. Rather, having within each issue arena or interest sector at least some different organizational alternatives may generate greater pressure for organizations to be responsive and accountable to their constituencies, because those constituencies have other options to which they can turn for representation. In this sense, some degree of competition between organizations may be healthy and may be conducive to competition within organizations as well. To the extent that the norms and structures of a civic community emerge, such pluralism need not obstruct the ability of these different organizations to cooperate for common ends. Moreover, pluralism diffuses risk in any given interest sector: the decline or extinction of one organization as a result of leadership mismanagement or abuse, co-optation, or repression does not mean the end of effective organized representation for the interest.

✓ The fifth and final feature is density. Civil society serves democracy best when it is dense in the sheer number of associations. The greater the density of associational life, the more memberships the average citizen is likely to have, and the wider the range of societal interests and activities that will find organizational expression. The more associations in civil society, the more likely that associations will develop specialized agendas and purposes that do not seek to swallow the lives of their members in one all-compassing organizational framework. More generally, as Tocqueville so trenchantly recognized with respect to democracy in America, the disposition to form and join organizations seems to be a habit, a core feature of political culture. The density of voluntary associational life has three important spillover effects. First, the more there are, the more likely that people will develop the trust, confidence, and skill to cooperate to form new associations, when new needs arise. For this reason, Putnam treats the density of associational life as a key indicator of a civic community and the formation of social capital. This leads to the second spillover: the denser a country's associational life, the more democratic the political culture is likely to be in generating political knowledge, interest, efficacy, trust, and tolerance. Third, one reason why tolerance is greater in densely populated civil societies is because multiple memberships reflect and reinforce cross-cutting patterns of cleavage that expose citizens to a wider array of interests, backgrounds, and perspectives.

Civil Society and Democratic Transitions

✓ Civil society advances democracy in two generic ways: by helping to generate a transition from authoritarian rule to (at least) electoral democracy and by deepening and consolidating democracy once it is established. Because of the long-standing tendency in the scholarly literature to emphasize the primary role of elites in leading, crafting, negotiating (or imposing) democratic transitions, it is important to stress how crucial has been the role of "the public"—organized and mobilized through civil society—in many cases of third-wave democratization.

With the Southern European and Latin American transitions of the 1970s and early 1980s in mind, Guillermo O'Donnell and Philippe Schmitter advance a model based on the sweeping assertion that "there is no transition whose beginning is not the consequence—direct or indirect—of important divisions within the authoritarian regime itself, principally along the fluctuating cleavage between hard-liners and soft-liners."[22] "Once something has happened" along these lines (once the soft-liners in the regime have sufficiently prevailed to widen the space for independent political expression and activity), then citizenship is revived, civil society is resurrected, and a "general mobilization is likely to occur," or even to snowball into a "popular upsurge" that pushes "the transition further than it otherwise would have gone."

Although this sequential model has generally been considered valid for the Southern European and Latin American transitions, it is now being questioned even for those foundational cases. In Spain, Peru, and Argentina, Ruth Collier and James Mahoney argue that protests and strikes led by trade unions "were crucial in destabilizing authoritarianism and opening the way for democratization," fostering divisions among authoritarian incumbents and pressing them to surrender power in a "defensive extrication" when they had not yet "formulated a reform project." And where, as in Uruguay and Brazil, the transition games more closely approximated "the standard model" of elite initiation and strategic interactions between authoritarian and democratic party elites, mass popular opposition in general and labor protest in particular played a crucial role in undermining the "legitimation projects" of the two regimes and their "attempts to control and limit the party system."[23]

In fact, the elite-centered model of democratic transitions poorly comprehends the dynamics of many third-wave cases, in which either the sequence is turned on its head (and it is the mobilization and then the upsurge of civil society that generates divisions in the ruling regime) or the causal dynamics are more intricate and subtle (with the growth in civil society pluralism, autonomy, and resistance advancing incrementally and interactively with political liberalization from above and with shifting or intermittent regime divisions over the pace of that liberalization). In particular, when authoritarian rule has been highly personalistic and decadent (to the point of what Linz calls "sultanistic"[24] and others "neopat-

rimonial"), the real impetus for democratic change tends to originate
outside of the regime in the mobilization of civil society. This has been
the case in much of Africa. Elsewhere, rapid economic development has
generated a more complex class structure and diverse associations and
movements, which functioned somewhat independently to induce or
widen political opening from above in a reciprocal or dialectical process.
Thus, although Taiwan is often viewed as a paradigmatic case of controlled political opening from above by a strong and self-confident ruling party, the social movements and protests of the 1980s "translated
long-suppressed popular discontent into ardent social forces that eroded the effectiveness of one-party rule and softened the resolve of the state
elite to retain the authoritarian arrangements."[25]

In a number of prominent cases, civil society has played a crucial role,
if not the leading role, in producing a transition to democracy. It was only
the courageous mobilization of hundreds of thousands of citizens surg-
ing into the streets to reclaim their stolen election that enabled the rebellion of military reformers to survive in the Philippines and forced Fer-
dinand Marcos from power, in what came to be known as the Miracle at
Edsa. If civil society had not organized massively through the umbrella
organization, NAMFREL, to monitor those 1986 presidential elections,
they would never have been able to document to the world Marcos's massive electoral fraud and, thus, to rally U.S. and other international support to their cause.

A year later, in South Korea, enormous student and worker demonstrations combined with the more sober pressure of middle-class business and professional groups and opposition politicians to force the authoritarian regime to yield to demands for true democratic change
(signified by direct election of the president).[26] The petition campaign
of early 1987 demanding direct election (which gathered over a million
signatures) can be seen as a classic moment of civil society upsurge, in
which traditionally reserved or compliant middle-class groups and newspapers were emboldened to challenge the authoritarian regime and its
propaganda.[27] But by then authoritarian rule had been heavily stripped
of legitimacy not only by its own acts of repression but also by the mobilization of a civil society coalition of unprecedented breadth, including
not only student and labor organizations but peasants, writers, journalists, academics, and "most of the country's Buddhist, Protestant, and
Roman Catholic clergy and lay groups."[28] The breadth, vigor, and, moral
legitimacy of this mobilization, combined with the rapid expansion
of Korea's economy and international engagement (with the Olympics

headed for Seoul in 1988), all raised the costs of repression enormously. By April 1987, in the face of massive prodemocracy demonstrations, the authoritarian president, Chun Doo-Hwan, cut off negotiations over democratic reform and appeared ready to launch a wave of repression. It was during those spring months of peak civil society mobilization, with labor unrest and student demonstrations exploding in number and scale and public protest gathering support from a growing array of previously quiescent establishment groups, that the regime suffered its most serious split. On June 29, Chun's close associate and hand-picked presidential successor, Roh Tae Woo, broke ranks with the regime and embraced opposition demands for democratic reforms, paving the way for full participation in the December 1987 founding elections of a new Korean democracy.[29]

In Chile, the stunning defeat of the Pinochet dictatorship in the October 1988 plebiscite was achieved against enormous odds only by the heroic organization of a remarkably broad range of independent organizations that united in the Crusade for Citizen Participation. This case perhaps more closely follows the Schmitter–O'Donnell model, in that there were well-known divisions within the military regime of General Pinochet pitting his loyalists against soft-liners, but mass mobilization emerged only with the political liberalization of the plebiscite. In any case, it was a gamble that Pinochet did not expect to lose at the polls, and he would not have lost it (and Chile would not have democratized when it did) without unprecedented civic unity and mobilization. At the same time, the communist regime in Poland was crumbling as a result of a decade of independent organization and publishing, particularly through the broad trade union front, Solidarity. When the walls finally came crashing down around all the Eastern European communist regimes in 1989, many credited Soviet leader Mikhail Gorbachev for refusing to intervene, but the revolutionary ground had been forcefully tilled and regime legitimacy undermined by courageous networks of dissidents, autonomous groups, and underground publications that represented the reemergence of civil society.[30]

Spawned in the wreckage left by predatory and incompetent states, the catalyzing role of civil society mobilization against dictatorship has perhaps been most striking in Africa. In a wide range of countries in sub-Saharan Africa (including Benin, Cameroon, Nigeria, Niger, Ghana, Kenya, South Africa, Zambia, Zimbabwe, Malawi, and even Zaire), the initial impetus for democratic change emanated from a vast panoply of autonomous actors in civil society: students, churches, professional associations, women's groups, trade unions, human rights organizations, producer groups, intellectuals, journalists, civic associations, and informal networks.[31] In contrast to the O'Donnell–Schmitter model, in the African regime transitions of the early 1990s, "'the popular upsurge' preceded elite concessions and was an important factor driving African political leaders to open the door to liberalization."[32] Particularly crucial in leveraging protest into regime change was the formation of broad coalitions of civil society actors and of linkages between these various groups and powerful, resourceful international actors. Not since the struggle for decolonization in the 1950s and 1960s have Africans united so broadly across ethnic, regional, religious, sectoral, and occupational divides for a common—and not coincidentally, similar—purpose: political liberation. This coalitional breadth created not only opportunities to oust authoritarian regimes but also posttransition challenges and dilemmas.

Unfortunately, even very courageous and wide civil society (and political) mobilization does not always bring an end to authoritarian rule and a transition to democracy. When an authoritarian regime has internal unity, vastly superior resources, at least some measure of international support, and the capacity and will to use brutal repression, it may prevail indefinitely against even a very broad base of societal opposition. Such has been the tragedy of Burma, where the National League for Democracy (NLD) of Aung San Suu Kyi won most of the seats in the 1990 parliamentary elections, which the regime then annulled. Although the NLD was able to forge an ethnically broad resistance through the Democratic Alliance of Burma (DAB), it had to do so from exile, and resistance to the regime has been weakened by military pressure, the resurgence of religious and ethnic rivalries (fanned by the regime), and the lack of support from neighboring Asian states and from powerful Western states eager to do business with resource-rich Burma, no matter who governs.[33] A similar situation prevailed in Nigeria, where, following the annulment of the 1993 opposition electoral victory, ethnic and factional divisions within the democratic movement and international eagerness to mine and market the country's oil wealth left the military dictatorship firmly in control (until the dictator, Sani Abacha, suddenly died in mid-1998).[34]

What purpose is left to civil society in the wake of such apparent defeat? It is important to take a long-term, developmental perspective: even when authoritarianism resurges, civil society may continue to function, both through religious, professional, cultural, social, and human rights organizations (which may be monitored, subverted, and harassed but which are tolerated) and through covert means, such as underground media. In Nigeria, human rights organizations continued to research, publicize, expose, lobby, and organize, sometimes treading more carefully while still facing arrest and imprisonment. A pirate radio station broadcast news, information, and inspiration from the democratic movement with the support of Western democratic donors; and banned news magazines continued to be produced by plucky journalists who had to investigate, write, edit, publish, sleep, and eat in hiding, on the run. This and other civil society activity pressured the Nigerian military to withdraw from power. Throughout the authoritarian, war-torn, and pseudodemocratic states of Africa, civil society organizations and media struggle against great odds to keep democratic hope and principles alive, to counter the Orwellian propaganda of the regime, to raise the consciousness of society, to preserve some ethic of truthfulness and commitment to the public good, and to contain the worst abuses of the regime (in part by exposing and documenting them to the international community).

Such efforts, however quixotic they may appear at the time, till the soil for a new democratic transition at some point in the future. They limit the capacity of the authoritarian regime to legitimate and consolidate its rule and to browbeat the public into total resignation. Not least, in the most pervasively corrupt and abusive contexts (as in Burma, Nigeria, and Zaire), civil society organizations (both to resist authoritarianism and to cooperate for development apart from the state) preserve some kernel of civicness in the culture, some seeds of honesty, trust, solidarity, efficacy, and hope. Some such alternative to the prevailing corruption, cynicism, exploitation, and powerlessness is vital if a society is to have some chance of constructing democracy, not simply replacing one form of authoritarianism with another when the opportunity for regime change next presents itself.

A long-term, developmental view of democracy stresses the importance of systematic, grassroots efforts to build social capital and cultivate democratic networks, norms, and expectations. An important example of such an effort is the work of the Zimbabwean human rights organization, Zimrights, which not only engages in traditional human rights reporting and legal defense but also raises political consciousness and inculcates democratic habits through innovative civic education programs. Zimrights first gets people to talk about and portray the everyday shortcomings of gov-ernance and public life; then links those complaints to more systemic issues of human rights, accountability, citizen responsibility, and good governance; then sponsors the collective writing and staging of a community play. In a week in a community, Zimrights activists begin to lift the fog of civic apathy, resignation, and fear and to generate a public expectation and demand for real democracy. As the corruption and arrogance of the country's longtime ruling party deepens (following a life cycle strikingly similar to that of neighboring African states), Zimrights' grassroots work at civic education and mobilization is sowing the seeds for an eventual transition to democracy.[35]

Civil society faces the most trying circumstances in collapsed and war-ravaged states. Yet even here it may have the potential to make a positive, even dramatic, contribution. Religious, human rights, women's groups, student groups, trade unions, and other civic organizations for peace and reconciliation can play a crucial role in helping to provide a neutral framework for negotiation between warring parties and then helping to administer the process of political and societal reconstruction, including the rehabilitation and reintegration into society of former combatants. Such has been the case in Liberia, where hundreds of nongovernmental organizations (NGOs) have been operating amid the chaos of the civil war, providing job training, counseling, food, and medicine to ex-combatants.[36] In Chad, the civic organization Chad Non-Violence is working with other NGOs to teach principles of human rights, nonviolence, and peaceful conflict resolution to youth, women, and the military. Such groups may seem to provide a thin reed of hope in a society in which arms are plentiful, frustrations pervasive, and state elites abuse human rights. But a culture of peace and accommodation can only be developed gradually, and the work of civil society organizations is vital to this transformation.

How Civil Society Promotes Democratic Development and Consolidation

A vibrant civil society serves the development, deepening, and consolidation of democracy in many ways. The first and most basic democratic function of civil society is to provide "the basis for the limitation of state power, hence for the control of the state by society, and hence for democratic political institutions as the most effective means of exercising that control."[37] After the transition, this involves checking, monitoring, and restraining the exercise of power by formally democratic states and holding them accountable to the law and public expectations of responsible government. Few developments are more destructive to the legitimacy of new democracies than blatant and pervasive political corruption, particularly during periods of painful economic restructuring, when many social groups are being asked to sustain tremendous economic and social sacrifices. New democracies, following long periods of arbitrary and statist authoritarian rule, lack the legal and bureaucratic institutions to contain corruption at the outset. Without a vigorously free, independent, and investigative press, and civic groups pressing for institutional reform, corruption is likely to flourish, as it has in Brazil, Argentina, Turkey, Pakistan, Thailand, and most African and post-Soviet states.

The function of checking and limiting the power of the state overlaps with the civic function of institutionally reforming the state. A growing number of civic organizations are turning their agendas to the pursuit of reforms to deter and control political and bureaucratic corruption. But increasingly, as with IDASA in South Africa and the Evelio B. Javier Foundation in the Philippines, they are also monitoring the performance of government bodies and even assessing the performance of individual government ministers and representatives. Wider, freer, more open, and independent flows of information are the indispensable foundation for civil society checks against the abuse of state power. In this sense, specialized publications and journals that make the conduct of government affairs accessible to the more educated and informed public of opinion leaders, academics, associational officers, and the like play a crucial role in facilitating scrutiny and critical evaluation.

The mass media in general play a vital role. In a democracy, the abuse of power thrives behind a veil of secrecy and opaque procedures. Transparency is a precondition for accountability and reform (the most important anticorruption organization in the world has chosen the name Transparency International). Investigation and exposure does not guarantee popular reaction, punishment, disgrace, and deterrence, but it can facilitate it and galvanize a civil society into motion. The gathering public and civil society pressure to reform Mexico's political institutions and push the country past the threshold of real electoral democracy owes in part to the emergence of a press that has broken free of the historic chains of deference, dependence, co-optation, and corruption that made Mexican newspapers accomplices of the state and the ruling party. With the awakening of organized forces in civil society and the liberalization of the Mexican economy and polity, financially autonomous and politically independent newspapers have emerged to take on previously taboo subjects, such as drug trafficking, official corruption, electoral fraud, opposition protest, political repression, and the Mexican military.[38] At least, the struggle is now engaged and out in the open. A similar effect has been observable—within a much more democratic context—in South Korea, where growing press freedom, pluralism, and assertiveness has brought about much more frequent exposure of government corruption and a significantly lower threshold of public tolerance for it. This, in conjunction with the mobilization of civic organizations and the close cooperation between them and the independent press, helped produce reform laws to make banking and real estate transactions more transparent.[39]

The "checking and limiting" function of civil society is a particularly clear manifestation of the "reserve of influence" that organized citizens retain but only periodically exercise with vigor in the civic culture.[40] Monitoring is a constant task for the press and various civic, interest, and watchdog groups. But broad civic mobilization to contain or punish abuse occurs only in cases of serious abuse, where the institutions of "horizontal accountability" (the courts, audit and counter-corruption agencies, the central bank, and so on) are either implicated themselves or too weak and compromised to act on their own. The broad outpouring of press scrutiny and opinion and organizational mobilization against the corruption and illegal acts of Presidents Richard Nixon in the United States (in 1974), Fernando Collor de Mello in Brazil (in 1992), and Carlos Andres Pérez in Venezuela (in 1992–93) in each case induced the legislature to move toward impeachment, removing Pérez and prompting Collor and Nixon to resign in disgrace.

The sting of civil society readiness to criticize and mobilize over perceived abuse of state authority was repeatedly felt by President Kim Young Sam of Korea, who began as a popular political reformer but was increasingly forced to backtrack and humbly apologize in the face of public scandals and controversies during the latter half of his five-year term (1993–98). In a particularly momentous showdown, President Kim and his party were forced to back down in early 1997 after they passed new labor reform and national security laws in a secretive predawn meeting of the National Assembly with opposition party members absent. The actions triggered several weeks of labor strikes (the largest and costliest in the country's history), public demonstrations joined by tens of thousands of students, support from the church and other middle-class sympathizers, and vociferous condemnation from both the Korean and international press. What fueled the scope and intensity of public outrage was not so much the labor reform itself (the reform made it easier for business to lay off workers, which Korean organized labor had long opposed but which was badly needed to improve the Korean economy's sagging competitiveness). Rather, civil society was provoked by what it perceived as violations of democratic principle: the rushed and furtive manner in which the bill was passed; the deferral for five years of a parallel promised reform, sought by labor, that would have made it easier for unions to organize (by lifting the old corporatist prohibition on more than one union in an industry); and the passage during that secret session of other legislation, including a bill to give broad new investigative powers to the nation's intelligence agency.[41]

A second democracy-building function of civil society is to supplement the role of political parties in stimulating political participation, increasing the political efficacy and skill of democratic citizens, and promoting an appreciation of the obligations as well as rights of democratic citizenship. For too many Americans (barely half of whom vote in presidential elections), this seems merely a quaint homily. But for civil society leaders like Poland's Bronislaw Geremek, who risked everything in the struggle for democracy, "there is no greater threat to democracy than indifference and passivity on the part of citizens."[42] A century and a half ago, the voluntary participation of citizens in all manner of associations outside the state struck Tocqueville as a bedrock of democratic practice and culture, and of independent economic vitality, in the young United States. Voluntary "associations may therefore be considered as large free schools, where all the members of the community go to learn the general theory of association."[43] And in particular, voluntary participation in horizontal networks breeds the social capital that spawns wider participation and cooperation.

The generation of democratic habits and skills is not merely (or inevitably) a fortuitous by-product of associational activity. Civil society can also be a vital and intentional arena for inculcating not only the participatory habits, interests, and skills of democratic citizenship but also the deeper values of a democratic political culture, such as tolerance, moderation, a willingness to compromise, and a respect for opposing viewpoints. These values and norms become most stable when they emerge through intense practice, and organizational participation in civil society provides an important form of practice in political advocacy and contestation (particularly if authority relations within the organization are structured along horizontal rather than hierarchical, domineering lines). Beyond this, many civic organizations, such as Conciencia (a network of women's organizations that began in Argentina and has since spread to fourteen other Latin American countries), are working directly in the schools and among groups of adult citizens to cultivate democratic norms and values through interactive programs that demonstrate the dynamics of reaching consensus in a group, the possibility for respectful debate between competing viewpoints, and the means by which people can cooperate to solve the problems of their own communities.[44]

Third, more than ever before, education for democracy has become an explicit project of civil society organizations in new democracies and also an international cause. Beginning in 1996, with support from the United States Information Agency, regional and international networks under the rubric of CIVITAS have begun to meet and organize to share techniques, strategies, and curricula for democratic civic education, to be employed both in formal schooling at all grade levels and in a variety of informal civil society programs to socialize young people and adults and stimulate their active participation in community affairs.[45] Over the long run, this could lead to profound cultural changes, reshaping the way children are educated and relate to authority, the way they understand their country's political history, and their readiness to trust and cooperate with their peers.

Increasingly, civic organizations and state educational officials (as well as official multilateral donors, like the Inter-American Development Bank, and to some extent private enterprise) are cooperating in reforming curricula, training civics teachers, writing standards for teaching civics and government, and creating new instructional materials for teaching participatory democracy, economic citizenship, and human rights. This nicely demonstrates an essential point of this chapter: that if civil society is to help develop and consolidate democracy, its mission cannot simply be to check, criticize, and resist the state. It must also complement and improve the state and enhance its democratic legitimacy and effectiveness.

A fourth way in which civil society may serve democracy is by structuring multiple channels, beyond the political party, for articulating, aggregating, and representing interests. This function is particularly important for providing traditionally excluded groups, such as women and racial or ethnic minorities, access to power that has been denied them in the upper institutional echelons of formal politics. Even where (as in South America) women have played, through various movements and organizations, prominent roles in mobilizing against authoritarian rule, democratic politics and governance after the transition have typically reverted to previous exclusionary patterns. In Eastern Europe, there are many signs of deterioration in the political and social status of women after the transition. Only with sustained, organized pressure from below, in civil society, can political and social equality be advanced and thus the quality, responsiveness, and legitimacy of democracy be deepened.[46]

This points to a fifth, related way that civil society can deepen democracy: by effecting what Jonathan Fox calls a "transition from clientelism to citizenship" at the local level. Democratization inevitably proceeds unevenly, and "authoritarian enclaves" frequently persist most stubbornly at the local or provincial level, especially in rural and less developed areas of a country. In Mexico and Brazil, India and Pakistan, Thailand and the Philippines, Nigeria and Ghana, Turkey and Russia, the story is more or less the same. It is the local level that provides the anchor, the social foundation for national chains of patron-client relations. It is at the locality where lords, *caciques*, chiefs, and bosses purchase deference and control through the particularistic dispensation of material rewards. It is at the local level where the horizontal ties and autonomous participation of democratic citizenship are blocked by the vertical dependence of clientelism.[47] Just as horizontal relations of trust and reciprocity are the building blocks of the civic community, so the "vertical relations of authority and dependency, as embodied in patron-client networks," are the building blocks of the uncivic community.[48] The autonomous organization of historically marginalized and dependent people—landless laborers, indigenous peoples, women, the poor in general—represents a watershed in the struggle for democracy and social justice, for a society in which citizens can advance and defend "their own interests and identities without fear of external intervention and punishment."[49] At one and the same time it empowers the powerless to advance their interests and it severs the psychological and structural bonds of clientelism that have historically locked them in a dependent and subordinated status, isolated from one another and unable to rally around their common material or cultural interests.

As Fox emphasizes, the struggle for empowerment and citizenship at the local level is not smooth and pretty but dialectical and often violent, "constructed gradually and unevenly through cycles of conflict that leave nascent democratic forces with political resources to draw on in successive rounds."[50] That is why, as in India and Brazil, conflicts may intensify and human rights violations increase as newly conscious groups organize autonomously to assert their rights and deepen democracy. However, movements of the poor and marginal have two assets that were not nearly so widely available in previous eras: international media and political attention to their plights, which often constrains the state's ability to utilize or condone repression against them; and linkages to a growing array of international civil society organizations (concerned with human rights, indigenous rights, the rights of women and children, sustainable development, and the environment). The growing density of these transnational civil-society linkages (often completely skipping over the political level of the nation-state) has significantly strengthened the ability of marginalized groups to defend their cultures, identities, lands, environments, and human rights (and in extreme cases their very lives) against abuses by landlords, developers, miners, security forces, and other agents of state authority.[51] In India and elsewhere, these transnational linkages are effectively grinding to a halt the formidable momentum of the post–World War II period for the construction of large-scale dams.[52]

✓ Sixth, a rich and pluralistic civil society, particularly in a relatively developed economy, tends to generate a wide range of interests that may cross-cut, and so mitigate, the principal polarities of political conflict. As new class-based organizations and issue-oriented movements arise, they draw together new constituencies that cut across long-standing regional, religious, ethnic, or partisan cleavages. In toppling communist (and other) dictatorships and mobilizing for democracy, these new formations may generate a more liberal type of citizenship that transcends historic divisions and preempts the resurgence of narrow, ethnically exclusivist, nationalist impulses.[53] To the extent that individuals have multiple interests and join a wide variety of organizations to pursue and advance those interests, they are more likely to associate with people with divergent political interests and opinions. These attitudinal cross-pressures will tend to soften the militancy of their own views, generate a more expansive and sophisticated political outlook, and so encourage tolerance for differences and a greater readiness to compromise.[54]

✓ A seventh function of a democratic civil society is recruiting and training new political leaders. In a few cases, this is a deliberate purpose of civic organizations. As they grow beyond election monitoring and voter education, a number of civic organizations in new democracies conduct (typically with support from international foundations) training programs, on a nonpartisan basis, for local and state elected officials and candidates, emphasizing not only technical and administrative skills but also normative standards of public accountability and transparency.[55] More often, recruitment and training are merely a by-product of the successful functioning and engagement with the state of civil society organizations over a long period of time.

✓ Civil society leaders and activists acquire (through rising in the internal politics of their organization and through articulating and representing the interests of their members in public policy arenas) the leadership and advocacy skills (and self-confidence) that qualify them for service in government and party politics. They learn how to organize and motivate people, debate issues, raise and account for funds, craft budgets, publicize programs, administer staffs, canvass for support, negotiate agreements, and build coalitions. At the same time, their work on behalf of their constituency, or of what they see to be the public interest, and their articulation of clear and compelling policy alternatives may gain for them a wider political following. Interest groups, social movements, and community efforts may therefore train, toughen, and thrust into public notice a richer (and more representative) array of potential new political leaders than might otherwise be recruited by political parties. Because of the traditional dominance by men of the corridors of power, civil society is a particularly important base for the training and recruitment of women (and members of other marginalized groups) into positions of formal political power. When the recruitment of new political leaders within the established political parties has become narrow or stagnant, this function of civil society may play a crucial role in revitalizing democracy and renewing its legitimacy.

Eighth, many civic organizations, institutes, and foundations have explicit democracy-building purposes, beyond leadership training. Nonpartisan election-monitoring efforts have been critical to deterring fraud, enhancing confidence in the electoral process, affirming the legitimacy of the result, and (as in the case of the Philippines in 1986 and Panama in 1989) demonstrating an opposition victory despite government fraud. This function is particularly crucial in founding elections like those that initiated democracy in Chile, Nicaragua, Bulgaria, Zambia, and South Africa.[56] Democracy institutes and think tanks are working in a number of countries to reform the electoral system, democratize political parties, decentralize and open up government, strengthen the legislature, and enhance government accountability.[57] Even to stimulate debate on and awareness of institutional alternatives is an important contribution to the improvement of democracy.

Civil society organizations mobilize the broad public support and pressure that is vital to win the adoption of institutional reforms that may not be appealing to politicians as a group. One recent historic instance of this was the concerted public mobilization of the Citizen's Coalition for Economic Justice and other civic groups to reform Korea's banking and real estate registration laws so as to require that the real names of the transacting parties be recorded. An important legal tool in the battle against corruption, this reform was adopted by the new Kim Young Sam government soon after it came to power, in 1993, as a way of demonstrating its democratic commitment and reformist credentials. Human rights organizations also play a crucial role in democratic reform and deepening, even after the transition to formal democracy, lobbying for greater judicial efficiency and impartiality, improved prison conditions, justice for particular individuals, increased public awareness of human rights, and greater institutionalized respect for individual liberties and minority rights. In Taiwan, the independent Judicial Reform Foundation, with extensive participation from lawyers, law professors, and the bar association, is campaigning to improve the capacity, professionalism, efficiency, and transparency of the country's antiquated judicial system.

Ninth, a vigorous civil society widely disseminates information and so empowers citizens in the collective pursuit and defense of their interests and values. While civil society groups may sometimes prevail temporarily through the raw political power of their numbers (e.g., in strikes and demonstrations), they generally cannot be effective in contesting government policies or defending their interests unless they are well informed. This is strikingly true in debates over military and national security policy, in which civilians in developing countries have generally been lacking woefully in even the most elementary knowledge. An autonomous and pluralistic press is only one way of providing the public with news and alternative perspectives. Independent organizations may also provide citizens information about government activities that does not depend on what government says it is doing but rather on exhaustive and enterprising investigation. This is a vital technique of human rights organizations: By contradicting the official story, they make it more difficult to cover up repression and abuses of power.

The mobilization of new information and understanding are essential to the achievement of economic reform in a democracy, and this is a tenth function that civil society can play. While economic stabilization policies typically must be implemented quickly and forcefully by elected executives in crisis situations, without widespread consultation, more structural economic reforms, like privatization and trade and financial liberalization, appear to be more sustainable and far-reaching (or in many postcommunist countries, only feasible) when they are pursued through the democratic process.[58]

Successful economic reform requires the support of political coalitions in society and the legislature. These coalitions do not emerge spontaneously; they must be fashioned. Here, the problem is not so much the scale, autonomy, and resources of civil society as the distribution across interests. Old, established interests that stand to lose from reform tend to be well organized into, for example, state-sector trade unions and networks that tie the managers of state enterprises or owners of favored industries to ruling party bosses. These are precisely the interests that stand to lose from economic reforms that close down inefficient industries, reduce state intervention, and open the economy to greater domestic and international competition. Newly emergent and more diffuse interests that stand to gain from reform (for example, farmers, small-scale entrepreneurs, and consumers) tend to be weakly organized and poorly informed about how new policies will ultimately affect them. In Asia, Latin America, and Eastern Europe, new actors in civil society—economic policy think tanks, chambers of commerce, and economically literate journalists, commentators, and television producers—are beginning to overcome the barriers to information and organization, mobilizing support for (and neutralizing resistance to) reform policies.[59]

Eleventh, a growing number of civil society organizations (emanating especially from the religious and human rights communities) are developing techniques for conflict mediation and resolution and offering these services. Some of these efforts involve formal programs and training of trainers to relieve political and ethnic conflict and teach groups to solve their disputes through bargaining and accommodation. When a wide range of political actors come to trust these organizations—believing in their integrity, credibility, and political neutrality—the organizations gain a "reserve of influence" that can be drawn on in a political crisis. This was the case in the Central African Republic, where the Ligue Centrafricaine des Droits de l'Homme (LCDH) played a crucial mediating rule during two army uprisings in 1996. During the first mutiny, in April 1996 (which claimed at least ten lives), Ligue officials played the chief mediating role between the mutineers and the government, drafting the protocols to provide the soldiers their back pay "and ultimately persuading the soldiers to lay down their arms." The subsequent military coup attempt (May 18–28) threatened not only democracy but even civil war with its ethnic overtones, internal military divisions, distribution of arms, demands for the resignation of the president, looting, and terrorizing of the civilian population. Although this uprising was ultimately put down by French military intervention, its political resolution, which saw the society rally behind democracy, was catalyzed by the Ligue's declared support for the regime and its mediation of negotiations between government and opposition forces within the political arena as well as between the regime and the military rebels. The Ligue drafted and won acceptance for "the political accord, including amnesty, disarmament, and resignation of the head of the army, that actually resolved the crisis." The ability of the Ligue to perform this democracy-saving role owed to the "consistent neutrality and objectivity" and widespread image of "moral credibility" it had established during the country's previous five years of democratic struggle.[60]

Twelfth, a vigorous civil society can strengthen the social foundations of democracy even when its activities focus on community development and have no explicit connection to or concern with political democracy per se. Effective grassroots development efforts may relieve the burden of expectations fixed on the state and so relieve the intensity of politics. At the same time, they build social capital by bringing citizens together to cooperate as peers for their common advancement. A particularly noteworthy example of this is the general phenomenon of microenterprise lending and the specific success of the Grameen Bank in Bangladesh. The bank lends money in small amounts to two million poor people in Bangladesh to enable them to start small enterprises (farming, livestock raising, food processing, petty trade, and so on). By dispersing access to capital that has typically been monopolized by rural elites, the bank is not only fighting poverty but undermining the deeply entrenched dependence of the rural poor on local elites for credit, wages, and agricultural inputs. At the same time that it weakens vertical chains of clientage, it builds new horizontal solidarities by using peer monitoring to substitute for the physical and monetary collateral that the poor cannot provide. In this peer system, poverty-stricken loan recipients are organized into groups of five, "and any unpaid loans become the responsibility of the whole group." That such an institutional innovation can change lives and build social capital is attested to by the exceptional loan-recovery rate of the bank—98 percent.[61]

A final, overarching function of civil society derives from the success of the above twelve. "Freedom of association," Tocqueville mused, may, "after having agitated society for some time . . . strengthen the state in the end."[62] By enhancing the accountability, responsiveness, inclusiveness, effectiveness, and hence legitimacy of the political system, a vigorous civil society gives citizens respect for the state and positive engagement with it. In the end, this improves the ability of the state to govern and to command voluntary obedience from its citizens. In addition, "by bringing people together in endless combinations for a great diversity of purposes, a rich associational life may not only multiply demands on the state, it may also multiply the capacities of groups to improve their own welfare, independently of the state, especially at the local level."[63]

Dilemmas and Caveats

To the above list of democratic functions of civil society I attach some dilemmas and caveats. To begin with, associations and mass media can only perform their democracy-building roles if they have autonomy in their financing, operations, and legal standing. Democracies vary in the degree to which they structure interest representation on pluralist as opposed to corporatist lines. However, while corporatist-style pacts or contracts between the state and peak interest associations may make for stable macroeconomic management, corporatist arrangements pose a serious threat to democracy in transitional or newly emerging constitutional regimes. The risk appears greatest in countries with a history of authoritarian state corporatism, such as Mexico, Egypt, and Indonesia, where the state has created, organized, licensed, funded, subordinated, and controlled "interest" groups (and also most of the mass media that it does not officially own and control), with a view to co-optation, repression, and domination rather than to ordered bargaining.

By contrast, the transition to a democratic form of corporatism "seems to depend very much on a liberal-pluralist past," which most developing and postcommunist states lack.[64] Limited economic development, or the absence of a fully functioning market economy, further increases the danger that corporatism will stifle civil society, even under a formally democratic framework, because there are fewer autonomous resources and less interest pluralism in society. Even in countries that have vigorous market economies and now rate as liberal democracies, like South Korea and Taiwan, the state corporatist legacy casts a neoauthoritarian shadow over the structure of interest representation. Experience teaches that state corporatist structures and rules must be completely dismantled if a fully democratic system is to be constructed. Only after that dismantling, on wholly new foundations, is a *democratic* corporatist pattern of interest representation likely to be feasible (if it is even preferred).

By co-opting, preempting, or constraining the most serious sources of potential challenge to its domination (and thus minimizing the amount of repression that has to be employed), state corporatist regimes may purchase a longer lease on authoritarian life. However, such regimes eventually come under pressure from social, economic, and demographic forces.

Socioeconomic development, as in Mexico and Indonesia, produces a profusion of authentic civil society groups that demand political freedom and autonomy, protected by law—especially when economic crisis hits. Social and economic decay, along with massive political corruption, weaken the hold of the authoritarian corporatist state, undermine the legitimacy of its sponsored associations, and may give rise to revolutionary movements, like the Islamic fundamentalist movements in Egypt and Algeria, that promise popular redemption through a new form of state hegemony.

Societal autonomy can go too far, however, even for the purposes of democracy. This is a second caveat. A hyperactive, confrontational, and relentlessly rent-seeking civil society can overwhelm a weak, penetrated state with the diversity and magnitude of its demands, saddling the state with unsustainable and inflationary fiscal obligations and leaving little in the way of a truly public sector that is concerned for the overall welfare of society. The state itself must have sufficient autonomy, legitimacy, capacity, and support to mediate among the various interest groups, to implement policies, and to allocate resources in ways that balance the claims of competing groups against one another and against the interests of society as a whole. This is a particularly pressing dilemma for new democracies that seek to implement much-needed economic reform programs in the face of stiff opposition from trade unions, pensioners, and the state-protected bourgeoisie, which is why countervailing forces in civil society must be educated and mobilized.

In many new democracies emerging out of long periods of totalitarian, highly repressive, or abusive rule, there is a deeper problem, stemming from the orientation of civil society as movements of resistance to the state or disengagement from its authority. As Geremek observes, this revives the original eighteenth-century conception of civil society as *in opposition* to the state.[65] When authoritarian rule is arbitrary, lawless, and exploitative, social mobilization against it tends to be not merely risky but even lawless, angry, and anomic, or in Putnam's term, "uncivic." The legacy in much of Africa is what Célestin Monga calls a civic deficit. "Thirty years of authoritarian rule have forged a concept of indiscipline as a method of popular resistance. In order to survive and resist laws and rules judged to be antiquated, people have had to resort to the treasury of their imagination. Given that life is one long fight against the state, the collective imagination has gradually conspired to craftily defy everything which symbolizes public authority."[66]

In many respects, a similar broad cynicism, indiscipline, and alienation from state authority—indeed from politics altogether—was bred by decades of communist rule in Eastern Europe and the former Soviet Union, though it led to somewhat different (and in Poland, much more broadly organized) forms of dissidence and resistance. Some countries, like Poland, Hungary, the Czech Republic, and the Baltic states, had previous civic traditions that could be recovered. These countries have generally made the most progress (though still quite partial) toward reconstructing state authority on a democratic foundation while beginning to constitute a modern, liberal-pluralist civil society. Those states in which civic traditions were weakest and predatory rule greatest—Romania, Albania, Russia, the Central Asian republics, and most of sub-Saharan Africa—face a far more difficult time, with independent organized life still fragmented and emergent market economies still heavily outside the framework of law—and thus "uncivil."[67]

This civic deficit constitutes a third major caveat with respect to the positive value of civil society for democracy. Civil society must be independent from the state but not alienated from it. It must be watchful but respectful of state authority; it must manifest balance between the subject and participant orientations. The image of a noble, vigilant, organized civil society checking at every turn the predations of a self-serving state, preserving a pure detachment from its corrupting embrace, is highly romanticized and misleading; it does not contribute to the construction of a viable democracy.

A fourth caveat or dilemma concerns a different and growing type of dependence—not on the state but on the international community. The character and possibilities of civil society mobilization in nascent democracies and less developed countries have been transformed in the past few decades by three dramatic changes in the world system: the rapid growth of transnational linkages among civil society organizations from different countries, the emergence of truly international movements and organizations (such as Amnesty International, Transparency International, Survival International, the World Council of Churches, and the World Council of Indigenous Peoples), and the explosion of democracy assistance programs in the wealthier democracies.[68] From the international environment, civil society organizations have drawn ideas, inspiration, skills, and most of all funding. This has facilitated activity on a scale that would otherwise have been unimaginable in poorer countries, where resources in the private sector are scarce or are controlled by authoritarian elites, or where (as in most of Latin America) there simply is not a tradition of large-scale private philanthropy for civic purposes. In many less developed countries, a number of civil society organizations have sprung into being because international funding was available.

✓   International support is enabling, but it also imposes, actively or passively, an agenda of its own. At one level, there is a philosophical or conceptual problem: to what extent are today's nongovernmental organizations in less developed countries self-generating, given that they are so heavily reliant on support from abroad? It depends. Some NGOs really are creatures of international support and have at best a thin base of indigenous initiative, support, and organization. This does not mean that they do not do valuable work for democracy and development (this varies widely), but it may call into question the extent to which they are truly civil society actors *of* their own country.[69] Other NGOs are no less heavily dependent on international funding but have a broad base of participation and a consciousness and an agenda that are clearly self-generated. And there are many collective actors who inhabit a gray zone in between. To some extent, this is a dilemma or challenge for international civil society: to carefully evaluate applicants for funding to determine what base they have in their own society and whom they represent (if, really, anybody beyond themselves).

✓   Representation is another horn of the international dilemma. Popular constituencies may be organized by a variety of groups, which then compete to speak for the entire constituency on the international stage (and to receive international funding to advance its cause domestically). International organizations sometimes also compete for influence on the ground (even out of good intentions). These forms of competition may foster healthy pluralism in interest representation, or they may unwittingly heighten a divisiveness that disperses scare human resources and weakens the voice and impact of the movement.

✓   The question of voice can be particularly crucial. Effective transnational linkages require the ability to communicate with sophisticated interlocutors and funders in the developed world. But the more representative social movement leaders are of marginalized and oppressed peoples, the less effectively they may be able to present their cause to the outside world. The poignancy of this dilemma, which has also fanned division in the movements of indigenous peoples, has been captured by Alison Brysk: "Those with the skills to lead internationally may be the least 'representative': for example, one extremely effective Indian leader encountered at the UN Working Group [on Indigenous Peoples] was a law student, another was a former congressional representative in his country, and a third was one of his people's eight college graduates. Conversely, one of the few truly grassroots delegates at the UN [meeting]—an Andean peasant woman—was ultimately unable to deliver her prepared statement."[70]

Beyond all questions of organizational authenticity, legitimacy, and voice, there is the simple existential problem of surviving in the face of changing international funding priorities and diminishing assistance budgets. In a context in which the state is manifestly repressive and unrepresentative, development assistance increasingly gravitates to NGOs as vehicles for raising human capacities (economic and political) and improving the quality of life. As authoritarian rule liberalizes to allow more space for civil society, more international donor funding is channeled to NGOs. And then, at that historic moment when the transition is clearly "on," when voters must be educated and trainers and monitors mobilized on a crash basis, the channels of funding swell into a mighty river. Participation in civil society (separate and apart from party politics) rises, and the civic quest to build democracy reaches new heights. Then the transition happens and the bubble bursts. Some international donors move on to political dramas in other countries, while many transfer their attention and investment to the (now presumably legitimate) governmental agencies of the new democracy.

This cycle of international enthusiasm for civil society has two major consequences. For a great many NGOs, it means extinction. For others, it means a growing dependence on agencies of the state as the primary alternative source of funding. The posttransition recession of civil society has greatly concerned democratic activists and thinkers in South Africa, where human rights and developmental NGOs and more loosely structured, grassroots "community-based organizations" (CBOs) proliferated in the later years of the antiapartheid struggle with the dramatic expansion of international donor support.

> Immediately preceding the April 1994 [founding] elections, the sector was probably at its peak, with approximately 54,000 NGOs and CBOs, of which about 20,000 could be considered to be development-oriented. These organizations provided a broad range of services, from educational support and training (particularly for blacks) to rural development and media services; many were involved in the promotion of human rights. Since the elections, a significant number of NGOs, including many that had existed for a long time, have closed or drastically curtailed their operations.[71]

And many others fell into dire financial straits. As Wilmot James and Daria Caliguire note, it is natural that a legitimate government, more concerned with real and equitable development, will become more active in service delivery after the transition. But the legitimacy, networks, expertise, and experience of NGOs make them important intermediaries and partners in this task, and in any case, the need for effective organization and representation of a myriad of grassroots interests does not cease with the transition to democracy. Moreover, in many former statist and communist systems, the posttransitional shrinkage of civil society is also apparent, even though economic reforms often shrink the state's involvement in delivering social services.

Domestic political dynamics, flowing from what seems to be an internal life cycle of many democratic transitions, also weaken civil society. Once the authoritarian regime disappears, the focus of political life shifts from a unifying struggle against an odious enemy to a much more dispersed and normal competition among parties and interests in the emerging democratic state. Inevitably, civil society and especially democratizing and single-issue social movements lose their primacy. Political parties and more conventional interest groups take center stage, and many individuals and groups turn to more "private-regarding" concerns as "the mere advent of democracy satisfies some of the most passionate revindications of movements."[72] The euphoria of the immediate posttransition period quickly wanes, and the broad associational fronts that struggled against authoritarian rule break apart.

"What had been 'moral political societies' became political blocs" in Europe's postcommunist states, and in Africa as well.[73] Class and ethnic divisions once again fragmented society, and the leadership ranks (and thus operational capacities) of civil society organizations were rapidly depleted as activists were massively drawn into politics, government, and (in Europe) business. The social inheritances of communism in Europe and neopatrimonial statism in Africa also reasserted themselves in renewed state dependence, co-optation, mistrust, and societal atomization, revealing the scarcity of social capital and "the lack of a culture of a free collective activity."[74] In fact, preliberal, illiberal, and uncivic cultural orientations constitute a major obstacle to democratic consolidation in much of Africa and the postcommunist world. In both regions as well, civil society has been further hampered after the transition by the harsh economic conditions of the 1990s, which have driven people to more urgent preoccupations with the exigencies of daily survival and have rendered African associations much more vulnerable to the compromising blandishments of domineering states.

Many of those NGOs that did not die after the transition have had to adapt their mission fairly dramatically in order to continue to function on anything like their existing scale. Adaptation is a dimension of institutionalization and can be a healthy phenomenon: after some period, voter education becomes a less compelling priority and the autonomous public procedures for free and fair elections may become institutionalized. At that point, civil society organizations need to tackle other challenges to deepen democracy. But where adaptation diminishes autonomy, shrinks the grassroots base, and dilutes the democratic zeal of the organization, it comes at a price.

Chile is another instance of a civil society that had an intense romance with the international donor community and then was jilted after the transition. For international donors with limited and even declining budgets, the impulse to withdraw is even more powerful in upper-middle-income countries like Chile, because the assumption is that political repression is the main obstacle to a vibrant civil society, and once the lid of authoritarianism is lifted the country ought to be rich enough to support its own NGOs. The problem in such countries (including, prominently, Argentina) is that they are weak in the social capital and public-spiritedness which enable civil society organizations to raise substantial funds from the private sectors of their own countries. Moreover, many of the most important NGOs represent women, youth, informal workers, the poor, ethnic minorities, and others who tend to lack the material resources to sustain collective organization on a large scale. Thus, NGOs often turn to the state to survive.

Chile's PARTICIPA evolved from a focus on citizenship education and participation to a wider range of strategic goals concerned with youth, local development, social integration, and public sector training. When international funding for these programs (primarily from the U.S. Agency for International Development) dried up, PARTICIPA began to secure contracts from its own government to continue these efforts. Now, "PARTICIPA's role as an implementing agent of government policy may limit its role as a critic of those policies. Time will tell whether the survival of the institution alters its role as an independent agent of social change."[75] As major international funding dries up for civil society organizations in South Africa, they face a similar dilemma. Many are already evolving in a similar direction, with possibly greater dangers to autonomy given the proclivity to corporatist relations of both government and many civil society leaders, and given as well the constraining hangover of "repressive policies, laws, and structures inherited from the old regime."[76]

There is no easy answer for this dilemma of international dependence. My own view is that civil society organizations are likely to have more space to act independently and define their own agendas when their financial dependence is on foreign donors rather than their own government, especially when that international dependence is dispersed among a number of donors (public and private) from many countries. In that case, no established democracy or donor organization is in a position to dictate an agenda, and the loss of one large grant does not threaten the survival of the organization. For that reason—and because NGOs in most developing and postcommunist countries are unlikely to be able to raise from their own societies the funding they need to perform the democracy-building functions they are capable of performing on the scale of which they are capable—international donor priorities and strategies need to be rethought. In some cases, even modest grants from prestigious international foundations can give NGOs the credibility and leverage they need to raise greater funding from corporations and foundations in their own society. (This is a strategy that the Taiwan Association for Human Rights is now pursuing.) Relative to the massive aid that flows to government programs and agencies, international donor funding for civil society is a small trickle. A modest shift in the balance between state and civil society, coupled with a reconsidered willingness to remain engaged longer with the civil societies of some more advanced developing countries, could make possible substantial continuing investments in building the civic infrastructure of democracy.

Without question, civil society makes its deepest, most organic, and most sustainable contribution to democracy when it cultivates a significant base of financial support among a broad and indigenous constituency. Beyond the greater autonomy it confers, this is true for two additional reasons. When members give money voluntarily to an organization, they are more likely to feel identity with it and ownership of it. Ironically, perhaps, this is particularly true for members of modest means, who are able to give only small amounts (as opposed to upper-middle-class Americans who write checks to dozens of organizations a year). When such financial donations are combined with broad grassroots organization and participation, they are likely to produce a particularly strong membership commitment and demand for democratic control. This is why a mass-membership campaign is a shrewd long-run tactic for organizational development.

In the case of the Zimbabwean human rights organization, Zim-rights, the annual dues of thousands of members account for only a small portion of the total budget, but they generate a widely dispersed base of committed supporters.[77] Beyond the depth of commitment that is generated, raising indigenous financial contributions creates cultural norms of cooperation, trust, reciprocity, and public-spiritedness; it generates social as well as financial capital. This is why international support for civil society organizations should increasingly focus on strategies to encourage and institutionalize this giving. Matching funding provides one potential method: if an NGO can honestly say it will receive ten dollars in international support for every dollar it raises locally, that sharply increases the incentive of the organization to raise locally and of local donors to give. (It also increases the efficacy of small donors, who see their contributions multiplied.) Another method is building endowments (in part with matching or challenge grants) for the most pivotal democracy-building civil society organizations by motivating and assisting owners of great private wealth to create, contribute to, or develop philanthropic trusts as an enduring legacy for their society. Efforts by the Ford Foundation and the Asia Foundation to strengthen and professionalize private philanthropy in emerging democracies constitute one of the most significant and potentially long-lasting forms of aid to civil societies.

Institutionalization raises a fifth dilemma or caveat for civil society. A social or political movement is only sustainable with organization. Organization means, to some extent, bureaucratization: the development of a complex vertical structure and the hiring of a permanent and professional staff. This returns us to Michels' dilemma: "Who says organization says oligarchy."[78] This dimension of the organizational life cycle parallels and interacts with the diminution of autonomy. Again, the evolution of Chile's PARTICIPA provides a graphic illustration. "Once PARTICIPA became an institution, questions of membership and control became important issues. As is usually the case when volunteer movements become institutionalized, a certain tension developed between the role of the professionals and the volunteers, which in the case of PARTICIPA has been resolved through the professionalization of the organization."[79] This has led to a distinctly less mass-based organization, utilizing fewer volunteers.

A sixth caveat concerns the role of politics. Interest groups and civic organizations cannot substitute for coherent political parties with broad and relatively enduring bases of popular support, for interest groups cannot aggregate interests as broadly across social groups and political issues as political parties can. Nor can they provide the discipline necessary to form and maintain governments and pass legislation. In this respect (and not only this one), one may question the thesis that a strong civil society is strictly complementary to the political and state structures of democracy. To the extent that interest groups dominate, enervate, or crowd out political parties as conveyors and aggregators of interests, they can present a problem for democratic consolidation. And in an age when the electronic media, increased mobility, and the profusion and fragmentation of discrete interests are all undermining the organizational bases for strong parties and party systems, this is something democrats everywhere need to worry about.[80]

✓   In fact, a stronger and broader generalization appears warranted: the single most important and urgent factor in the consolidation of democracy is not civil society but political institutionalization. If consolidation is the process by which democracy becomes the only game in town, broadly and profoundly legitimate at both the elite and mass levels, cultural change is crucial. But it must be reinforced by a political system that works to deliver the political goods of democracy and, eventually, the economic and social goods people expect, as well. The normalization of politics and entrenchment of legitimacy that consolidation entails requires the expansion of citizen access, the development of democratic citizenship and culture, the broadening of leadership recruitment and training, and other functions that civil society performs. But it also requires orderly and effective democratic governance, and that is something that civil society cannot in and of itself provide. Political institutions (parties, legislatures, judicial systems, local governments, and the bureaucratic structures of the state more generally) must become more capable, complex, coherent, and responsive.

✓   Despite their impressive capacity to survive years (even decades) of social strife and economic instability and decline, many new democracies in Latin America, Eastern Europe, Asia, and Africa will probably break down in the medium to long run unless they can reduce their often appalling levels of poverty, inequality, and social injustice and, through market-oriented reforms, lay the basis for sustainable growth. For these and other policy challenges, strong parties and effective state institutions are vital. They do not guarantee wise and effective policies, but they do ensure that government will make and implement policies of some kind and not flail about, impotent or deadlocked.

✓   These caveats and dilemmas are sobering, but they do not nullify my principal thesis. Civil society can, and typically must, play a central role in building and consolidating democracy. Its role is not decisive, not even the most important, at least not initially. However, the more active, pluralistic, resourceful, institutionalized, and internally democratic civil society is, and the more effectively it balances the tensions in its relations with the state (between autonomy and cooperation, vigilance and loyalty, skepticism and trust, assertiveness and civility), the more likely democracy will be to emerge and endure.

7

A Fourth Wave?

As the previous chapters have shown, the third wave of democratization has drawn to a halt, and the key challenge in the coming years will be to prevent a third reverse wave of democratic breakdowns. That is why democratic consolidation forms the central concern of this book. But what about the longer term? Will there be a fourth wave of democratization? If so, when and why?

The very breadth of the third wave may, ironically, suggest gloomy prospects for a fourth. Almost all of the countries that had favorable economic, social, and cultural conditions for democracy have democratized. Most of those countries that did not democratize do not seem promising candidates for democratic transition in the next decade or two. In several of the most repressive countries in the world, particularly Iraq, Syria, Libya, North Korea, and Cuba, even modest political liberalization will probably require the death or overthrow of the long-ruling tyrant or clique. Aside from Kuwait, the oil-rich monarchies of the Persian Gulf, led by Saudi Arabia, have so far shown little appetite for any kind of political opening.

For most of the fifty-three "not free" states, the prospects for democratization appear bleak for some time to come. As Freedom House noted in its report on 1994, forty-nine of these states share one or more of the following three characteristics:

— They have a majority Muslim population and often strong Islamic fundamentalist pressures.
— They have deep ethnic divisions without a single, dominant ethnic group (that has over two-thirds of the population).
— They have neocommunist or postcommunist regimes with a strong hangover of diffuse, one-party domination.[1]

Many of these countries have two (a few have three) of these characteristics. In addition, the "not free" states are disproportionately poor (twenty of them are classified as low-income by the World Bank). Poverty in itself does not preclude democratic development, but it does significantly shorten the average life expectancy of a democracy, especially in the absence of sustained economic growth.[2] When it is combined with one or more of the other conditions above, it greatly diminishes the democratic prospect.

However, no calculus of regime futures should dismiss the possibility for surprise. Few foresaw the collapse of Soviet and East European communist regimes, and the rise of democracy in Russia in particular. Not many Asia specialists were predicting in the mid-1990s that General Suharto would be ignominiously toppled from power. Few were the Africanists in 1990 anticipating an imminent "second liberation." Many democratic transitions during the third wave figured to happen sooner or later, when dictators died, military rulers exhausted the patience of previously democratic societies, or international backing for authoritarian rule peeled away. But others were simply unexpected.

A number of the most repressive regimes in the world are brittle. If a broad domestic crisis grips the economy or society, and if international support or tolerance erodes, they are vulnerable to collapse. When Indonesian President Suharto celebrated the thirtieth anniversary of his rule in March 1996, he seemed "secure in his control," the regime looked "solid and highly efficient," and the country appeared further away from democracy than it had been just a few years before.[3] Barely two years later, popular protests resulting from a devastating financial crisis forced Suharto to resign and his chosen successor to pledge new, democratic elections. Burma and Nigeria have articulate democratic movements with passionate support in their societies, and some combination of domestic mobilization, internal divisions in the regime, and international pressure could trigger democratic change. The sudden death in June 1998 of Nigerian military dictator Sani Abacha (who had already been nominated as the presidential candidate of all five political parties in a pseudotransition) opened possibilities for a more authentic transition to civilian, democratic rule. Authoritarian regimes in Kenya and Cameroon were thrown on the defensive and nearly toppled by domestic and international pressure in the early 1990s. They will face new and serious challenges again at some point in the years ahead.

Even with the growth of comparative research, statistical methods, and country-specific expertise, we cannot confidently predict where and when a combination of unforeseen events, regime divisions, and popular protest might open a game of democratic transition. The element of surprise thus justifies some broad distribution of democracy promotion efforts, so that repression is condemned, democratic opposition is encouraged, and foundations for pluralism are fostered in as many non-democracies as possible. This increases the odds that authoritarian regime crises will lead to democracy when they do emerge unexpectedly. In addition, international pressure for democracy and human rights will be more credible and effective to the extent that it has some consistency across different regional and political circumstances.

Still, most democracy promotion efforts directed at today's authoritarian regimes will at best till the soil for longer-term political change. Their strategic aim should be to help gradually lay the foundations for market economies, constrained centers of power, rules of law, more resourceful civil societies, and the incremental development of competitive electoral processes. For countries (like China) in which economic growth promises to produce better educated, more informed, diverse, and assertive societies in the coming generation, what Minxin Pei terms "creeping democratization" seems a realistic prospect and a compelling rationale for long-term engagement by the established, wealthy democracies.[4]

In fact, the "long term" may not be that long. Assuming that China and Indonesia sustain relatively high growth rates in per capita income (averaging 4.5% annually), Henry Rowen projects that, by 2020, they will have per capita incomes (in 1990 dollars, expressed in purchasing power parity, or PPP) of $6,600 and $8,800, respectively.[5] These income levels lie in the middle to upper-middle reaches of economic development, which Samuel Huntington has identified as the characteristic "zone" for democratic transitions in the third wave.[6] According to Rowen, Taiwan, South Korea, Spain, Portugal, Chile, and Argentina "all made the democratic transition in this range" of $5,000 to $7,000 in per capita income.[7] In fact, $7,000 (in 1990 PPP dollars) is roughly equivalent to the threshold at which Adam Przeworski and his colleagues argue that (based on the 1950–90 experience of regime change) "democracies are impregnable and can be expected to live forever."[8]

Of course, predicting the future can be a dangerous business. The outbreak in late 1997 of the East Asian financial crisis has underscored how tenuous linear projections of past performance can be. By mid-1998, Indonesia's currency, per capita income, and financial institutions had suffered such staggering declines that projections even for long-term development had to be sharply reconsidered. Yet the collapse of the Indonesian miracle, combined with long-standing public frustration over massive corruption and nepotism, only accelerated pressures for democratization. Skeptics were predicting economic troubles for China as well, which could have a similar effect in undermining the stability of Communist Party rule. If popular and intellectual mobilization for democratization did erupt in China, it is not clear whether the regime would respond with liberalization or with the kind of brutal crackdown it launched on the Tiananmen protests in 1989.

China's Democratic Prospects

All that can be said in confidence now is that China is starting to liberalize politically as it crosses the threshold of $2,500 per capita income.[9] This was the same income level at which political opening and pluralization began to gather momentum in Taiwan in the early 1970s.[10] In a loose parallel to Taiwan, a key early element of political change lies in the increasing autonomy of local-level authority and the introduction of at least partially competitive and free elections for local governing bodies at the village level. Although competitive elections for village head and committee are now in place for probably no more than a third of China's nearly one million villages, the process has been mandated by national law for more than a decade, and some villages have now experienced four rounds of such contests. In some regions the nomination process is becoming distinctly fairer and more open, and the procedures and values of a secret-ballot election, with political competition and choice, appear to be improving and taking root. Gradually, authority relations at the micro level are being transformed, and the Communist Party monopoly on village administration is loosening. China's central government is actively working to improve and standardize competitive village elections—and even seeking international assistance in the process—for the same reason it initiated them in 1987: it needs this democratic vehicle to control corruption, channel peasant frustrations, generate greater efficiency and legitimacy at the local level, and thus maintain political stability.[11]

Political decompression in China has other dimensions as well. Modest competition has been introduced for election to the party congress. The National People's Congress and especially some provincial and local people's congresses are evolving from rubber stamps into more autonomous, professional, and inquisitive bodies, and delegates at all levels are pressing for further reform. The decentralization of economic and political responsibility to provincial and lower-level governments is giving rise to a "nascent federalist structure." Rule is becoming more institutionalized, less personalized, with the enforcement of mandatory retirement ages and two-term limits on officials. A "system of law" is beginning to emerge, partly through a law on administrative litigation (implemented in 1990) that enables citizens to sue government agencies and officials for abuse of state power. By the mid-1990s, the number of lawsuits continued to rise, and more than a third led to relief for the plaintiffs, either through a favorable court decision or through an out-of-court settlement.

Chinese citizens are becoming more aware of their political and economic rights and more assertive in defending them. This is due in part to economic reform and development—which are breeding other changes in state-society relations—and to limits to central state power. Access to independent information is expanding, and so is the number of semiofficial and private (as opposed to state or party-controlled) associations—such as those of lawyers, private entrepreneurs, consumers, and environmentalists—that are "civic" in their concerns to articulate interests and affect public policy as well as in their creation of social capital through the horizontal organization of individuals as self-motivated citizens. Finally, "in the 1990s, China's elite political culture has begun to change. Democracy has begun to be enshrined as an ultimate goal for China."[12]

To be sure, China remains an authoritarian, one-party state with strong corporatist controls over civil society and appalling human rights violations.[13] The current shift involves only a partial and tentative opening, a transition from totalitarianism to some form of what Robert Scalapino calls "authoritarian pluralism," in which one-party rule and constraints on liberty coexist with certain institutional limits on arbitrary authority and some space for independent organization, initiative, and thought.[14] Most observers do not think the trends and challenges will lead to the democratization of China any time soon.[15] But sooner or later, economic development will generate growing pressures (and possibilities) for China to make a more definitive regime change, to democracy.

In China (as in Taiwan and Korea and before that most classically in Spain), economic development is creating a more complex, pluralistic, self-confident, resourceful society, which cannot be managed with the old patterns of monolithic and highly repressive and arbitrary state domination.[16] With communist ideology spent in its potential to legitimate Communist Party rule, the regime increasingly recognizes that it must provide institutional mechanisms to limit corruption and abuse of power and to enable citizens to express their concerns and challenge state actions. Without this adaptation and normalization of state-society relations, societal acceptance of the regime could evaporate, protests over unemployment, dislocation, corruption, and inequality could spin out of control, and Communist Party rule could be swept away in a sudden, violent eruption. Thus, the Chinese Communist Party is in "a race against time" to establish new, more participatory, decentralized, and law-based institutions before the old ones give way to a "crisis of governability."[17]

In attempting to preserve its dominance, the Chinese communist leaders will face a difficult quandary. They must continue reforming politically, introducing higher and wider levels of political competition, freer flows of information, more space for independent organization, and a more autonomous, authentic system of justice. But if they do keep liberalizing politically, they will be riding a tiger they cannot dismount. More and more citizens and groups will have acquired a stake in institutions that give them some political voice, freedom, predictability, and choice, and it will become increasingly costly and dangerous to take these away. As the new institutions are practiced with growing scope and sophistication around the country, they will generate democratic norms and expectations, and a demand for further expansion of democratic practices and procedures. (This process will clearly occur much sooner in Hong Kong than the rest of China, and the potential diffusion effects emanating from democratization or rising democratic pressure in Hong Kong should not be underestimated. Neither should the demonstration effect of a successful Chinese democracy in Taiwan.)

It is possible that all of this will merely produce a steady (though hardly smooth and linear) expansion of political pluralism and civil freedom, perhaps for a generation, until China reaches a "magic moment" in its level of economic development. More likely, however, at some point sooner, political and social change will cumulate—and possibly intersect with economic stress or social turmoil—to produce a regime crisis. Such a crisis could lead to a transition to democracy, depending on how regime leaders divide and nonregime forces align. But it could just as likely lead to a new form of authoritarianism, or a period of contested rule and social and fiscal disarray, or simply a ruthless crackdown that would set the country back in every respect.

No matter which scenario unfolds, China will not remain the same politically, and how it evolves will powerfully influence political trends in Asia and the rest of the world. For China is not just another country. It is a rising superpower. It is a major civilization. It is a fifth of humanity. In a narrow demographic sense, one could argue that the successful democratization of China would, in itself, constitute a "wave" of democratic change. Certainly its impact on global political models and power relations would be profound.

If China undergoes substantial political liberalization in the next two decades (improving its average freedom score to, say, 4 on the 7-point Freedom House scale), and even more so if China becomes an electoral democracy at the national level, the diffusion effects throughout East Asia and beyond could be powerful enough to launch a fourth wave of global democratization.

Other East Asian Prospects

Even more modest continued political opening in China will likely co-exist with similar, and in some cases, more rapid or decisive democratizing trends in other East Asian countries. Indonesia may or may not make a transition to democracy (which may or may not succeed), but student, labor, and middle-class pressure for democratization will likely persist in some form. Prolonged economic contraction in Malaysia could also topple the autocratic Prime Minister Mahathir Mohamad and stimulate pressure for real democratization. Economic crisis has blown off course Rowen's estimate for Thailand (that it will have a per capita income of $17,000, in 1990 PPP dollars, by 2020—equivalent to Italy's 1990 development level). But Thailand is already a robust (if roguish) electoral democracy, and it will recover from the East Asian economic crisis faster than authoritarian Indonesia. In another generation, Thailand's levels of income and education will make much more difficult the levels of neopatrimonial relations, vote buying, and military influence that constrain the quality of democracy in Thailand today. At such a level of development, a military coup would be unthinkable—something that no country with even half that level of projected per capita wealth has experienced.

The same assumption of high growth (averaging 4.5% annually) would lift Vietnam to $2,600 per capita income in 2020, at the level of China today. But Vietnam is likely to be more democratic in 2020 than China is today, given the evolution it has already undergone (similar to

China in many respects) to expand the role of the National Assembly, to separate the party bureaucracy from the operation of government, to decentralize political administration, to implement a market economy and attract foreign investment, and to redefine its legitimacy on bases other than Marxist ideology. As in China, severe human rights violations persist. However, Frederick Brown concludes, "Many within the VCP [Vietnamese Communist Party] recognize that Marxist-Leninist ideology is succumbing to the forces of science, education, cultural exchange, and the marketplace. These fact of modern life would appear to make 'peaceful evolution' in Vietnam inevitable, leading initially to a softer authoritarianism and perhaps later to a more sophisticated participatory system of governance."[18]

No such process of liberalization is yet discernible in North Korea, which remains the world's last truly Stalinist regime. No political system in the world today is more closed, more brutally repressive and inhumane, more totally and obsessively controlling than North Korea's.[19] By mid-1998, the North Korean regime was giving hints of interest in limited economic liberalization, as its economy was plunging deeper into total dysfunction and mass starvation. However, it is doubtful whether the North Korean communist regime can, at this late date, negotiate a gradual transition from Stalinist totalitarianism to a more pluralist authoritarianism. There is a strong possibility that at some point in the next few years the North Korean regime will simply collapse, generating political and economic burdens on the South that dwarf what Germany experienced in its unification. Whether political change comes (and it must) through reform or breakdown, stability on the Korean peninsula will be served to the extent that the people of the North gain more access to information and some initial awareness of the alternatives that political and economic freedom present.

Some time in the next decade or two, Singapore's uniquely anomalous status as the world's richest nondemocracy (the one true exception to the "threshold" thesis of development and democracy) also seems likely to yield to changing realities. The maturation of a new generation, socialized into affluence with more "postmaterialist" values, will produce broader resentment of rigid, hierarchical, state control, paternalistic dictation from the ruling party, and lack of the accountability that comes from real political competition. Already, the popular vote for the ruling People's Action Party has declined from its 70 percent-plus levels of the 1968–80 period—and this with virtually no effective opposition party. The passing from the scene of the grand architect of the system, Lee

Kuan Yew, could aggravate tensions within the regime over leadership succession. Finally, there is much to suggest that the stability of pseudo-democracy in Singapore has derived not from nondemocratic and deeply rooted "Asian values" but from a pragmatic bargain, in which the regime produced dynamic material progress and the people offered political compliance and quiescence in exchange—but only for those policies and institutions that could be rationalized as necessary for continuing the economic miracle.[20] If the miracle fades, if economic growth declines from the 7 percent annual rate that Singapore averaged in the 1980s and early 1990s to the 2–3 percent growth rates more characteristic of advanced industrial societies (not to mention the possibility of stagnation or a prolonged recession), the historic bargain of "pragmatic materialism" will fray and quite possibly unravel. In any case, pressure for a freer, more competitive political system can be expected to rise.[21]

Global Democratic Prospects

Although it is much poorer and weaker in its state structures, Africa is another major frontier for democratic expansion in the next generation. Since the "second liberation" began in Africa in 1990, about a dozen African countries have made a transition to electoral democracy. Many more have liberalized politically to some degree. Most of Africa is in flux politically today. A great opportunity for democracy derives from the profound discredit that has befallen all forms of authoritarianism—military, personal, and one-party. Increasingly, Africans attribute the calamities of the postindependence era—economic destitution, humanitarian crisis, ethnic violence, civil war, and state decay—to the absence of the constitutionalism and accountability that democracy provides. A growing array of elites and organizations recognize that economic development and political stability require good governance, which in turn encompasses political choice and inclusion, freedom of expression and organization, a rule of law—in essence some form of democracy.

If the results of Africa's wave of transitions in the 1990s have been "generally disappointing" (to quote Richard Joseph), they have not been completely so. The states of Africa are taking divergent political paths. Many are stuck in pseudodemocracy or have reverted to one form or another of authoritarian rule or chronic instability. But others (including new democracies in South Africa, Ghana, and Benin) are beginning to institutionalize democracy and a rule of law. In these states, and in politics, civil society, and public opinion elsewhere on the continent, there has been what Gyimah-Boadi calls a "rebirth of liberalism"—a renewed concern for constitutionalism; the dogged persistence and growth of independent organizations and media committed to democracy and human rights; and more autonomous, assertive, and skillful parliaments. Even in many of Africa's nondemocratic states, these trends are apparent to some degree and may sink roots for the growth of democratic culture and practice. If these roots are watered with international support and attention, they are likely to bring forth new (and probably more successful) attempts at democratic transition in the coming generation. A new wave of African democratization will be even more likely if the democratic states on the continent follow Botswana in becoming models of competent governance and economic growth.[22]

In the Islamic Middle East, democracy seems at least plausible in the long run. Culturally and historically, this has been the most difficult terrain in the world for political freedom and democracy. But Islamists, increasingly, do not speak with one voice, and democratic pluralist currents are emerging. A "growing group of Islamic reformers" is struggling with "the question of how to modernize and democratize political and economic systems in an Islamic context."[23] Moreover, democratic reforms have already progressed significantly in Jordan, which now has the most liberal average freedom score (4) of any Arab country and has undergone some evolution toward constitutional monarchy and electoral democracy. With the unexpected election to the presidency of a political and social moderate, Ayatollah Khatami, in 1997, Iran also took some steps toward civil and political liberalization, although these were fiercely resisted by the country's conservative ruling clergy.

In the predominantly Muslim states of the Arab world, if democratization is to be sustainable (or even feasible), it will probably need to unfold in what Bernard Lewis calls "gradual and unforced change" that proceeds "in slow stages" through reforming autocracy to more open and competitive political systems.[24] An abrupt democratic opening could trigger either a neoauthoritarian reaction from a faction of the ruling elite or a breakthrough to an Islamic fundamentalist regime that would have no use for democracy or liberalism. Yet even incremental democracy must give a wide berth to social criticism, political dissent, and independent associations and parties. Except for Jordan, Lewis's other two examples of "modernizing autocracies" that are "moving toward greater freedom"—Morocco and Egypt—as yet offer little or no scope for the people to change their government or to mobilize peacefully for fundamental reform.

The time to begin a process of real political liberalization in these and other Middle Eastern countries is long overdue. Most of the authoritarian regimes in the Middle East are highly corrupt and are experiencing growing challenges to their legitimacy. Continued decadent and repressive rule enables Islamic fundamentalist movements, which take refuge in the mosque and alternative networks of support and exchange in the economy, to establish themselves as the principle alternative to unpopular regimes that permit no other avenue of change. Ignoring these trends could be costly for the global cause of democracy.

In the near term, there are clearly other serious challenges and potential dangers. Many Asian political leaders and intellectuals will continue to challenge "Western" notions of what constitutes good government and to advance models of "democracy" that vary from illiberal to entirely illusory. In the midst of prolonged economic stagnation, inequality, corruption, and massive crime, democracy in Russia could still give way to some kind of nationalist or neocommunist dictatorship, with demonstration effects and reintegrationist pressures reverberating through the region. If it is blocked by the military from democratizing, Nigeria could drift from military dictatorship to anarchy or even civil war, dragging down the prospects for democratic development throughout West Africa.

Still, the possibility of a fourth wave of democratization in the world rests most pivotally on the future of China. Factional political leadership struggles in China could interrupt or reverse political liberalization, producing a repressive, hostile, and nationalistic China that intimidates democracies (and potential democracies) throughout the region. The long shadow of Chinese hostility to democracy will, in the short term, hang over Hong Kong and Taiwan in any case. But if the West in general and the United States in particular assume that China seeks an authoritarian and expansionist regional hegemony, and if they pursue overt policies to "contain" the presumed Chinese "threat," they are much more likely to turn the regime away from internal reform and external accommodation. Peaceful engagement with China, and separation of trade relations from human rights and security concerns, does not require that the West abandon its principled commitments to human rights—and its steady work to get China to live up to its own commitments in this regard.

Unless the established democracies fumble into a new cold war along civilizational lines with China, East Asia, or Islamic Middle Eastern states, most of the above potential setbacks to freedom figure to be limited in duration and scope. If more and more countries continue to liberalize and open their economies in ways that create secure property rights and expanded trade and investment, there could well be, as Henry Rowen predicts, an extraordinary period of "world wealth expanding" ahead, in which much of the developing and postcommunist world experiences dramatic gains in per capita income within a generation. In addition, it is almost certain, as Rowen shows, that educational levels will steadily rise in developing countries. Together, these two forces are going to generate, as Rowen argues and much other evidence suggests, highly propitious conditions for democracy. This will particularly be so in the part of the world where growth will be most rapid and socially transformative—East Asia—although the pace of progress will surely be slowed if not temporarily reversed by the economic crisis of the late 1990s.[25] Within a generation, East Asia's richest emerging economies— Taiwan and South Korea, possibly Thailand as well—will likely be not just electoral democracies but consolidated liberal democracies. And several of today's Asian autocracies will be moving toward democracy.

In the long run, the expansion of world wealth and education will be the most powerful structural factor facilitating the expansion and deepening of democracy. But as I emphasize throughout this volume, democratic development is probabilistic, open-ended, and reversible. Economic and social development will help, but ultimately political leadership, choice, and action at many levels will make the difference. This imposes strong obligations not only on government officials, political parties, interest groups, and civic organizations in developing democracies but also on institutions in rich, established ones.

Perhaps the most distinctive feature of the third wave is the considerable contribution that international actors have made to democratic development by enhancing the resources, skills, techniques, ideas, linkages, and legitimacy of civil society organizations, civic education efforts, the mass media, legislatures, local governments, judicial systems, political parties, and election commissions in the developing and postcommunist worlds. The prospects for democracy in the world will be much brighter if these many currents of practical engagement are sustained, refined, and widened. This is why continued and increased funding is needed for the democratic assistance programs of official aid agencies, regional and international organizations, publicly funded democracy foundations (such as the U.S. National Endowment for Democracy, Britain's Westminster Foundation, and the German party foundations), private foundations (such as the Soros Foundation network), and a wide array of smaller nongovernmental organizations in the established democracies.[26]

Seeking a More Democratic World

Democrats throughout the world increasingly share a vision of a world system that is democratic in two senses: one that is composed of free societies and democratic states; and one in which relations between states and among peoples are constrained by law and by common principles of decency and justice. The world community is embracing a shared normative expectation that all states seeking international legitimacy should manifestly "govern with the consent of the governed"—in essence, a "right to democratic governance," a legal entitlement.[27] A growing international architecture of collective institutions and formal agreements is gradually emerging, enshrining both the principles of democracy and human rights and the legitimacy of international action to promote and defend them.[28] In the next generation, we have an historic opportunity to bring a truly democratic world into being.

That quest encompasses three core challenges: first, to deepen and consolidate democracy where it has formally come into being; second, to continue to build and reinforce the cooperative structures and institutional rules of democracy at the level of regional and international organizations; and third, to encourage the many disparate currents of change that could at some point in the future gather into a fourth wave of democratization.

None of this is inevitable. The most dangerous intellectual temptation for democrats is teleology—to think that the world is *necessarily* moving toward some natural democratic end state. Too many international policy makers have taken electoral democracy as an end state in itself. Too many citizens blithely take the current state of their own established democracies as an end point of political evolution, the best democracy can do, even though it leaves them cynical and detached. Some observers seem to assume that democratic consolidation is bound to follow transition in much of the world.

These assumptions are false and counterproductive. Democracy can deteriorate at any point in its development; its quality and stability can never be taken for granted. No deus ex machina—economic or otherwise—will deliver democracy with some hidden hand. As Samuel Huntington observed in the last sentence of his seminal book, *The Third Wave*, "History . . . does not move forward in a straight line, but when skilled and determined leaders push, it does move forward."[29] In previous chapters, I highlight the key imperatives for consolidating new democracies and preempting a third reverse wave. I conclude here with some thoughts on how the established democracies might push democracy forward in the coming decades, toward a fourth wave of democratic expansion.

Heavy and sustained investment in democracy promotion is vital, but it will not be sufficient. To be credible, and to provide an appealing model and vision of a global democratic future, the established democracies—not least the United States—must attend to the quality of democracy in their own countries. It is wrong to think that democracy is the only model of governance with any power and legitimacy in the world today. Communism may be dead, but Leninism lives on. And there is still a powerful attraction in Asia and elsewhere to what may be termed the "Singaporean" model—a form of pseudodemocracy that offers real economic freedom but only a thin veneer of electoral competition and constitutionalism, behind which a hegemonic state and ruling party firmly control and constrain political life. Even as it begins to fray in Iran, the Islamic fundamentalist model is still very much alive in a crucial part of the world. Then there is the eternal danger of bigotry and intolerance. In the face of social and economic stress, democracy will always struggle against one or another form of ethnic or nationalist chauvinism, which exalts some defined "we" by demonizing and persecuting some perceived "they."

If democratic progress is to continue in the next century, it must continue at the core, in the most economically advanced countries. As Philippe Schmitter has observed, "their ability to adjust their well-entrenched rules and practices to accommodate the growing disaffection of their citzenries will determine the prospects for democracy worldwide."[30] The established liberal democracies need renewed and more vigorous engagement of citizens in public life. They need to nurture and revitalize the associational structures through which citizens participate and cooperate directly, as political equals, and which breed the cultural foundations of a healthy democracy: trust, tolerance, efficacy, reciprocity, honesty, and respect for law.[31] In the United States especially—the most radically individualist of all major democracies—the culture of rights must be tempered by rejuvenating the spirit of civic obligation to the community.

Across the democracies of the world, rich and poor, there is accumulating a large agenda for democratic reform. Access to power must continue to expand to women and minorities. Political parties must find new ways to elicit commitment and engagement from citizens. Many systems of party and campaign finance must be reformed to reinvigorate political competition, curb the raw purchase of political influence, and restore a sense of political ownership of the process on the part of ordinary citizens. Continued economic dynamism must be secured through needed economic reforms, including the restructuring of welfare and social security systems that are fiscally unsustainable. Yet at the same time, democracies everywhere in the world need to worry about the yawning gaps between rich and poor and to make the investments in human capital that are needed to narrow them.

A second imperative is to help create the economic conditions that will not only consolidate the third wave but help to bring into being a fourth. New democracies have persisted in the third wave in the face of economic hardships that many believed they could not endure. Now, after painful economic reforms, a number of postcommunist, Latin American, and even African states are experiencing real, even vigorous growth. International assistance can help to foster the market-oriented reforms that are driving this growth and that are necessary to quicken and sustain it. But ultimately, the most powerful initiative the industrialized democracies can take to foster growth in the emerging democracies is to open their markets and to compel the emerging democracies to open their own markets, while observing international standards of trading conduct and labor rights. Open economies are the institutional companion of open societies and free political systems. As communities of nations liberalize and eliminate their barriers to trade, they draw closer politically and culturally as well. The European Union is the single greatest and most important community of democracies in the history of the world. Two of the highest strategic priorities for the advance of democracy in the world are (1) to expand that union to incorporate the postcommunist states and (2) to bring about a true common market in the Americas.

The latter is a feasible and urgently important goal for the next decade. There is now in the Americas a growing network of free-trade agreements, anchored by NAFTA (the North American Free Trade Agreement) in the north and Mercosur in the south. The goal of an enduringly democratic Western Hemisphere could be powerfully boosted by the construction of a free-trade community uniting North, Central, and South America and conditioning membership—as does the EU—on democracy and respect for fundamental human rights. There is already an evolving political architecture for such a system in the Organization of American States and in its explicit readiness to collectively defend democracy (as in Guatemala, Peru, Haiti, and Paraguay).

For the major democratic powers, and especially for the United States, dealing with the next world's next superpower, China, is likely to be the most formidable international challenge. It is vitally important that China continue to develop economically, and nothing would be gained for democracy or other U.S. interests to use trade as a weapon to punish China for its reprehensible record on human rights. Relations with China must recognize contradictory trends and, therefore, must move on multiple tracks. On the one hand, China is not only growing richer rapidly, as a result of dramatic (albeit still partial) market reforms; at a slower pace, it is also making some significant political reforms. At the same time, however, ugly parallel realities persist: the brutal suppression of political dissent; the persecution of religious belief and practice; the systematic repression of independent labor organization; the torture and mistreatment of prisoners and political activists; forced abortions and coercive birth control; the sale of organs of executed prisoners; the continual efforts to control and restrict the flow of information; and the genocidal campaign, through terror, domination, and inward migration, to erase the independent identity of the Tibetan people. These grave violations of human rights must be exposed and condemned. Moral and diplomatic pressure must be mounted through a variety of means and forums to persuade China to cease these abuses.

However, international moral outrage alone will not change China. If it is not balanced by engagement and dialogue it could provoke a nationalist reaction that would freeze or derail political reform in the country. While protesting abuses in the short term, international democrats must encourage the longer-term process of social and political change in China. That involves working with reformist elements in various state and semiofficial institutions, to quietly provide technical assistance and support for the types of political reform mentioned above. It involves exchanges to broaden contact between organizations, leaders, and thinkers in China and their counterparts in Western democracies. It involves support for Chinese organizations and intellectuals abroad who are providing various actors in China with ideas, strategies, information, exchanges, and tools for democratic change. And it involves the investment and trade that, by accelerating economic growth in China, is creating a more sophisticated, pluralistic, informed, and autonomously organized society. Balance of this kind will also be needed to engage and pressure other authoritarian regimes in which change is possible but democratization seems a distant prospect.

In Africa, the established democracies have more scope to pressure for democratic reforms than in China, because they exercise much greater power. The dependence of African states on international aid, finance, and investment makes it possible to provide tangible incentives for liberalizing reforms and to impose penalties on those regimes that cling to corrupt and abusive practices. Concerted international pressure on authoritarian elites could reinforce domestic pressures and persuade authoritarian elites that the costs of resisting demands for democracy exceed the benefits they expect to reap. At a minimum, international pressure can narrow the base of support for the regime and induce it to negotiate with the opposition for a new democratic framework, as happened in South Africa, Zambia, and Malawi. But international sanctions and inducements can work only if they are consistently applied and broadly adhered to by the major powers.

A new bargain is needed between Africa and the West, swapping debt for democracy and development for good governance. Aid should be conditioned on economic liberalization, political freedom and accountability, and redirection of budgetary priorities away from military and other unproductive spending and toward human and physical capital. Those governments that are serious about development and good governance deserve more aid, including debt relief, as a transitional boost to sustainable development. Those that are not should be denied international aid and loans. Even in the most authoritarian situations, however, the international community needs to seek out and support civil society groups that are serious about development, democratization, and accountability. If international actors are to promote democratization, they must affect the domestic political context; this means strengthening prodemocratic forces from below and giving wavering and divided regime elites incentives to tilt toward democracy.

The possibilities for democracy are shaped by many grand historical and social forces: the failure of empires, the diffusion of models, the movement of peoples, the change of generations, the transformation of values and class structures that comes with economic development. These forces, especially economic development, are going to generate new pressures for democratization in the twenty-first century. But in the end, democracy is won or lost, invented or squandered, perfected or perverted, by individuals and groups and by their choices and actions.

In the near term, democrats around the world confront a historic opportunity and imperative: to prevent a third reverse wave of democratic breakdowns by moving the values, practices, laws, and institutions of new and unstable democracies toward consolidation. If, in the coming decade or two, some large portion of the third-wave democracies can be deepened and consolidated, the "established democracies" will be greatly enlarged in number and the world will be transformed.

Increasingly, universal norms of democracy and human rights will become embedded in international dialogue and action. And many of the newly established democracies will become important sources of diffusion and promoters of democracy themselves. As democracy—indeed, *liberal* democracy—takes root in many parts of the world where it was scarcely present before, its universality will be affirmed, and the specter of a clash of civilizations will be laid to rest. Pressure will grow on the world's remaining dictatorships, and resources and moral inspiration will flow to the movements, thinkers, parties, and politicians that are seeking democratic change. No doubt, many of them will fail. But within a generation, enough of them will succeed to generate a fourth wave of global democratization and a spread of democracy throughout the world that few liberals would have dared imagine in 1974, when the third wave began.

Appendix

Classification of Regimes
at the End of 1997

States are listed in order of their average Freedom House score on political rights and civil liberties at the end of 1997. "Free" states (those with average freedom scores of 1.0–2.5) are listed here as *liberal democracies.* The list of *electoral democracies* is from Freedom House, *Freedom in the World: The Annual Survey of Political Rights and Civil Liberties, 1997–1998* (New York: Freedom House, 1998), 605–9. Classification of the remaining countries into *pseudodemocracies* and *authoritarian regimes* is by the judgment of the author.

Liberal
Democracies

1.0
Andorra
Australia
Austria
Barbados
Belize
Canada
Cyprus (Greek)
Denmark
Dominica
Finland
Iceland
Ireland
Kiribati
Liechtenstein
Luxembourg

Malta
Marshall Islands
Netherlands
New Zealand
Norway
Portugal
San Marino
Sweden
Switzerland
Tuvalu
United States

1.5
Bahamas
Belgium
Cape Verde
Costa Rica
Czech Republic
Estonia

France
Germany
Grenada
Hungary
Italy
Japan
Latvia
Lithuania
Mauritius
Micronesia
Monaco
Palau
Poland
St. Kitts & Nevis
St. Lucia
St. Vincent &
    Grenadines
Sao Tome &
    Principe

Slovenia
Solomon Islands
South Africa
Spain
Trinidad &
    Tobago
United Kingdom
Uruguay

2.0
Benin
Bolivia
Botswana
Chile
Greece
Guyana
Israel
Korea, South
Nauru

279

Romania
Taiwan
Vanuatu
Western Samoa

2.5
Argentina
Bulgaria
El Salvador
Honduras
Jamaica
Malawi
Mongolia
Namibia
Panama
Philippines
Venezuela

3.0
Mali

**(Nonliberal)
Electoral
Democracies**

3.0
Bangladesh
Dom Republic
Ecuador
Ghana
India
Madagascar
Nicaragua
Papua New
   Guinea
Seychelles
Slovakia
Suriname
Thailand

3.5
Brazil
Fiji
Georgia
Guatemala
Guinea-Bissau

Macedonia
Moldova
Mozambique
Nepal
Paraguay
Russia
Sri Lanka
Ukraine

4.0
Albania
Central African
   Republic
Colombia
Croatia
Kyrgyz Republic
Lesotho

4.5
Haiti
Liberia
Pakistan
Turkey

5.0
Bosnia-
   Herzegovina

**Pseudo-
democracies**

3.5
Antigua &
   Barbuda
Mexico

4.0
Jordan
Senegal
Tonga
Uganda

4.5
Armenia
Burkina-Faso
Comoros

Ethiopia
Gabon
Malaysia
Peru
Zambia

5.0
Azerbaijan
Côte D'Ivoire
Morocco
Singapore
Tanzania
Zimbabwe

5.5
Chad
Guinea
Kazakhstan
Lebanon
Togo
Tunisia
Yemen

6.0
Algeria
Angola
Belarus
Cameroon
Congo
   (Brazzaville)
Egypt
Indonesia
Kenya
Mauritania
Niger
Yugoslavia

6.5
Cambodia
Gambia

**Authoritarian
Regimes
(one-party or
no-party)**

4.5
Kuwait

5.0
Eritrea

5.5
Djibouti
Swaziland
United Arab
   Emirates

6.0
Brunei
Maldives
Oman
Tajikistan

6.5
Bahrain
Congo (Kinshasa)
Iran
Laos
Nigeria
Qatar
Rwanda
Sierra Leone
Uzbekistan

7.0
Afghanistan
Bhutan
Burma
Burundi
China
Cuba
Equatorial Guinea
Iraq
Korea, North
Libya
Saudi Arabia
Somalia
Sudan
Syria
Turkmenistan
Vietnam

NOTES

Chapter 1. Defining and Developing Democracy

1. Samuel P. Huntington, *The Third Wave: Democratization in the Late Twentieth Century* (Norman: University of Oklahoma Press, 1991). Treating earlier historical developments somewhat differently, Philippe C. Schmitter labels this period the "fourth wave" of global democratization, but this does not alter the trends and issues analyzed here. See Schmitter, "The International Context of Contemporary Democratization," *Stanford Journal of International Affairs* 2, no. 1 (1993): 1–34. Robert A. Dahl, by contrast, defines three historical waves of democratization based on the type of political transformation that was initiated: from hegemonies into competitive oligarchies (first wave, nineteenth century); from near polyarchies into full polyarchies (second wave, early twentieth century); and further democratization of full polyarchies (before and after World War II). Dahl, *Polyarchy: Participation and Opposition* (New Haven: Yale University Press, 1971), 10–11.

2. Huntington, *The Third Wave*, 15.

3. Gabriel A. Almond, "Political Science: The History of the Discipline," in *A New Handbook of Political Science*, edited by Robert E. Goodin and Hans-Dieter Klingemann (Oxford: Oxford University Press, 1996), 53–61. See also David Held, *Models of Democracy* (Stanford: Stanford University Press, 1987), chaps. 1, 2.

4. Aristotle, *The Politics*, edited by Stephen Everson (Cambridge: Cambridge University Press, 1988), 1292.

5. The relationship between a liberal, democratic polity and a liberal economy in this regard touches on some of the oldest issues in political theory and is beyond the scope of this book. There are not only organic links between the two phenomena but also contradictions. As Dahl notes in *Polyarchy* (2), a "full" or nearly perfect democracy would require that all the differing preferences of citizens be weighed equally, which in turn requires full political equality. But this would require economic equality among citizens, which is incompatible with a liberal economy (and in any case, unattainable, I believe, in any complex society).

6. Robert A. Dahl, *Democracy and Its Critics* (New Haven: Yale University Press, 1989), chap. 8; quotations at 88 and 89.

7. There are certain economic, social, and cultural conditions for democracy to be viable, but they are often overstated, and we should be cautious about positing them as "prerequisites." See Larry Diamond, "Economic Development and Democracy Reconsidered," in *Reexamining Democracy: Essays in Honor of Seymour Martin Lipset,* edited by Gary Marks and Larry Diamond (Newbury Park, Calif.: Sage, 1992), 93–139.

8. Dahl, *Polyarchy,* 26.

9. Quoted in U.S. Department of State, *Country Reports on Human Rights Practices for 1996* (Washington, D.C.: Government Printing Office, 1997), xxi.

10. François Furet, "Democracy and Utopia," *Journal of Democracy* 9, no. 1 (1998): 65–79.

11. Fareed Zakaria, "The Rise of Illiberal Democracy," *Foreign Affairs* 76, no. 6 (1997): 22–43.

12. And even these governments are not very liberal, for the same reason that liberal autocracy is generally not possible: when Antiguans and Tongans demand real democracy, they are harassed by the state or the ruling party. Freedom House, *Freedom in the World: The Annual Survey of Political Rights and Civil Liberties, 1996–1997* (New York: Freedom House, 1997), 125, 488. As I explain in greater detail below, each year Freedom House rates countries on a scale from 1 to 7 on two measures, political rights and civil liberties (1 being most liberal). It also classifies all the countries in the world as to whether or not they are electoral democracies. Of the countries that are not electoral democracies, only the above two have scores of 3 on civil liberties (and none has better than 3).

13. Marc F. Plattner, "Liberalism and Democracy," *Foreign Affairs* 77, no. 2 (1998): 171–80; quotation on 175.

14. Ibid., 173.

15. Russell Bova, "Democracy and Liberty: The Cultural Connection," *Journal of Democracy* 8, no. 1 (1997): 115, table 1. The difference in average rating on the Humana human rights scale between countries that clearly have electoral democracy and those that clearly do not is enormous: 85 to 35. For a description of this 100-point scale (with 100 being the top score), see Charles Humana, *World Human Rights Guide,* 3d ed. (New York: Oxford University Press, 1992).

16. Bruce Russett, *Grasping the Democratic Peace: Principles for a Post–Cold War World* (Princeton: Princeton University Press, 1993), 119. The statistical evidence is summarized in tables 1.2 and 4.1. For a recent overview of theory and evidence, see James Lee Ray, "The Democratic Path to Peace," *Journal of Democracy* 8, no. 2 (1997): 49–64. For a more wide-ranging analysis, which departs from much of the existing literature in suggesting that democracies are intrinsically less inclined toward aggressive violence, see the many works by Rudolph J. Rummel, including, *Power Kills: Democracy as a Method of Nonviolence* (New Brunswick, N.J.: Transaction, 1997); Rummel, "Democracies ARE Less War-

like than Other Regimes," *European Journal of International Relations* 1, no. 4 (1995): 457–79.

17. Boutros Boutros-Ghali, *An Agenda for Democratization* (New York: United Nations, 1996); quotations at 7, 8.

18. Ted Robert Gurr, *Minorities at Risk: A Global View of Ethnopolitical Conflicts* (Washington, D.C.: U.S. Institute of Peace, 1993), 137.

19. Ibid., 290–313; Donald Horowitz, *Ethnic Groups in Conflict* (Berkeley: University of California Press, 1985), 583- 680; Horowitz, *A Democratic South Africa: Constitutional Engineering in a Divided Society* (Berkeley: University of California Press, 1991), 124–226; Horowitz, "Ethnic Conflict Management for Policymakers" and "Making Moderation Pay," both in *Conflict and Peacemaking in Multiethnic Societies,* edited by Joseph V. Montville (Lexington, Mass: Lexington Books, 1990), 115–30, 451–76; Arend Lijphart, *Democracy in Plural Societies* (New Haven: Yale University Press, 1977); Lijphart, "The Power-Sharing Approach," in Montville, *Conflict and Peacemaking,* 491–509.

20. Larry Diamond and Marc F. Plattner, *Nationalism, Ethnic Conflict, and Democracy* (Baltimore: Johns Hopkins University Press, 1994), xxiii–xxix. See also the country and regional case studies in ibid.

21. For a discussion of electoral system design, see chapter 3. For the role that international mediation of a fair electoral process can play to help resolve violent conflict, see Jennifer McCoy, Larry Garber, and Robert Pastor, "Poll-watching and Peacemaking," *Journal of Democracy* 2, no. 4 (1991): 102–14.

22. Rudolph J. Rummel, "Power, Genocide, and Mass Murder," *Journal of Peace Research* 31, no. 1 (1994): 1.

23. For a summary of the evidence and conclusions, see ibid. The full presentation (and review of the literature) appears in Rummel, *Power Kills.* Adding up what revolutionary movements, totalist ideologies, totalitarian regimes, and chauvinistic nationalisms have wrought in this century through wars of aggression and fanaticism and various campaigns of mass murder of civilians, Zbigniew Brzezinski estimates that "no less than 167,000,000 lives . . . were deliberately extinguished in politically motivated carnage." Brzezinski, *Out of Control: Global Turmoil on the Eve of the 21st Century* (New York: Scribners, 1993), 17. Noting the unique proclivity of autocracies to mass murder, Dahl argues that open political contestation and full participation prevent the use of "extreme sanctions" against more than a very small percentage of the population. Dahl, *Polyarchy,* 27.

24. Rummel, "Power, Genocide, and Mass Murder," 8.

25. Rodger A. Payne, "Freedom and the Environment," *Journal of Democracy* 6, no. 3 (1995): 41–55.

26. Adam Przeworski and Fernando Limongi, "Democracy and Development," in *Democracy's Victory and Crisis,* edited by Axel Hadenius (Cambridge: Cambridge University Press, 1997), 172.

27. Ibid., 171–79; Adam Przeworski and Fernando Limongi, "Political Regimes and Economic Growth," *Journal of Economic Perspectives* 7, no. 3 (1993):

51–69. This does not mean that there is no relationship at all between regimes and growth performance. As Przeworski and Limongi speculate in "Democracy and Development," it may well be the case that "democracies are less likely to generate both miracles and disasters than dictatorships" (166). In this regard, they warn, social scientists should be careful about equating growth with human welfare. People may value an assured minimum steady growth over a high average with wide variation.

28. Przeworski and Limongi, "Democracy and Development," 178.

29. Partha Das Gupta, *An Inquiry into Well-being and Destitution* (Oxford: Clarendon, 1993), 116–21.

30. David Collier and Steven Levitsky, "Democracy with Adjectives: Conceptual Innovation in Comparative Research," *World Politics* 49, no. 3 (1997): 430–51. For the full list of subtypes, see Collier and Levitsky's unpublished paper of the same title, Department of Political Science, University of California at Berkeley.

31. Severe, persistent socioeconomic inequality may well be (as some scholars find) a major threat to political democracy. But to establish this, we must first have a measure of democracy that is limited to features of the political system. For an effort exhibiting this approach (and finding), see Zehra F. Arat, *Democracy and Human Rights in Developing Countries* (Boulder, Colo.: Lynne Rienner, 1991). For a critique of the incorporation of socioeconomic criteria into the definition of democracy, see Terry Lynn Karl, "Dilemmas of Democratization in Latin America," *Comparative Politics* 23, no. 1 (1990): 2.

32. Joseph Schumpeter, *Capitalism, Socialism, and Democracy*, 2d ed. (New York: Harper, 1947), 269. For Schumpeter, Held explains, "the democratic citizen's lot was, quite straightforwardly, the right periodically to choose and authorize governments to act on their behalf" (*Models of Democracy*, 165). Schumpeter was clearly uneasy with direct political action by citizens, warning that "the electoral mass is incapable of action other than a stampede" (283). Thus, his "case for democracy can support, at best, only minimum political involvement: that involvement which could be considered sufficient to legitimate the right of competing elites to rule" (ibid., 168). This is, indeed, as spare a notion of democracy as one could posit without draining the term of meaning.

33. Huntington, *The Third Wave*, 5–13, esp. 6; Samuel P. Huntington, "The Modest Meaning of Democracy," in *Democracy in the Americas: Stopping the Pendulum*, edited by Robert A. Pastor (New York: Holmes and Meier, 1989), 15. For similar conceptions of democracy based on competitive elections, see Seymour Martin Lipset, *Political Man: The Social Bases of Politics* (Baltimore: Johns Hopkins University Press, 1981), 27; Lipset, "The Social Requisites of Democracy Revisited," *American Sociological Review* 59, no. 1 (1994): 1; Juan J. Linz, *The Breakdown of Democratic Regimes: Crisis, Breakdown, and Reequilibration* (Baltimore: Johns Hopkins University Press, 1978), 5–6; J. Roland Pennock, *Democratic Political Theory* (Princeton: Princeton University Press, 1979), 7–15; G.

Bingham Powell, *Contemporary Democracies: Participation, Stability, and Violence* (Cambridge: Harvard University Press, 1982), 3; Tatu Vanhanen, *The Process of Democratization: A Comparative Study of 147 States, 1980–88* (New York: Crane Russak, 1990), 17–18; Giuseppe Di Palma, *To Craft Democracies: An Essay on Democratic Transitions* (Berkeley: University of California Press, 1991), 16; Adam Przeworski, *Democracy and the Market: Political and Economic Reforms in Eastern Europe and Latin America* (Cambridge: Cambridge University Press, 1991), 10–11.

34. Dahl, *Polyarchy*, 2–3. Dahl uses the term *polyarchy* to distinguish these systems from a more ideal form of democracy, "one of the characteristics of which is the quality of being completely or almost completely responsive to all its citizens" (2).

35. Ibid., app. A; Michael Coppedge and Wolfgang H. Reinecke, "Measuring Polyarchy," in *On Measuring Democracy: Its Consequences and Concomitants*, edited by Alex Inkeles (New Brunswick, N.J.: Transaction, 1991), 47–68.

36. Adam Przeworski, Michael Alvarez, José Antonio Cheibub, and Fernando Limongi, "What Makes Democracies Endure?" *Journal of Democracy* 7, no. 1 (1996): 50–51. Their methodology is more comprehensively explained in Michael Alvarez, José Antonio Cheibub, Fernando Limongi, and Adam Przeworski, "Classifying Political Regimes for the ACLP Data Set," Working Paper 4, Chicago Center on Democracy, University of Chicago. Many other approaches to conceiving and measuring democracy in quantitative, cross-national analyses have also tended to rely on indicators of competition and participation (whether dichotomous, categorical, or continuous), but some of these were gravely flawed by their incorporation of substantively inappropriate indicators, such as voter turnout or political stability. (On this and other conceptual and methodological problems, see Kenneth A. Bollen, "Political Democracy: Conceptual and Measurement Traps," in Inkeles, *Measuring Democracy*, 3–20.)

As an alternative approach that explicitly includes the behavioral, noninstitutional dimensions of democracy, the combined Freedom House scales of political rights and civil liberties, described below, are increasingly being used in quantitative analysis. For examples, see Henry S. Rowen, "The Tide Underneath the 'Third Wave,'" *Journal of Democracy* 6, no. 1 (1995): 52–64; Surjit S. Bhalla, "Freedom and Economic Growth: A Virtuous Cycle?" in Hadenius, *Democracy's Victory and Crisis*, 195–241. While the Freedom House data is available annually, it goes back in time only to 1972, and the criteria for scoring have become stricter over time (particularly in the 1990s), creating problems for interpreting changes in scores over time. The appeal of a simple dichotomous measure such as that used by Przeworski and his colleagues is precisely the relative simplification of data collection and regime classification and the ability to conduct a straightforward "event history" analysis that analyzes changes toward and away from democratic regime forms. Encouragingly, the Freedom House ratings and other measures of democracy are generally highly correlated with one another (Alex Inkeles, introduction to *Measuring Democracy*). In fact, Przeworski et al. report that the Freedom House combined ratings for 1972 to 1990 predict 93 percent of their regime classifications during this period ("What Makes Democracies Endure?" 52). However, as we see in chapter 2, since 1990 the formal properties and the liberal substance of democracy have increasingly diverged. Thus, the substantive validity of measures that focus mainly on formal competition may be particularly suspect after 1990.

37. Terry Lynn Karl, "Imposing Consent? Electoralism versus Democratization in El Salvador," in *Elections and Democratization in Latin America, 1980–1985*, edited by Paul Drake and Eduardo Silva (San Diego: Center for Iberian and Latin American Studies, Center for US/Mexican Studies, University of California at San Diego, 1986), 9–36; Karl, "Dilemmas of Democratization in Latin America," 14–15; Karl, "The Hybrid Regimes of Central America," *Journal of Democracy* 6, no. 3 (1995): 72–86.

38. Philippe C. Schmitter and Terry Lynn Karl, "What Democracy Is . . . and Is Not," *Journal of Democracy* 2, no. 3 (1991): 78.

39. Collier and Levitsky, "Democracy with Adjectives." A seminal discussion of reserved domains appears in J. Samuel Valenzuela, "Democratic Consolidation in Post-Transitional Settings: Notion, Process, and Facilitating Conditions," in *Issues in Democratic Consolidation: The New South American Democracies in Comparative Perspective*, edited by Scott Mainwaring, Guillermo O'Donnell, and J. Samuel Valenzuela (Notre Dame: University of Notre Dame Press, 1992), 64–66. See also Huntington, *The Third Wave*, 10; Schmitter and Karl, "What Democracy Is," 81; Guillermo O'Donnell, "Illusions about Consolidation," *Journal of Democracy* 7, no. 2 (1996): 34–51; Juan J. Linz and Alfred Stepan, *Problems of Democratic Transition and Consolidation: Southern Europe, South America, and Post-Communist Europe* (Baltimore: Johns Hopkins University Press, 1996), 3–5.

40. On the Polity III data set, see Keith Jaggers and Ted Robert Gurr, "Tracking Democracy's Third Wave with the Polity III Data," *Journal of Peace Research* 32, no. 4 (1995): 469–82. On the Polity II data (which Polity III corrects and updates to 1994), see Ted Robert Gurr, Keith Jaggers, and Will H. Moore, "The Transformation of the Western State: The Growth of Democracy, Autocracy, and State Power since 1800," in Inkeles, *Measuring Democracy*, 69–104. Although it does not measure civil liberties, the democracy measure of the polity data sets goes beyond electoral competitiveness to measure institutional constraints on the exercise of executive power (the phenomenon of "horizontal accountability").

41. Among the expanded procedural definitions that appear to bear a strong affinity to the conception of liberal democracy articulated here, but that are somewhat cryptic or ambiguous about the weight given to civil liberties, are Karl, "Dilemmas of Democratization in Latin America," 2; Dietrich Rueschemeyer, Evelyne Huber Stephens, and John D. Stephens, *Capitalist Development and Democracy* (Chicago: University of Chicago Press, 1992), 43–44, 46.

42. Obviously, the independent power of the legislature to "check and balance" executive power will differ markedly between presidential and parliamentary regimes. However, even in parliamentary regimes, democratic vigor requires striking a balance between disciplined parliamentary support for the governing party and independent capacity to scrutinize and question the actions of cabinet ministers and executive agencies. For the political quality of democracy, the most important additional mechanism of horizontal accountability is an autonomous judiciary, but crucial as well are institutionalized means (often in a separate, autonomous agency) to monitor, investigate, and punish government corruption at all levels. On the concept of lateral, or "constitutional," accountability and its importance, see Richard L. Sklar, "Developmental Democracy," *Comparative Studies in Society and History* 29, no. 4 (1987): 686–714; Sklar, "Towards a Theory of Developmental Democracy," in *Democracy and Development: Theory and Practice*, edited by Adrian Leftwich (Cambridge: Polity Press, 1996), 25–44. For the concept and theory of "horizontal accountability," see Guillermo O'Donnell, "Delegative Democracy," *Journal of Democracy* 5, no. 1 (1994): 60–62, and "Horizontal Accountability and New Polyarchies," in Andreas Schedler, Larry Diamond, and Marc F. Plattner, eds., *The Self-Restraining State: Power and Accountability in New Democracies* (Boulder, Colo.: Lynne Rienner, forthcoming).

43. For an important explication of the rule of law and its related concepts, see Guillermo O'Donnell, "The (Un)Rule of Law in Latin America," in *The Rule of Law and the Underprivileged in Latin America*, edited by Juan Méndez, Guillermo O'Donnell, and Paulo Sérgio Pinheiro (Notre Dame: University of Notre Dame Press, forthcoming).

44. This is a particular emphasis of Schmitter and Karl, "What Democracy Is," 78–80, but it has long figured prominently in the work and thought of democratic pluralists such as Robert A. Dahl. In addition to his *Polyarchy*, see Dahl, *Who Governs?* (New Haven: Yale University Press, 1961); Dahl, *Dilemmas of Pluralist Democracy: Autonomy versus Control* (New Haven: Yale University Press, 1982).

45. Juan J. Linz, "Democracy Today: An Agenda for Students of Democracy," *Scandinavian Political Studies* 20, no. 2 (1997): 120 21.

46. Richard Rose, William Mishler, and Christian Haerpfer, *Democracy and Its Alternatives: Understanding Post-Communist Societies* (Oxford: Polity Press, 1998).

47. Linz, "Democracy Today," 118.

48. The larger raw-point scores from which the two scales derive are constructed by assigning 0 to 4 points to each country on each of thirteen checklist items for civil liberties and each of eight checklist items for political rights. Further minor adjustments may be made for severe instances of cultural destruction or other violence. For a full account of the methodology see, Freedom House, *Freedom in the World, 1996–1997*, 572–78, and the similar chapters in previous years of the annual volume.

49. Juan J. Linz, "Types of Political Regime and Respect for Human Rights: Historical and Cross-National Perspectives," in *Conditions for Civilized Politics: Political Regimes and Compliance with Human Rights*, edited by Asbjørn Eide and Bernt Hagtvet (Oslo: Scandinavian University Press, 1996), 186; see also 183.

50. Ibid., 187.

51. Thus Linz concludes that "democracies can fail in relation to human rights more by inaction than by action," in neglecting acute social and economic problems and the violations of public order by antisystem groups. Ibid., 191.

52. Guillermo O'Donnell, "Illusions about Consolidation," *Journal of Democracy* 7, no. 2 (1996): 34–51.

53. Ibid., 36. While O'Donnell is sympathetic to the conception of liberal democracy articulated here and sees a strong affinity with the way he defines polyarchy, differences derive from where one marks the cutting point on the continuum of civil and political freedom. Like many substantial conceptual approaches, O'Donnell's cutting point is the combination of "inclusive, fair, and competitive elections" and "basic accompanying freedoms," which can be read (although O'Donnell may not mean it to be read so restrictively) as freedoms to facilitate "inclusive, fair, and competitive elections" (ibid., 36). This was the way Diamond, Linz, and Lipset defined democracy (competition, participation, and "liberties . . . sufficient to ensure the integrity of competition and participation"), until a subsequent "precising" identified the need for liberties to enable citizens "to develop and advocate their views and interests and contest policies" between elections. Larry Diamond, Juan J. Linz, and Seymour Martin Lipset, preface to *Democracy in Developing Countries: Asia, Africa, and Latin America* (Boulder, Colo.: Lynne Rienner, 1989), xvi; Larry Diamond, Juan J. Linz, and Seymour Martin Lipset, "What Makes for Democracy?" in *Politics in Developing Countries: Comparing Experiences with Democracy*, edited by Diamond, Linz, and Lipset (Boulder, Colo.: Lynne Rienner, 1995), 7.

54. O'Donnell, "Illusions about Consolidation," 45–46.

55. For a perspective that does just this, see Joseph Chan, "Hong Kong, Singapore, and Asian Values: An Alternative View," *Journal of Democracy* 8, no. 2 (1997): 35–48. One can have a political system that meets the ten criteria of liberal democracy I outline but that is culturally conservative or restrictive in some policies. The key test is whether those who disagree with these policies have full civic and political freedom to mobilize to change them.

56. Diamond et al., "What Makes for Democracy?" 8.

57. Giovanni Sartori, *Parties and Party Systems: A Framework for Analysis* (Cambridge: Cambridge University Press, 1976), 230–38.

58. See appendix. Taking seriously Collier and Levitsky's appeal to reduce the conceptual clutter in comparative democratic studies, we relate our categories here to similar concepts in other studies, particularly the "diminished subtypes" of democracy. Those subtypes that are missing the attribute of free elections or relatively fair multiparty contestation are pseudodemocracies. Those

that have real and fair multiparty competition but with limited suffrage constitute exclusionary, or oligarchic, democracy, which is not relevant to the contemporary era of universal suffrage. Those regimes without adequate civil liberties or civilian control of the military may nevertheless be electoral democracies.
Care is needed to empirically apply concepts, however. For example, Donald K.
Emmerson's category of "illiberal democracy" would seem to be coincident with
"electoral democracy" in my framework. However, as Emmerson applies the
concept to what he calls "one-party democracy" in Singapore and Malaysia, the
coincidence breaks down. Civil and political freedoms are so constrained in these
two countries that the minimum criterion of electoral democracy (a sufficiently
level electoral playing field to give opposition parties a chance at victory) is
not met. See Emmerson, "Region and Recalcitrance: Rethinking Democracy
through Southeast Asia," *Pacific Review* 8, no. 2 (1995): 223–48.

59. Both the term *developmental* and my emphasis on the continuous and
open-ended nature of change in the character, degree, and depth of democratic
institutions owe heavily to the work of Richard Sklar. See Sklar, "Developmental Democracy"; Sklar, "Towards a Theory of Developmental Democracy."
Readers will nevertheless note important differences in our perspectives.

60. E. Gyimah-Boadi, "The Rebirth of African Liberalism," *Journal of
Democracy* 9, no. 2 (1998): 18–31.

61. Karl, "The Hybrid Regimes of Central America," 82–83.

62. I am grateful to Sunita Parikh for calling my attention to this point.

63. Philippe C. Schmitter, "Interest Systems and the Consolidation of
Democracies," in Marks and Diamond, *Reexamining Democracy*, 160.

64. Linz, *The Breakdown of Democratic Regimes*, 97. Emphasis is mine.

65. Schmitter and Karl, "What Democracy Is," 85–87.

66. On civic competence and the challenges to improving it in contemporary, large-scale, complex, media-intensive, and information-saturated societies,
see Robert A. Dahl, "The Problem of Civic Competence," *Journal of Democracy*
3, no. 4 (1992): 45–59.

67. In their comparative study of the restructuring of property relations in
postsocialist Eastern Europe, *Postsocialist Pathways* (Cambridge: Cambridge
University Press, 1997), Laszlo Bruszt and David Stark argue that policy coherence, effectiveness, and sustainability are fostered when executives are constrained and reform policies are negotiated between governments and "deliberative associations."

68. Robert D. Putnam with Robert Leonardi and Raffaella Y. Nanetti,
Making Democracy Work: Civic Traditions in Modern Italy (Princeton: Princeton
University Press, 1993), 181; see also Putnam, "Bowling Alone: America's Declining Social Capital," *Journal of Democracy* 6, no. 1 (1995): 65–78. See also
chapter 6, this volume.

69. Sklar, "Developmental Democracy."

70. Such a developmental perspective may help to inoculate democratic

theory against the tendency toward teleological thinking that Guillermo O'Donnell discerns in the literature on democratic consolidation: that is, the underlying assumption that there is a particular natural path and end state of democratic development.

71. Giuseppe Di Palma, *To Craft Democracies* (Berkeley: University of California Press); Michael Burton, Richard Gunther, and John Higley, "Elite Transformations and Democratic Regimes," in *Elites and Democratic Consolidation in Latin America and Southern Europe*, edited by John Higley and Richard Gunther (Cambridge: Cambridge University Press, 1992).

72. Steven Fish, *Democracy from Scratch: Opposition and Regime in the New Russian Revolution* (Princeton: Princeton University Press, 1995).

Chapter 2. Is the Third Wave of Democratization Over?

1. Samuel P. Huntington, *The Third Wave: Democratization in the Late Twentieth Century* (Norman: University of Oklahoma Press, 1991), counts thirty democracies in 1973 with populations over one million but does not list them. Presumably, he does not count as democracies the Chilean and Uruguayan regimes that broke down in 1973, so the discrepancy could be due to his classification of some ambiguous regimes (notably Malaysia) as democratic at the time. In classifying ambiguous regimes in 1974, I follow Adam Przeworski's principle that "democracy is a system in which parties lose elections" (*Democracy and the Market: Political and Economic Reforms in Eastern Europe and Latin America* [Cambridge: Cambridge University Press, 1991], 10). In ambiguous cases, I classify civilian, multiparty, electoral regimes as democratic only if the ruling party lost power in an election at some point or clearly allowed itself to be at risk of electoral defeat. Mexico, Singapore, Malaysia (after 1969), and Senegal all failed this rule in 1974. Freedom House's 1990 classification of regimes as formally democratic or not follows this principle.

2. These eleven democracies in mid-1974 were Bahamas, Barbados, Botswana, Fiji, the Gambia, Iceland, Luxembourg, Malta, Mauritius, Nauru, and Trinidad and Tobago. Maldives and Grenada could be considered near democracies. The twenty-eight democracies with populations of more than one million at the start of the third wave were Australia, Austria, Belgium, Canada, Colombia, Costa Rica, Denmark, Finland, France, West Germany, India, Ireland, Israel, Italy, Jamaica, Japan, Lebanon, Netherlands, New Zealand, Norway, Papua New Guinea, Sri Lanka, Sweden, Switzerland, Turkey, United Kingdom, United States, and Venezuela.

3. Huntington, *The Third Wave*, 25-26.

4. Larry Diamond, "The Globalization of Democracy," in *Global Transformation and the Third World*, edited by Robert O. Slater, Barry R. Schutz, and Steven R. Dorr (Boulder, Colo.: Lynne Rienner, 1993), 41, table 3.2.

5. Table 2.5 includes Nigeria because for much of this period it appeared

to be moving toward democracy. It had constructed most of the architecture of electoral democracy by 1993, when the military annulled the results of a free and fair presidential election and then ultimately scrapped the whole emergent electoral system in a November coup. The subsequent drastic reduction in freedom and Nigeria's ongoing political crisis stands in sharp contrast to developments in Africa's other most influential country, South Africa. Moreover, the Nigerian experience has probably encouraged military coups and democratic setbacks in Gambia in 1995 and in Niger in 1996.

6. It must be noted that Freedom House has become more sensitive in its scoring in recent years, and in the 1990s its ratings appear to reflect a greater tendency to downgrade freedom scores in electoral democracies for problems of human rights abuses, electoral violence, military influence, and generally poor and corrupt functioning of democratic institutions. Nevertheless, I believe the overall implication of the trends in freedom scores—that political rights and especially civil liberties have deteriorated since the mid-1980s in many prominent electoral democracies—is valid and is supported by other evidence and analysis (see below).

7. Human Rights Watch, *World Report 1998* (New York: Human Rights Watch, 1997), 283; Freedom House, *Freedom in the World: The Annual Survey of Political Rights and Civil Liberties, 1994–1995* (New York: Freedom House, 1995), 567.

8. Human Rights Watch, *World Report 1998*, 284–85. In late 1995, Human Rights Watch estimated that the civil war in southeastern Turkey had claimed "over 19,000 deaths, including some 2,000 death-squad killings of suspected PKK sympathizers, two million displaced, and more than 2,200 villages destroyed, most of which were burned down by Turkish security forces." Human Rights Watch Arms Project, *Weapons Transfers and Violations of the Laws of War in Turkey* (New York: Human Rights Watch, 1995), 1. Human Rights Watch reported some efforts in 1997 to contain and correct abuses by the police and state security forces, but the dominant trend was "a continual back-and-forth between signs of improvement and abuse" (*World Report 1998*, 283). For other documentation and accounts, see Human Rights Watch, annual *World Reports*, and U.S. Department of State, *Country Reports on Human Rights Practices for 1996* (Washington, D.C.: Government Printing Office, 1997). The latter frankly notes the persistence of torture and excessive use of force, despite the close security and economic ties between the United States and Turkey that might have induced a more charitable assessment by the U.S. Department of State.

9. Human Rights Watch, *World Report 1996*, 239.

10. Abraham Lowenthal, "Latin America: Ready for Partnership?" *Foreign Affairs* 72, no. 1 (1992–93): 75.

11. President Bill Clinton, address to the nation on Haiti, September 15, 1994, in *New York Times*, Sept. 17, 1994.

12. Larry Diamond, "Democracy in Latin America: Degrees, Illusions,

and Directions for Consolidation," in *Beyond Sovereigny: Collectively Defending Democracy in the Americas*, edited by Tom Farer (Baltimore: Johns Hopkins University Press, 1996), 52–104.

13. Again, it is difficult to compare scores within countries across this span of time because the standards of the freedom survey rose somewhat in this period. Nevertheless, I discount here the decline of Costa Rica from an average score of 1.5 to 2 (which was explicitly identified by Freedom House as methodological change); the decline of Guatemala from 3 to 3.5, since the latter score, for 1996, denotes a marked improvement from recent years (and probably from what prevailed in 1987); and the decline of Cuba from 6 to 7, which would also seem to involve a shift in rating standards. The nine countries that improved in freedom from 1987 are Uruguay, Chile, Bolivia, Panama, El Salvador, Nicaragua, Mexico, Paraguay, and Haiti. The nine that declined are Trinidad and Tobago, Argentina, Jamaica, Venezuela, Dominican Republic, Ecuador, Brazil, Colombia, and Peru. See table 2.6.

14. Jonathan Hartlyn, "Democracies in Contemporary South America: Convergences and Diversities," in *Argentina: The Challenges of Modernization*, edited by Joseph Tulchin and Allison M. Garland (Wilmington, Del.: Scholarly Resources, 1997), 90.

15. See in particular Karen L. Remmer, "Democracy and Economic Crisis: The Latin American Experience," *World Politics* 42, no. 3 (1990): 315–35; Remmer, "The Political Impact of Economic Crisis in Latin America," *American Political Science Review* 85 (1991): 777–800; Remmer, "Democratization in Latin America," in Slater et al., *Global Transformation*, 91–111.

16. Barbara Geddes, "Challenging the Conventional Wisdom," in *Economic Reform and Democracy*, edited by Larry Diamond and Marc F. Plattner (Baltimore: Johns Hopkins University Press, 1995), 67.

17. Guillermo O'Donnell, "Delegative Democracy," *Journal of Democracy* 5, no. 1 (1994): 55–69.

18. Lowenthal, "Latin America," 83; Francisco C. Weffort, "New Democracies: Which Democracies?" in *The Bold Experiment: South Africa's New Democracy*, edited by Hermann Giliomee and Lawrence Schlemmer (Johannesburg: Southern Book Publishers, 1994), 39–40; Terry Lynn Karl, "The Hybrid Regimes of Central America," *Journal of Democracy* 6, no. 3 (1995): 72–86. An earlier, somewhat more extended (and widely circulated) version of Weffort's essay was released in January 1992 as a working paper for the Woodrow Wilson Center for International Scholars, Washington, D.C.

19. In addition to O'Donnell, "Delegative Democracy," see also O'Donnell's earlier and more extended version, "Delegative Democracy?" Working Paper 173, Kellogg Institute, Notre Dame University, March 1992.

20. O'Donnell, "Delegative Democracy," 62; see also Weffort, "New Democracies," 38–39. As Weffort notes in the 1992 version of his essay (44), however superficial these delegative democracies may be, they are procedurally

democratic in a way that the facade, or oligarchical, democracies of the late nineteenth and early twentieth centuries were not.

21. Weffort, "New Democracies," 39.

22. Kenneth Roberts, "Neoliberalism and the Transformation of Populism in Latin America: The Peruvian Case," *World Politics* 48, no. 1 (1995): 111–12. The same has been true of President Rafael Caldera in Venezuela. For a comparison of the leadership styles of Fujimori and Caldera (and their impacts on democracy in Peru and Venezuela), see Anibal Romero, "Leadership and Political Learning: The Contrasting Approaches of Rafael Caldera in Venezuela and Alberto Fujimori in Peru," paper presented to the First Conference of the Americas, cosponsored by the Hoover Institution and the University of the Americas, Cholula, Mexico, 1996.

23. O'Donnell, "Delegative Democracy," 61–62. Of course, in parliamentary systems, there can be effective representative democracy without separation of powers in the sense envisioned by the U.S. Constitution. However, in such systems the cabinet, including the prime minister, is accountable before parliament and can be regularly and vigorously questioned by it. Moreover, while there is not separation of executive and legislative power, European parliamentary democracies do have independent judiciaries, which are able to protect individual rights and enforce basic constitutional principles. Delegative democracies do not provide executive accountability to the legislature, the courts, or civil society.

24. See Stephan Haggard and Robert R. Kaufman, *The Political Economy of Democratic Transitions* (Princeton: Princeton University Press, 1995); Larry Diamond, "Democracy and Economic Reform: Tensions, Compatibilities, and Strategies for Reconciliation," in *Economic Transition in Eastern Europe and Russia: Realities of Reform*, edited by Edward Lazear (Stanford: Hoover Institution Press, 1995), 107–58; Larry Diamond and Marc F. Plattner, eds., *Economic Reform and Democracy* (Baltimore: Johns Hopkins University Press, 1995); Luiz Carlos Bresser Pereira, José María Maravall, and Adam Przeworski, *Economic Reforms in New Democracies: A Social Democratic Perspective* (Cambridge: Cambridge University Press, 1993); Jorge I. Domínguez, "Free Politics and Free Markets in Latin America," *Journal of Democracy* 9, no. 4 (1998): 70–84.

25. Jonathan Hartlyn and Arturo Valenzuela, "Democracy in Latin America since 1930," in *The Cambridge History of Latin America*, edited by Leslie Bethell (Cambridge: Cambridge University Press, 1994), 6: 106.

26. Weffort, "New Democracies."

27. Cynthia McClintock, "Peru's Fujimori: A Caudillo Derails Democracy," *Current History* 92, no. 572 (1993): 112–19; McClintock, "Presidents, Messiahs, and Constitutional Breakdowns in Peru," in *The Failure of Presidential Democracy: The Case of Latin America*, edited by Juan J. Linz and Arturo Valenzuela (Baltimore: Johns Hopkins University Press, 1994), 286–321.

28. David Scott Palmer, "Peru: Collectively Defending Democracy in the Western Hemisphere," in Farer, *Beyond Sovereignty*, 267; McClintock, "Presidents, Messiahs."

29. McClintock, "Presidents, Messiahs." The latter quotation is from Roberts, "Neoliberalism," 100.

30. Terry Lynn Karl, "The Venezuelan Petro-State and the Crisis of 'Its' Democracy," in *Democracy under Pressure: Politics and Markets in Venezuela*, edited by Jennifer McCoy et al. (Transaction Press, 1994); see also Karl, *The Paradox of Plenty: Oil Booms and Petro-States* (Berkeley: University of California Press, 1997); Moisés Naim, *Paper Tigers and Minotaurs: The Politics of Venezuela's Economic Reforms* (Washington, D.C.: Carnegie Endowment, 1993), esp. chap. 2.

31. Judith Ewell, "Venezuela in Crisis," *Current History* 92, no. 572 (1993); 121.

32. Ibid., 122. See also Michael Coppedge, "Venezuela's Vulnerable Democracy," *Journal of Democracy* 3, no. 4 (1992): 32–44.

33. Coppedge, "Venezuela's Vulnerable Democracy," 37; Michael Coppedge, *Strong Parties and Lame Ducks: Presidential Partyarchy and Factionalism in Venezuela* (Stanford: Stanford University Press, 1994). See also Karl, "The Venezuelan Petro-State."

34. Ewell, "Venezuela in Crisis," 124.

35. Anibal Romero, "Venezuela: Democracy Hangs On," *Journal of Democracy* 7, no. 4 (1996): 32.

36. Ibid.

37. Jonathan Hartlyn, "Explaining Crisis-Ridden Elections in a Fragile Democracy: Presidentialism and Electoral Oversight in the Dominican Republic, 1978–1994," paper presented to the annual meeting of the American Political Science Association, New York, 1994; Hartlyn, "The Dominican Republic: Contemporary Problems and Challenges," in *Democracy in the Caribbean: Political, Economic, and Social Perspectives*, edited by Jorge I. Domínguez, Robert A. Pastor, and R. DeLisle Worrell (Baltimore: Johns Hopkins University Press, 1993), 150–72. See also the country entries in the annual surveys by Freedom House, *Freedom in the World*.

38. The historical establishment of a "reasonably effective" rule of law distinguishes Uruguay, Chile, and Costa Rica from all other countries in Latin America, but in Chile this legacy suffered lasting distortions as a result of the constitutional constraints and authoritarian-minded judges imposed by the Pinochet military regime. Guillermo O'Donnell, "The (Un)Rule of Law in Latin America," in *The Rule of Law and the Underprivileged in Latin America*, edited by Juan Mendéz, Guillermo O'Donnell, and Paulo Sérgio Pinheiro (Notre Dame: University of Notre Dame Press, forthcoming).

39. Freedom House, *Freedom in the World, 1994–1995*, 107. By 1997 the situation had changed little, as Menem continued to manipulate the judicial system (including the Supreme Court he had stacked with his political cronies and loyalists) to block any effective probe of high-level government corruption. Freedom House, *Freedom in the World, 1996–1997*, 127.

40. Edgardo Buscaglia Jr., Maria Dakolias, and William Ratliff, *Judicial Reform in Latin America: A Framework for National Development* (Stanford, Calif.: Hoover Institution, 1995).

41. Freedom House, *Freedom in the World, 1994–1995*, 108.

42. Freedom House, *Freedom in the World, 1993–1994*, 120; Pepe Eliaschev, "Argentina's War on Journalists," *New York Times*, Sept. 22, 1993.

43. U.S. State Department, *Country Reports for 1996*, 341.

44. Kathryn Sikkink, "Nongovernmental Organizations, Democracy, and Human Rights in Latin America," in Farer, *Beyond Sovereignty*, 150–68.

45. The first quotation is from Human Rights Watch, *World Report 1993*, 69. The second is from Freedom House, *Freedom in the World, 1994–1995*, 17.

46. Human Rights Watch, *World Report 1998*, 85.

47. U.S. State Department, *Country Reports for 1995*. On the problems of judicial delays, inertia, inefficiency, and malfunctioning, see Buscaglia et al., *Judicial Reform in Latin America*. In 1992, they note, more than a million cases were pending in the federal courts of Argentina (a country with less than 35 million people). U.S. State Department, *Country Reports for 1995*, 366, notes a backlog of over one million legal cases in Colombia (which has slightly over 35 million people). In Bolivia, an estimated 85–90 percent of all persons in custody have yet to be sentenced (ibid., 334), while in Ecuador only 37 percent of prisoners had been convicted of a crime (402). In Colombia, 97 percent of all crimes go unpunished (363). The term *social cleansing* originated in Colombia, where it is used to describe "the killing of street children, prostitutes, homosexuals, and others deemed socially undesirable" by vigilante groups, which are "often supported or ignored by the police and the military" (363).

48. O'Donnell, "Polyarchies and the (Un)Rule of Law," 18 (March 1998 unpublished manuscript).

49. Human Rights Watch, *World Report 1996*, 64.

50. Human Rights Watch, *World Report 1997*, 116–19, 133–38; U.S. State Department, *Country Reports for 1996*, 455–56, 540.

51. U.S. State Department *Country Reports for 1996*, 475, 477–78. By July 1997, only 25 percent of urban Haitians judged Haiti to be a democracy, down from 58 percent in October 1995. U.S. Information Agency, "The People Have Spoken: Global Views of Democracy," Office of Research and Media Reaction, January 1998, 45.

52. Human Rights Watch, *World Report 1993*, 76; *Economist*, June 19, 1993, 45.

53. Human Rights Watch, *World Report 1993*, 70, 80–81, *World Report 1996*, 65, 70–72; see also the relevant U.S. State Department *Country Reports*. A Brazilian congressional commission in March 1992 reported 4,611 children (mostly teenage males) killed between 1988 and 1990, 82 percent of them black (*Country Reports for 1993*, 81). In Brazil's most populous state, São Paulo, military police killed 338 people in the first half of 1995 and appeared to be dumping corpses at a clandestine site outside the city (Human Rights Watch, *World Report 1996*, 71).

54. Human Rights Watch, *World Report 1993*, 71, 82–83; indigenous communities have also been attacked with impunity by miners and loggers in Brazil.

55. Ibid., 71–72, 86–90 (and other years). A Colombian nongovernmental organization reported 1,288 politically motivated murders in the first half of 1995 alone, and the U.S. State Department reported some 216 political killings in Guatemala in 1995 (*Country Reports for 1996*, 363, 419).

56. See the annual reports of Human Rights Watch and the U.S. State Department. In Peru, the so-called "faceless courts" were set up in 1992 to engineer summary trials of suspected terrorists, yielding "hundreds of arbitrary convictions after unfair trials," and these, along with secret military tribunals, have continued even though the country has supposedly turned the corner in its fifteen-year war against the guerrilla group, Sendero Luminoso. Human Rights Watch, *World Report 1996*, 116–17.

57. Human Rights Watch, *World Report 1993*, 88.

58. Ibid., 70, 80–81, 89–90, 106–9, 112–16; Freedom House, *Freedom in the World, 1992–1993*, 104; and subsequent annual reports of Human Rights Watch, Freedom House, and the U.S. State Department.

59. J. Samuel Fitch, "Democracy, Human Rights, and the Armed Forces in Latin America," in *The United States and Latin America in the 1990s: Beyond the Cold War*, edited by Jonathan Hartlyn, Lars Schoultz, and Augusto Varas (Chapel Hill: University of North Carolina Press, 1993), 200.

60. John Higley and Richard Gunther, eds., *Elites and Democratic Conslidation in Latin America and Southern Europe* (Cambridge: Cambridge University Press, 1992); see in particular the introductory and concluding essays by Michael Burton, Richard Gunther, and John Higley.

61. Ergun Özbudun, "Turkey: How Far from Consolidation?" *Journal of Democracy* 7, no. 3 (1996): 126, 136–37.

62. Freedom House, *Freedom in the World, 1994–1995*, 445–46; U.S. State Department, *Country Reports for 1995*, 1334–35, 1339, *Country Reports for 1996*, 1464–65, 1469; Paula Newburg, "The Two Benazir Bhuttos," *New York Times*, Feb. 11, 1995.

63. U.S. Information Agency, "The People Have Spoken," 26.

64. U.S. State Department, *Country Reports for 1996*, 1154; Human Rights Watch, *World Report 1997*, 240–41, *World Report 1998*, 283–87.

65. Human Rights Watch, *World Report 1996*, 240; see also U.S. State Department, *Country Reports for 1995*, 1060–74, *Country Reports for 1996*, 1153–73. The Committee to Protect Journalists reported that 135 journalists were detained in Turkey in 1996, 14 of them arbitrarily, and that there were nineteen reported instances of physical assault as well as one instance of kidnapping directed against journalists during the year. U.S. State Department, *Country Reports for 1996*, 1164.

66. U.S. State Department, *Country Reports for 1996*, 1163–66.

67. Human Rights Watch, *World Report 1996*, 165–68, *World Report 1997*,

175–80; U.S. State Department, *Country Reports for 1995*, 1335–46, *Country Reports for 1996*, 1464–83.

68. U.S. State Department, *Country Reports for 1996*, 1464, 1466, 1468–69.

69. Human Rights Watch, *World Report 1998*, 201.

70. Human Rights Watch, *World Report 1996*, 171–75, *World Report 1997*, 182–86, *World Report 1998*, 205–8; U.S. State Department, *Country Reports for 1995*, 1352–61, *Country Reports for 1996*, 1483–95.

71. U.S. State Department, *Country Reports for 1996*, 1438–39.

72. Freedom House, *Freedom in the World, 1994–1995*, 296–97; Human Rights Watch, *World Report 1998*, 186. Although the TADA lapsed in 1995, detentions continued for offenses allegedly committed before that.

73. U.S. State Department, *Country Reports for 1996*, 1445–46; Human Rights Watch *World Report 1998*, 186–87.

74. U.S. State Department, *Country Reports for 1995*, 697–706, 721–25, *Country Reports for 1996*, 752–64, 778–89.

75. Carolina G. Hernandez, "The Philippines in 1997: A House Finally in Order?" *Asian Survey* 37, no. 2 (1997): 204–11.

76. U.S. State Department, *Country Reports for 1995*, 989, *Country Reports for 1996*, 1082–91. Human Rights Watch estimates that between 18,500 and 80,000 civilians were killed from the outbreak of the war in Chechnya in December 1994 to the end of 1996. *World Report 1997*, 231.

77. Human Rights Watch, *World Report 1997*, 232.

78. U.S. Information Agency, "The People Have Spoken," 17, 19. Public evaluation of progress toward the rule of law was virtually identical in Ukraine. Three-fourths of Russians also said that the Russian state is unable to maintain law and order.

79. Alexander Motyl, "Soviet Remnants," *Freedom Review* 27, no. 1 (1996): 30–34.

80. Michael McFaul, "Russia's Rough Ride," in *Consolidating the Third Wave Democracies: Regional Challenges*, edited by Larry Diamond, Marc F. Plattner, Yun-han Chu, and Hung-mao Tien (Baltimore: Johns Hopkins University Press, 1997), 64–94.

81. George Zarycky, "Along Russia's Rim: The Challenges of Statehood," *Freedom Review* 27, no. 1 (1996): 34–43. See also the ratings and country reports in Freedom House, *Freedom in the World, 1995–1996, Freedom in the World, 1996–1997*; U.S. State Department, *Country Reports for 1995*, and subsequent years.

82. U.S. State Department, *Country Reports for 1996*, 1000–1001; Human Rights Watch, *World Report 1998*, 265–66.

83. U.S. State Department, *Country Reports for 1996*, 898–900, 894.

84. Human Rights Watch, *World Report 1996*, xxv.

85. Zarycky, "Along Russia's Rim," 42. In September 1996, Armenian president Levon Ter-Petrosian was returned to power in a "flagrantly undemocrat-

ic" election. Ian Bremmer and Cory Welt, "Armenia's New Autocrats," *Journal of Democracy* 8, no. 3 (1997): 77–91, 78.

86. Zarycky, "Along Russia's Rim," 38.

87. The countries are Senegal, Côte d'Ivoire, Burkina Faso, Ghana (in 1992 but not 1996), Togo, Cameroon, Gabon, Zimbabwe, Kenya, Ethiopia, Chad, Equatorial Guinea, the Gambia, Mauritania, Niger, and Zambia. Particularly significant has been the recent trend toward subversion of the electoral process (in Chad, the Gambia, Niger, and nearly in Nigeria) "to clothe army coup-makers in civilian legitimacy that places little restraint on repressive rule." Thomas R. Lansner, "Africa: Between Failure and Opportunity," *Freedom Review* 28, no. 1 (1997): 133.

88. Michael Bratton, "Second Elections in Africa," *Journal of Democracy* 9, no. 3 (1998): 51–66. On Ghana's breakthrough, see two articles under the heading "Ghana's Encouraging Elections": Terence Lyons, "A Major Step Forward," and E. Gyimah-Boadi, "The Challenges Ahead," *Journal of Democracy* 8, no. 2 (1997): 65–91.

89. For a balanced assessment of Uganda's distinctive electoral regime, see Nelson Kasfir, "'No-Party Democracy' in Uganda," *Journal of Democracy* 9, no. 2 (1998): 49–63.

90. Huntington, *The Third Wave*, 87–98, 284–87.

91. This trend has been particularly the case with France, whose initial flirtation with democracy promotion in Africa, in 1991, proved highly superficial and fleeting. For a more detailed treatment of democracy promotion in Africa, see Larry Diamond, "Promoting Democracy in Africa: U.S. and International Policies in Transition," in *Africa in World Politics: Post–Cold War Challenges*, 2d ed., (Boulder, Colo.: Westview, 1995), 250–77. The more powerful or strategically significant the authoritarian state (such as China and Saudi Arabia), the less inclined the established democracies have been to use their own power resources to press for democracy.

92. See Larry Diamond, "Promoting Democracy in the 1990s: Actors, Instruments, and Issues," in *Democracy's Victory and Crisis*, edited by Axel Hadenius (Cambridge: Cambridge University Press, 1997), 311–70.

93. The literature on these facilitating factors is vast. For a recent brief overview, see Larry Diamond, Juan J. Linz, and Seymour Martin Lipset, "What Makes for Democracy?" in Diamond, Linz, and Lipset, *Politics in Developing Countries: Comparing Experiences with Democracy* (Boulder, Colo.: Lynne Rienner, 1995), 1–67.

94. For evidence of the negative effects of poverty and increasing income inequality on the likelihood of democratic endurance, see Adam Przeworski, Michael Alvarez, José Antonio Cheibub, and Fernando Limongi, "What Makes Democracies Endure?" *Journal of Democracy* 7, no. 1 (1996): 50–51.

95. For an influential and stunning assessment, see Alex Inkeles, "The Emerging Social Structure of the World," *World Politics* 47, no. 4 (1975): 467–95.

Of course, the growth in global communciations—not just telephone, radio, TV, and now computer network linkages but also book and periodical translations and business and satellite communications—has been especially breathtaking, generating closer interdependence and "the emergence, for the first time in human history, of a truly universal world culture." Alex Inkeles, "Linking the Whole Human Race: The World as a Communications System," in *Business in the Contemporary World*, edited by Herbert L. Sawyer (Lanham, Md.: University Press of America, 1988), 161.

96. Thomas Franck, "The Emerging Right to Democratic Governance," *American Journal of International Law* 86, no. 46 (1992): 50.

97. For some evidence of these trends, see the collection of essays, "International Organizations and Democracy," *Journal of Democracy* 4, no. 3 (1993): 3–69; Larry Diamond, *Promoting Democracy in the 1990s: Actors and Instruments, Issues and Imperatives* (New York: Carnegie Corporation, 1995), 31–38.

98. John W. Meyer, "The Changing Cultural Content of the Nation-State: A World Society Perspective," in *State and Culture*, edited by G. Steinmetz (Ithaca: Cornell University Press, forthcoming). The quotation is from the January 1996 typescript draft, 2.

99. A classic work demonstrating the impact of modern social structural settings (in particular education) on attitudes and values is Alex Inkeles and David H. Smith, *Becoming Modern* (Cambridge: Harvard University Press, 1974). The role and limits of convergence in producing more similar social and political systems is discussed in Alex Inkeles, "The Emerging Social Structure of the World," *World Politics* 27, no. 4 (1975): 467–95; Inkeles, "Convergence and Divergence in Industrial Societies," in *Directions of Change: Modernization Theory, Research, and Realities*, edited by Mustafa O. Attir, Burkart Holzner, and Zdenek Suda (Boulder, Colo.: Westview, 1981), 3–38.

100. This was the hypothesis advanced by Inkeles in his 1975 and 1981 essays (see previous note), when communist systems still manifested "evident durability."

101. Alex Inkeles and Jon C. Hooper, "A Century of Procedural Due Process Guarantees in Constitutions Worldwide: Testing the World Polity and Convergence Models," *Tocqueville Review* 14, no. 2 (1993): 3–51.

102. Inkeles and Hooper (ibid.) analyzed the extant constitutions in the world at twenty-year intervals between 1870 and 1970. However, 1970 was just about the nadir of the second reverse wave, and if diffusion or convergence do generate over time greater constitutional protection for human rights, 1970 would have been one of the least likely times to observe it. With the explosion in the number of democracies in the world during the third wave, and with the relatively liberal character of the democracies that came into being in most of Central and Eastern Europe, I suspect that one would find a dramatic increase by the early 1990s in the percentage of constitutions affirming each of the fourteen due process rights that Inkeles and Hooper measured.

103. These were India, the Philippines, Thailand, Papua New Guinea, Brazil, Bolivia, Colombia, Venezuela, Peru, Ecuador, the Dominican Republic, the Gambia, and (in 1998) Argentina.

104. Samuel P. Huntington, "Armed Forces and Democracy: Reforming Civil-Military Relations," *Journal of Democracy* 6, no. 4 (1995): 13.

105. Unfortunately, the inhibitions against renewed military intervention appear to be considerably weaker in Africa than in other regions, because most African militaries have far less corporate professionalism and sense of mission and are riven with ethnic, factional, and personalistic divisions and motivations. And the persistence of military rule in Nigeria, in the face of rhetorically strident but effectively mild international pressure, appears to have had its own demonstration effects, encouraging militaries in West Africa in particular to seize power (as in the Gambia and Niger).

106. "Bangladesh's Reluctant Army," *Economist*, Feb. 24, 1996, 35–36.

107. Huntington, "Armed Forces and Democracy," 9–12. I do not think the trends in civil-military relations in third-wave (or existing Third World) democracies are as broadly encouraging as Huntington portrays them, however. Undeniable progress in a number of cases, such as South Korea, the Philippines, and Poland, is counterbalanced by stagnation or regression in some others, as discussed below. In particular, the state of civil-military relations in Latin America "remains decidedly mixed for the fundamental reason that it is not obvious what an appropriate role for [the military] should be that would facilitate their removal from active involvement in domestic politics" (Hartlyn, "Democracies in Contemporary South America," 17). Like many other students of Latin America, Hartlyn believes that the militarization of the drug war (supported by the United States) has impeded the transition to a more democratically responsible and professionally constrained military.

108. The absence of military regimes in the postcommunist states of the former Soviet Union and the former Yugoslavia—where state authority is weak and fragmented and civilian, multiparty regimes take the form of pseudodemocracy (or a very illiberal electoral democracy)—may owe to the radically antipolitical atmosphere, "the near total flight from the public world as such." This, Charles Fairbanks speculates, produces leaders of militias and irregular armies "driven by the desire for money or raw power or by pointless grudges rather than by the ambition that builds states" ("The Postcommunist Wars," *Journal of Democracy* 6, no. 4 [1995]: 28, 30). In Russia, a major reason that the military has not seized power, in Huntington's view ("Reforming Civil-Military Relations," 14), is that it is no longer capable of doing so, given the dramatic declines in its coherence, organization, professionalism, and morale since the breakup of the Soviet Union.

109. Philippe C. Schmitter, "Democracy's Future: More Liberal, Preliberal, or Postliberal?" *Journal of Democracy* 6, no. 1 (1995): 17.

110. For a trenchant analysis linking Colombia's democratic regression to

murderous violence, wholesale impunity of state security forces, and "a reassertion of military authority and autonomy," despite a succession of reformist presidents, see Marc W. Chernick, "Colombia's Fault Lines," *Current History* 95, no. 598 (1996): 76–81.

Chapter 3. Consolidating Democracy

1. Samuel P. Huntington, "Democracy for the Long Haul," *Journal of Democracy* 7, no. 2 (1996): 5.

2. I am grateful to Guillermo O'Donnell for emphasizing this point to me and for identifying the apparent circularity in an earlier formulation of my definition.

3. Three widely influential definitions of legitimacy along these lines are found in Seymour Martin Lipset, *Political Man: The Social Bases of Politics* (Baltimore: Johns Hopkins University Press, 1981), 64; Juan J. Linz, *The Breakdown of Democratic Regimes: Crisis, Breakdown, and Reequilibration* (Baltimore: Johns Hopkins University Press, 78), 16–18; Robert A. Dahl, *Polyarchy: Participation and Opposition* (New Haven: Yale University Press, 1971), 129–31. One value of this conceptual approach is that it enables us to apply the notion of consolidation, and its relationship to regime persistence and stability, to nondemocratic (or semidemocratic) as well as democratic regimes. For elaboration of this broader conception of legitimacy and application to the (mainly less-than-democratic) regimes of Southeast Asia, see Muthiah Alagappa, ed., *Political Legitimacy in Southeast Asia: The Quest for Moral Authority* (Stanford: Stanford University Press, 1995). Because democratic institutions have greater capacity for adaptation and self-correction, and are less dependent for their legitimation on personalities and immediate economic performance, democracies are capable of more enduring legitimation than nondemocracies and, hence, of managing political strains and institutional crises without experiencing deconsolidation. But this by no means guarantees that any particular democracy will achieve such lasting legitimation/consolidation, and the hypothesis raises a host of issues beyond the scope of this analysis.

4. Juan J. Linz and Alfred Stepan, *Problems of Democratic Transition and Consolidation: Southern Europe, South America, and Post-Communist Europe* (Baltimore: Johns Hopkins University Press, 1996), 5–7; Linz and Stepan, "Toward Consolidated Democracies," *Journal of Democracy* 7, no. 2 (1996): 14–16. For other conceptualizations of consolidation that are similar to, or at least not inconsisent with, this emphasis, see Adam Przeworski, *Democracy and the Market: Political and Economic Reforms in Eastern Europe and Latin America* (Cambridge: Cambridge University Press, 1991), 26–34; Guillermo O'Donnell, "Transitions, Continuities, and Paradoxes," in *Issues in Democratic Consolidation: The New South American Democracies in Comparative Perspective*, edited by Scott Mainwaring, Guillermo O'Donnell, and J. Samuel Valenzuela (Notre Dame: Notre Dame University

Press, 1992), 48–49; J. Samuel Valenzuela, "Democratic Consolidation in Post-Transitional Settings: Notion, Process, and Facilitating Conditions," in Mainwaring et al., *Issues in Democratic Consolidation*, 69; Philippe C. Schmitter, "Interest Systems and the Consolidation of Democracies," in *Reexamining Democracy: Essays in Honor of Seymour Martin Lipset*, edited by Gary Marks and Larry Diamond (Newbury Park, Calif.: Sage, 1992), 158–59; Richard Gunther, Hans-Jürgen Puhle, and P. Nikiforos Diamandouros, eds., introduction to *The Politics of Democratic Consolidation: Southern Europe in Comparative Perspective* (Baltimore: Johns Hopkins University Press, 1995), 7–10. One important difference among these perspectives involves the extent to which consolidation rests on normative and attitudinal foundations. Przeworski, *Democracy and the Market*, avoids the invocation of norms and values, instead construing democratic consolidation as a self-enforcing "equilibrium of the decentralized strategies of all relevant political forces," shaped by institutions that are sufficiently "fair" so that they "make even losing under democracy more attractive than a future under nondemocratic alternatives" (26 and 33). I believe consolidation cannot be measured and understood without reference to political attitudes and values.

5. Dankwart Rustow, "Transitions to Democracy: Toward a Dynamic Model," *Comparative Politics* 2, no. 3 (1970): 337–63.

6. Laurence Whitehead, "The Consolidation of Fragile Democracies: A Discussion with Illustrations," in *Democracy in the Americas: Stopping the Pendulum*, edited by Robert A. Pastor (New York: Holmes and Meier, 1989), 79.

7. Linz, *The Breakdown of Democratic Regimes*, 16, 29–30, 36–37.

8. Robert A. Dahl, *Polyarchy: Participation and Opposition* (New Haven: Yale University Press, 1971), 128.

9. A partial exception is the work of John Higley and Michael Burton, but this is mainly focused on the choices and decisions that produce procedural consensus and increased integration among elites. See, for example, Michael Burton, Richard Gunther, and John Higley, "Introduction: Elite Transformations and Democratic Regimes," in *Elites and Democratic Consolidation in Latin America and Southern Europe*, edited by John Higley and Richard Gunther (Cambridge: Cambridge University Press, 1992), 1–37. Gunther et al., *The Politics of Democratic Consolidation*, 13, usefully urge attention to the symbolic gestures, public rhetoric, official documents, and ideological declarations of leaders and organizations.

10. Linz, *The Breakdown of Democratic Regimes*, 28–38.

11. Of course, the absence of antisystem parties does not necessarily mean that democracy has become consolidated. Otherwise, it would be easy to accept Guillermo O'Donnell's assertion that the term has no useful meaning. See his "Illusions about Consolidation," *Journal of Democracy* 7, no. 2 (1996): 34–51. This is why we must study norms and behaviors at the mass level and not simply look for overt, immediate signs of contempt for democracy at the level of elites or organizations.

12. Gunther et al., *The Politics of Democratic Consolidation*, 8.

13. In their seminal formulation, Linz and Stepan distinguish a third "constitutional" dimension. However, this is another dimension of behavior, involving the habitual resolution of conflicts within the "specific laws, procedures, and institutions sanctioned by the democratic process." Their behavioral dimension is indicated when no significant actors spend significant resources trying to create a nondemocratic regime. I believe these two dimensions can be usefully combined with no real loss of explanatory power. They both involve behavioral support for democracy—its institutions and constraints. Linz and Stepan, *Problems of Democratic Transition and Consolidation*, 6.

14. Barry R. Weingast, "The Political Foundations of Democracy and the Rule of Law," *American Political Science Review* 91, no. 2 (1997): 251.

15. O'Donnell, "Illusions about Consolidation," 39.

16. Ibid.

17. Samuel P. Huntington, *The Third Wave: Democratization in the Late Twentieth Century* (Norman: University of Oklahoma Press, 1991), 266–67.

18. For evidence of rising levels of political alienation, detachment, and cynicism in Venezuela, and the increasing separation between the society and an ossified party system, see Anibal Romero, "Venezuela: Democracy Hangs On," *Journal of Democracy* 7, no. 4 (1996): 30–42; and the various contributions in Louis W. Goodman, Johanna Mendelson Forman, Moisés Naím, Joseph S. Tulchin, and Gary Bland, eds., *Lessons of the Venezuelan Experience* (Washington, D.C.: Woodrow Wilson Center Press, 1995). India, by contrast, has been witnessing a fragmentation and deconsolidation of its political party system but not of its democracy per se.

19. These criteria of institutionalization are elaborated in Samuel P. Huntington, *Political Order in Changing Societies* (New Haven: Yale University Press, 1968), 12–26.

20. Dahl, *Polyarchy*, 15–16, 36–37. Mutual security may be seen as the ability of contending political forces, in government and opposition and within factions of the opposition, to tolerate one another: the confidence that they may oppose, protest, and contest for power without risk to their political existence or other basic interests.

21. See, for example, Stephan Haggard and Robert R. Kaufman, *The Political Economy of Democratic Consolidation* (Princeton: Princeton University Press, 1995); Larry Diamond and Marc F. Plattner, eds., *Economic Reform and Democracy* (Baltimore: Johns Hopkins University Press, 1995).

22. I borrow the term *partial regimes* from Philippe Schmitter, although he applies it more narrowly to "distinctive sites for the representation of social groups and the resolution of their ensuing conflicts." Schmitter, "Interest Systems and the Consolidation of Democracy," 160.

23. Lipset, *Political Man*, 67–71.

24. For a seminal discussion of these causal interactions, see Linz, *The Breakdown of Democratic Regimes*, 18–23.

25. Leonardo Morlino and José R. Montero, "Legitimacy and Democracy in Southern Europe," in Gunther et al., *The Politics of Democratic Consolidation*, 231–60. For more details, see chap. 5, this volume.

26. Adam Przeworski, Michael Alvarez, José Antonio Cheibub, and Fernando Limongi, "What Makes Democracies Endure?" *Journal of Democracy* 7, no. 1 (1996): 41–42.

27. John Williamson, "Democracy and the 'Washington Consensus,'" *World Development* 21, no. 8 (1993): 1329–36; Henry S. Rowen, "World Wealth Expanding: Why a Rich, Democratic, and (Perhaps) Peaceful Era Is Ahead," in *The Mosaic of Economic Growth*, edited by Ralph Landau, Timothy Taylor, and Gavin Wright (Stanford: Stanford University Press, 1996), 93–95.

28. Stephan Haggard and Robert R. Kaufman, eds., *The Politics of Economic Adjustment* (Princeton: Princeton University Press, 1992); Luis Carlos Bresser Pereira, José Maria Maravall, and Adam Przeworski, *Economic Reforms in New Democracies: A Social-Democratic Approach* (Cambridge: Cambridge University Press, 1993); Joan Nelson, ed., *A Precarious Balance: Democracy and Economic Reforms in Latin America*, 2 vols. (San Francisco: Institute for Contemporary Studies and Washington, Overseas Development Council, 1994); Joan Nelson et al., *Intricate Links: Democratization and Market Reforms in Latin America and Eastern Europe* (Washington, D.C.: Overseas Development Council, 1994); Haggard and Kaufman, *The Political Economy of Democratic Transitions*; Larry Diamond, "Democracy and Economic Reform: Tensions, Compatibilities, and Strategies for Reconciliation," in *Economic Transition in Eastern Europe and Russia: Realities of Reform*, edited by Edward P. Lazear (Stanford, Calif.: Hoover Institution, 1995), 107–58.

29. Karen L. Remmer, "Democracy and Economic Crisis: The Latin American Experience," *World Politics* 42, no. 3 (1990): 315–35; Remmer, "The Political Impact of Economic Crisis in Latin America," *American Political Science Review* 85 (1991): 777–800; Remmer, "Democratization in Latin America," in *Global Transformation and the Third World*, edited by Robert O. Slater, Barry M. Schutz, and Steven R. Dorr (Boulder, Colo.: Lynne Rienner, 1993), 91–111.

30. See World Bank, *World Development Report 1996* (New York: Oxford University Press, 1996), 196–97, table 5 (or any other recent year of that annual report), for country data on income distributions. As Rowen observes, "The ratio of incomes of the richest 20 percent of the population to the poorest 20 percent is 4 to 11 times in a set of East Asian countries and 11 to 26 times in a set of Latin American ones." Rowen, "World Wealth Expanding," 102, n. 9. Indeed, as Rowen notes in his table 2, that ratio is an incredible 32 in Brazil. Nora Lustig reports that the overall Latin American ratio of the top fifth to bottom fifth income shares is 10, compared to 6.7 in other low- and middle-income countries; Nora Lustig, ed., *Coping with Austerity: Poverty and Inequality in Latin America* (Washington, D.C.: Brookings, 1995), 2.

31. Jonathan Hartlyn, "Democracies in Contemporary South America:

Convergences and Diversities," in *Argentina: The Challenges of Modernization*, edited by Joseph Tulchin and Allison M. Garland (Wilmington, Del.: Scholarly Resources, 1997), 95, table 3. The Inter-American Dialogue estimated that about half of the roughly 180 million poor Latin Americans live in such abject poverty that they do not have enough to eat and that in many countries (including Brazil and Peru) "a substantial majority of the population is impoverished." *Convergence and Community: The Americas in 1993* (Washington, D.C.: Inter-American Dialogue, 1992), 43.

32. Lustig, *Coping with Austerity*, 4–5, 16.

33. Inter-American Dialogue, *The Americas in 1994: A Time for Leadership* (Washington, D.C.: Inter-American Dialogue, 1994), 3.

34. World Bank, *World Development Report 1998*, table 5. Brazil is the only country in the world with a Gini index of income inequality of more than 0.60 (for the Gini index, 0 indicates perfect equality and 1 perfect inequality). Brazil is also the only one of the sixty-five low- and middle-income countries (not to mention the twenty much more egalitarian high-income countries) in which the top 10 percent of individuals capture more than half of all income. Moreover, income inequality has evidently been increasing, and "in the 1980s the increase in inequality was particularly perverse, hurting the poorest segments of the population the most." Ricardo Paes de Barros, Rosanne Mendonça, and Sonia Rocha, "Brazil: Welfare, Inequality, Poverty, Social Indicators, and Social Programs in the 1980s," in Lustig, *Coping with Austerity*, 248.

35. Bolivar Lamounier, "Inequality against Democracy," in *Politics in Developing Countries: Comparing Experiences with Democracy*, edited by Larry Diamond, Juan J. Linz, and Seymour Martin Lipset (Boulder, Colo.: Lynne Rienner, 1995), 119–70.

36. "Unambiguous evidence" of intensifying poverty during the 1980s and erosions of income for all but the top tenth of income earners in Brazil is presented in de Barros et al., "Brazil in the 1980s," 250–51. Inequality even increased during the last half of the decade, "when the government was giving great emphasis to social programs" (270). For evidence of Brazilians' weaker support for democracy, see chap. 5.

37. Armando Castelar Pinheiro, "Brazil's Economy in the 1990s: Looking Back and Forwards," in *Comparing Brazil and South Africa: Two Transitional States in Political and Economic Perspective*, edited by Steven Friedman and Riaan de Villiers (Johannesburg: Centre for Policy Studies and the Foundation for Global Dialogue; and São Paulo: Instituto de Estudos Econômicos, Sociais, e Politicos de São Paulo, 1996), 249–83.

38. Charles Simkins, "The New South Africa: Problems of Reconstruction," *Journal of Democracy* 7, no. 1 (1996): 83.

39. Only about 13 percent of South Africa's population is White, about 76 is Black African, and the remainder is Colored and Asian. For data and further analysis of the historical implications of this massive inequality, see Steven Fried-

man, "South Africa: Divided in a Special Way," in Diamond et al., *Politics in Developing Countries*, 531–81.

40. Gustavo Marquez, "Venezuela: Poverty and Social Policies in the 1980s," in Lustig, *Coping with Austerity*, 400.

41. Ibid., 430, 433.

42. Terry Lynn Karl, *The Paradox of Plenty: Oil Booms and Petro-States* (Berkeley: University of California Press, 1997), chap. 8.

43. Adolfo Figueroa, "Peru: Social Policies and Economic Adjustment," in Lustig, *Coping with Austerity*, 392.

44. Ibid., 376–81.

45. These figures were for September 1990. By March 1992, a month before the Fujimori coup, the respective confidence figures had plummeted to 12 percent and 14 percent, and to 17 percent for congress (from 45% in September 1990). Cynthia McClintock, "Presidents, Messiahs, and Constitutional Breakdowns in Peru," in *The Failure of Presidential Democracy: The Case of Latin America*, edited by Juan J. Linz and Arturo Valenzuela (Baltimore: Johns Hopkins University Press, 1994), 286–321.

46. Cynthia McClintock, "La voluntad política presidencial y la ruptura constitucional de 1992 en al Perú," in *Los Enigmas del Poder* (Lima: Fundación Friedrich Ebert, 1996), 53–77, quotation on 57–58.

47. Lustig, *Coping with Austerity*, 16.

48. Samuel A. Morley, *Poverty and Inequality in Latin America: Past Evidence and Future Prospects*, Policy Essay 13 (Washington, D.C.: Overseas Development Council, 1994), 1. In fact, Morley emphasizes, so critically important is the overall context of growth that "no social emergency program or special antipoverty social policy can completely offset the effect on the poor of a macroeconomic downturn" (69).

49. Rowen, "World Wealth Expanding," 101–8. In Latin America, Chile and Costa Rica stand out for their ability to rebound through adjustment policies, precisely because their sustained high levels of social investment in mass education "gave both countries a flexibility and an ability to develop new and promising export opportunities created by the reform process." Morley, *Poverty and Inequality*, 73. On the role of human capital investment in the East Asian experience, see World Bank, *The East Asian Miracle: Economic Growth and Public Policy* (New York: Oxford University Press, 1993).

50. Jeffrey Puryear and José Joaquín Brunner, "An Agenda for Educational Reform in Latin America and the Caribbean," Policy Brief, Inter-American Dialogue, Washington, D.C., 1994. On overall underfinancing of education (as a result of the low tax base in the region), see Fernando Reimers, "Education Finance in Latin America: Perils and Opportunities," in *Key Issues*, vol. 1 of *Education, Equity, and Economic Competitiveness in the Americas*, edited by Jeffrey M. Puryear and José Joaquín Brunner (Washington, D.C.: Organization of American States, 1995), 9–65.

51. Carol Graham, *Social Safety Nets, Politics, and the Poor: Transitions to Market Economies* (Washington, D.C.: Brookings, 1994).

52. Juan Linz and Alfred Stepan, "Political Crafting of Democratic Consolidation or Destruction: European and South American Comparisons," in Pastor, *Democracy in the Americas*, 41–61. Linz and Stepan, *Problems of Democratic Transition*, 108–15.

53. World Bank, *World Development Report 1983*, 148–49, table 1. Spain's per capita GNP of $5,640 in 1981 ranked it 23d of 119 countries for which such data was available.

54. Felipe Agüero, "Chile: South America's Success Story?" *Current History* 92, no. 572 (1993): 130. The data on Chile's macroeconomic performance, 1990–94, are from World Bank, *World Development Report 1996*, 209, table 11.

55. The decline in value of the New Taiwan dollar (18%) was the second lowest among major East Asian currencies in 1997 (it was 51% for South Korea and Thailand); unemployment in early 1998 was less than 3 percent, and foreign debt was also unusually low. While social spending is increasing in Taiwan, macroeconomic prudence and fiscal restraint have basically been maintained under democracy. *China Post* (Taipei), Jan. 24, 1998.

56. *The Republic of China Yearbook 1996* (Taipei: Government Information Office, 1996), 153.

57. Yun-han Chu, "The Political Economy of Democratic Transition in East Asia," in *Constructing Democracy and Markets: East Asia and Latin America* (Washington, D.C. and Los Angeles: International Forum for Democratic Studies and Pacific Council on International Policy, 1996), 26–38. On the growing problem of money and corruption in Taiwan's politics, see also Chu, "Taiwan's Unique Challenges," *Journal of Democracy* 7, no. 3 (1996): 69–82. The 4.98-fold difference in income shares between the top and bottom fifths still leaves Taiwan with one of the more egalitarian income distributions in the world. Taiwan's gap between rich and poor is smaller than in the typical industrialized country, less than in the typical postcommunist country, and virtually identical to India's. See World Bank, *World Development Report 1998*, table 5, for comparisons.

58. Chu, "Taiwan's Unique Challenges," 78. As he indicates there, "most voters distrust not only the legislature as a whole but their own representatives as well."

59. Samuel P. Huntington, "Reforming Civil-Military Relations," *Journal of Democracy* 6, no. 4 (1995): 15.

60. Przeworski et al., "What Makes Democracies Endure?" For low- and middle-income countries, purchasing power parity (PPP) estimates of GNP per capita are typically 1.5 to 2 times larger than reported GNP per capita. Thus, the Przeworski et al. threshold of $6,000 in PPP (1985 dollars) would be lower if figured in nominal dollars but would also then need to be adjusted upward for inflation. The Przeworski et al. threshold is therefore still considerably higher than Huntington's "coup attempt ceiling" but probably below the PPP GNP per capi-

ta of a number of upper-middle-income countries, including South Korea, Argentina, Chile, Mauritius, and the Czech Republic. See World Bank, *World Development Report 1996*, table 1, for PPP estimates for 1994.

61. Larry Diamond, "Economic Development and Democracy Reconsidered," in Marks and Diamond, *Reexamining Democracy*, 93–139.

62. Bresser Pereira et al., *Economic Reforms in New Democracies*, 215–16.

63. Linz, *The Breakdown of Democratic Regimes*, 23, 56–61. "Paradoxically, a democratic regime might need a larger number of internal security forces than a stabilized dictatorship, since it cannot count on the effect of fear. Its reactions to violence require massive but moderate responses; only numerical superiority can prevent the deadly reactions of overpowered agents of authority" (61).

64. Juan J. Linz, "State Building and Nation Building," *European Review* 1, no. 4 (1993): 355–69.

65. For evidence of a "dramatic post-conflict crime wave" that gripped El Salvador (and that became one of the principal performance challenges for its new democracy), see Chuck Call, "Incorporating Former Enemies into the Police: National Reconciliation and Police Reform in Post-Conflict El Salvador," paper prepared for the MacArthur Consortium Workshop on Democratization and Internal Security, Stanford University, 1996 (permission to cite this paper has been granted by the author). In addition to the other crime-inducing legacies of civil war mentioned in the text, Call notes the transformation of some death squads into organized criminal gangs.

66. This problem appears most serious in Brazil, where there are an estimated seven to ten million urban street children and where there appears to be extensive and even increasing murderous violence against civilians by both state and military police, with many bodies being dumped at clandestine sites. Human Rights Watch, *World Report 1996* (New York: Human Rights Watch, 1995), 65, 70–72; *World Report 1993*, 80–81. In Colombia, the prevalence of these police violations of human rights "led the U.N. special rapporteurs for extrajudicial executions and torture to issue a joint report characterizing the situation as 'alarming'" (*World Report 1996*, 65). In El Salvador, the postconflict crime wave led to popular support for vigilante justice, and it rekindled military role expansion as the military began to fill the demand for greater internal security (Call, "National Reconciliation"). Popular vigilante street retribution against suspected criminals is also increasingly common in South Africa, as are illiberal government responses, such as an act to make bail more difficult for suspected violent criminals (*World Report 1996*, 48).

67. U.S. Information Agency, "The People Have Spoken: Global Views of Democracy," Office of Research and Media Reaction, January 1998, 9, 14, 26, 34, 43. The various surveys were conducted in 1996 and 1997 (in Korea in September 1997, two months before the financial crash). The trends and determinants of public support for democracy are explored in greater depth in chapter 5.

68. Catharin Dalpino, "Political Corruption: Thailand's Search for Accountability," *Journal of Democracy* 2, no. 4 (1991): 62.

69. Larry Diamond, "Political Corruption: Nigeria's Perennial Struggle," *Journal of Democracy* 2, no. 4 (1991): 73–85; Diamond, "Nigeria: The Uncivic Society and the Descent into Praetorianism," in Diamond et al., *Politics in Developing Countries*, 437–40, 447–52, 468–72

70. Andrew Reynolds, "Electoral Systems and Democratic Consolidation in Southern Africa" (Ph.D. diss., Department of Political Science, University of California at San Diego, 1996), 78; Freedom House, *Freedom in the World: The Annual Survey of Political Rights and Civil Liberties, 1995–1996* (New York: Freedom House, 1996), 502–3. As Reynolds notes, since 1993, President Chiluba "has been forced to fire four senior cabinet ministers and over 20 other senior officials enmeshed in corruption scandals. However, this has failed to cleanse the international perception that the MMD government is rotten to the core." For assessments of Zambia's democratic deterioration in comparative perspective, see Richard Joseph, "Africa 1990–1997: From Abertura to Closure," *Journal of Democracy* 9, no. 2 (1998): 3–17; Michael Bratton, "Second Elections in Africa," *Journal of Democracy* 9, no. 3 (1998).

71. Stephan Haggard and Robert R. Kaufman, "Institutions and Economic Adjustment," in Haggard and Kaufman, *The Politics of Economic Adjustment*, 25. The term is originally Miles Kahler's.

72. Linz and Stepan, *Problems of Democratic Transition*, 11.

73. This theme has been emphasized increasingly by the scholarly and policy literatures in recent years and emerges as a major recurrent theme among the essays in Diamond and Plattner, *Economic Reform and Democracy*. See in particular Moisés Naím, "Latin America: The Second Stage of Reform," 28–44; Also see Naím, "Latin America's Journey to the Market: From Macroeconomic Shocks to Institutional Therapy," Occasional Paper 62, International Center for Economic Growth, San Francisco, 1995.

74. For a case demonstration, see Call, "National Reconciliation."

75. The Washington Office on Latin America (WOLA), "The International Community, Police Reform and Human Rights in Central America and Haiti," November 1995. The quotes are from a discussion of U.S. assistance programs, p. 27, and from page 17, respectively.

76. Ibid., 18.

77. Andreas Schedler, "Under- and Overinstitutionalization: Some Ideal Typical Propositions Concerning New and Old Party Systems," Working Paper 213, Helen Kellogg Institute for International Studies, Notre Dame University, 1995.

78. Michael Coppedge, *Strong Parties and Lame Ducks: Presidential Partyarchy and Factionalism in Venezuela* (Stanford: Stanford University Press, 1994).

79. Juan J. Linz, "Change and Continuity in the Nature of Contemporary Democracies," in Marks and Diamond, *Reexamining Democracy*, 184–90.

80. Seymour Martin Lipset, "The Social Requisities of Democracy, Revisited," *American Sociological Review* 59, no. 1 (1994): 114. For a cogent and more extended recent treatment of this classic proposition linking the strength of parties and party systems to the stability of democracy, see Scott Mainwaring and Timothy R. Scully, eds., *Building Democratic Institutions: Party Systems in Latin America* (Stanford: Stanford University Press, 1995), 1–34.

81. Philippe C. Schmitter, "Intermediaries in the Consolidation of New Democracies: The Role of Parties, Associations, and Movements," in *Political Parties and Democracy*, edited by Larry Diamond and Richard Gunther (forthcoming).

82. Larry Diamond "Rethinking Civil Society: Toward Democratic Consolidation," *Journal of Democracy* 5, no. 3 (1994): 15.

83. Larry Diamond, Juan J. Linz, and Seymour Martin Lipset, "What Makes for Democracy?" in Diamond et al., *Politics in Developing Countries*, 34.

84. Mainwaring and Scully, *Building Democratic Institutions*, 4–5. Among the conditions (indicators) of party system institutionalization they also list actor commitment to the legitimacy of the multiparty electoral process, but that is a dimension of democratic consolidation itself.

85. Haggard and Kaufman, *The Political Economy of Democratic Transitions*, 370. See also 170–74, 355–64, and passim.

86. Giovanni Sartori, *Parties and Party Systems: A Framework for Analysis* (Cambridge: Cambridge University Press, 1976); Linz, *The Breakdown of Democratic Regimes*, 24–27; Mainwaring and Scully, *Building Democratic Institutions*, 32–33. On the poor fit between presidentialism and multipartism in Latin America, see Scott Mainwaring, "Presidentialism, Multipartism, and Democracy: The Difficult Combination," *Comparative Political Studies* 26 (1993): 198–228.

87. Naìm, "Latin America's Journey to the Market"; Naìm, "Latin America: The Second Stage of Reform."

88. Giovanni Sartori, *Comparative Constitutional Engineering: An Inquiry into Structures, Incentives, and Outcomes* (New York: New York University Press, 1994).

89. More generally, it appears that while institutional configurations are not fixed at the moment of transition, "the extent of post-transition constitutional revision in our cases is surprisingly limited and that the initial political bargains struck at the time of the transition had important implications for the subsequent path of political development." Haggard and Kaufman, *The Political Economy of Democratic Transitions*, 371.

90. In Bolivia, the congress chooses between the top three presidential candidates if no candidate wins a majority of the popular vote. Although the congress cannot subsequently remove the president by a vote of no confidence, this unusual provision for executive selection (which defines a particular type of hybrid regime that Shugart and Carey term "assembly independent") provides an incentive for formation of cross-party congressional coalitions much stronger

than is found in purely presidential systems. See Matthew Soberg Shugart and John M. Carey, *Presidents and Assemblies: Constitutional Design and Electoral Dynamics* (Cambridge: Cambridge University Press, 1992). Shugart and Carey are generally skeptical of pure parliamentarism and inclined toward the French-style, premier-presidential system; Sartori, in *Comparative Constitutional Engineering*, takes a similar stance. The most important critique of presidentialism and the case for the parliamentary alternative is Juan J. Linz and Arturo Valenzuela, eds., *The Failure of Presidential Democracy: Comparative Perspectives*, vol. 1, and *The Case of Latin America*, vol. 2 (Baltimore: Johns Hopkins University Press, 1994), and especially the essays by Linz, "Parliamentary or Presidential Democracy: Does It Make a Difference?" 3–87 (both vols.), and Valenzuela, "Party Politics and the Crisis of Presidentialism in Chile: A Proposal for a Parliamentary Form of Government," 2: 91–150. An earlier and abbreviated version of Linz's essay, "The Perils of Presidentialism," appeared in the *Journal of Democracy* 1, no. 1 (1990), 51–70.

91. Rein Taagapera and Matthew Soberg Shugart, *Seats and Votes: The Effects and Determinants of Electoral Systems* (New Haven: Yale University Press, 1989), 218; see also Arend Lijphart, *Electoral Systems and Party Systems: A Study of Twenty-seven Democracies, 1945–1990* (Oxford: Oxford University Press, 1994), 151.

92. Key works, in addition to Sartori's *Comparative Constitutional Engineering*, exploring the effects, advantages, and disadvantages of different electoral systems are Maurice Duverger, *Political Parties: Their Organization and Activity in the Modern State* (New York: Wiley, 1963); Douglas Rae, *The Political Consequences of Electoral Laws* (New Haven: Yale University Press, 1967); Arend Lijphart, *Democracies: Patterns of Majoritarian and Consensus Government in Twenty-one Democracies* (New Haven: Yale University Press, 1984); Bernard Grofman and Arend Lijphart, eds., *Electoral Laws and Their Consequences* (New York: Agathon, 1986); Taagepera and Shugart, *Seats and Votes;* Donald Horowitz, *A Democratic South Africa: Constitutional Engineering in a Divided Society* (Berkeley: University of California Press, 1991); Shugart and Carey, *Presidents and Assemblies;* Lijphart, *Electoral Systems and Party Systems.* For a debate on the merits of proportional representation versus plurality systems, see the essays by Arend Lijphart, Guy Lardeyret, Quentin Quade, and Ken Gladdish in *The Global Resurgence of Democracy,* edited by Larry Diamond and Marc F. Plattner (Baltimore: Johns Hopkins University Press, 1996), 162–206.

93. "Effective number of parties" is a technical expression for measuring the degree of fragmentation in parliament (or in the popular vote for parliament). Although it is a continuous scale, it might be thought of as roughly the number of parties significant enough to shape the formation of government and the dynamics of the political system. Lijphart, *Electoral Systems and Party Systems*, table 5.1 and passim, provides clear evidence of the greater tendency of proportional representation toward multipartism.

94. Shugart and Carey, *Presidents and Assemblies*, 7.
95. The seminal exposition of the majoritarian and consensual models is Lijphart, *Democracies*. For an application of the institutional alternatives and their implications, see Andrew Reynolds, *Electoral Systems and Democratization in Southern Africa* (Oxford: Oxford University Press, 1998).
96. According to Joel Barkan, in relatively poor agrarian communities, such as predominate in the typical African country, accountability is particularly important because voters mainly care about delivery of the basic infrastructure of economic development, and thus service to the constituency is the main criterion by which candidates and parties are evaluated. Barkan, "Elections in Agrarian Societies," *Journal of Democracy* 6, no. 4 (1995): 106–16. However, as Sartori observes, the linkage between voter and representative weakens as the number of voters per district increases. Sartori, *Comparative Constitutional Engineering*, 56.
97. For a description of how the system works in practice, see Taagepera and Shugart, *Seats and Votes*, 26–28; Lijphart, *Electoral Systems and Party Systems*, 157–59.
98. See Reynolds, *Electoral Systems*.
99. Taagepera and Shugart, *Seats and Votes*, 228 and 229.
100. Ken Gladdish, "Choosing an Electoral System: The Primacy of the Particular," *Journal of Democracy* 4, no. 1 (1993): 53–65.
101. Sartori, *Parties and Party Systems;* see also Linz, *The Breakdown of Democratic Regimes*, 26.
102. Vincent T. Maphai, "The New South Africa: A Season for Power-Sharing," *Journal of Democracy* 7, no. 1 (1996): 67.
103. Although they differ significantly in their preferred institutional approaches and formulas, this is a common, underlying assumption in the work of both Arend Lijphart and Donald Horowitz. See for example Arend Lijphart, *Democracy in Plural Societies* (New Haven: Yale University Press, 1977); Lijphart, *Democracies;* Lijphart, "The Power-Sharing Model," in *Conflict and Peacemaking in Multiethnic Societies*, edited by Joseph V. Montville (Lexington, Mass: Lexington Books, 1990); Donald Horowitz, *Ethnic Groups in Conflict* (Berkeley: University of California Press, 1985); Horowitz, "Ethnic Conflict Management for Policymakers," in Montville, *Conflict and Peacemaking;* Horowitz, "Democracy in Divided Societies," *Journal of Democracy* 4, no. 4 (1993): 18–38, also in *Nationalism, Ethnic Conflict, and Democracy*, edited by Larry Diamond and Marc F. Plattner (Baltimore: Johns Hopkins University Press, 1994).
104. See Lijpart, *Democracy in Plural Societies*, for the consociational model. The record of consociationalism in the developing world (as in Lebanon) does not inspire confidence. This is true because the model can rigidify in ways that are difficult to modify with social change, because it relies heavily on elite control over ethnic or political groups, and because it can give rise to a lack of democracy and debate within political parties and, thus, to an elite cartel from which

new generations and socioeconomic interests are alienated. This has been one of the problems with Colombia's 1958 semiconsociational pact, which brought political stability in the 1960s but began to wear thin in the late 1970s and 1980s.

105. Reynolds, "Electoral Systems," 507.

106. With the proportional representation systems used in the founding elections in Namibia and South Africa, 99 percent of the votes in Namibia (and an even higher percentage in South Africa) went toward electing a representative. This was partly due to the very low threshold (less than 1% of the vote) for winning legislative representation. Andrew Reynolds, "Constitutional Engineering in Southern Africa," *Journal of Democracy* 6, no. 2 (1995): 90–91.

107. Although the African National Congress got relatively few White votes, it did garner about 30 percent of Indian and Colored votes in the 1994 founding elections, and a disproportionately large number of White candidates were prominent on its party lists. The National Party broadened its base to garner about half its votes from non-White groups. Reynolds, "Electoral Systems."

108. Ibid., 509.

109. On some of these problems with the German-style electoral system, see Vernon Bogdanor, "The Electoral System, Government, and Democracy," in *Israeli Democracy under Stress*, edited by Ehud Sprinzak and Larry Diamond (Boulder, Colo.: Lynne Rienner, 1993), 92–94. With regard to the complexity of the system, he cites survey evidence showing that comparatively few voters understand the difference between the two ballots they cast.

110. In "The Case for Proportionality," *Journal of Democracy* 6, no. 4 (1995): 123, Andrew Reynolds proposes something close to this system for South Africa: a Finnish-style system in which three hundred members of the National Assembly would be elected (in open-list proportional representation) from districts, each one sending from five to twelve members, with overall proportionality achieved by appointing the "best losers" from each party's other candidates to fill the remaining seats. By drawing from the best losers, this system would further enhance local accountability. Yet there is something to be said for the stimulus to party coherence that would come from enabling the national party to designate and even rank candidates on a national list for perhaps a quarter of the seats. Moreover, when the number of a district's representatives rises much beyond five, the lines of accountability between voters and representatives blur.

111. Arend Lijphart, "Constitutional Choices for New Democracies," *Journal of Democracy* 2, no. 1 (1991): 81. Taagepera and Shugart, *Seats and Votes*, 236, take a similar approach when they recommend, in generic terms for new democracies, some form of proportional representation in low-magnitude districts (such as three or five seats). Sartori takes an even more emphatic view, arguing that "in its pure form PR generally backfires" into polarization and paralysis, while "in its impure forms it generally obtains a satisfactory blending of adequate representation and sufficient governability" (*Comparative Constitutional Engineering*, 73–74).

112. Sartori, *Comparative Constitutional Engineering*, 77, n. 7.

113. Bolivar Lamounier, "Brazil at an Impasse," *Journal of Democracy* 5, no. 3 (1994): 80.

114. Ibid.

115. Mainwaring and Scully, "Party Systems in Latin America," 29. For a full list of the parties and their seats, see Arthur S. Banks, *Political Handbook of the World 1994–1995* (Binghamton, N.Y.: CSA Publications, 1995), 111. Eight of the parties won five seats or fewer; each equaled less than 1 percent of the chamber.

116. "Election Watch," *Journal of Democracy* 6, no. 1 (1995): 181.

117. Lijphart shows, in *Electoral Systems and Party Systems*, that the "effective threshold" (i.e., the combination of district magnitude and the formal electoral threshold, if it exists) is the electoral system variable with the greatest influence on the number of parties in parliament; its effect on the degree of proportionality of election outcomes is strong.

118. Lamounier, "Brazil at an Impasse," 86. An important principle of institutional reform is to avoid *over*correcting for existing flaws. Brazil might therefore be well advised to avoid giving the central leaders of the parties complete control over the selection of candidates. This could be done either by holding primary elections within the parties to select and rank the candidates for the state party lists or by giving voters the option of reranking the candidates on the party list they select. Although the latter would still be an open-list system, it would emphasize personalities less than the current system because voters would be voting for an entire party list, and in the typical open-list proportional representation system "the official ranking may prevail more often than not." Taagapera and Shugart, *Seats and Votes*, 25. In the context of reapportioning the allocation of lower-house seats among the current electoral districts (the states), Brazil might also be well served by breaking up the larger states into smaller, multimember districts, to provide greater accountability of representatives to the voters.

119. Ephraim Yuchtman-Yaar and Yochanan Peres, "Trends in the Commitment to Democracy: 1987–1990," in Sprinzak and Diamond, *Israeli Democracy under Stress*, 221–34. Although Israelis remained steadfast during this period in their overwhelming support for democratic freedoms, the percentage preferring democracy even if it opposed one's personal opinions declined from 69 percent in 1987 to 46 percent in 1989–90 (231).

120. See for example, Bogdanor, "The Electoral System"; Arend Lijphart, "Israeli Democracy and Democratic Reform in Comparative Perspective"; and Larry Diamond and Ehud Sprinzak, "Directions for Reform"; all in Sprinzak and Diamond, *Israeli Democracy under Stress*, 83–106, 107–24, 361–74. Bogdanor also proposes opening up the closed party lists and breaking up Israel's single electoral constituency into a number of smaller districts (of variable size), topping off with the best losers or by drawing from a national list in order to restore some of the proportionality lost by moving to smaller districts.

121. Duverger's psychological effect, however, is the impact on voters over time, which could further reduce party fragmentation in Israel (*Political Parties*); see also Taagepera and Shugart, *Seats and Votes*, 65.

122. Although the new executive structure is far from presidential, in that the directly elected prime minister can (with political cost to the legislators, namely, dissolution of parliament) be brought down by a vote of no confidence, it does suffer from some of the same problems that plague presidentialism, such as the tendency to weaken parties, personalize politics, and confer on the prime minister a plebiscitarian mandate open to demagogy and abuse and entirely at odds with the logic of a parliamentary system. For a discussion of the strengths and weaknesses of this innovation and of an alternative, more modest reform proposal for strengthened prime ministerial government, see Diamond and Sprinzak, "Directions for Reform," 364–69.

123. Reynolds, "Constitutional Engineering in Southern Africa," 89.

124. On this problem, see Lijphart, *Electoral Systems and Party Systems*, 40–42; Taagepera and Shugart, *Seats and Votes*, 28. Political parties in Taiwan have sought to deal with this dilemma by nominating the "optimum" number of candidates they are likely to be able to elect in the district and then finding a way (for example, by geographically zoning the district among the multiple candidates) to divide the party vote evenly among their multiple candidates. Nevertheless, the plan may not work if party strategists miscalculate their electoral base in a district, if additional party candidates run in defiance of the establishment, or if individual party candidates seek to maximize their chances by garnering as large a vote as possible for themselves. John Fuh-sheng Hsieh, "The SNTV System and Its Political Implications," in *Taiwan's Electoral Politics and Democratic Transition: Riding the Third Wave*, edited by Hung-mao Tien (Armonk, N.Y.: M. E. Sharpe, 1996), 199–200.

125. Hsieh, "The SNTV System," 208. See also Yun-han Chu, "SNTV and the Evolving Party System in Taiwan," *Chinese Political Science Review* 22 (1994): 35–39; Ming-tong Chen, "Local Factions and Elections in Taiwan's Democratization," in Tien, *Taiwan's Electoral Politics*, 174–92.

126. Frank McNeil, "Update on Japan: Rock of Sisyphus or Road to Reform?" *Journal of Democracy* 5, no. 3 (1994): 104. As passed in January 1994, the reform legislation also introduced public financing of campaigns and required that all private political contributions over a certain amount be made public.

127. Taagepera and Shugart, *Seats and Votes*, 236.

128. Chu, "Taiwan's Unique Challenges," 76–78.

129. Sartori is particularly critical of systems that deliberately mix the logics of proportional representation, with its "sincere voting" to express preferences, and the plurality SMD system, with "strategic voting" that inclines not to waste a vote on a likely loser. This, he insists, confuses the behavior of voters and produces "parliaments that cannot serve any purpose." Sartori, *Comparative Constitutional Engineering*, 75. In fact, we do not yet know what the effects will be

(and whether they will be the same across countries). A vast natural experiment is occurring as institutional forms proliferate and change. I suspect that in the cases of Italy and Japan (and Taiwan, too, if it should reform), the mixed systems will not produce the disastrous consequences Sartori anticipates. In Italy, it appears to have produced a more coherent government.

130. Interview with member of the Control Yuan, April 22, 1998. The Control Yuan (which, in its obligation to receive and investigate complaints against public officials, is similar to an ombudsman commission) has twenty-nine members (in effect, ombudsmen) but only about forty investigators. New legislation (long sought by the Control Yuan) will more than double the number of investigators, but the inability to punish offenders leads many to regard the body as a toothless tiger.

131. Felipe Agüero, *Soldiers, Civilians, and Democracy: Post-Franco Spain in Comparative Perspective* (Baltimore: Johns Hopkins University Press, 1995); Agüero, "Toward Civilian Supremacy in South America," in *Consolidating the Third Wave Democracies: Themes and Perspectives*, edited by Larry Diamond, Marc F. Plattner, Yun-han Chu, and Hung-mao Tien (Baltimore: Johns Hopkins University Press, 1997), 177–206.

132. In addition to the works by Agüero, see also Harold Crouch, "Civil-Military Relations in Southeast Asia," in Diamond et al., *Consolidating the Third Wave Democracies*, 207–35.

133. Alfred Stepan, *Rethinking Military Politics: Brazil and the Southern Cone* (Princeton: Princeton University Press, 1988), 138–39.

134. Wendy Hunter, "Contradictions of Civilian Control: Argentina, Brazil, and Chile in the 1990s," *Third World Quarterly* 15, no. 4 (1994): 633–53.

135. "Bangladesh's Reluctant Army," *Economist*, Feb. 24, 1996, 35.

136. Huntington, *The Third Wave*, 231. For extended treatment of these problems and strategies for democratizing civil-military relations, see ibid., 211–53; Stepan, *Rethinking Military Politics*; Diamond, "Democracy in Latin America," 86–91; Agüero, *Soldiers, Civilians, and Democracy*.

137. Stepan, *Rethinking Military Politics*, 128–45.

138. Agüero, *Soldiers, Civilians, and Democracy*, 33.

139. Samuel P. Huntington, "Reforming Civil-Military Relations," in *Civil-Military Relations and Democracy*, edited by Larry Diamond and Marc F. Plattner (Baltimore: Johns Hopkins University Press, 1996), 3–11.

140. On the positive effects of NATO membership for developing civilian supremacy and capacity and for consolidating democracy in Spain, Portugal, and Greece, see Agüero, *Soldiers, Civilians, and Democracy*, 203–6, 232–33, 243–44.

Chapter 4. Size and Democracy

1. Of the eight states with between a half million and a million population, six are not democracies and only one is a liberal democracy. However, of the nine

states with one to two million population, six are electoral democracies and five are liberal democracies. Grouping together all seventeen of these states, we find eight electoral democracies (47%) and seven liberal democracies (41%), figures much closer to those for all the countries of the world and very different from the thirty-three states with less than a half million population.

2. Robert A. Dahl and Edward R. Tufte, *Size and Democracy* (Stanford: Stanford University Press, 1973).

3. I include, as former "Anglo-American" colonies or dependencies, forty-five members of the Commonwealth (excluding Britain, Canada, Australia, and New Zealand), the other two former British colonies of Burma and Sudan, the former U.S.-administered states in the Pacific (the Philippines, the Marshall Islands, Micronesia, Palau, and Tuvalu), and the former Australian-administered Nauru. I exclude other more temporary and superficial former British-administered lands, like the Middle Eastern lands under British mandate following World War I. Needless to say, inclusion of these would diminish further the proportion of democracies in former Anglo-American colonies with populations above one million. See Arthur S. Banks et al., *Political Handbook of the World, 1995–1996* (Binghamton, N.Y.: CSA Publications, 1996).

4. For arguments about the expected benefits of decentralizing responsibility for local infrastructural services, see Dennis Rondinelli, *Decentralizing Urban Development Programs: A Framework for Analyzing Policy* (Washington, D.C.: U.S. Agency for International Development, 1990).

5. Whereas only 22 percent of the population in the world's less developed regions lived in cities and towns in 1960, this number increased to 52 percent over the next thirty years. Urban population growth in these areas is expected to increase by eighty million annually between 1990 and 2020. United Nations, *World Urbanization Prospects, 1990: Estimates and Projections of Urban and Rural Populations and of Urban Agglomerations* (New York: United Nations, 1991).

6. R. Andrew Nickson, *Local Government in Latin America* (Boulder: Lynne Rienner, 1995), 22.

7. World Bank, *Sub-Saharan Africa: From Crisis to Sustainable Growth* (Washington, D.C.: World Bank, 1989).

8. Harry Blair, "Supporting Democratic Local Governance: Lessons from International Donor Experience, Initial Concepts and Some Preliminary Findings," paper presented to the annual meeting of the American Political Science Association, San Francisco, 1996.

9. Cited in Thomas G. Kingsley, "Perspectives on Devolution," *Journal of the American Planning Association* 62, no. 4 (1996): 419–27.

10. Robert J. Bennett, *Local Government and Market Decentralization* (Tokyo: United Nations, 1994), 19–23.

11. John Stuart Mill, *Considerations on Representative Government* (New York: Liberal Arts Press, 1958), 214.

12. Ibid., 215.

13. Benjamin Barber, *Strong Democracy* (Berkeley: University of California Press, 1984), 268.

14. Dilys M. Hill, *Democratic Theory and Local Government* (London: Allen and Unwin, 1974), 22.

15. Robert D. Putnam with Robert Leonardi and Raffaella Y. Nanetti, *Making Democracy Work: Civic Traditions in Modern Italy* (Princeton: Princeton University Press, 1993), chap. 5.

16. Ibid., 28–29.

17. Robert A. Dahl, *Dilemmas of Pluralist Democracy: Autonomy versus Control* (New Haven: Yale University Press, 1982), 144.

18. Robert A. Dahl, "The Problem of Civic Competence," *Journal of Democracy* 3, no. 4 (1992): 52–53.

19. Anne Phillips, "Feminism and the Attractions of the Local," in *Rethinking Local Democracy*, edited by Desmond King and Gerry Stoker (London: Macmillian, 1996), 119.

20. Personal communication from Eliza Willis, March 25, 1998.

21. Putnam et al., *Making Democracy Work.*

22. Phillips, "Feminism and the Attractions of the Local," 115.

23. Mill, *Considerations on Representative Government,* 212.

24. Putnam et al., *Making Democracy Work,* 54.

25. The margins of difference ranged from 7 to 10 percentage points. In 1996, 55 percent of Turks had confidence in their local government, 46 percent in the national government. "Turks Support Democratic Ideals, Criticize Own System," *Opinion Analysis, U.S. Information Agency,* Oct. 18, 1996, 2.

26. The levels of efficacy were low everywhere, but if we include those who responded that they could influence a decision even "some of the time" as opposed to "never," the responses (in Sept.–Oct. 1994) for the national and local levels were El Salvador, 38%, 40%; Panama, 46%, 49%; Romania, 49%, 57%; and Ukraine, 24%, 33%. "Benchmarks in Democracy Building: Public Opinion and Global Democratization: A Case Study of Four Countries." Special Report Prepared for USAID by the Office of Research and Media Reaction, U.S. Information Agency, August 15, 1996. Also at http://www.civnet.org/teaching/research/bench.htm

27. Josephine Andrews and Kathryn Stoner-Weiss, "Regionalism and Reform in Provincial Russia," *Post-Soviet Affairs* 11, no. 4 (1995): 384–406.

28. "Provincial Politics in South Africa: Powers, Performance and Public Opinion," *Public Opinion Service Report* 7 (Cape Town: Institute for Democracy in South Africa, 1996): 4.

29. Ibid., 8. Only 8 percent supported reducing provincial powers vis-à-vis the national government.

30. "Voter Education and the 1995 Local Government Elections," *Public Opinion Service Reports* 6 (1996): 8–10.

31. Public approval of government performance (which dropped for all lev-

els of government between 1995 and 1997) stood at 47 percent for the national government, 36 percent for provincial governments, and 30 percent for local governments. The perception that government was interested in their opinion stood at 48 percent for national government, 40 percent for provincial, and 36 percent for local. Robert Mattes and Hermann Thiel, "Consolidation and Public Opinion in South Africa," *Journal of Democracy* 9, no. 1 (1998): 106.

32. Kyoung-Ryung Seong, "Delayed Decentralization and Incomplete Consolidation of Democracy: The Case of Korean Local Autonomy," in *Institutional Reform and Democratic Consolidation in Korea*, edited by Doh Chull Shin and Larry Diamond (Stanford, Calif.: Hoover Institution Press, forthcoming).

33. David Beetham, "Theorising Democracy and Local Government," in King and Stoker, *Rethinking Local Democracy*, 38.

34. David Everatt, Grace Rapholo, Celinda Lake, and Mark Orkin, *Finishing the Job? Deepening Democracy and Delivering Benefits through Successful Local Government Elections* (Cape Town: Project Vote, 1994), 27.

35. Dahl and Tufte, *Size and Democracy*, 76.

36. The ratio of population per legislator is not to be confused with constituency size. In single-member district systems (with relatively equally sized districts), as in the United States, the United Kingdom, and India, the figures are more or less the same. However, where legislators are elected from multimember districts, as in Taiwan, or especially where most national legislators are elected under proportional representation from a relatively small number of constituencies (37 in Poland in 1991, the 26 states in Brazil, the 9 regions in South Africa), the population size of the constituency is much larger, and the difficulty of communication and accountability between the people and their representatives is considerably greater.

37. Dahl and Tufte, *Size and Democracy*, 62–64.

38. Lawrence Rose, Stanislav Buchta, György Gajduschek, Miroslav Grochowski, and Ondrej Hubacek, "Political Culture and Citizen Involvement," in *Local Democracy and the Processes of Transformation in East-Central Europe*, edited by Harald Baldersheim, Michael Illner, Audun Offerdal, Lawrence Rose, and Pawel Swianiewicz (Boulder: Westview, 1996), 76–78, 81 83, 93 95.

39. Dahl and Tufte, *Size and Democracy*, 66–78.

40. Everatt et al., *Finishing the Job?* 30–31.

41. Dahl and Tufte, *Size and Democracy*, 75–76.

42. Alexis de Tocqueville, *Democracy in America* (New York: Knopf, 1945 [1840]), 1:281–82.

43. Guillermo O'Donnell and Philippe C. Schmitter, *Transitions from Authoritarian Rule: Tentative Conclusions about Uncertain Democracies* (Baltimore: Johns Hopkins University Press, 1986); Adam Przeworski, "Some Problems in the Study of Transition to Democracy," in *Transitions from Authoritarian Rule: Comparative Perspectives*, edited by Guillermo O'Donnell, Philippe Schmitter, and Laurence Whitehead (Baltimore: Johns Hopkins University Press, 1986).

44. James Manor, "India Defies the Odds: Making Federalism Work," *Journal of Democracy* 9, no. 3 (1998): 23.

45. Larry Diamond, Juan J. Linz, and Seymour Martin Lipset, "What Makes for Democracy?" in *Politics in Developing Countries: Comparing Experiences with Democracy*, edited by Diamond, Linz, and Lipset (Boulder, Colo.: Lynne Rienner, 1995), 45.

46. Jonathan Fox, "Latin America's Emerging Local Politics," *Journal of Democracy* 5, no. 2 (1994): 105–16.

47. Ibid.

48. Personal communication from Eliza Willis, March 25, 1998.

49. Putnam et al., *Making Democracy Work*, 61.

50. Diana Jean Schemo, "Colombia's Death-Strewn Democracy: Party Born of Peace Talks Decimated," *New York Times*, July 24, 1997.

51. Fox, "Latin America's Emerging Local Politics," 107.

52. Human Rights Watch, *World Report 1997* (New York: Human Rights Watch 1996), 82.

53. Nickson, *Local Government in Latin America*, 84.

54. Gerry Stoker, "Normative Theories of Local Government and Democracy," in King and Stoker, *Rethinking Local Democracy*, 15.

55. Phillips, "Feminism and the Attractions of the Local," 120.

56. Blair, "Supporting Democratic Local Governance," 14.

57. Artashes Gazaryan, "Local Government in Lithuania in the Transition Period," in *Local Government in Eastern Europe*, edited by Andrew Coulson (Hants, England: Edward Elgar, 1995), 143.

58. Juan J. Linz and Alfred Stepan, *Problems of Democratic Transition and Consolidation: Southern Europe, South America, and Post-Communist Europe* (Baltimore: Johns Hopkins University Press, 1996), 415.

59. Ibid., 423.

60. Daniel C. Bach, "Indigeneity, Ethnicity, and Federalism," in *Transition without End: Nigerian Politics and Civil Society under Babangida*, edited by Larry Diamond, Anthony Kirk-Greene, and Oyeleye Oyediran (Boulder: Lynne Rienner, 1997), 333–49.

61. Lawrence Prachett and David Wilson, "Local Government under Siege," in *Local Democracy and Local Government*, edited by Prachett and Wilson (London: Macmillan, 1996), 6–7; Nickson, *Local Government in Latin America*, 1–25, 43–59.

62. Nickson, *Local Government in Latin America*, 55.

63. Desmond King, "Conclusion," in King and Stoker, *Rethinking Local Democracy*, 218.

64. Ibid., 225.

65. Eliza J. Willis, Christopher Garman, and Stephan Haggard, "The Politics of Decentralization in Latin America," *Latin American Research Review* (in press); Alfred Stepan, "Toward a New Comparative Analysis of Democracy and

Federalism: Demos Constraining and Demos Enabling Federations," paper presented to the meeting of the International Political Science Association, Seoul, 1997; Scott Mainwaring and David Julian Samuels, "Robust Federalism and Democracy in Contemporary Brazil," paper presented to the meeting of the International Political Science Association, Seoul, 1997.

66. Joel Migdal, *Strong Societies and Weak States* (Princeton: Princeton University Press, 1988).

67. Philip Mawhood, ed., *Local Government in the Third World* (Pretoria: Africa Institute of South Africa, 1993), ix.

68. Garman et al., "The Politics of Decentralization in Latin America."

69. Blair, "Supporting Democratic Local Governance," 17.

70. Linz and Stepan, *Problems of Democratic Transition.*

71. Mawhood, *Local Government in the Third World*, 38–40.

72. Lilean Bobea, "An Experiment in Local Democracy," *NACLA Report on the Americas* 30, no. 5 (1997): 27–31.

73. Richard Bird, Caroline Freund, and Christine Wallich, "Decentralization of Intergovernmental Finance in Transition Economies," *Comparative Economic Studies* 36, no. 4 (1994): 151.

74. William Tordoff, "Decentralisation: Comparative Experience in Commonwealth Africa," *Journal of Modern African Studies* 32, no. 4 (1994): 578. See also Mawhood, *Local Government in the Third World*, 41.

75. Prachett and Wilson, "Local Government under Siege," 6. Even when local government is heavily dependent on central government transfers, the design of these transfers affects the degree to which local autonomy is compromised. To the extent, as in Brazil, that transfers from the central government are automatic and permit subnational governments considerable spending discretion, the central government's power over the lower levels may not increase much. Whether such transfers promote local accountability, however, is another matter. See Willis, Garman, and Haggard, "The Politics of Decentralization in Latin America."

76. Mawhood, *Local Government in the Third World*, 41.

77. Jane Guyer, "Local Government, Chiefs, and Officeholders in a Rural Area: An Interpretation Based on Ibarapa, Oyo State," in Diamond et al., *Transition without End* (Ibadan, Nigeria: Vantage Publishers, 1997): 423–49.

78. Bird et al., "Decentralization of Intergovernmental Finance," 154.

79. Ibid., 156.

80. Nickson, *Local Government in Latin America*, 47.

81. Bird et al., "Decentralization of Intergovernmental Finance," 157.

82. Ibid.; Nickson, *Local Government in Latin America*, 54–55.

83. Eliza Willis found this effect in her recent research on decentralization of health services in Brazil. Personal communication, March 25, 1998.

84. Andrew Coulson, "From Democratic Centralism to Local Democracy," in Coulson, *Local Government in Eastern Europe*, 3

85. Alan Norton, "What East European Democracies Might Learn from the West," in Coulson, *Local Government in Eastern Europe*, 271–72.

86. Coulson, "From Democratic Centralism," 11.

87. World Bank, *Better Urban Services: Finding the Right Incentives* (Washington, D.C.: World Bank, 1995).

88. Robert J. Bennett, ed., *Local Government in the New Europe* (London: Belhaven, 1993), 190–94. Turnout in the first Polish and Hungarian local elections was around 40 percent.

89. *Republic of China Yearbook 1997* (Taipei: Government Information Office, 1997), 102–5; Linda Chao and Ramon H. Myers, *The First Chinese Democracy* (Baltimore: Johns Hopkins University Press, 1998), 284–85, table 14.

90. Colin Rallings, Michael Temple, and Michael Thrasher, "Participation in Local Elections," in Prachett and Wilson, *Local Democracy and Local Government*, 64, table 4.1.

91. For case evidence on Ecuador and Guatemala, see Nickson, *Local Government in Latin America*, 175, 189.

92. Ibid., 152–53.

93. Bennett, *Local Government in the New Europe*, 188.

94. Rose et al., "Political Culture and Citizen Involvement," 74–88. The countries surveyed were the Czech and Slovak Republics, Hungary, and Poland, but only the Hungarian sample was national.

95. Blair, "Supporting Democratic Local Governance," 19.

96. Barber, *Strong Democracy*, 290. Anne Phillips counters that multi-choice referenda could be developed that would then be able to "capture the intensity of support and opposition, and the kind of urgency or priority people give to each issue," but the referendum is generally a blunt instrument that is not suited to this type of nuance, much less to a negotiated compromise on an issue. Phillips, "Why Does Local Democracy Matter?" in Prachett and Wilson, *Local Democracy and Local Government*, 33.

97. Phillips, "Why Does Local Democracy Matter?", 34.

98. Stoker, "Redefining Local Democracy," 198–99.

99. G. Jones and J. Stewart, quoted in Prachett and Wilson, "Local Government under Siege," 14.

100. Ibid., 13. The figure is for 1994.

101. France has 110 citizens per councillor; Sweden, 270; Germany, 400; the United States, 490; and Britain, 1,800. Nickson, *Local Government in Latin America*, 65.

102. Time-series data of voting in one county in England shows that in years in which a national election coincided with a municipal election, turnout was above average and that it fell back sharply the following election. Rallings et al., "Participation in Local Elections," 74.

103. Harald Baldersheim, Gejza Blaas, Tamas M. Horvath, Michal Illner,

and Pawel Swianiewicz, "New Institutions of Local Government: A Comparison," in Baldersheim et al., *Local Democracy*, 35.

104. Rallings et al. cite a recent study showing that (ceteris paribus) voter turnout is 7 percent higher in proportional representation systems than in first-past-the-post ones. "Participation in Local Elections," 63.

105. Ibid., 66.

106. Ibid., 79.

107. Peter Ordeshook and Olga Shvetsova, "Federalism and Constitutional Design," *Journal of Democracy* 8, no. 1 (1997): 36.

108. Norton, "What East European Democracies Might Learn," 278.

109. William H. Riker, "Federalism," in *Governmental Institutions and Processes*, edited by Fred Greenstein and Nelson Polsby (Reading, Mass.: Addison-Wesley, 1975), 5:101.

110. Robert A. Dahl, *Democracy, Liberty, and Equality*. (Oslo: Norwegian University Press, 1986), 114.

111. Barry R. Weingast, "The Political Foundations of Democracy and the Rule of Law," *American Political Science Review* 91, no. 2 (1997): 245–63.

112. William H. Riker, *Federalism: Origin, Operation, Significance* (Boston: Little, Brown, 1964), 14.

113. Stepan, "Toward a New Comparative Analysis," 3; emphasis in original.

114. Donald L. Horowitz, *Ethnic Groups in Conflict* (Berkeley: University of California Press, 1985); Horowitz, "Democracy in Divided Societies," *Journal of Democracy* 4, no. 4 (1993): 18–38. Also in *Nationalism, Ethnic Conflict, and Democracy*, edited by Larry Diamond and Marc F. Plattner (Baltimore: Johns Hopkins University Press, 1994).

115. Juan Linz, "Democracy, Multinationalism, and Federalism," paper presented to the meeting of the International Political Science Association, Seoul, 1997, 15–16.

116. Horowitz, *Ethnic Groups in Conflict*, 598–613.

117. Diamond et al., "What Makes for Democracy?" 45; Jyotirindra Das Gupta, "Democratic Becoming and Developmental Transition," in Diamond et al., *Politics in Developing Countries*, 263–322; Larry Diamond, "Nigeria: The Uncivic Society and the Descent into Praetorianism," in Diamond et al., *Politics in Developing Countries*, 417–92; Robert L. Hardgrave Jr., "India: The Dilemmas of Diversity," *Journal of Democracy* 4, no. 4 (1993): 54–68; Rotimi T. Suberu, "The Travails of Federalism in Nigeria," *Journal of Democracy* 4, no. 4 (1993): 39–53; Manor, "India Defies the Odds."

118. Horowitz, *Ethnic Groups in Conflict*, 613–21; Horowitz, "Democracy in Divided Societies."

119. Charles Tiebout, "A Pure Theory of Local Expenditures," *Journal of Political Economy* 64 (1956): 414–24.

120. Barry R. Weingast, "The Economic Role of Political Institutions: Market-Preserving Federalism and Economic Development," *Journal of Law, Economics, and Organization* 11 (1995): 1–31.

121. Ibid., 4. See also Gabriella Montinola, Yingyi Qian, and Barry R. Weingast, "Federalism, Chinese Style: The Political Basis for Economic Success in China," *World Politics* 48, no. 1 (1995): 50–81.

122. Yingyi Qian and Barry R. Weingast, *China's Transition to Markets: Market-Preserving Federalism, Chinese Style*, Essays in Public Policy 55 (Stanford, Calif.: Hoover Institution, 1995).

123. Jonathan Rodden and Susan Rose-Ackerman, "Does Federalism Preserve Markets?" *Virginia Law Review* 83, no. 7 (1997): 1565.

124. Ibid., 1553.

125. Manor, "India Defies the Odds," 22.

126. Juan Linz, "Democratization and Types of Democracies: New Tasks for Comparativists," paper presented to the annual meeting of the Political Science Association, University of Glasgow, 1996.

127. Linz, "Democracy, Multinationalism, and Federalism," 43.

128. Ronald Grigor Suny, *Revenge of the Past* (Stanford: Stanford University Press, 1993).

129. Stepan, "Toward a New Comparative Analysis." Many of India's worst problems of ethnic group estrangement and separatist violence have been aggravated not by the presence of autonomy but by its absence or interruption, particularly in the loosely constructed and frequently abused provisions enabling a federal government to intervene and displace a state government through "president's rule." For a description of this, see 39. See also Manor, "India Defies the Odds."

130. Stepan, "Toward a New Comparative Analysis ," 50–51.

131. Horowitz, *Ethnic Groups in Conflict*, 625–26.

132. Linz and Stepan, *Problems of Democratic Transition*, 98–107.

133. Ibid., 33, 35, 106.

134. Horowitz, *Ethnic Groups in Conflict*, 617–19.

135. Riker, *Federalism*, 5.

136. Stepan, "Toward a New Comparative Analysis," 8–9.

137. Arend Lijphart, *Democracies: Patterns of Majoritarian and Consensus Government in Twenty-one Countries* (New Haven: Yale University Press, 1984).

138. Ronald L. Watts, "Contemporary Views on Federalism," in *Evaluating Federal Systems*, edited by Bertus De Villiers (Cape Town: Juta, 1994).

139. Jenna Bednar, William N. Eskridge Jr., and John Ferejohn, "A Political Theory of Federalism," in *Constitutions and Constitutionalism*, edited by John Ferejohn, Jack Rakove, and Jonathan Riley (New York: Cambridge University Press, 1998).

140. Riker, *Federalism*, 86.

141. Ibid., 93.

142. Ordeshook and Shvetsova, "Federalism and Constitutional Design," 34.

143. Of course, simultaneous elections are impossible to institutionalize in a parliamentary system, in which the terms of national and state parliaments are not fixed. On the other hand, parliamentary systems generate other incentives to party coherence.

144. Ordeshook and Shvetsova, "Federalism and Constitutional Design," 38–41.

145. Stepan, "Toward a New Comparative Analysis," 28–49.

146. For an extended treatment of this problem, see Horowitz, *Ethnic Groups in Conflict*, 628–51.

147. On the limits to decentralization in nondemocratic contexts, see Blair, "Supporting Democratic Local Governance"; Joel Barkan, "Decentralization, Democratization, Déjà Vu? Contemporary Lessons from Anglophone Africa," paper presented to the annual meeting of the American Political Science Association, San Francisco, 1996

Chapter 5. Political Culture

1. Robert A. Dahl, *Polyarchy* (New Haven: Yale University Press, 1971), 129–40; Juan J. Linz, *The Breakdown of Democratic Regimes: Crisis, Breakdown, and Reequilibration* (Baltimore: Johns Hopkins University Press, 1978).

2. Gabriel A. Almond and Sidney Verba, *The Civic Culture: Political Attitudes and Democracy in Five Nations* (Princeton: Princeton University Press, 1963); Alex Inkeles and David Smith, *Becoming Modern: Individual Change in Six Developing Nations* (Cambridge: Harvard University Press, 1974); Alex Inkeles, "Participant Citizenship in Six Developing Countries," *American Political Science Review* 63, no. 4 (1969): 1120–41.

3. Seymour Martin Lipset, *Political Man: The Social Bases of Politics* (Baltimore: Johns Hopkins University Press, 1981), 27–63. New supporting evidence for the overall relationship and the intervening role of political culture appears in Larry Diamond, "Economic Development and Democracy Reconsidered," in *Reexamining Democracy: Essays in Honor of Seymour Martin Lipset*, edited by Gary Marks and Larry Diamond (Newbury Park, Calif.: Sage, 1992), 93–139.

4. Alex Inkeles and Larry Diamond, "Personal Qualities as a Reflection of Level of National Development," in *Comparative Studies in the Quality of Life*, edited by Frank Andrews and Alexander Szalai (London: Sage, 1980), 73–109.

5. Ronald Inglehart, *Culture Shift in Advanced Industrial Countries* (Princeton: Princeton University Press, 1990), 45. See also Inglehart, "The Renaissance of Political Culture," *American Political Science Review* 82, no. 4 (1988): 1203–30.

6. Harry Eckstein, "A Culturalist Theory of Political Change," *American Political Science Review* 82, no. 2 (1988): 790. The relatively firm and enduring character of these orientations (for which "early learning conditions later learning") generates "economy of action and predictability in interaction" in Eckstein's "culturalist theory" (792).

7. Almond and Verba, *The Civic Culture*, 15; Gabriel Almond, "The Intellectual History of the Civic Culture Concept," in *The Civic Culture Revisited*, edited by Gabriel A. Almond and Sidney Verba (Boston: Little, Brown, 1980), 27–28; Gabriel A. Almond, *A Discipline Divided: Schools and Sects in Political Science* (Newbury Park, Calif.: Sage, 1990), 153.

8. Lucian W. Pye, "Political Culture and Political Development," in *Political Culture and Political Development*, edited by Lucian W. Pye and Sidney Verba (Princeton: Princeton University Press, 1965), 7. In a more recent consideration, however, Pye warns that "logically coherent views do not necessarily prevail and that people, in their collective moods and inclinations, are quite capable of adhering to contradictory positions." Pye, *Asian Power and Politics: The Cultural Dimensions of Authority* (Cambridge: Harvard University Press, 1985), 29. An especially strong articulation of the coherence of political cultures (as diffuse "ways of life") is advanced by Aaron Wildavsky, "Choosing Preferences by Constructing Institutions: A Cultural Theory of Preference Formation," *American Political Science Review* 81, no. 1 (1987): 3–21.

9. For a discussion of this point, with reference to the evidence in Almond and Verba, *The Civic Culture*, see Michael Thompson, Richard Ellis, and Aaron Wildavsky, *Cultural Theory* (Boulder, Colo.: Westview, 1990), 247–59. In fact, cultural theory posits as a central premise that none of the basic cultural orientations would be viable in a society without the presence of alternative ones and, hence, that differentiation and "conflict among cultures is a precondition of cultural identity." Wildavsky, "Choosing Preferences," 7.

10. A more recent theory of distinctive national political cultures, reminiscent of the literature on national character, is Pye, *Asian Power and Politics*, which identifies shared ways of viewing power and authority relations within Asian nations and across Asia.

11. See, for example, Howard Wiarda, ed., *Politics and Social Change in Latin America: The Distinct Tradition* (Amherst: University of Massachusetts Press, 1974). See also the works cited in John A. Booth and Mitchell A. Seligson, "Paths to Democracy and the Political Culture of Costa Rica, Mexico, and Nicaragua," nn. 4, 10, 11, and 12, in *Political Culture and Democracy in Developing Countries*, edited by Larry Diamond (Boulder, Colo.: Lynne Rienner, 1993), 107–38.

12. Pye, *Asian Power and Politics*, quotations on 20 and vii; see also 12–53, passim. Although his essay is entitled "A Culturalist Theory of Political Change," Eckstein shares with Pye an emphasis on the pattern-maintaining qualities of political culture and a profound skepticism about the possibilities for short-term, "revolutionary" transformations of the core (value) features of political culture (no doubt in part because of his shared emphasis on early socialization).

13. Almond, *A Discipline Divided*, 144–47; quotations on 144.

14. Inglehart, *Culture Shift*, 17.

15. Harry Eckstein, "Social Science as Culture Science, Rational Choice as Metaphysics," in *Culture Matters: Essays in Honor of Aaron Wildavsky*, edited by

Richard J. Ellis and Michael Thompson (Boulder, Colo.: Westview, 1997), 25. See also Eckstein, "A Culturalist Theory of Political Change," 796.

16. Larry Diamond, Juan J. Linz, and Seymour Martin Lipset, *Democracy in Developing Countries: Africa, Asia, and Latin America* (Boulder, Colo.: Lynne Rienner, 1988 and 1989). On the role of the international system in promoting political culture change, see Samuel P. Huntington, *The Third Wave: Democratization in the Late Twentieth Century* (Norman: University of Oklahoma Press, 1991); Lucian W. Pye, "Political Science and the Crisis of Authoritarianism," *American Political Science Review* 84, no. 1 (1990): 8–9; Larry Diamond, "The Globalization of Democracy: Trends, Types, Causes, and Prospects," in *Global Transformation and the Third World*, edited by Robert Slater, Barry Schutz, and Stephen Dorr (Boulder, Colo.: Lynne Rienner, 1992), 31–69. The role of economic growth and social change is demonstrated in Inglehart, *Culture Shift*.

17. See Almond and Verba, *The Civic Culture*, 489–93; Sidney Verba, "Comparative Political Culture," in Pye and Verba, *Political Culture and Political Development*, 544–50; Lipset, *Political Man*, 78–79; Dahl, *Polyarchy*; Alex Inkeles, "National Character and Modern Political Systems," in *Psychological Anthropology: Approaches to Culture and Personality*, edited by Francis L. K. Hsu (Homewood, Ill.: Dorsey, 1961), 193–99. Also see Larry Diamond, "Three Paradoxes of Democracy," *Journal of Democracy* 1, no. 3 (1990): 56–58. For an earlier, political and psychological treatment that influenced several of the above approaches, see Harold Lasswell, *The Political Writings of Harold Lasswell* (Glencoe, Ill.: Free Press, 1951), 465–525.

18. Pye, "Political Science and the Crisis of Authoritarianism," 15.

19. Verba, "Comparative Political Culture," 546.

20. Lasswell, *Political Writings*, quotation on 502; Almond and Verba, *The Civic Culture*; Verba, "Comparative Political Culture"; Dahl, *Polyarchy*; Robert D. Putnam with Robert Leonardi and Raffaella Y. Nanetti, *Making Democracy Work: Civic Traditions in Modern Italy* (Princeton: Princeton University Press, 1993). For an analysis emphasizing the implications of trust and social capital for economic scale, efficiency, and flexibility, see Francis Fukuyama, *Trust: The Social Virtues and the Creation of Prosperity* (New York: Free Press, 1995).

21. Inkeles, "National Character," 195–98.

22. Sidney Hook, *Reason, Social Myth, and Democracy* (New York: Humanities, 1950), cited in Inkeles, "National Character," 196.

23. Jacques Maritain is quoted in Inkeles, "National Character," 195–96; see also J. Roland Pennock, *Democratic Political Theory* (Princeton: Princeton University Press, 1979), 240–41.

24. Pye, *Asian Power and Politics*, vii; see also 18–19, 22- 29, 326–41.

25. Ibid., 341.

26. Pennock, *Democratic Political Theory*, 257, 245–46, 258- 59. On the importance of public-spiritedness and civic engagement, see also Putnam et al., *Making Democracy Work*.

27. Thompson et al., *Cultural Theory*, 256–57.

28. Linz, *Breakdown of Democratic Regimes*, 16; Lipset, *Political Man*, 64.

29. Although they do not use the term *legitimacy*, this conception of support for democracy as inherently comparative in nature drives the theory and methodology of Richard Rose, William Mishler, and Christian Haerpfer in their analysis of attitudinal trends in the postcommunist states. See their *Democracy and Its Alternatives: Understanding Post-Communist Societies* (Oxford: Polity Press, 1998).

30. A particularly suspect feature of this item as a measure of democracy is that supporters of the governing party evince substantially higher levels of satisfaction with democracy than do supporters of the opposition party, irrespective of whether it is the left or the right that is governing. In some cases, these differences are very large (30–40 percentage points). Dieter Fuchs, Giovanna Guidorossi, and Palle Svensson, "Support for the Democratic System," in *Citizens and the State*, edited by Hans-Dieter Klingemann and Dieter Fuchs (Oxford: Oxford University Press, 1995), 345–46. Typical of the misuse of this item is an otherwise rigorous and widely cited study of "legitimation," which takes satisfaction with the way democracy works as equivalent to other, more appropriate, measures of legitimacy. Frederick D. Weil, "The Sources and Structure of Legitimation in Western Democracies: A Consolidated Model Tested with Time-Series Data in Six Countries since World War II," *American Sociological Review* 54, no. 4 (1989): 682–706.

31. Rose et al., *Democracy and Its Alternatives*, 99–101.

32. José María Maravall, *Regimes, Politics, and Markets: Democratization and Economic Change in Southern and Eastern Europe* (Oxford: Oxford University Press, 1997), 204.

33. Lipset, *Political Man*, 68–70.

34. Weil, "The Sources and Structure of Legitimation."

35. Fuchs et al., "Support for the Democratic System," 328.

36. Two exceptions are a series of Spanish surveys that asked whether "democracy is the best system for a country like ours," and the New Korea Barometer, which asks Koreans to rate from 1 to 10 how "suitable" democracy was for the country during the authoritarian era and is today. José Ramón Montero, Richard Gunther, and Mariano Torcal, "Democracy in Spain: Legitimacy, Discontent, and Disaffection," Estudio/Working Paper 1997/100, Centro de Estudios Avanzados en Ciencias Sociales, Instituto Juan March de Estudios e Investigaciones, 1997, 5; Doh Chull Shin and Peter McDonough, "The Dynamics of Popular Reaction to Democratization in Korea: A Comparative Perspective," unpublished draft, December 1997, Department of Political Science, University of Illinois at Springfield.

37. This is the principal criticism of the standard research approach advanced in Arthur H. Miller, Vicki L. Hesli, and William M. Reisinger, "Understanding Democracy: A Comparison of Mass and Elite in Post-Soviet Russia and

Ukraine," Studies in Public Policy 247, Centre for the Study of Public Policy, University of Strathclyde, 1995. In Russia and Ukraine, elite and mass have different conceptions of democracy, and "beliefs about democracy vary across demographic and political categories rather than reflecting a shared common culture" (16). Rose et al., *Democracy and Its Alternatives*, avoid or diminish potential ambiguity in interpreting a commitment to "democracy" by specifying the system as involving "free elections and many parties" or by specifying concrete types of authoritarian alternatives.

38. Alex Inkeles, "Participant Citizenship in Six Developing Countries," *American Political Science Review* 63, no. 4 (1969): 1120–41.

39. Almond and Verba, *The Civic Culture*, 19.

40. Ibid., 482, 490.

41. Terry Lynn Karl, "Dilemmas of Democratization in Latin America," in *Comparative Political Dynamics*, edited by Dankwart A. Rustow and Kenneth Paul Erickson (New York: Harper/Collins, 1991), 168. For the original argument against preconditions, see Dankwart A. Rustow, "Transitions to Democracy: Toward a Dynamic Model," *Comparative Politics* 2, no. 3 (1970): 337–63.

42. Dahl, *Polyarchy*, 36–47; Almond and Verba, *The Civic Culture*, 7–8; Rustow, "Transitions to Democracy."

43. Dahl, *Polyarchy*, 36.

44. Guillermo O'Donnell, Philippe Schmitter, and Laurence Whitehead, eds., *Transitions from Authoritarian Rule* (Baltimore: Johns Hopkins University Press, 1986), in particular the volume by O'Donnell and Schmitter, *Tentative Conclusions about Uncertain Democracies*; Adam Przeworski, *Democracy and the Market: Political and Economic Reforms in Eastern Europe and Latin America* (Cambridge: Cambridge University Press, 1991).

45. For an excellent treatment of this process, see Nancy Bermeo, "Democracy and the Lessons of Dictatorship," *Comparative Politics* 26, no. 3 (1992): 273–91.

46. Michael G. Burton, Richard Gunther, and John Higley, "Elite Transformations and Democratic Regimes," in *Elites and Democratic Consolidation in Latin America and Southern Europe*, edited by John Higley and Richard Gunther (Cambridge: Cambridge University Press, 1992), 1–37. See also John Higley and Michael G. Burton, "The Elite Variable in Democratic Transitions and Breakdowns," *American Sociological Review* 54, no. 1 (1989): 17–32; Michael G. Burton and John Higley, "Elite Settlements," *American Sociological Review* 52, no. 3 (1987): 295–307.

47. For critiques, see Alan Knight, "Mexico's Elite Settlement: Conjuncture and Consequences," and John Peeler, "Elite Settlements and Democratic Consolidation: Colombia, Costa Rica, and Venezuela," both in Higley and Gunther, *Elites and Democratic Consolidation*; Larry Diamond, "Political Culture and Democracy," in Diamond, *Political Culture and Democracy in Developing Countries*, 5–6.

48. Laurence Whitehead, "The Consolidation of Fragile Democracies: A

Discussion with Illustrations," in *Democracy in the Americas: Stopping the Pendulum*, edited by Robert A. Pastor (New York: Holmes and Meier, 1989), 76–95; Giuseppe Di Palma, *To Craft Democracies: An Essay on Democratic Transitions* (Berkeley: University of California Press, 1990).

49. Juan J. Linz and Alfred Stepan, *Problems of Democratic Transition and Consolidation: Southern Europe, South America, and Post-Communist Europe* (Baltimore: Johns Hopkins University Press, 1996). In his other writings, Richard Gunther also gives explicit attention to mass political culture as a crucial factor in determining democratic consolidation. See for example Montero et al., "Democracy in Spain," and Richard Gunther, P. Nikiforos Diamandouros, and Hans-Jürgen Puhle, eds., *The Politics of Democratic Consolidation: Southern Europe in Comparative Perspective* (Baltimore: Johns Hopkins University Press, 1995).

50. Quoted in Pennock, *Democratic Political Theory*, 211, from Mill's essay, "On Representative Government."

51. See Leonardo Morlino and José Ramón Montero, "Legitimacy and Democracy in Southern Europe," in Gunther, Diamandouros, and Puhle, *The Politics of Democratic Consolidation*, 236, table 7.1. For the exact wording of the complete survey item, see 458, n. 21.

52. Fuchs, Guidorossi, and Svensson, "Support for the Democratic System," 349, table 11.6.

53. Linz and Stepan, *Problems of Democratic Transition*, 110; for data, see 108–9, tables 6.4 and 6.5. See also Montero et al., "Democracy in Spain," 5–6, tables 1, 2.

54. Morlino and Montero, "Legitimacy and Democracy," 244. Legitimacy also increased in the face of a steep decline in political trust during this period of economic turmoil in Spain. For the data on trust, see Weil, "The Sources and Structures of Legitimation," 694.

55. Montero et al., "Democracy in Spain," 3.

56. Morlino and Montero, "Legitimacy and Democracy," 236–41; see in particular 241, table 7.5. Rejection of democratic efficacy is indicated by the response: "Our democracy is getting worse, and soon it will not work at all," as opposed to agreeing with either the proposition: "Our democracy works well," or the proposition: "It has many defects, but it works."

57. Maravall, *Regimes, Politics, and Markets*, 221.

58. Ibid., 218, 249.

59. Morlino and Montero, "Legitimacy and Democracy," 243.

60. Linz and Stepan, *Problems of Democratic Transition*, chap. 10.

61. Marta Lagos, "Latin America's Smiling Mask," *Journal of Democracy* 8, no. 3 (1997): 133, table 3.

62. For the Uruguayan data, see Linz and Stepan, *Problems of Democratic Transition*, 160–61; for the comparative data on ideology and legitimacy, see Morlino and Montero, "Legitimacy and Democracy," 241, table 7.5.

63. Lagos, "Latin America's Smiling Mask," 128–29.

64. For Linz's seminal formulation of loyalty to the democratic regime (and its rules, procedures, and norms) as a key foundation for stable democracy, see Linz, *The Breakdown of Democratic Regimes*, 27–38. See also Linz and Stepan, *Problems of Democratic Transition*, chap. 10.

65. Morlino and Montero, "Legitimacy and Democracy," 236. As their data show, even though Italians were markedly more dissatisfied with their democracy than the other three Southern European publics, they were just about as likely (65%) as citizens in Spain or Portugal to see their democratic system as working, even if with defects.

66. Linz and Stepan, *Problems of Democratic Transition*, 163.

67. Between 1976 and 1991, the average level of satisfaction with democracy among the twelve EC countries ranged between 49 and 59 percent, with an overall mean of 57 percent. Only in Northern Ireland and Italy were the fifteen-year national averages below 50 percent. Greece, Spain, and Portugal averaged 56, 58, and 63 percent satisfaction, respectively, during the 1980s. Fuchs, Guidorossi, and Svensson, "Support for Democracy," 332–34, 337–42.

68. For an application to Korea of the survey most widely used in the post-communist world, see Doh Chull Shin and Richard Rose, "Koreans Evaluate Democracy: A New Korea Barometer Survey," Studies in Public Policy 292, Centre for the Study of Public Policy, University of Strathclyde, 1997.

69. For the trend data on all of these questions in Central and Eastern Europe for the four surveys from 1991 to 1995, see Richard Rose and Christian Haerpfer, "Change and Stability in the New Democracies Barometer: A Trend Analysis," Studies in Public Policy 270, Centre for the Study of Public Policy, University of Strathclyde, 1996, 22–41.

70. Max Kaase, "Political Culture and Political Consolidation in Central and Eastern Europe," *Research on Democracy and Society* 2 (1994): table 10.

71. Rose et al., *Democracy and Its Alternatives*, chap. 5.

72. Rose and Haerpfer, "Change and Stability in the New Democracies Barometer," fig. 2.8; Richard Rose and Evgeny Tikhomirov, "Trends in the New Russia Barometer, 1992–1995," Studies in Public Policy 256, Centre for the Study of Public Policy, University of Strathclyde, 1995, 29, figure II.4. The Russian figure is for spring 1994, and all the rest are for autumn 1995.

73. Rose et al., *Democracy and Its Alternatives*, 23, fig. 2.1; Rose and Tikhomirov, "Trends in the New Russia Barometer," 17, table 2.1.

74. Rose and Haerpfer, "Change and Stability," 34–37, figs. 2.7, 2.8; Richard Rose and William Mishler, "What Are the Alternatives to Democracy in Post-Communist Societies," Studies in Public Policy 248, Centre for the Study of Public Policy, University of Strathclyde, 1995, 12, table 1; Rose and Tikhomirov, "Trends in the New Russia Barometer," 24–25, fig. 2.2. Although Rose and Tikhomirov emphasize the lack of clear support for any particular authoritarian alternative, their spring 1995 survey actually detects some decline in support for democracy, which was not high to begin with. The proportion of

"democrats" who evaluated the current regime positively but not the preperestroika communist regime fell from 21 percent in 1994 to 7 percent. Reactionaries (the reverse) increased from 36 to 48 percent. The percentage saying, "We should try some other system of government [if the current one] can't produce results soon," increased from 55 percent in 1994 to 68 percent.

75. Stephen Whitefield and Geoffrey Evans, "Support for Democracy and Political Opposition in Russia, 1993–1995," *Post-Soviet Affairs* 12, no. 3 (1996): tables 2, 5.

76. James L. Gibson, "Mass Opposition to the Soviet Putsch of August 1991: Collective Action, Rational Choice, and Democratic Values in the Former Soviet Union," *American Political Science Review* 91, no. 3 (1997): 671–84.

77. Adrian Karatnycky, "Freedom on the March," in Freedom House, *Freedom in the World: The Annual Survey of Political Rights and Civil Liberties, 1996–1997* (New York: Freedom House, 1997), 10.

78. Shin and Rose, "Koreans Evaluate Democracy," 11.

79. Doh Chull Shin, "The Evolution of Popular Support for Democracy during the Kim Young Sam Government," paper presented to the conference, Institutional Reform and Democratic Consolidation in Korea, Hoover Institution, 1998, table 6.

80. Shin and Rose, "Koreans Evaluate Democracy," 24; Doh Chull Shin and Huoyan Shyu, "Political Ambivalence in South Korea and Taiwan," *Journal of Democracy* 8, no. 3 (1997): 112–13.

81. Shin, "The Evolution of Popular Support for Democracy." Belief in the suitability of democracy is indicated when respondents choose a point from 6 to 10 on a 10-point scale. See Shin and Rose, "Koreans Evaluate Democracy," 25.

82. Shin, "The Evolution of Popular Support for Democracy," fig. 4.

83. Question wording was slightly different in Taiwan but still comparable. For the Korean data and response wording, see Shin and Rose, "Koreans Evaluate Democracy," 19–20. For the data and wording from the Taiwanese questionnaire, see ibid., table 5.

84. Pye, *Asian Power and Politics*. In Lee Kuan Yew's famous interview, "Culture Is Destiny," he rejects the notion of a single Asian model, but the interview is full of generalizations about nondemocratic values that are "widely shared in East Asia." *Foreign Affairs* 73, no.2 (1994): 109–26; 113.

85. William L. Parish and Charles Chi-hsiang Chang, "Political Values in Taiwan: Sources of Change and Constancy," in *Taiwan's Electoral Politics and Democratic Transition: Riding the Third Wave*, edited by Hung-mao Tien (Armonk, N.Y.: M. E. Sharpe, 1996), 27–41. The evolution of political values is part of a much larger process of cultural change in Taiwan as a result of modernization and integration with the West. For example, such traditional Confucian values as unconditional filial piety, nepotism, fatalism, conformity, and male primacy have eroded to the point at which only four of sixteen traditional-value statements find majority agreement in Taiwan. By huge majorities, Taiwanese disagree that one should always favor a relative or friend, that one should do what

parents say, and that it is better to have a son than a daughter. Huoyan Shyu, "Neo-Traditionalism in a Modernizing Confucian Society: Value Change in Taiwan," paper presented to the meeting of the Association of Asian Studies, Washington, D.C., 1995.

86. Hu Fu and Yun-han Chu, "Neo-Authoritarianism, Polarized Conflict and Populism in a Newly Democratizing Regime: Taiwan's Emerging Mass Politics," *Journal of Contemporary China* 5, no. 11 (1996): 31.

87. Huoyan Shyu, "Empowering the People: The Role of Elections in Taiwanese Democratization," paper presented to the workshop, Power and Authority in the Political Cultures: East Asia and the Nordic Countries Compared, Nordic Institute of Asian Studies, Copenhagen, 1997, table 3.

88. For excellent overviews of these milestones in Taiwan's democratic development, see Hung-mao Tien, "Taiwan's Transformation," in *Consolidating the Third Wave Democracies: Regional Challenges*, edited by Larry Diamond, Marc F. Plattner, Yun-han Chu, and Hung-mao Tien (Baltimore: Johns Hopkins University Press, 1997), 123–61; Linda Chao and Ramon H. Myers, *The First Chinese Democracy: Political Life in the Republic of China on Taiwan* (Baltimore: Johns Hopkins University Press, 1998), esp. 13, fig. 2.

89. Shin and Shyu, "Political Ambivalence," 114–15.

90. This is a major insight of Chao and Myers, *The First Chinese Democracy.*

91. Shin and Shyu, "Political Ambivalence," 117.

92. In 1966, only 35 percent of Spaniards agreed that "decisions should be taken by a group of people elected by the citizens" (as opposed to a single person). This democratic response grew to 60 percent in 1974 and to 78 percent by May 1976 (six months after the death of Franco), after which it leveled off. More qualitative evidence suggests the majority political culture during the Franco era was illiberal, "defensive and authoritarian." Yet in 1973, as that era was ending, pollsters were beginning to find support for various political freedoms among large majorities of the public. José Ramón Montero and Mariano Torcal, "Voters and Citizens in a New Democracy: Some Trend Data on Political Attitudes in Spain," *International Journal of Public Opinion Research* 2, no. 2 (1990): 119–20.

93. This emphasis on adult political learning figures prominently in the works of Montero and his colleagues (Montero et al., "Democracy in Spain"; Morlino and Montero, "Legitimacy and Democracy"; Montero and Torcal, "Voters and Citizens in a New Democracy"); and of Rose et al., *Democracy and Its Alternatives.* Even stronger versions of political culture theory recognize some scope for adult resocialization. See Almond, *A Discipline Divided;* Eckstein, "A Culturalist Theory."

94. Shin and Shyu, "Political Ambivalence," 122.

95. Among the small Asian population in South Africa, support for democracy plummeted from 55 to 27 percent. Robert Mattes and Hermann Thiel, "Consolidation and Public Opinion in South Africa," *Journal of Democracy* 9, no. 1 (1998): 100, table 1.

96. The mean score on the 4-point scale of satisfaction (with 4 being "very satisfied") was 2.75 for Black ANC supporters and 2.41 for Black supporters of the rival Inkatha Freedom Party. (Private communication from Robert Mattes, November 14, 1997.) This compares with overall 1993 means of 1.9 for Poland, 2.0 for Hungary, 2.1 for Slovakia, and 2.5 for the Czech Republic. Gabor Toka, "Political Support in East-Central Europe," in Klingemann and Fuchs, *Citizens and the State*, 362, table 12.2.

97. Shin and McDonough, "The Dynamics of Popular Reactions." External efficacy—the perception that government has an effect on them as individuals—also emerged as a significant element of "democratic experience" affecting change in support for democracy.

98. "Parliamentary Ethics and Government Corruption: Playing with Public Trust," Institute for Democracy in South Africa, *Public Opinion Service Reports* 3 (1996): 12–13.

99. "The Public's View of Parliament," *Public Opinion Service Reports* 1 (1996): app. 2, 11.

100. Maravall, *Regimes, Politics, and Markets*, 239.

101. The evaluation of the current regime appears similar in wording to measures of satisfaction with how democracy is working, but in the patterns of response by country it is closer to measures of legitimacy. The responses in 1993 on satisfaction with the way democracy works, regime approval, and rejection of all authoritarian alternatives are as follows:

Country	Satisfaction with Democracy (%)	Approve Current Regime (%)	Disapprove Suspension of Parliament (%)
Czech Republic	53	78	72
Hungary	29	51	70
Poland	26	69	71
Slovakia	27	52	76

Sources: For satisfaction, Gabor Toka, "Political Support in East-Central Europe," in Klingemann and Fuchs, *Citizens and the State*, 364–65, table 12.3; Rose and Haerpfer, "Change and Stability in the New Democracies Barometer," figs. 2.1 and 2.7.

102. Rose et al., *Democracy and Its Alternatives*, tables 7.2, 8.4, 9.2. The standardized regression coefficients (betas) for the combined test of economic and political (table 8.4) are evaluation of communist regime (-.22), more perceived freedom now (.14), patience (.11), and destitution (-.09). Trust in institutions, income, future expectations of household finance, and future expectations for the national economy have significant but weaker effects (.03 to .06). For the data on political patience, see also Richard Rose and William Mishler, "Political Patience in Regime Transformation: A Comparative Analysis of Post-Communist Citizens," Studies in Public Policy 274, Centre for the Study of Public Policy, University of Strathclyde, 28, table 4.

103. Rose et al., *Democracy and Its Alternatives*, tables 7.2, 8.4, 9.2. The "increased fairness" item measured whether the current regime was regarded as better, equal, or worse than the previous one in "treating everybody equally and fairly."

104. Michael McFaul, "Russia: Transition without Consolidation," in Freedom House, *Freedom in the World, 1996–1997*, 14–25. Support for political liberty in Russia (and by extension, democracy) appears to be contingent on the political context. In a 1996 survey, only 30 percent said they would oppose martial law if there was widespread political unrest. The more that Russians perceive a threat to order, the more they are willing to support the suspension of political rights and freedoms, a worrisome sign given the weakness of legal institutions. James L. Gibson, "The Struggle between Order and Liberty in Contemporary Russian Political Culture," *Australian Journal of Political Science* 32, no. 2 (1997): 271–90.

105. Geoffrey Evans and Stephen Whitefield, "The Politics and Economics of Democratic Commitment: Support for Democracy in Transition Societies," *British Journal of Political Science* 25 (1995): 503. Their conclusion closely parallels Weil's in his analysis of the survey evidence for the United States, Britain, France, Germany, Italy, and Spain: "Citizens judge democracy less by what it 'gives' them than by whether it presents them with real (but not polarized) alternatives and responds to their choices." Weil, "The Sources and Structures of Legitimation," 699.

106. Lagos, "Latin America's Smiling Mask." See also Marta Lagos, "The Latinobarometro: Media and Political Attitudes in South America," paper presented to the annual meeting of the American Political Science Association, San Francisco, 1996.

107. Linz and Stepan, *Problems of Democratic Transition*, 210. For their conceptual treatment of the problem, see 3–5, 207–11.

108. Richard Rose, "Freedom as a Fundamental Value," *International Social Science Journal* 145 (1995): table 2. For additional raw data drawn from the New Democracies Barometer III of Rose and Haerpfer, see Linz and Stepan, *Problems of Democratic Transition*, 443, table 21.3. For the full raw data, see Richard Rose and Christian Haerpfer, "New Democracies Barometer III: Learning from What Is Happening," Studies in Public Policy 230, Centre for the Study of Public Policy, University of Strathclyde, 1994, questions 35–42.

109. U.S. Information Agency, "The People Have Spoken: Global Views of Democracy," Office of Research and Media Reaction, January 1998.

110. Rose et al., *Democracy and Its Alternatives*, fig. 7.3. The New Democracies Barometer III, which they use, lists only five dimensions of freedom. Of those feeling freer on all five, 65 percent were positive about the current regime, while those who felt freer on only one or no dimension were 19 percent and 16 percent, respectively, positive about democracy.

111. Richard Rose, "Postcommunism and the Problem of Trust," *Journal of Democracy* 5, no. 3 (1994): 25.

112. Richard Rose and Christian Haerpfer, "New Democracies Barometer IV: A 10-Nation Survey," Studies in Public Policy 262, Centre for the Study of Public Policy, University of Strathclyde, 1996, 41, table 3.1.

113. Alexander J. Motyl, "The Non-Russian States: Soviet Legacies, Post-Soviet Transformations," in *Freedom in the World, 1996–1997*, 26–31.

114. Russell Bova, "Democracy and Liberty: The Cultural Connection," *Journal of Democracy* 8, no. 1 (1997): 112–26.

115. Rose et al., *Democracy and Its Alternatives*, 140.

116. Ibid., tables 6.3, 9.2.

117. Geoffrey Evans, "Mass Political Attitudes and the Development of Market Democracy in Eastern Europe," Discussion Paper 39, Centre for European Studies, Nuffield College, Oxford University, 1995, table 11. The scale includes not only democratic political orientations but also social tolerance. This scale is also consistently negatively associated with age across all ten countries. Studies also found consistent, significant positive effects of education (and negative effects of age) on democratic orientations in Russia, Ukraine, and Lithuania in 1991, 1992, and 1995. Arthur H. Miller, Vicki L. Hesli, and William M. Reisinger, "Reassessing Mass Support for Political and Economic Change in the Former USSR," *American Political Science Review* 88, no. 2 (1994): 406–7, and their "Understanding Political Change in Post-Soviet Societies: A Further Commentary on Finifter and Mickiewicz," *American Political Science Review* 90, no. 1 (1996): 157–58; William M. Reisinger, Arthur H. Miller, Vicki L. Hesli, and Kristen Hill Maher, "Political Values in Russia, Ukraine, and Lithuania: Sources and Implications for Democracy," *British Journal of Political Science* 24 (1994): 183–223.

118. The discrepancy between the findings of Rose et al., *Democracy and Its Alternatives*; Evans, "Mass Political Attitudes," and Miller et al., "Reassessing Mass Support," with respect to age may owe to the wider range of democratic values and orientations probed in the latter two groups of studies.

119. Evans, "Mass Political Attitudes," 37.

120. Parish and Chang, "Political Values in Taiwan," 31–34.

121. Shyu, "Empowering the People," table 4.

122. Yun-han Chu, "The Transformation of Civic Culture in Mainland China, Taiwan, and Hong Kong," paper presented to the convention of the Association of Asian Studies, Honolulu, 1996, 13.

123. Alex Inkeles, *Continuity and Change in Popular Values on the Pacific Rim* (Stanford, Calif.: Hoover Institution Press, 1997), 20.

124. Montero et al., "Democracy in Spain," 13–15. For further evidence of the impact of economic conditions and of public evaluations of government policies and political performance on democratic satisfaction, see Maravall, *Regimes, Politics, and Markets*, 230, table 5.6.

125. For example, in both sets of democracies, only about 25–35 percent felt (in 1991) that "most elected officials care what people like me think." The

outliers on the low end are Italy (15%) and European Russia (20%) and on the high end is the United States (45%). Kaase, "Political Culture and Political Consolidation," table 7.

126. Toka, "Political Support," 363–67.

127. Kaase, "Political Culture and Political Consolidation," 255, 269.

128. Rose and Haerpfer, "Change and Stability," 49, fig. 3.4. Here, I take as indicators of satisfaction the ratings of how the system of government and the economy work (at present and in the past and future) on the "heaven/hell" scale from plus 100 to minus 100, with positive ratings indicating satisfaction or approval.

129. Ibid., 38.

130. Rose et al., *Democracy and Its Alternatives*, tables 7.2, 8.4, 9.2.

131. Rose and Haerpfer, "Change and Stability," 39, fig., 2.9; Rose and Tikhomirov, "Trends in the New Russia Barometer," 27, fig. 2.3.

132. In Russia, Ukraine, and Belarus, 53 percent expected to approve of the political regime in five years' time, compared to a 79 percent mean for CEE; 45 percent in those three countries expected to approve of the economic system in five years, compared to a 72 percent mean for CEE.

133. Montero et al., "Democracy in Spain," 12.

134. In addition to the analyses cited above, a recent study finds that, in every one of eleven Western European countries surveyed by the Eurobarometer in 1990, evaluations of both national economic performance and the respondent's own personal economic performance have statistically significant positive effects on satisfaction with democracy. By contrast, the standard demographic variables (even education) virtually never register significant effects. Christopher J. Anderson and Christine A. Guillory, "Political Institutions and Satisfaction with Democracy: A Cross-National Analysis of Consensus and Majoritarian Systems," *American Political Science Review* 91, no. 1 (1997): 74, table 1.

135. Montero et al., "Democracy in Spain," 16.

136. See Lagos, "The Latinobarometro," figs. 7, 8, 9. No doubt, Uruguay would be similar to Chile in belief about clean elections, but data for Uruguay were not presented in this comparison.

137. Seymour Martin Lipset and William Schneider, *The Confidence Gap* (New York: Free Press, 1983).

138. Rose, "Postcommunism and the Problem of Trust," 19.

139. Rose et al., *Democracy and Its Alternatives*, chap. 7, fig. 7.4.

140. Ibid., fig. 7.5, table 9.2. The step pattern also holds for rejection of all authoritarian alternatives.

141. Across three time points in the first decade of Spanish democracy, trust in government was significantly positively correlated (.37 to .40) with democratic satisfaction. Peter McDonough, Samuel H. Barnes, and Antonio López Pina, "The Growth of Democratic Legitimacy in Spain," *American Political Science Review* 80, no. 3 (1986): 747, table 5.

142. The Czech Republic had the lowest level of overall distrust (18%) and was the only one of the nine countries in which distrust did not exceed trust. William Mishler and Richard Rose, "Trust, Distrust, and Skepticism: Popular Evaluations of Civil and Political Institutions in Post-Communist Societies," *Journal of Politics* 59, no. 2 (1997): fig. 2.

143. Lagos, "The Latinobarometro"; Lagos, "Latin America's Smiling Mask," table 1; Shin and Rose, "Koreans Evaluate Democracy"; Richard Rose and Doh C. Shin, "Discerning Qualities of Democracy in Korea and Post-Communist Countries," paper presented to the International Political Science Association Meeting, Seoul, 1997, 21–22. The Korean figures on institutional trust are not strictly comparable because the response categories were structured differently.

144. Montero et al., "Democracy in Spain."

145. Lagos, "Latin America's Smiling Mask." The low levels of interpersonal trust appear quite stable: the figures Lagos reports for 1996 for Mexico (21%) and Argentina (23%) are about the same as what was reported for those two countries in the 1981–91 period (18% and 21%, respectively). For the latter figures, see Edward N. Muller and Mitchell A. Seligson, "Civic Culture and Democracy: The Question of Causal Relationships," *American Political Science Review* 88, no. 3 (1994): 648, table A-1. As that table makes clear, except for Scandinavia, interpersonal trust is not particularly high even in the established democracies, but their median level of more than 40 percent is much higher than in South America.

146. Rose, "Postcommunism and the Problem of Trust."

147. Mishler and Rose, "Trust, Distrust, and Skepticism," 441; see also tables 3 and 4. Political trust (like democratic satisfaction) may also have a partisan dimension. Between 1978 and 1984 in Spain, people were much more likely to trust in government if the party they supported governed. McDonough et al., "Democratic Legitimacy in Spain," table 2.

148. Muller and Seligson, "Civic Culture and Democracy." Frederick D. Weil, however, finds that interpersonal trust has a positive effect on democratic values in Germany (though not significantly so in East Germany). Weil, "Will Democracy Survive Unification in Germany? Extremism, Protest, and Legitimation Three Years after the Fall of the Berlin Wall," paper presented to the annual meeting of the American Sociological Association, Miami, 1993, table 2.

149. This is essentially the finding of Muller and Seligson, who show (for twenty-seven countries in Europe and Central America) that interpersonal trust is an effect, not a cause, of democracy (the number of years of continuous democracy since 1900). They conclude that "the institutional opportunities for peaceful collective action afforded by democratic regimes could be expected to promote relatively high levels of interpersonal trust." "Civic Culture and Democracy," 647.

150. Lagos, "Latin America's Smiling Mask," 128–30.

151. Montero et al., "Democracy in Spain," 22. While their analysis is convincing, one may question just how low political efficacy in Spain really is. On two other measures of political efficacy, Spaniards appear much more confident of their ability to have some impact on the political system. In 1991, 47 percent disagreed that "people like me don't have any say about what the government does," and 78 percent agreed that "voting gives people like me some say about how the government runs things" (table 5.8). The latter percentage was (with France) the highest among six Western publics and more than 20 percentage points higher than in Britain. The former response may seem low, but it was higher than in the United States, Britain, and West Germany.

152. Maravall, *Regimes, Politics, and Markets,* 234–37.

153. Montero et al., "Democracy in Spain," 20–21. The Taiwanese data are from the 1996 National Taiwan University survey, "The Changing Political System and Electoral Behavior." The questions used in the two countries were virtually identical.

154. Evans and Whitefield, "The Politics and Economics of Democratic Commitment," tables 1, 4, 5.

155. James L. Gibson, "Democratic Political Culture in the Transitional Russian Polity," paper presented to the annual meeting of the American Political Science Association, San Francisco, 1996, 8–9, table 1.

156. Weil, "Will Democracy Survive Unification?"

157. Evans, "Mass Political Attitudes"; Evans and Whitefield, "The Politics and Economics of Democratic Commitment; "Miller et al., "Reassessing Mass Support."

158. Rose et al., *Democracy and Its Alternatives,* chaps., 7, 9.

159. Anderson and Guillory, "Political Institutions."

160. In Weil's research, "The Sources and Structures of Legitimation," 697, incoherent party systems, with high levels of political polarization and legislative fractionalization, appear negatively associated with democratic satisfaction and legitimacy in Western Europe. This coincides with other analytic inferences about the relationship between party system coherence and government performance, for example with respect to economic reform. See Stephan Haggard and Robert R. Kaufman, *The Political Economy of Democratic Transition* (Princeton: Princeton University Press, 1995). It also coincides with evidence that Brazil and Peru (with uncertain legitimacy) have two of the most volatile and least institutionalized party systems in Latin America (compared to democratically consolidated Uruguay and Costa Rica), while Russia has one of the least institutionalized party systems of any democracy analyzed. Scott Mainwaring, *The Party System and Democratization in Brazil: Rethinking Party Systems* (Stanford: Stanford University Press, forthcoming).

161. Miller et al. find that Russians and Ukrainians who identify with a political party are more likely to emphasize freedom and majority rule and signifi-

cantly less likely to make negative comments when asked about the meaning of democracy. "Understanding Democracy," 20.

162. Maravall, *Politics, Regimes, and Markets*, 208–11; quotation on 210.

163. Montero et al., "Democracy in Spain," 31.

164. Rose et al., *Democracy and Its Alternatives;* Whitefield and Evans, "Support for Democracy," table 241.

165. Weil, "Will Democracy Survive Unification?" 3; Frederick D. Weil, "The Development of Democratic Attitudes in Eastern and Western Germany in a Comparative Perspective," *Research on Democracy and Society* 1 (1993): 195–225. See also Weil, "Sources and Structure of Legitimation," 699–700. Whitefield and Evans come to an entirely different conclusion about the relative weight of historical/cultural factors versus more recent, performance-based effects. In analyzing differences in support for democracy between their Czech and Slovak national samples in 1994, they find that the effect of country melts away when measures of democratic performance (system efficacy, personal efficacy, and evaluation of democratic practice) are added to the regression and, again, when economic assessments are added in. Stephen Whitefield and Geoffrey Evans, "Political Culture versus Rational Choice: Explaining Responses to Transition in the Czech Republic and Slovakia," *British Journal of Political Science* (forthcoming). However, both national samples shared an earlier national experience with democracy in the interwar Czechoslovak Republic, and it is this common experience that Rose et al. (*Democracy and Its Alternatives*) speculate accounts for the considerable effect that living in the Czech Republic or Slovakia has on support for democracy and rejection of authoritarian alternatives in their wider sample of postcommunist publics.

166. I am grateful to José Ramón Montero for expressing this point to me.

167. Maravall, *Politics, Regimes, and Markets*, 23

Chapter 6. Civil Society

1. Michael G. Burton, Richard Gunther, and John Higley, "Elite Transformations and Democratic Regimes," in *Elites and Democratic Consolidation in Latin America and Southern Europe*, edited by John Higley and Richard Gunther (Cambridge: Cambridge University Press, 1992). See also Michael G. Burton and John Higley, "Elite Settlements," *American Sociological Review* 52, no. 3 (1987): 295–307; Higley and Burton, "The Elite Variable in Democratic Transitions and Breakdowns," *American Sociological Review* 54, no. 1 (1989): 17–32.

2. Guillermo O'Donnell, Philippe C. Schmitter, and Laurence Whitehead, eds. *Transitions from Authoritarian Rule* (Baltimore: Johns Hopkins University Press, 1986), particularly volume by O'Donnell and Schmitter, eds., *Tentative Conclusions about Uncertain Democracies;* Adam Przeworski, "The Games of Transition," in *Issues in Democratic Consolidation: The New South American Democracies in Comparative Perspective*, edited by Scott Mainwaring, Guillermo

O'Donnell, and J. Samuel Valenzuela (Notre Dame: University of Indiana Press, 1992), 105–52; Donald Share, "Transitions to Democracy and Transition through Transaction," *Comparative Political Studies* 19 (1987): 525–48; Terry Lynn Karl, "Dilemmas of Democratization in Latin America," *Comparative Politics* 23, no. 1 (1990): 1–21; Samuel P. Huntington, *The Third Wave: Democratization in the Late Twentieth Century* (Norman: University of Oklahoma Press, 1991); Higley and Gunther, *Elites and Democratic Consolidation*.

3. Naomi Chazan, "Africa's Democratic Challenge: Strengthening Civil Society and the State," *World Policy Journal* 9 (Spring 1992): 279–308; S. N. Eisenstadt, "Civil Society," in *The Encyclopedia of Democracy*, edited by Seymour Martin Lipset (Washington, D.C.: Congressional Quarterly, 1995), 1: 240–42; Edward Shils, "The Virtue of Civil Society," *Government and Opposition* 26, no. 1 (1991): 9–10, 15–16; Peter Lewis, "Political Transition and the Dilemma of Civil Society in Africa," *Journal of International Affairs* 27, no. 1 (1992): 31–54; Marcia A. Weigle and Jim Butterfield, "Civil Society in Reforming Communist Regimes: The Logic of Emergence," *Comparative Politics* 25, no. 1 (1992): 3–4; Philippe C. Schmitter, "Civil Society East and West," in *Consolidating the Third Wave Democracies: Themes and Perspectives*, edited by Larry Diamond, Marc F. Plattner, Yun-han Chu, and Hung-mao Tien (Baltimore: Johns Hopkins University Press, 1997), 240–62.

4. Eisenstadt, "Civil Society," 240. For an exposition of Metzger's "three marketplaces" (economic, political, and ideological), see Thomas Metzger and Ramon H. Myers, "Introduction: Two Diverging Societies," in Myers, ed., *Two Societies in Opposition* (Stanford: Hoover Institution Press, 1991): xiii–xiv.

5. To a considerable degree, this is what Schmitter means by "nonusurpation." "Civil Society East and West," 240.

6. Of course, corporatist systems of interest representation are distinctive in that they deliberately grant monopolies of interest representation to peak associations that represent all the constituent organizations within particular sectors of the economy. If these arrangements are arrived at through a democratic process, then the resulting actors constitute part of civil society. The nature of this process and the degree to which interest organizations with such broad "encompassing scope" (Schmitter's term) are independent of the state constitute the key distinction between democratic (societal) corporatism and authoritarian (state) corporatism. For his latest perspective, see ibid., 246–47.

7. Chazan, "Africa's Democratic Challenge," 288–89; Lewis, "Political Transition," 35–36.

8. Seymour Martin Lipset, *Political Man: The Social Bases of Democracy*, 2d ed. (Baltimore: Johns Hopkins University Press, 1981), 74–75.

9. Gabriel A. Almond and Sidney Verba, *The Civic Culture: Political Attitudes and Democracy in Five Nations* (Boston: Little, Brown, 1965), 16–30, 346–47, 350.

10. Robert D. Putnam with Robert Leonardi and Raffaella Y. Nanetti,

Making Democracy Work: Civic Traditions in Modern Italy (Princeton: Princeton University Press, 1993), quotations from 167, 173.

11. Ibid., 177.

12. This was the finding of an assessment of international donor support for civil society, based on evaluations of programs in Bangladesh, Chile, El Salvador, Kenya, and Thailand and sponsored by the U.S. Agency for International Development. Few civil society organizations "observed across the five countries exhibited any serious internal democracy, but this did not appear to inhibit their effectiveness at moving democracy forward and playing democratic politics." Nondemocratic civil society organizations can generate democratic interest competition and responsiveness to the needs of various communities if there is pluralism and space for different interests to organize and be heard. But this leaves open the important question of the longer-term implications for democratic culture change and social capital accumulation of having mainly autocratic patterns of governance within organizations. Harry Blair, "Civil Society and Building Democracy: Lessons from International Donor Experience," paper presented to the annual meeting of the American Political Science Association, Chicago, 1996, 14.

13. I offer this mainly as a theoretical observation, with only scanty empirical support. Almond and Verba show that membership in voluntary associations promotes greater social trust, political participation, political knowledge, and political efficacy ("subjective civic competence"). And membership in a politically oriented organization breeds political opinions, participation, and self-confidence even more readily. *The Civic Culture*, chap. 10. Putnam and colleagues, too, find a correlation between associational activity and civic culture, although the finding is more inferential. The prevalence of associations is one of four components of their civic community index, and elite and mass attitudes and values appear markedly more civic (more trusting, efficacious, law-abiding, cooperative, and politically satisfied) in the regions that are structurally and behaviorally more civic. *Making Democracy Work*, 91–115. What does not seem to exist is any direct test of whether members of associations that are more democratically governed manifest more democratic norms and values than members of associations that are more hierarchically and arbitrarily governed. The one inference that can be drawn comes again from Almond and Verba, *The Civic Culture* (260–61): members who have held an official position in their organization are much more likely to have a sense of political efficacy than passive members (and passive members more than nonmembers). Democratic organizations that frequently rotate individuals in and out of offices will advance this element of democratic culture and, one may surmise, others as well.

14. Samuel P. Huntington, *Political Order in Changing Societies* (New Haven: Yale University Press, 1968), 12–24.

15. Interview with Kang Moon-Kyu, chairperson, and Soh Kyung-Suk, secretary-general, KCCM, May 7, 1998. See also, Kyoung-Ryung Seong,

"Civil Society and Democratic Consolidation in Korea, 1987–1996: Great Achievements and Remaining Problems," in *Consolidating Korean Democracy*, edited by Larry Diamond and Byung-Kook Kim, manuscript in preparation.

16. Neil Nevitte and Santiago Canton, "Rethinking Election Observation," *Journal of Democracy* 8, no. 3 (1997): 47–61. See also the first-person accounts of organizational evolution beyond an initial focus on founding elections in Larry Diamond, ed., *The Democratic Revolution: Struggles for Freedom and Pluralism in the Developing World* (New York: Freedom House, 1992): María Rosa de Martini, "Civil Participation in the Argentine Democratic Process," 29–52; Dette Pascual, "Building a Democratic Culture in the Philippines," 53–72; Monica Jiménez de Barros, "Mobilizing for Democracy in Chile: The Crusade for Citizen Participation and Beyond," 73–88.

17. Information on these ongoing activities is available from IDASA's regular publications, *Parliamentary Whip*, *Budget Watch*, and *Public Opinion Service Reports*.

18. In the end, some types of organizations and movements are likely to lose relevance and others figure to gain as the political context changes after the transition. An instructive case study is Sunhyuk Kim, "State and Civil Society in South Korea's Democratic Consolidation: Is the Battle Really Over?" *Asian Survey* 37, no. 12 (1997): 1135–44.

19. Schmitter, "Civil Society East and West," 246–47, 249.

20. Robert Michels, *Political Parties: A Sociological Study of the Oligarchical Tendencies of Modern Democracy* (Glencoe, Ill.: Free Press, 1949). Formal organization, Michels laments, inevitably "gives birth to the dominion of the elected over the electors. . . . Who says organization says oligarchy" (401).

21. Seymour Martin Lipset, Martin A. Trow, and James S. Coleman, *Union Democracy* (Garden City, N.Y.: Anchor, 1962).

22. O'Donnell and Schmitter, *Tentative Conclusions*, 19; subsequent quotations from 48, 54, and 56.

23. Ruth Berins Collier and James Mahoney, "Adding Collective Actors to Collective Outcomes: Labor and Recent Democratization in South America and Southern Europe," *Comparative Politics* 29, no. 3 (1997): 287, 295. Their interpretation of the Spanish case, in particular, challenges the conventional theoretical interpretation, but they note that even before the death of Franco labor protest "produced a severe challenge to the regime" and altered the terms of elite political calculations (288). Moreover, their arguments accord with historical evidence from earlier periods and other cases that emphasize the role of organized labor (and other mass-based collective actors) in generating and deepening democratization. See Dietrich Rueschemeyer, Evelyne Huber Stephens, and John D. Stephens, *Capitalist Development and Democracy* (Chicago: University of Chicago Press, 1992).

24. Juan J. Linz, "Totalitarian and Authoritarian Regimes," in *Handbook of*

344 + Notes to Pages 235–237

Political Science, edited by Fred I. Greenstein and Nelson W. Polsby (Reading, Mass.: Addison-Wesley, 1975), 3: 175–411.

25. Yun-han Chu, *Crafting Democratization in Taiwan* (Taipei: Institute for National Policy Research, 1992), 99. See also Linda Chao and Ramon H. Myers, *The First Chinese Democracy: Political Life in the Republic of China on Taiwan* (Baltimore: Johns Hopkins University Press, 1998), chap. 6.

26. Hsin-Huang Michael Hsiao and Hagen Koo, "The Middle Classes and Democratization," in Diamond et al., *Consolidating the Third Wave Democracies*, 312–33.

27. David I. Steinberg, "The Republic of Korea: Pluralizing Politics," in *Politics in Developing Countries: Comparing Experiences with Democracy*, edited by Larry Diamond, Juan J. Linz, and Seymour Martin Lipset (Boulder, Colo.: Lynne Rienner, 1995), 385.

28. Sunhyuk Kim, "Civil Society in South Korea: From Grand Democracy Movements to Petty Interest Groups?" *Journal of Northeast Asian Studies* 15, no. 2 (1996): 91.

29. See Steinberg, "The Republic of Korea," 385–86; and for a more detailed account of the civil society dynamics during 1984–87, Sun-hyuk Kim, "From Resistance to Representation: Civil Society in South Korean Democratization" (Ph.D. diss., Stanford University, 1996), chap. 5. The sequence of civil society mobilization in Korea also challenges the assumption that the "privileged sectors" of private "industrialists, merchants, bankers, and landowners" assume "a crucial role in the earliest stages of the transition," owing to "their superior capacity for action, their lesser exposure to the risks of repression, and their sheer visibility." O'Donnell and Schmitter, *Tentative Conclusions*, 50. While this was true to some considerable degree in the Philippines and in other "sultanistic" states in which a decadent personal ruler and ruling party preyed upon private capital, in Korea big capital backed the regime, sat on the sidelines, or defected only in the final moments. As Hsiao and Koo note ("The Middle Classes and Democratization"), in both Korea and Taiwan it was the professional and intellectual classes and petty bourgeoisie, not big business, that led, supported, and financed the democratic movements.

30. Christine Sadowski, "Autonomous Groups as Agents of Democratic Change in Communist and Post-Communist Eastern Europe," in *Political Culture and Democracy in Developing Countries*, edited by Larry Diamond (Boulder, Colo.: Lynne Rienner, 1993), 163–97.

31. Lewis, "Political Transition and the Dilemma of Civil Society in Africa"; Chazan, "Africa's Democratic Challenge"; Naomi Chazan, "Between Liberalism and Statism: African Political Cultures and Democracy," in Diamond, *Political Culture and Democracy in Developing Countries*, 67–105; Michael Bratton and Nicholas van de Walle, "Toward Governance in Africa: Popular Demands and State Response," in *Governance and Politics in Africa*, edited by Goran Hyden and Michael Bratton (Boulder, Colo.: Lynne Rienner, 1992), 27–56;

Michael Bratton, "Civil Society and Political Transitions in Africa," and E. Gyimah-Boadi, "Associational Life, Civil Society, and Democratization in Ghana," both in *Civil Society and the State in Africa*, edited by John W. Harbeson, Donald Rothchild, and Naomi Chazan (Boulder, Colo.: Lynne Rienner, 1994); Michael Bratton and Nicholas van de Walle, *Democratic Experiments in Africa* (Cambridge: Cambridge University Press, 1997); E. Gyimah-Boadi, "Civil Society in Africa," *Journal of Democracy* 7, no. 2 (1996): 118–32.

    32. Bratton, "Civil Society and Political Transitions," 63.

    33. Josef Silverstein, "Burma's Uneven Struggle," *Journal of Democracy* 7, no. 4 (1996): 88–102.

    34. For a detailed exploration of the failed transition, see Larry Diamond, Anthony Kirk-Greene, and Oyeleye Oyediran, *Transition without End: Nigerian Politics and Civil Society under Babangida* (Boulder, Colo.: Lynne Rienner, 1997). On the obstruction of democratic transition under the successor regime of General Abacha, see Diamond's concluding chapter, in ibid.; Julius Ihonvbere, "Are Things Falling Apart? The Military and the Crisis of Democratisation in Nigeria," *Journal of Modern African Studies* 34, no. 2 (1996): 193–225; Peter Lewis, "From Prebendalism to Predation: The Political Economy of Decline in Nigeria," *Journal of Modern African Studies* 34, no. 1 (1996); Paul A. Beckett and Crawford Young, eds., *Dilemmas of Democracy in Nigeria* (Rochester: University of Rochester Press, 1997).

    35. Zimrights Executive Director David Chimhini and Zimrights community theater specialists, interviews by author, Harare, March 17–19, 1997.

    36. David Peterson, "Liberia: Crying for Freedom," *Journal of Democracy* 7, no. 2 (1996): 148–58.

    37. Samuel P. Huntington, "Will More Countries Become Democratic?" *Political Science Quarterly* 99, no. 2 (1984): 204. See also Lipset, *Political Man*, 52.

    38. Chappell Lawson, "New Media, New Democracies: Political Transition and the Emergence of a Free Press" (Ph.D. diss., Stanford University, 1998).

    39. Seong, "Civil Society and Democratic Consolidation"; David Steinberg, "Continuing Democratic Reform: The Unfinished Symphony," in Diamond and Byung-Kook Kim, *Consolidating Korean Democracy*.

    40. Almond and Verba, *The Civic Culture*, 347.

    41. "South Korea: Culture Clash," *Economist*, Jan. 11, 1997, 35–36; "Seoul Leader Fails to Halt Labor Strife," *New York Times*, Jan. 23, 1997; "Labor Rivals Team Up in South Korea," *San Francisco Chronicle*, Jan. 27, 1997.

    42. Bronislaw Geremek, "Problems of Postcommunism: Civil Society Then and Now," *Journal of Democracy* 3, no. 2 (1992): 11.

    43. Alexis de Tocqueville, *Democracy in America* (New York: Vintage, 1945 [1840]): 2: 124.

    44. María Rosa de Martini and Sofía de Pinedo, "Women and Civic Life in Argentina," *Journal of Democracy* 3, no. 3 (1992): 138–46; María Rosa de Marti-

ni, "Civic Participation in the Argentine Democratic Process," in Diamond, *The Democratic Revolution*, 29–52.

45. On June 2–6, 1995, civic activists, educators, education officials, and thinkers from fifty-two countries met in Prague to initiate CIVITAS, "an international consortium for civic education that aims to strengthen effective education for informed and responsible citizenship in new and established democracies." This was followed by regional meetings in Latin America, Africa, and Asia. The CIVITAS project is significant for the scope and depth of its emphasis on "education for democracy" through a variety of means and also for the international cooperation that represents one dimension of the rapid growth of international civil society. For further information, see http://www.civnet.org.

46. Georgina Waylen, "Women and Democratization: Conceptualizing Gender Relations in Transition Politics," *World Politics* 46, no. 3 (1994): 327–54. Although Waylen is correct that O'Donnell and Schmitter speak to the dangers of excessive popular mobilization during the transition, her criticism of the democracy literature as a whole for trivializing the role of civil society is unfairly overgeneralized and certainly inapplicable to work on Africa. Moreover, accepting her challenge to treat civil society as a centrally important phenomenon in democratization does not require one to accept her insistence on defining democracy to include economic and social rights as well as political ones.

47. Jonathan Fox, "The Difficult Transition from Clientelism to Citizenship: Lessons from Mexico," *World Politics* 46, no. 2 (1994): 151–84; Fox, "Latin America's Emerging Local Politics," *Journal of Democracy* 5, no. 2 (1994): 105–16.

48. Putnam et al., "Making Democracy Work," 101.

49. Fox, "The Difficult Transition," 152.

50. Ibid., 155.

51. Kathryn A. Sikkink, "Nongovernmental Organizations, Human Rights, and Democracy in Latin America," in *Beyond Sovereignty: Collectively Defending Democracy in the Americas*, edited by Tom Farer (Baltimore: Johns Hopkins University Press, 1996), 150–68; Allison Brysk, "Turning Weakness into Strength: The Internationalization of Indian Rights," *Latin American Perspectives* 23, no. 2 (1996): 38–57.

52. Sanjeev Khagram, "Dams, Development, and Democracy: Transnational Struggles for Power and Water" (Ph.D. diss., Stanford University, 1998).

53. On the important distinction between *political* (liberal, inclusionary) nationalism and *ethnic* (exclusivist) nationalism, see Ghia Nodia, "Nationalism and Democracy," *Journal of Democracy* 3, no. 4 (1992): 3–22. Nodia argues that it was precisely "totalitarianism's decades-long assault on the structures of civil society" and the "rubble" it left behind "of atomized individuals searching frantically for a common principle" that made conditions ripe for a revival of ethnic nationalism (18).

54. Lipset, *Political Man*, 70–79.

55. The Evelio B. Javier Foundation was a relatively early entrant into this type of activity. Dette Pascual, "Organizing People Power in the Philippines," *Journal of Democracy* 1, no. 1 (1990): 102–9.

56. Larry Garber and Glenn Cowan, "The Virtues of Parallel Vote Tabulations," *Journal of Democracy* 4, no. 2 (1993): 94–107.

57. Arye Carmon, "Israel's 'Age of Reform,'" *Journal of Democracy* 4, no. 3 (1993): 114–23; Chai-Anan Samudavanija, "Promoting Democracy and Building Institutions in Thailand," in Diamond, *The Democratic Revolution*, 125–44.

58. See the works cited in chap. 3, n. 28, and the essays in Larry Diamond and Marc F. Plattner, eds., *Economic Reform and Democracy* (Baltimore: Johns Hopkins University Press, 1995).

59. John Sullivan, "Democratization and Business Interests," in Diamond and Plattner, *Economic Reform and Democracy*, 182–96. More information on these organizations and efforts can be obtained from supporting foundations such as the Center for International Private Enterprise (http://www.cipe.org).

60. David Peterson, private communication with author, August 1996.

61. Yasmen Murshed and Nazim Kamran Choudhury, "Bangladesh's Second Chance," *Journal of Democracy* 8, no. 1 (1997): 80.

62. Tocqueville, *Democracy in America*, 2: 126.

63. Larry Diamond, "Civil Society and the Struggle for Democracy," in Diamond, *The Democratic Revolution*, 11.

64. Philippe C. Schmitter, "Still the Century of Corporatism?" in *Private Interest Government: Beyond Market and State*, edited by Wolfgang Streeck and Philippe C. Schmitter (Beverly Hills, Calif.: Sage, 1984), 126. On the important distinction between societal (democratic) and state corporatism, see 102–8.

65. Geremek, "Civil Society Then and Now."

66. Célestin Monga, "Civil Society and Democratisation in Francophone Africa," *Journal of Modern African Studies* 33, no. 3 (1995): 363. See also Monga, *Anthropologie de la Colère: Société et Démocratie en Afrique Noire* (Paris: L'Harmattan, 1994), and the English-language edition, *The Anthropology of Anger* (Boulder, Colo.: Lynne Rienner, 1996).

67. Richard Rose, "Toward a Civil Economy," *Journal of Democracy* 3, no. 2 (1992): 13–26.

68. Larry Diamond, *Promoting Democracy in the 1990s: Actors and Instruments, Issues and Imperatives* (New York: Carnegie Corporation of New York, 1995). Also at http://www.ccpdc.org/pubs/diamond/diaframe.htm.

69. In one sense, the problem was much more severe during the Cold War, when the Soviet Union (and its communist allies) and the United States (and its allies) covertly supported front organizations that did their bidding in the struggle for international supremacy. Today, assistance to NGOs is mainly overt rather than covert and is much less driven by strategic calculations. Still, even if money is given openly and with idealistic intentions, those intentions impose priorities and conditions on recipients and favor some activities over others.

70. Brysk, "Turning Weakness into Strength," 52.

71. Wilmot James and Daria Caliguire, "The New South Africa: Renewing Civil Society," *Journal of Democracy* 7, no. 1 (1996): 61.

72. Schmitter, "Civil Society East and West," 242.

73. Aleksander Smolar, "Civil Society after Communism: From Opposition to Atomization," *Journal of Democracy* 7, no. 1 (1996): 29. See also Gyimah-Boadi, "Civil Society in Africa."

74. Smolar, "Civil Society after Communism," 33.

75. Joel M. Jutkowitz, "Civil Society and Democratic Development in Chile," paper presented to the annual meeting of the American Political Science Association, Chicago, 1995, 21.

76. James and Caliguire, "The New South Africa," 64.

77. With its six thousand plus members (as of March 1997) and organizers in eight of eleven provinces, Zimrights represents the most substantial grassroots political base of any organization in the country, outside of the country's ruling party. Zimrights Executive Director David Chimhini and Zimbabwean journalists and political scientists, interviews by author, March 17–19, 1997.

78. Michels, *Political Parties*, 401.

79. Jutkowitz, "Civil Society and Democratic Development in Chile," 19.

80. Juan J. Linz, "Change and Continuity in the Nature of Contemporary Democracies," in *Reexamining Democracy: Essays in Honor of Seymour Martin Lipset*, edited by Gary Marks and Larry Diamond (Newbury Park, Calif.: Sage, 1992), 184–9

Chapter 7. A Fourth Wave?

1. Freedom House, *Freedom in the World: The Annual Survey of Political Rights and Civil Liberties, 1994–1995* (New York: Freedom House, 1995), 6.

2. This is a central finding of Adam Przeworski, Michael Alvarez, José Antonio Cheibub, and Fernando Limongi, "What Makes Democracies Endure?" *Journal of Democracy* 7, no. 1 (1996): 50–51.

3. R. William Liddle, "Indonesia: Suharto's Tightening Grip," *Journal of Democracy* 7, no. 4 (1996): 59, 70. However, in this article and in numerous other writings, Liddle was among the scholars of Indonesia most sensitive to the social and political forces that might undermine military domination and ignite a transition from authoritarianism.

4. Minxin Pei, "'Creeping Democratization' in China," *Journal of Democracy* 6, no. 4 (1995); 65–79.

5. Henry S. Rowen, "World Wealth Expanding: Why a Rich, Democratic, and (Perhaps) Peaceful Era Is Ahead," in *The Mosaic of Economic Growth*, edited by Ralph Landau, Timothy Taylor, and Gavin Wright (Stanford: Stanford University Press, 1996), 112. Although an economic downturn or implosion in China is certainly conceivable, resulting from a deep political, environmental,

or financial system crisis, the assumption of another generation of 4.5 percent average annual growth in real per capita income in China seems attainable. Since 1979, China has averaged 5 percent annual growth in per capita income, and it has been higher in recent years. Henry S. Rowen, "The Short March: China's Road to Democracy," *National Interest* (Fall 1996): 61.

6. Samuel P. Huntington, *The Third Wave: Democratization in the Late Twentieth Century* (Norman: University of Oklahoma Press, 1991), 61.

7. Henry S. Rowen, "Why a Rich, Democratic, and (Perhaps) Peaceful Era, with More Advanced Weapons in More Hands, Is Ahead," paper presented to the annual meeting of the American Political Science Association, San Francisco, 1996, 7.

8. Przeworski et al., "What Makes Democracies Endure?" 41.

9. China's per capita gross national product in 1995 was estimated at $2,920 in purchasing power parity (1995 U.S. dollars). World Bank, *World Development Report 1997* (New York: Oxford University Press, 1997), 214, table 1.

10. Rowen, "The Short March," 67.

11. Kevin J. O'Brien, "Implementing Political Reform in China's Villages," *Australian Journal of Chinese Affairs*, no. 32 (July 1994): 33–60; Lianjiang Li and Kevin J. O'Brien, "The Struggle over Village Elections," Department of Political Science, University of California, Berkeley, October 21, 1997; Melanie Manion, "The Electoral Connection in the Chinese Countryside," *American Political Science Review* 90, no. 4 (1996): 736–48; Jean Oi, "Economic Development, Stability, and Democratic Village Self-Governance," *China Review* (1996): 125–44; Carter Center, "Village Elections in China, March 2–15, 1998," Carter Center Delegation Report, Atlanta, Georgia, March 25, 1998; International Republican Institute (IRI), "Village Committee Elections in the People's Republic of China," Washington, D.C., January 1997; IRI, "Election Observation Report: Fujian, People's Republic of China," May 1997.

12. See Pei, "Creeping Democratization in China"; Minxin Pei, "Is China Democratizing?" *Foreign Affairs* 77, no. 1 (1998): 68–82; Minxin Pei, "Citizens versus Mandarins: Administrative Litigation in China," *China Quarterly* 152 (Dec. 1997): 832–62; Minxin Pei, "Chinese Civic Associations: An Empirical Analysis," *Modern China* 24, no. 3 (1998): 285–318; Minxin Pei, *From Reform to Revolution: The Demise of Communism in China and the Soviet Union* (Cambridge: Harvard University Press, 1994), chap. 5; Chih-Yu Shih, "The Institutionalization of China's People's Congress System: The Views of People's Deputies," *International Politics* 33 (1996): 145–62; Yingyi Quian and Barry R. Weingast, *China's Transition to Markets: Market-Preserving Federalism, Chinese Style* (Stanford, Calif: Hoover Institution Press, 1995); Michel Oksenberg, "Will China Democratize? Confronting a Classic Dilemma," *Journal of Democracy* 9, no. 1 (1998): 27–40, quotation on 30.

13. In addition to the annual human rights report of Amnesty International, Human Rights Watch, and the U.S. Department of State, see Amnesty In-

ternational, *China: No One Is Safe* (New York: Amnesty International, 1996); Martin King Whyte, "Social Trends and the Human Rights Situation in the PRC," paper presented to the Twenty-seventh Sino-American Conference on Contemporaty China, Institute of International Relations, Taipei, 1998.

14. Robert A. Scalapino, "Will China Democratize? Current Trends and Future Prospects," *Journal of Democracy* 9, no. 1 (1998): 35–40.

15. See the entire collection of essays, "Will China Democratize?" *Journal of Democracy* 9, no. 1 (1998): 3–64.

16. Przeworski et al. ("What Makes Democracies Endure?") argue that the strong relationship between economic development and democracy is attributable entirely to the steadily increasing life expectancy of democratic regimes as per capita income levels rise. Finding no relationship between income level and the probability of a democratic transition, they conclude that the genetic, or "endogenous," assumption of "modernization" theory is untenable. Rising income (modernization) does not make a democratic transition more likely (as Lipset, Huntington, Rowen, and I have all predicted), it just makes democracy more likely to endure if it comes into being for other reasons. For a more extended presentation of the evidence and argument, see Adam Przeworski and Fernando Limongi, "Modernization: Theory and Facts," *World Politics* 49, no. 2 (1997): 155–83. However, their determination of life expectancies for authoritarian regimes is heavily distorted by the prevalence in their sample of rich dictatorships. In fact, eighteen of their twenty-five cases of "highest levels of per capita income under which dictatorships survived" in their forty-year time period (table 3) ultimately made transitions to democracy. To weigh the Przeworski and Limongi argument, we should exclude the Soviet puppet states, which could not democratize because of Soviet military domination (but then democratized soon after it was lifted). We should further exclude or discount oil states, which—because they rank lower on key dimensions of human development (such as education) than on per capita income and because the state dominates the economy and society—do not experience the stimulus to democratization of civil society growth and political culture change to the extent that other modernizing states do. For this argument, see Larry Diamond, "Economic Development and Democracy Reconsidered," in *Rethinking Democracy: Essays in Honor of Seymour Martin Lipset*, edited by Gary Marks and Larry Diamond (Newbury Park, Calif.: Sage, 1992), 93–139. If we reassess the Przeworski and Limongi data in light of these qualifications, only three serious exceptions are left standing: Singapore (the outstanding exception to the Lipset thesis), Malaysia, and Mexico, which is moving toward democracy partly because of the greater pluralism of economic and associational life generated by economic development.

In the paradigmatic cases of Taiwan and South Korea, which are no less likely to be harbingers of China's political evolution than is Singapore, there is widespread scholarly consensus that economic development made an important contribution to political liberalization, and then democratization, by creating a more functionally complex, better educated, more socially mobilized and organized society, with more independent centers of power that could not be controlled by the state. See Yun-han Chu, *Crafting Democratization in Taiwan* (Taipei: Institute for National Policy Research, 1992); Tun-jen Cheng, "Democratizing the Quasi-Leninist Regime in Taiwan," *World Politics* 42, no. 4 (1989): 471–99; Hung-mao Tien, *The Great Transition: Political and Social Change in the Republic of China* (Stanford, Calif.: Hoover Institution Press, 1989); David Steinberg, "The Republic of Korea: Pluralizing Politics," in *Politics in Developing Countries: Comparing Experiences with Democracy*, edited by Larry Diamond, Juan J. Linz, and Seymour Martin Lipset (Boulder, Colo.: Lynne Rienner, 1995), 369–416; Michael Hsiao and Hagen Koo, "The Middle Class and Democratization in East Asian NICs," in Larry Diamond, Juan J. Linz, and Seymour Martin Lipset, *Consolidating the Third Wave Democracies: Themes and Perspectives*, edited by Larry Diamond, Juan J. Linz, and Seymour Martin Lipset (Baltimore: Johns Hopkins University Press, 1997), 312–33.

17. Pei, "Creeping Democratization," 77.

18. Frederick Z. Brown, "Vietnam's Tentative Transition," *Journal of Democracy* 7, no. 4 (1996): 86.

19. For a perspective from the accounts of former political prisoners and prison guards, see "Voice from the North Korean Gulag," *Journal of Democracy* 9, no. 3 (1998): 82–96.

20. Solomon Lefler, "Singapore's 'Pragmatic Materialism': Why Non-Liberal Government Persists," Department of Political Science, Stanford University, 1996. See also Cong Ching Liang, "Authoritarianism as Expediency: The Group-Oriented Singaporeans and Their Social Choices" (master's thesis, University of Oregon, 1995).

21. Chua Beng-Huat, "Arrested Development: Democratisation in Singapore," *Third World Quarterly* 15, no. 4 (1994): 668. In the framework of Chua's skeptical analysis, I suggest that the growth of civil society and a greater propensity to risk taking by individuals in it will break the cycle of apathy that has led to a resigned (as Chua emphasizes, by no means enthusiastic) acceptance of restricted liberty and People's Action Party hegemony.

22. For alternative views of Africa's ambiguities, see Richard Joseph, "Africa, 1990–1997: From *Abertura* to Closure," and E. Gyimah-Boadi, "The Rebirth of African Liberalism," *Journal of Democracy* 9, no. 2 (1998): 3–17, 18–31.

23. Robin Wright, "Islam and Liberal Democracy: Two Visions of Reformation," *Journal of Democracy* 7, no. 2 (1996): 64–75. Alternative perspectives on her interpretation are offered by Abdou Filali-Ansary, Mahamed Elhachmi Hamdi, and Laith Kubba, "Islam and Liberal Democracy," *Journal of Democracy* 7, no. 2 (1996): 76–89.

24. Bernard Lewis, "Islam and Liberal Democracy: A Historical Overview," *Journal of Democracy* 7, no. 2 (1996): 62–63.

25. Henry S. Rowen, "The Tide Underneath the 'Third Wave,'" *Journal of Democracy* 6, no. 1 (1995): 52–64; Rowen, "World Wealth Expanding."

26. On recent experience and future policy directions for international democracy promotion, see Larry Diamond, *Promoting Democracy in the 1990s: Actors and Instruments, Issues and Imperatives* (New York: Carnegie Corporation of New York, 1995); Thomas Carothers, *Assessing Democracy Assistance: The Case of Romania* (Washington, D.C.: Carnegie Endowment for International Peace, 1996); Kevin F. F. Quigley, *For Democracy's Sake: Foundations and Democracy Assistance in Central Europe* (Washington, D.C.: Woodrow Wilson Center Press, 1997); Joel D. Barkan, "Can Established Democracies Nurture Democracy Abroad? Lessons from Africa," in *Democracy's Victory and Crisis*, edited by Axel Hadenius (Cambridge: Cambridge University Press, 1997), 371–403; Michael Pinto-Duschinsky, "The Rise of 'Political Aid,'" in *Consolidating the Third Wave Democracies: Regional Challenges*, edited by Larry Diamond, Marc F. Plattner, Yun-han Chu, and Hung-mao Tien (Baltimore: Johns Hopkins University Press, 1997), 295–324.

27. Thomas Franck, "The Emerging Right to Democratic Governance," *American Journal of International Law* 86, no. 46 (1992): 50.

28. Diamond, *Promoting Democracy in the 1990s;* Morton H. Halperin and Kristen Lomasney, "Toward a Global 'Guarantee Clause,'" *Journal of Democracy* 4, no. 3 (1993): 60–69; Morton H. Halperin and Kristen Lomasney, "Guaranteeing Democracy," *Foreign Policy* 91 (Summer 1993): 105–22; Morton H. Halperin and Kristen Lomasney, "Guaranteeing Democracy: A Review of the Record," *Journal of Democracy* 9, no. 2 (1998): 134–47; Tom Farer, ed., *Beyond Sovereignty: Collectively Defending Democracy in the Americas* (Baltimore: Johns Hopkins University Press, 1996).

29. Huntington, *The Third Wave*, 316.

30. Philippe C. Schmitter, "Democracy's Future: More Liberal, Preliberal, or Postliberal?" *Journal of Democracy* 6, no. 1 (1995): 14–22.

31. Robert Putnam argues that social capital has actually been declining of late in important respects in the United States. See his "Bowling Alone: America's Declining Social Capital," *Journal of Democracy* 6, no. 1 (1995): 65–78.

INDEX

Control Yuan, 112, 316n.130
corporatism, 232, 341n.6
corruption, political, 91–93, 240–41; in
Asia, 52; in the former Soviet Union,
53–54, 93; in Mexico, 240
Costa Rica, 16, 40, 195
Country Reports on Human Rights Practices (U.S. State Department), 44
courts. *See* judicial system
crime, 90–91, 308n.65
Croatia, 54
Cuba, 43, 261
Czech Republic, 20–21, 79, 116, 127,
183–84, 185, 197, 216, 252, 340n.165

Dahl, Robert, 3, 8, 18, 66, 118, 123, 127,
129, 166, 172, 281nn.1, 5, 283n.23,
285n.34
decentralization: arguments for, 121–
32; challenges of, 138–45; as factor in
democracy, 120–21, 159–60; and federalism, 158; financing of, 140–42; in
postcolonial states, 138–39; problems
of, 132–38
delegative democracy, 34–42, 47,
49–50, 71, 293n.23
delegativismo, 40
democracies: crime in, 90–91; number
of, 1–2, 24–31, 61, 190n.1; rating of,
12–13, 282n.12, 291n.6, 292n.13. *See
also names of individual countries*
democracy: in Asia, 14–15; and authority, 167–68; as best form of government, 2–7; citizen involvement in,
145–49; classification of, 290n.1,
conceptualizations of, 7–17; cultural
correlates of, 165–74; dangers of decentralization, 132–38; deepening of,
74–76, 112–16, 130; delegative, 34–
42, 47, 49–50, 71, 293n.23; as developmental phenomenon, 17–19; diffusion of, 24, 55–60; efficacy as measure of, 208–12; electoral, 8–10, 19–
20, 24, 55–56, 61, 73, 289n.58; elites'
role in, 67–70, 173–74, 218–20; ethnic minorities in, 6, 9, 11, 134–35,
156–57, 243; evaluating, 200–206;

expansion of, 1–2, 22–23, 24–27; and
federalism, 120, 149–59; in former
Anglo-American colonies, 118–19,
317n.3; illiberal, 29, 42–50; in Latin
America, 14, 31–49, 70–71, 179–83,
195–96, 200, 204–5; legitimation of,
20, 21, 174–92, 212–17; liberal, 3, 4,
10–13, 19–20, 21, 25, 55, 61, 117,
219; and local government, 121–32,
138–45; measures of, 285–86n.36;
measuring support for, 192–200;
midrange conceptions, 13–15; participation in, 143–49, 242, 244; and political corruption, 240–41; private
philanthropy for, 258; promotion of,
56–57, 121–32, 239–50, 263, 272–
73; prospects for, 22–23, 159–60,
261–78; public support for, 174–92;
quality of, 28, 132; size as factor in,
117–21, 127–29; subtypes of, 7–8;
transition to, 233–39, 263; trust in,
206–8; values and norms of, 242–43,
278; women's role in, 243–44. *See also*
civil society; consolidation of democracy; decentralization; democratization; legitimacy, democratic; local
government; political culture;
pseudodemocracies; *and names of
individual countries*
Democratic Progressive Party (DPP)
(Taiwan), 132
democratization: in Africa, 55; and contingent consent, 130–32; education as
factor in, 199–200; in the former Soviet Union, 49, 53–55, process of, 5–
6; reverse waves of, 2, 5, 22, 64–65,
78; third wave of, 24–31, 56–63, 86–
87, 139–40, 220, 261, 272; waves of,
1–2, 22, 281n.1
devolution of power, 120–21, 126; in
South Korea, 130; in Taiwan, 130
Diamandouros, Nikiforos, 68
Diamond, Larry, 161
Di Palma, Guiseppe, 173
discrimination: against minorities,
134–35
Dominican Republic, 14, 39–40, 140

Library of Congress Cataloging-in-Publication Data

Diamond, Larry Jay.
   Developing democracy : toward consolidation / Larry Diamond.
      p.   cm.
   Includes bibliographical references and index.
   ISBN 0-8018-6014-8 (alk. paper)
   1. Democracy—History—20th century. 2. World politics—1989–
   I. Title.
   JC421.D4918   1999
   321.8′09′049—dc21   98-42981
                                                                              CIP